CISA – Certified Information Systems Auditor Study Guide

Aligned with the CISA Review Manual 2019 to help you audit, monitor, and assess information systems

Hemang Doshi

BIRMINGHAM - MUMBAI

CISA – Certified Information Systems Auditor Study Guide

Acquisition Editor: Karan Gupta
Content Development Editor: Kinnari Chohan
Senior Editor: Rohit Singh
Technical Editor: Pradeep Sahu
Copy Editor: Safis Editing
Project Coordinator: Deeksha Thakkar
Proofreader: Safis Editing
Indexer: Manju Arasan
Production Designer: Aparna Bhagat

First published: August 2020

Production reference: 1210820

Published by Packt Publishing Ltd.
Livery Place
35 Livery Street
Birmingham
B3 2PB, UK.

ISBN 978-1-83898-958-3

www.packt.com

`Packt.com`

Subscribe to our online digital library for full access to over 7,000 books and videos, as well as industry leading tools to help you plan your personal development and advance your career. For more information, please visit our website.

Why subscribe?

- Spend less time learning and more time coding with practical eBooks and Videos from over 4,000 industry professionals

- Improve your learning with Skill Plans built especially for you

- Get a free eBook or video every month

- Fully searchable for easy access to vital information

- Copy and paste, print, and bookmark content

Did you know that Packt offers eBook versions of every book published, with PDF and ePub files available? You can upgrade to the eBook version at `www.packt.com` and as a print book customer, you are entitled to a discount on the eBook copy. Get in touch with us at `customercare@packtpub.com` for more details.

At `www.packt.com`, you can also read a collection of free technical articles, sign up for a range of free newsletters, and receive exclusive discounts and offers on Packt books and eBooks.

Contributors

About the author

Hemang Doshi is a chartered accountant and a Certified Information System Auditor with more than 15 years' experience in the field of IS auditing/risk-based auditing/compliance auditing/vendor risk management/due diligence/system risk and control. He is the founder of www.cisaexamstudy.com and www.criscexamstudy.com, dedicated platforms for CISA and CRISC study, respectively. He has also authored other books on auditing.

I wish to thank those people who have been close to me and supported me, especially my wife, Namrata, and my parents.

About the reviewer

Gokhan Polat works in the consulting department of EY Turkey and, in addition to implementing business development activities for technology services, he has also managed projects on cybersecurity assessments and data privacy consultancy. Previously, he created an internal audit department at Bakirkoy Municipality and headed up this department for 3 years. He also has 14 years' experience in the Turkish Armed Forces as an officer involved in various assignments with multinational teams.

As a risk management professional, he has CISSP, CISA, CRISC, CDPSE, CIA, and CRMA qualifications, which bear testimony to his dedication to the profession. He has authored articles that have been published in the internal auditing magazine of IIA Turkey and the ISACA journal of ISACA Global. Currently, he is a member of the ISACA Istanbul Chapter and sits on the board of CSA Turkey.

Packt is searching for authors like you

If you're interested in becoming an author for Packt, please visit authors.packtpub.com and apply today. We have worked with thousands of developers and tech professionals, just like you, to help them share their insight with the global tech community. You can make a general application, apply for a specific hot topic that we are recruiting an author for, or submit your own idea.

Table of Contents

Section 2: Governance and Management of IT

Section 4: Information System Operations and Business Resilience

Section 5: Protection of Information Assets

Preface

Certified Information System Auditor (CISA) is one of the most sought-after courses in field of auditing, control, and information security. CISA is a globally recognized certification that validates your expertise and gives you the leverage you need in order to advance in your career. CISA certification is key to a successful career in IT.

CISA certification can showcase your expertise and assert your ability to apply a risk-based approach to planning, executing, and reporting on projects and engagements. It helps to gain instant credibility as regards your interactions with internal stakeholders, regulators, external auditors, and customers.

As per ISACA's official website (`www.isaca.org`), the average salary of a CISA holder is USD110,000 +.

Who this book is for

If you are a passionate auditor, risk practitioner, IT professional, or security professional, and are planning to enhance your career by obtaining a CISA certificate, this book is for you.

What this book covers

Chapter 1, *Audit Planning*, deals with the audit processes, standards, guidelines, practices, and techniques that an IS auditor is expected to use during audit assignments. An IS auditor must have a detailed knowledge of IS processes, business processes, and risk management processes in order to protect an organization's assets.

Chapter 2, *Audit Execution*, covers project management techniques, sampling methodology, and audit evidence collection techniques. It provides details regarding data analysis techniques, reporting and communication techniques, and quality assurance processes.

Chapter 3, *IT Governance*, provides an introduction to IT governance and aspects related to IT enterprise governance. Enterprise governance includes the active involvement of management in IT management. Effective IT governance and management involves an organization's structure as well as IT standards, policies, and procedures.

Chapter 4, *IT Management*, walks you through various aspects of designing and approving IT management policy and effective information security governance. It will also teach you to audit and evaluate IT resource management, along with services provided by third-party service providers, while also covering IT performance monitoring and reporting.

Chapter 5, *Information Systems Acquisition and Development*, provides information about project governance and management techniques. This chapter discusses how an organization evaluates, develops, implements, maintains, and disposes of its information systems and related components.

Chapter 6, *Information Systems Implementation*, covers various aspects of information systems implementation. The implementation process comprises a variety of stages, including system migration, infrastructure deployment, data conversion or migration, user training, post-implementation review, and user acceptance testing.

Chapter 7, *Information Systems Operations*, explains how to identify risk related to technology components and how to audit and evaluate IT service management practices, systems performance management, problem and incident management policies and practices, change, configuration, release and patch management processes, and database management processes.

Chapter 8, *Business Resilience*, covers all aspects of the business impact analysis, system resiliency, data backup, storage and restoration, the business continuity plan, and disaster recovery plans.

Chapter 9, *Information Asset Security and Control*, provides information about the information security management framework, privacy principles, physical access and environmental controls, and identity and access management.

Chapter 10, *Network Security and Control*, provides an introduction to various components of networks, network-related risks and controls, types of firewalls, and wireless security.

Chapter 11, *Public Key Cryptography and Other Emerging Technologies*, details various aspects of public key cryptography, cloud computing, virtualization, mobile computing, and the Internet of Things.

Chapter 12, *Security Event Management*, looks in depth at how to evaluate an organization's information security and privacy policies and practices. It also discusses various types of information system attack methods and techniques, and covers different security monitoring tools and techniques as well as evidence collection and forensics methodology.

To get the most out of this book

This book is aligned with ISACA's CISA Review Manual and covers all the topics that a CISA aspirant needs to understand in order to pass the CISA exam successfully. The key aspect of this book is its use of simple language, which makes this book ideal for candidates with non-technical backgrounds. At the end of each topic, key pointers from the CISA exam perspective are presented in table format. This is the unique feature of this book. It also contains 850 plus exam-oriented practice questions. The questions are designed in consideration of the language and testing methodology used in an actual CISA exam. This will help any CISA aspirant to face the CISA exam with increased confidence. For more practice questions along these lines, please refer to www.cisaexamstudy.com.

Download the color images

We also provide a PDF file that has color images of the screenshots/diagrams used in this book. You can download it here:

https://static.packt-cdn.com/downloads/9781838989583_ColorImages.pdf

Conventions used

There are a number of text conventions used throughout this book.

Bold: Indicates a new term, an important word, or words that you see on screen. For example, words in menus or dialog boxes appear in the text like this. Here is an example: "**Electromagnetic Interference (EMI)**: EMI generally results from electric storms or noisy electrical equipment. EMI may result in system corruption or damage."

Warnings or important notes appear like this.

Tips and tricks appear like this.

Get in touch

Feedback from our readers is always welcome.

General feedback: If you have questions about any aspect of this book, mention the book title in the subject of your message and email us at customercare@packtpub.com.

Errata: Although we have taken every care to ensure the accuracy of our content, mistakes do happen. If you have found a mistake in this book, we would be grateful if you would report this to us. Please visit www.packtpub.com/support/errata, selecting your book, clicking on the Errata Submission Form link, and entering the details.

Piracy: If you come across any illegal copies of our works in any form on the internet, we would be grateful if you would provide us with the location address or website name. Please contact us at copyright@packt.com with a link to the material.

If you are interested in becoming an author: If there is a topic that you have expertise in, and you are interested in either writing or contributing to a book, please visit authors.packtpub.com.

Reviews

Please leave a review. Once you have read and used this book, why not leave a review on the site that you purchased it from? Potential readers can then see and use your unbiased opinion to make purchase decisions, we at Packt can understand what you think about our products, and our authors can see your feedback on their book. Thank you!

For more information about Packt, please visit packt.com.

Section 1: Information System Auditing Process

1

This part contains 21 percent of the CISA exam, approximately 32 questions.

This part contains the following chapters:

- Chapter 1, *Audit Planning*
- Chapter 2, *Audit Execution*

1
Audit Planning

An audit plan is a step-wise approach to be followed to conduct an audit. It helps to establish the overall audit process in an effective and efficient manner. An audit plan should be aligned with the audit charter of the organization. To plan an audit, the IS auditor is required to have a thorough understanding of business processes, business applications, and relevant controls. Audit planning includes both short- and long-term planning.

The following topics will be covered in this chapter:

- The content of an audit charter
- Audit planning
- Business process applications and controls
- Types of controls
- Risk-based audit planning
- Types of audit and assessment

The content of an audit charter

An internal audit is an independent activity and it should ideally be reported to a board-level committee. In most organizations, the internal audit function reports to the audit committee of the board. This helps to protect the independence of the audit function.

The independence of the audit function is ensured through a management-approved audit charter.

The following figure shows the features of an audit charter:

The CISA candidate should note the following features of the audit charter:

- An audit charter is a formal document defining the internal audit's objective, authority, and responsibility. The audit charter covers the entire scope of audit activities.
- An audit charter must be approved by top management.
- An audit charter should not be changed too often and hence procedural aspects should not be included in it. Also, it is recommended to not include a detailed annual audit calendar including things such as planning, the allocation of resources, and other details such as audit fees, other expenses for the audit, and so on in an audit charter.
- An audit charter should be reviewed annually to ensure that it is aligned with business objectives.

Essentially, an auditor's activities are impacted by the charter of audit department, which authorizes the accountability and responsibility of the audit department.

An audit charter includes the following:

- The mission, purpose, and objective of the audit function
- The scope of the audit function
- The responsibilities of management

- The responsibilities of internal auditors
- The authorised personnel of the internal audit work

If an audit is outsourced to an audit firm, the objective of the audit, along with its detailed scope, should be incorporated in an audit engagement letter.

An audit charter forms the basis of structured audit planning. Activities relevant to audit planning are discussed in the next topic.

Key aspects from CISA exam perspective

The following table covers important aspects from the CISA exam perspective:

CISA questions	Possible answers
Who should approve the audit charter of an organization?	Senior management
What should the content of an audit charter be?	The scope, authority, and responsibilities of the audit function
What is the prime reason for review of an organization chart?	To understand the authority and responsibility of individuals
The actions of an IS auditor are primarily influenced by	Audit charter
Which document provides the overall authority for an auditor to perform an audit?	Audit charter
What is the primary reason for the audit function directly reporting to the audit committee?	The audit function must be independent of the business function and should have direct access to the audit committee of the board

Self-evaluation questions

1. **An audit charter should be approved by:**
    A. Higher management
    B. The head of audit
    C. The Information Security department
    D. The project steering committee

2. **The audit charter should**:
   A. Be frequently upgraded as per changes in technology and the audit profession
   B. Incorporate yearly audit planning
   C. Incorporate business continuity requirements
   D. Incorporate the scope, authority, and responsibility of the audit department

3. **The prime objective of an audit charter is to**:
   A. Document the procedural aspect of an audit
   B. Document system and staff requirements to conduct the audit
   C. Document the ethics and code of conduct for the audit department
   D. Document the responsibility and authority of the audit department

4. **The document that delegates authority to the audit department is**:
   A. The audit planner
   B. The audit charter
   C. The IT policy
   D. The risk assessment and treatment document

5. **The prime reason for the review of an organization chart is to**:
   A. Get details related to the flow of data
   B. Analyze the department-wise employee ratio
   C. Understand the authority and responsibility of individuals
   D. Analyze department-wise IT assets

6. **An IS auditor would be primarily influenced by**:
   A. The charter of the audit department
   B. The representation by management
   C. The structure of the organization
   D. The number of outsourcing arrangements

7. **Which of the following is the result of a risk management process?**
   A. A corporate strategic plan
   B. A charter incorporating the audit policy
   C. Decisions regarding the security policy
   D. Outsourcing arrangements

8. **Which of the following should be included in an audit charter?**
    A. Annual audit planning
    B. The audit function's reporting structure
    C. Guidelines for drafting audit reports
    D. An annual audit calendar

9. **The scope, authority, and responsibility of the IS audit function is defined by:**
    A. The approved audit charter
    B. The head of the IT department
    C. The operational head of the department
    D. The head of audit

10. **Which of the following functions is governed by the audit charter?**
    A. The information technology function
    B. The external audit function
    C. The internal audit function
    D. The information security function

11. **Which of the following covers the overall authority to perform an IS audit?**
    A. The audit scope with goals and objectives
    B. Management's request to perform an audit
    C. The approved audit charter
    D. The approved audit schedule

12. **The audit function should be reported to the audit committee of the board because**:
    A. The audit function has few resources
    B. The audit function must be independent of the business function and should have direct access to the audit committee of the board
    C. No other function should use the resources of the audit function
    D. The audit function can use their own authority to complete the audit on a priority basis.

13. **The best objective for the creation of an audit charter is to:**
    A. Determine the audit resource requirements
    B. Document the mission and long-term strategy of the audit department
    C. Determine the code of conduct for the audit team
    D. Provide the authority and responsibility of the audit function

Audit planning

CISA aspirants should understand the following important terms before reading about the different aspects of audit planning:

- **Audit universe**: An inventory of all the functions/processes/units under the organization.
- **Qualitative risk assessment**: In a qualitative risk assessment, risk is assessed using qualitative parameters such as high, medium, and low.
- **Quantitative risk assessment**: In a quantitative risk assessment, risk is assessed using numerical parameters and is quantified.
- **Risk factors**: Factors that have an impact on risk. The presence of those factors increases the risk, whereas the absence of those factors decreases the risk.

All of the preceding elements are important prerequisites for the design of a structured audit plan. Next, let's discuss the benefits of a structured and well-designed audit plan.

Benefits of audit planning

Audit planning is the initial stage of the audit process. It helps to establish the overall audit strategy and the technique to complete the audit. Audit planning aids in making the audit process more structured and objective oriented.

An audit plan helps to identify and determine the following aspects:

- The objectives of the audit
- The scope of the audit
- The periodicity of the audit
- The members of the audit team
- The method of audit

The following are some of the benefits of audit planning:

- It helps the auditor to focus on high-risk areas
- It helps in the identification of resource requirements to conduct the audit
- It helps to estimate the budget for the audit
- It helps to carry out audit work in a defined structure, which ultimately benefits the auditor as well as the auditee units

Selection criteria

An IS auditor should have a sufficient understanding about the various criteria for the selection of audit processes.

One of the criteria for audit planning is to have an audit universe. All of the significant processes of the enterprise's business should be included in the audit universe.

Each business process may undergo a qualitative or quantitative risk assessment by evaluating the risk in respect to relevant risk factors. Risk factors influence the frequency of the audit. After the risk is evaluated for each relevant factor, criteria may be defined to determine the risk of each process. The audit plan can then be designed to consider all the high-risk areas.

Reviewing audit planning

This audit plan should be reviewed and approved by top management. Generally, approval is obtained from the audit committee of the board.

The audit plan should be flexible enough to address the change in risk environment (that is, new regulatory requirements, changes in the market condition, and other risk factors).

The approved audit plan should be communicated promptly to the following groups:

- Senior management
- Business functions and other stakeholders
- The internal audit team

Individual audit assignments

The next step after doing the overall annual planning is to plan individual audit assignments. The IS auditor must understand the overall environment under review. While planning an individual audit assignment, an IS auditor should consider the following:

- Prior audit reports
- Risk assessment reports
- Regulatory requirements
- Standard operating processes
- Technological requirements

Like every other process, the audit process will also have some input and output. The following diagram will help you to understand input and output elements of the audit process:

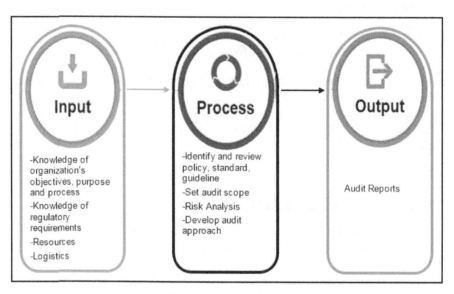

Figure 1.3 – Audit process flow

For effective audit planning, it is of utmost importance that the IS auditor has a thorough understanding of business process applications and controls. The basic architecture of some of the commonly used applications and their associated risks are discussed in the next topic.

Key aspects from CISA exam perspective

The following figure covers important aspects from the CISA exam perspective:

CISA questions	Possible answers
What is the first step in risk-based audit planning?	To identify areas of high risk
What is a major benefit of risk-based audit planning?	The utilization of resources for high-risk areas
What is the first step to conduct a data center review?	What is the first step to conduct a data center review?

Self-evaluation questions

1. **Which of the following is the first step in risk-based audit planning?**
   A. To identify the requirements of relevant stakeholders
   B. To identify high-risk processes in the company
   C. To identify the budget
   D. To identify the profit function

2. **Which of the following is a major advantage of a risk-based approach to audit planning?**
   A. Advance communication of the audit plan
   B. Completion of the audit exercise within the allotted time and budget
   C. The collection of audit fees in advance
   D. Optimum use of audit resources for high-risk processes

3. **Which of the following should be the first exercise while reviewing data center security?**
   A. The evaluation of the physical security arrangement
   B. The evaluation of vulnerabilities and threats to the data center location
   C. The evaluation of the business continuity arrangement for the data center
   D. The evaluation of the logical security arrangement

4. **Which of the following is the most important aspect of planning an audit?**
   A. Identifying high-risk processes
   B. Identifying the experience and capabilities of audit staff
   C. Identifying control testing procedures of the audit
   D. Determining the audit schedule

Business process applications and controls

Working knowledge of the business environment and business objectives is required to plan a risk-based audit. The IS auditor should have a sufficient understanding of the overall architecture and technological specifications of the various applications used by the organization and the risks associated with those applications.

In understanding the issues and current risks facing the business, the IS auditor should focus on the areas that are most meaningful to management. To effectively audit business application systems, an IS auditor is required to gain a thorough understanding of the system under the scope of the audit.

The following are some of the widely used applications in business processes. The CISA candidate should be aware of the risks associated with each of them.

E-commerce

Let's start with understanding how e-commerce works:

- Single-tier architecture runs on a single computer, that is, a client-based application
- Two-tier architecture includes a client and server
- Three-tier architecture consists of the following:
    - A presentation tier (for interaction with the user)
    - An application tier (for processing)
    - A data tier (for the database)

The risks are as follows:

- A compromise of confidential user data
- Data integrity issues due to unauthorized alterations
- The system being unavailable may impact business continuity
- The repudiation of transactions by either party

The IS auditor's roles are as follows:

- To review the overall security architecture related to firewalls, encryption, networks, PKI to ensure confidentiality, integrity, availability, and the non-repudiation of e-commerce transactions
- To review the process of log capturing and monitoring for e-commerce transactions
- To review the incident management process
- To review the effectiveness of the controls implemented for privacy laws
- To review anti-malware controls
- To review business continuity arrangements

Electronic Data Interchange (EDI)

Let's start with understanding how EDI works:

- EDI is the online transfer of data or information between two enterprises.
- EDI ensures an effective and efficient transfer platform without the use of paper.
- The traditional exchange of paper documents between organizations has been replaced with EDI platforms.
- EDI applications contain processing features such as transmission, translation, and the storage of transactions flowing between two enterprises.
- An EDI setup can be either traditional EDI (batch transmission within each trading partner's computers) or web-based EDI (accessed through an internet service provider).

The risks are as follows:

- One of the biggest risks applicable to EDI is transaction authorization.
- Due to electronic interactions, no inherent authentication occurs.
- There could be related uncertainty with a specific legal liability when we don't have a trading partner agreement.
- Any performance-related issues with EDI applications could have a negative impact on both parties.
- Other EDI-related risks include unauthorized access, data integrity and confidentiality, and the loss or duplication of EDI transactions.

The IS auditor's roles are as follows:

- To determine the data's confidentiality, integrity, and authenticity, as well as the non-repudiation of transactions
- To determine invalid transactions and data before they are uploaded to the system
- To determine the accuracy, validity, and reasonableness of data
- To validate and ensure the reconciliation of totals between the EDI system and the trading partner's system

The IS auditor should determine the use of some controls to validate the sender, as follows:

1. The use of control fields within an EDI message
2. The use of VAN sequential control numbers or reports
3. Acknowledgment transactions with the sender

The auditor should also determine the availability of the following controls:

Control requirements for inbound transactions:

- A log of each inbound transaction on receipt
- Segment count totals built into the transaction set trailer
- Checking digits to detect transposition and transcription errors

Control requirements for outbound transactions:

- Transactions to be compared with the trading partner's profile
- Proper segregation of duties for high-risk transactions
- A log to be maintained for outbound transactions

EDI audits also involve the use of audit monitors (to capture EDI transactions) and expert systems (to evaluate transactions).

Point of Sale (POS)

Let's start with understanding how POS works:

- Debit and credit card transactions are the most common examples of POS.
- Data is captured at the time and place of sale.

The risks of this are as follows:

- The risk of skimming, that is, the unauthorized capturing of card data with the purpose of duplicating the card
- The risk of the unauthorized disclosure of PINs

The IS auditor's objectives are as follows:

- To determine that data used for authentication (PIN/CVV) is not stored in the local POS system
- To determine that the cardholder's data (either at rest or in transit) is encrypted

Electronic banking

Let's start with understanding how it works:

- E-banking websites and mobile-based systems are integrated with the bank's core system to support automatic transactions without any manual intervention.
- Automated processing improves processing speed and reduces opportunities for human error and fraud.
- Electronic banking increases the dependence on internet and communication infrastructure.

Two of the risks of this are as follows:

- Heavy dependence on internet service providers, telecommunication companies, and other technology firms
- Cyber risks such as system hacking, system unavailability, and a lack of transaction integrity

The IS auditor's objectives are as follows:

- To determine the effectiveness of the governance and oversight of e-banking activities
- To determine arrangements for the confidentiality, integrity, and availability of e-banking infrastructure
- To determine the effectiveness of security controls with respect to authentication and the non-repudiation of electronic transactions
- To review the effectiveness of the controls implemented for privacy laws
- To review anti-malware controls
- To review business continuity arrangements

Electronic funds transfer (EFT)

Let's start with understanding how EFT works:

- Through EFT, money can be transferred from one account to another electronically, that is, without cheque writing and cash collection procedures.

Some of the risks are as follows:

- Heavy dependence on internet service providers, telecommunication companies, and other technology firms
- Cyber risks such as system hacking, system unavailability, and a lack of transaction integrity

The IS auditor's objectives are as follows:

- To determine the availability of two-factor authentication for secure transactions.
- To determine that systems and communication channels have undergone appropriate security testing.
- To determine that transaction data (either at rest or in transit) is encrypted.
- To determine the effectiveness of controls on data transmission.
- To review security arrangements for the integrity of switch operations. An EFT switch connects with all equipment in the network.
- To review the log capturing and monitoring process of EFT transactions. In the absence of paper documents, it is important to have an alternate audit trail for each transaction.

Image processing

Let's start with understanding how it works:

- An image processing system processes, stores, and retrieves image data.
- An image processing system requires huge amounts of storage resources and strong processing power for scanning, compression, displays, and printing.
- Such systems are capable of identifying colors and shades.
- The use of image processing (in place of paper documents) can result in increased productivity, the immediate retrieval of documents, enhanced control over document storage, and efficient disaster recovery procedures.

Some of the risks are as follows:

- Implementation without appropriate planning and testing may result in system failure.
- The workflow system may need to be completely redesigned to integrate with the image processing system.

- Traditional controls and audit processes may not be applicable to image processing systems. New controls must be designed for automated processes.
- Cyber risks such as system hacking, system unavailability, and a lack of transaction integrity.

The IS auditor's objectives are as follows:

- To determine the effectiveness of controls on the inputs, processing, and outputs of image processing systems
- To determine the reliability of the scanners used for image processing
- To review the retention process for original documents
- To determine that original documents are retained at least until a good image has been captured
- To review the confidentiality, integrity, and availability arrangements of image processing systems
- To review the training arrangements for employees to ensure that the processes of image scanning and storing are maintained as per the quality control matrix

Artificial intelligence and expert systems

Artificial intelligence and expert systems do the following:

- Capture and utilize the knowledge and experience of individuals
- Improve performance and productivity
- Automate skilled processes without manual intervention

A knowledge base in AI contains information about a particular subject and rules for interpreting that information. The components of a knowledge base include the following:

- **Decision trees**: Questions to lead the user through a series of choices
- **Rules**: Rules that use "if" and "then" conditions
- **Semantic nets**: A knowledge base that conveys meaning
- **Knowledge interface**: Stores expert-level knowledge
- **Data interface**: Stores data for analysis and decision making

The risks are as follows:

- Incorrect decisions or actions performed by the system due to incorrect assumptions, formulas, or databases in the system
- Cyber risks such as system hacking, system unavailability, and a lack of transaction integrity

The IS auditor's roles are as follows:

- To assess the applicability of AI in various business processes and determine the associated potential risks
- To review adherence to documented policies and procedures
- To review the appropriateness of the assumptions, formulas, and decision logic built into the system
- To review the change management process for updating the system
- To review the security arrangements to maintain the confidentiality, integrity, and availability of the system

Once the IS auditor understands the basic architecture of the business applications and associated risks, the next step is to understand the appropriateness and effectiveness of the implemented controls to mitigate the risks.

Key aspects from CISA exam perspective

The following covers the important aspects from a CISA exam perspective:

CISA questions	Possible answer
What is the major risk of EDI transactions?	The absence of agreement (in the absence of a trading partner agreement, there could be uncertainty related to specific legal liability).
What is the objective of encryption?	To ensure the integrity and confidentiality of transactions.
How are inbound transactions controlled in an EDI environment?	Inbound transactions are controlled via logs of the receipt of inbound transactions, the use of segment count totals, and the use of check digits to detect transposition and transcription errors.

What is the objective of key verification control?	Key verification is a method where data is entered a second time and compared with the initial data entry to ensure that the data entered is correct. This is generally used in EFT transactions, where another employee re-enters the same data to perform this check before any money is transferred.
What is the objective of non-repudiation?	Nom-repudiation ensures that a transaction is enforceable and that the claimed sender cannot later deny generating and sending the message.
What is the most important component of the artificial intelligence/expert system area?	Knowledge base (The knowledge base contains specific information or fact patterns associated with a particular subject matter and the rules for interpreting these facts; therefore, strict access control should be implemented and monitored to ensure the integrity of the decision rules)

Self-evaluation questions

1. **Which of the following is the area of greatest concern in an EDI process?**
    A. No logging and monitoring of EDI transactions.
    B. Senior management has not approved the EDI process.
    C. The contract for a trading partner has not been entered.
    D. EDI using a dedicated channel for communication.

2. **Encryption helps in achieving which of the following objectives in an EDI environment?**
    A. Ensuring the confidentiality and integrity of transactions
    B. Detecting invalid transactions
    C. Validating and ensuring the reconciliation of totals between the EDI system and a trading partner system
    D. Providing functional acknowledgment to the sender

3. **In an EDI environment, which of the following procedures ensures the completeness of an inbound transaction?**
    A. The process for transaction authentication
    B. The build segment count coming to the transaction set trailer of the sender
    C. An audit trail
    D. The segregation of duties for high-risk transactions

4. **In which of the following processes are details entered by one employee re-entered by another employee to check their accuracy?**
    A. Reasonableness check
    B. Key verification
    C. Control total
    D. Completeness check

5. **Which of the following is used in an e-commerce application to ensure that a transaction is enforceable?**
    A. Access control
    B. Authentication
    C. Encryption
    D. Non-repudiation

Types of controls

An internal control is a process that is used to safeguard the assets of an organization. Assets can include systems, data, people, hardware, or the reputation of the organization. Internal controls help in achieving the objectives of the organization by mitigating various risks.

Internal controls are implemented through policies, procedures, practices, and organizational structures to address risks. Internal controls provide reasonable assurance to management about the achievement of business objectives. Through internal controls, risk events are prevented or detected and corrected.

Top management is responsible for implementing a culture that supports efficient and effective internal control processes.

Effective controls in an organization can be categorized into the following types:

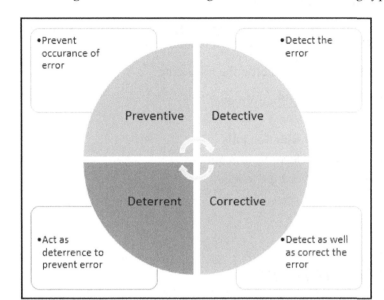

Let's discuss the control types in detail.

Preventive controls

Preventive controls are designed to be implemented in such a way that prevents a threat event and thus avoids any potential impact of that threat event.

Examples of preventive controls include the following:

- The use of qualified personnel
- The segregation of duties
- The use of SOPs to prevent errors
- Transaction authorization procedures
- Edit checks
- Access control procedures
- Firewalls
- Physical barriers

Detective controls

Detective controls are designed to detect a threat event once that event has occurred. Detective controls aim to reduce the impact of such events.

Examples of detective controls include the following:

- Internal audits and other reviews
- Log monitoring
- Checkpoints in production jobs
- Echo controls in telecommunications
- Error messages over tape labels
- Variance analysis
- Quality assurance

Corrective controls

Corrective controls are designed to minimize the impact of a threat event once it has occurred and help in restoring a business to normal operations.

Examples of detective controls include the following:

- Business continuity planning
- Disaster recovery planning
- Incident response planning
- Backup procedures

Deterrent controls

The purpose of a deterrent control is to give a warning signal to deter a threat event.

Examples of deterrent controls include the following:

- CCTV cameras or "under surveillance" signs
- Warning signs

The difference between preventive and deterrent controls

For the CISA exam, it is important to understand the difference between preventive and deterrent controls. When a preventive control is implemented, an intruder is prevented from performing an act. They do not have a choice in whether or not to perform the act.

When a deterrent control is implemented, the intruder is being given a warning. Here, the intruder has a choice: either to act as per the warning or ignore the warning.

A locked door to a room is a preventive control. Intruders cannot go through the door. On the other hand, just a warning sign that says "No Entry" is a deterrent control. Intruders can ignore the warning and enter the room.

Apart from the controls we have covered thus far, CISA candidates should also understand compensating controls. It should be noted that the absence of one control can be compensated for by having another strong control.

Compensating controls

Compensating controls are alternate measures that are employed to ensure that weaknesses in a system are not exploited. In many cases, a strong control in one area can compensate for a weakness in another area.

For example, in small organizations, the segregation of duties may not always be feasible. In such cases, compensatory controls such as reviews of logs should be implemented.

Similarly, some organizations may prefer to have alternate security measures in place of encryption.

Control objectives

A control objective is a reason why a control is implemented. Control objectives are linked to business objectives.

A control objective generally addresses the following:

- The effectiveness and efficiency of operational processes. For example, preventive controls attempt to prevent invalid transactions from being processed and assets from being misappropriated. However, detective controls have the objective of detecting errors or fraud that could result in the misstatement of financial statements.
- Adherence to regulatory requirements.
- The protection of assets.

It is advisable to document objectives for each and every control. Periodic reviews and monitoring of controls are required to validate results against these objectives.

Control measures

Control measures are implemented to achieve control objectives. Control measures are activities that are taken to prevent, eliminate, or minimize the risk of threat occurrence.

Key aspects from CISA exam perspective

The following table covers the important aspects from a CISA exam perspective:

CISA questions	Possible answer
Segregation of duties is an example of which type of control?	Preventive control
Controls that enable a risk or deficiency to be corrected before a loss occurs are known as what?	Corrective control
Controls that directly mitigate a risk or lack of controls directly acting upon a risk are know as what?	Compensating control

Self-evaluation questions

1. **Controls that are designed to prevent omissions, errors, or negative acts from occurring are which kind of controls?**
    A. Preventive controls
    B. Detective controls
    C. Corrective controls
    D. Compensating controls

2. **What are controls that are put in place to indicate or detect an error?**
    A. Preventive controls
    B. Detective controls
    C. Corrective controls
    D. Deterrent controls

3. **Which of the following is the segregation of duties an example of?**
    A. Preventive control
    B. Detective control
    C. Corrective control
    D. Deterrent control

4. **What is the process of using well-designed documentation to prevent errors an example of?**
    A. Preventive control
    B. Detective control
    C. Corrective control
    D. Deterrent control

5. **What kind of control is a control that enables a deficiency or another irregularity to be corrected before a loss occurs?**
    A. Preventive control
    B. Detective control
    C. Corrective control
    D. Deterrent control

6. **Utilizing a service of only qualified resource is an example of:**
    A. Preventive control
    B. Detective control
    C. Corrective control
    D. Internal control

7. **A check subroutine that identifies an error and makes a correction before enabling the process to continue is an example of what kind of control?**
    A. Preventive control
    B. Detective control
    C. Corrective control
    D. Deterrent control

8. **Barriers or warning signs are examples of what kind of control?**
    A. Preventive control
    B. Detective control
    C. Corrective control
    D. Deterrent control

9. **An "echo" message in a telecommunications protocol is an example of what kind of control?**
    A. Preventive control
    B. Detective control
    C. Corrective control
    D. Compensating control

10. **Checkpoints in a production job are examples of what kind of control?**
    A. Preventive control
    B. Detective control
    C. Corrective control
    D. Compensating control

11. **Controls that minimize the impact of a threat are what kind of controls?**
    A. Preventive controls
    B. Detective controls
    C. Corrective controls
    D. Compensating controls

12. **Controls that remedy problems observed by means of detective controls are what kind of controls?**
    A. Preventive controls
    B. Detective controls
    C. Corrective controls
    D. Compensating controls

13. **Controls that indirectly address a risk or address the absence of controls that would otherwise directly act upon that risk are what kind of controls?**
    A. Preventive controls
    B. Detective controls
    C. Corrective controls
    D. Compensating controls

14. **Controls that predict potential problems before their occurrence are what kind of controls?**
    - A. Preventive controls
    - B. Detective controls
    - C. Corrective controls
    - D. Compensating controls

15. **The requirement of biometric access for physical facilities is an example of what kind of control?**
    - A. Preventive control
    - B. Detective control
    - C. Corrective control
    - D. Deterrent control

16. **Which of the following risks represents a process failure to detect a serious error?**
    - A. Detective risk
    - B. Inherent risk
    - C. Sampling risk
    - D. Control risk

17. **Which of the following statements best describes detective controls and corrective controls?**
    - A. Both controls can prevent the occurrence of errors
    - B. Detective controls are used to avoid financial loss and corrective controls are used to avoid operational risks
    - C. Detective controls are used as a deterrent check and corrective controls are used to make management aware that an error has occurred
    - D. Detective controls are used to identify that an error has occurred and corrective controls fix a problem before a loss occurs

18. **Why are control objectives defined in an audit program?**
    - A. To give the auditor an overview for control testing
    - B. To restrict the auditor to testing only documented controls
    - C. To prevent management from altering the scope of the audit
    - D. To help the auditor to plan for the resource requirements

Risk-based audit planning

CISA aspirants are expected to understand the following aspects of risk-based audit planning:

- What is the risk?
- Vulnerabilities and threats
- Inherent risk and residual risk
- The advantages of risk-based audit planning
- Audit risk
- The steps of the risk-based audit approach
- The steps of risk assessment
- The four methodologies for risk treatment

What is risk?

Let's look at some of the widely accepted definitions of *risk*.

Most of the CISA questions are framed around **Risk**. CISA candidates should have a thorough understanding of the term *risk*. Multiple definitions/formulas are available for risk. If you look carefully, every definition speaks either directly or indirectly about two terms: **probability** and **impact**.

Some of the more commonly used definitions of risk are presented here:

- ERM-COSO defines risk as "Potential events that may impact the entity."
- The Oxford English Dictionary defines risk as "The probability of something happening multiplied by the resulting cost or benefit if it does."
- Business Dictionary.com defines risk as "The probability or threat of damage, injury, liability, loss, or any other negative occurrence that is caused by external or internal vulnerabilities, and that may be avoided through preventive action."
- ISO 31000 defines risk as "The effect of uncertainty on objectives."

In simple words, the 'risk' is the product of probability and impact:

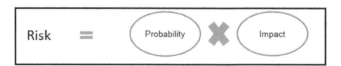

Probability and impact are equally important when identifying risk. For example, say that the probability or likelihood of a product being damaged is very high, with a value of "1"; however, say that product barely costs anything and so the impact is "0" even if the product is damaged.

So, the risk in this scenario would be calculated as follows:

Risk = P * I

Risk = 1 * 0 = 0

Understanding vulnerability and threat

Another way of understanding risk is by understanding the notion of vulnerability and threat. In simple terms, a vulnerability is a weakness and a threat is something that can exploit said weakness. Again, both elements (V and T) should be present in order to constitute a risk.

There is no threat to a useless system, even if it is highly vulnerable. As such, the risk for that system would be nil in spite of the high vulnerability:

Vulnerability	Threat
A weakness in a system. Generally, a vulnerability can be controlled by the organization.	An element that exploits a weakness. Generally, a threat is not in the control of the organization.
Vulnerabilities are mostly internal elements.	Threats are mostly external elements.
Examples include weak coding, missing anti-virus, weak access control, and others.	Examples include hackers, malware, criminals, natural disasters, and so on.

There are various definitions and formulas for risks. However, for the CISA certification, please remember only the following two formulas:

Risk = Probability*Impact

Risk = A*V*T

In the second formula, A, V, and T are the value of, vulnerability of, and threats to assets, respectively.

Understanding inherent risk and residual risk

A CISA candidate should understand the difference between inherent risk and residual risk:

Inherent risk	Residual risk
The risk that an activity poses, excluding any controls or mitigating factors	The risk that remains after taking controls into account
Gross risk – that is, the risk before controls are applied	Net risk – that is, the risk after controls are applied

The following is the formula for residual risk:

Residual Risk = Inherent Risk - Control

Advantages of risk-based audit planning

Risk-based audit planning is essential to determine an audit's scope (the areas/processes/assets to be audited) effectively. It helps to deploy audit resources to areas within an organization that are subject to the greatest risk.

The following are the advantages of risk-based audit planning:

- Effective risk-based auditing reduces the audit risk that arises during an audit.
- Risk-based auditing is a proactive approach that helps in identifying issues at an early stage.
- One of the major factors in a risk assessment is compliance with contractual and legal requirements. Risk-based auditing helps an organization to identify any major deviation from contractual and legal requirements. This improves compliance awareness throughout the organization.
- Risk-based auditing promotes preventive controls over reactive measures.
- Risk-based auditing helps to align internal audit activities with the risk management practices of the organization.

Audit risk

Audit risk refers to the risk that an auditor may not be able to detect material errors during the course of an audit. Audit risk is influenced by inherent risk, control risk, and detection risk. The following list describes each of these risks:

- **Inherent risk**: This refers to risk that exists before applying a control.
- **Control risk**: This refers to risk that internal controls fail to prevent or detect.
- **Detection risk**: This refers to risk that internal audits fail to prevent or detect.

The following figure explains the relationship between all three risks:

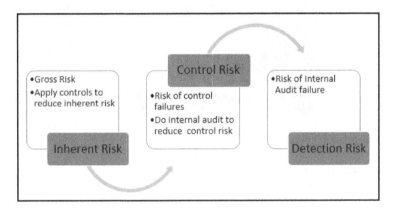

The following is the formulae for calculating the audit risk:

Audit Risk = Inherent Risk X Control Risk x Detection Risk

An IS auditor should have sound knowledge of the audit risk when planning auditing activities. Some ways to minimize audit risk are listed here:

- Conduct risk-based audit planning
- Review the internal control system

- Select appropriate statistical sampling
- Assess the materiality of processes/systems in the audit scope

It is the experience and expertise of the auditor that minimizes audit risk. However, it must be noted that the auditor is a watchdog and not a bloodhound.

Risk-based auditing approach

In a risk-based auditing approach, it is important to understand the steps to be performed by the IS auditor. The following structured approach will help to minimize the audit risk and provide assurance about the state of affairs of the auditee organization:

1. Step 1 – Acquire pre-audit requirements:
   - Knowledge about industry and regulatory requirements
   - Knowledge about applicable risk to the concerned business
   - Prior audit results
2. Step 2 – Obtain information about internal controls:
   - Get knowledge about the control environment and procedures
   - Understand control risks
   - Understand detection risks

3. Step 3 – Conduct compliance test:
   - Identify the controls to be tested
   - Determine the effectiveness of the controls
4. Step 4 – Conduct a substantive test:
   - Identify the process for the substantive test
   - See that the substantive test includes analytical procedures, detail tests of account balances, and other procedures

Risk assessments

A risk assessment includes the following steps:

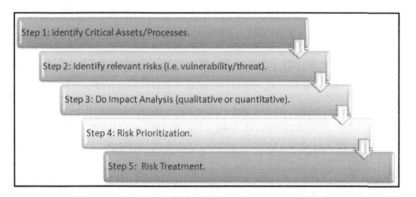

Risk assessments should be conducted at regular intervals to account for changes in risk factors. The risk assessment process has an iterative life cycle. Risk assessments should be performed methodically and the outputs should be comparable and reproducible.

Also, it is important to determine the risk appetite of the organization. Risk appetite helps to prioritize various risks for mitigation.

Risk response methodology

Risk response is the process of dealing with a risk to minimize its impact. It is a very important step in the risk management process. Here are the four main risk response methodologies:

- **Risk mitigation/risk reduction**: Take some action to mitigate/reduce the risk.
- **Risk avoidance**: Change the strategy or business process to avoid the risk.

- **Risk acceptance**: Decide to accept the risk.
- **Risk transfer**: Transfer the risk to a third party. Insurance is the best example.

The risk culture and risk appetite of the organization in question determines the risk response method. Of the preceding responses, the most widely used response is risk mitigation by implementing some level of controls.

Let's understand the preceding risk response methodologies with a practical example. Say that a meteorological department has forecasted heavy rain during the day and we need to attend CISA lectures. The risk of rain can be handled in the following manner:

- The majority of candidates will try to mitigate the risk of rain by arranging for an umbrella/raincoat to safeguard them from potential rain (mitigation of risk).
- Some courageous candidates won't worry about carrying an umbrella/raincoat (risk acceptance).
- Some candidates, such as me, will not attend classes (risk avoidance).

It's not always feasible to mitigate all the risk at an organizational level. Risk-free enterprise is an illusion.

You cannot run a business without taking risks. Risk management is the process of determining whether the amount of risk taken by an organization is in accordance with the organization's capabilities and needs.

Top-down and bottom-up approaches to policy development

Let's understand the difference between the top-down and bottom-up approaches to policy development.

The top-down approach

In the top-down approach, a policy is developed and designed from a senior management perspective. In a top-down approach, policies are developed and aligned with business objectives. Involvement of senior management in designing the risk scenario is of the utmost importance. One advantage of the top-down approach to developing organizational policies is that it ensures consistency across the organization.

The bottom-up approach

In the bottom-up approach, polices are designed and developed from the process owner's/employee's perspective. The bottom-up approach begins by defining operational-level requirements and policies. The bottom-up approach is derived from and implemented on the basis of the results of risk assessments.

The best approach

An organization should make use of both the top-down approach and the bottom-up approach when developing organizational policies. They are complementary to each other and should be used simultaneously. In a top-down approach, major risks to business objectives are addressed, whereas in the bottom-up approach, process-level risks are addressed.

Key aspects from CISA exam perspective

The following table covers the important aspects from the CISA exam perspective:

CISA questions	Possible answers
The most important step in a risk assessment is to identify	Threats and vulnerabilities
In risk-based audit planning, an IS auditor's first step is to identify what?	High risk areas
Once threats and vulnerabilities are identified, what should be the next step?	Identify and evaluate existing controls
What is the advantage of risk based audit planning?	Resources can be utilized for high risk areas
What does the level of protection of information assets depend on?	Criticality of assets
What is risk that is influenced by the actions of an auditor known as?	Detection risk
What is audit risk?	Audit risk is the sum total of inherent risk, control risk, and detection risk
What is risk the product of?	Probability and impact
What are the results of risk management processes used for?	Designing the control

Whose responsibility is the management of risk to an acceptable level?	Senior management
What is the absence of proper security measures known as?	Vulnerability
What is the advantage of the bottom-up approach for the development of organizational policies?	It ensures consistency across the organization.
What is risk before controls are applied known as?	Inherent risk/gross risk (after the implementation of controls, it is known as residual risk/net risk).

Self-evaluation questions

1. **Which of the following is the most critical aspect of a risk analysis?**
    A. Identifying competitors
    B. Identifying the existing controls
    C. Identifying vulnerabilities
    D. Identifying the reporting matrix of the organization

2. **What is the initial step in risk-focused audit planning?**
    A. Identifying the role and responsibility of the relevant function
    B. Identifying high-risk processes
    C. Identifying the budget
    D. Identifying the profit function

3. **What is the main objective of conducting a risk assessment?**
    A. To determine the segregation of duties for critical functions
    B. To ensure that critical vulnerabilities and threats are recognized
    C. To ensure that regulations are complied with
    D. To ensure business profitability

4. **What should be the next step of an IS auditor after identifying threats and vulnerabilities in a business process?**
    A. Identifying the relevant process owner
    B. Identifying the relevant information assets
    C. Reporting the threat and its impact to the audit committee
    D. Identifying and analyzing the current controls

5. **Which of the following is the main benefit of risk-based audit planning?**
    A. The communication of audit planning to the client in advance
    B. The completion of the audit activity within the allocated budget constraints
    C. The use of the latest auditing technology
    D. The focus on high-risk areas

6. **Which of the following should be the primary focus when considering the level of security of an IT asset?**
    A. The criticality of the IT asset
    B. The value of IT the asset
    C. The owner of IT the asset
    D. The business continuity arrangement for the IT asset

7. **The actions of the IS auditor is most likely to influence which of the following risks?**
    A. Inherent
    B. Detection
    C. Control
    D. Business

8. **What is the risk of an inadequate audit methodology known as?**
    A. The procedural aspect
    B. Control risk
    C. Detection risk
    D. Residual risk

9. **Particular threat of an overall business risk indicated as:**
    A. The product of the probability and impact
    B. The probability of threat realization
    C. The valuation of the impact
    D. The valuation of the risk management team

10. **Which of the following is the first step in performing risk assessments of information systems?**
    A. Reviewing the appropriateness of existing controls
    B. B. Reviewing the effectiveness of existing controls
    C. Reviewing the asset-related risk surveillance mechanism
    D. Reviewing the threats and vulnerabilities impacting the assets

11. **What is the first step in evaluating the security controls of a data center?**
    A. Determining the physical security arrangement
    B. Evaluating the threats and vulnerabilities applicable to the data center site
    C. Evaluating the hiring process of security staff
    D. Determining the logical security arrangements

12. **What does the classification of information assets help to ensure?**
    A. The protection of all IT assets
    B. That a fundamental level of security is implemented irrespective of the value of assets
    C. That information assets are subject to suitable levels of protection
    D. That only critical IT assets are protected

13. **Which of the following should be performed first in a risk-focused audit?**
    A. Analyzing inherent risk
    B. Analyzing residual risk
    C. Analyzing the controls assessment
    D. Analyzing the substantive assessment

14. **In a risk-focused audit, which of the following is the most critical step?**
    A. Determining the high-risk processes
    B. Determining the capability of audit resources
    C. Determining the audit procedure
    D. Determining the audit schedule

15. **Which of the following options best describes the process of assessing a risk?**
    A. Subject-oriented
    B. Object-oriented
    C. Mathematics-oriented
    D. Statistics-oriented

16. **What is the outcome of a risk assessment exercise utilized for?**
    A. Estimating profits
    B. Calculating the ROI
    C. Implementing relevant controls
    D. Conducting user acceptance testing

17. **With whom does the responsibility of managing risk to an acceptable level rest?**
    - A. The risk management team
    - B. Senior business management
    - C. The chief information officer
    - D. The chief security officer

18. **Which of the following is a major factor in the evaluation of IT risks?**
    - A. Finding vulnerabilities and threats that are applicable to IT assets
    - B. Analyzing loss expectancy
    - C. Benchmarking with industry
    - D. Analyzing previous audit reports

19. **An IS auditor has determined a few vulnerabilities in a critical application. What should their next step be?**
    - A. Reporting the risk to the audit committee immediately
    - B. Determining a system development methodology
    - C. Identifying threats and their likelihood of occurrence
    - D. Recommending the development of a new system

20. **What does a lack of appropriate control measures indicate?**
    - A. Threat
    - B. Magnitude of impact
    - C. Probability of occurrence
    - D. Vulnerability

21. **Which of the following is the first step in a risk management program?**
    - A. Determining a vulnerability
    - B. Determining existing controls
    - C. Identifying assets
    - D. Conducting a gap analysis

22. **What is the advantage of the bottom-up approach to the development of enterprise policies?**
    - A. They cover the whole organization.
    - B. They are created on the basis of risk analysis.
    - C. They are reviewed by top management.
    - D. They support consistency of procedure.

23. **The mitigation of risk can be done through which of the following?**
    A. Controls
    B. Outsourcing
    C. Audit and certification
    D. Service level agreements (SLAs)

24. **The most important factor when implementing controls is ensuring that the control does which of the following?**
    A. Helps to mitigate risk
    B. Does not impact productivity
    C. Is cost effective
    D. Is automated

25. **The absence of internal control mechanisms is known as what?**
    A. Inherent risk
    B. Control risk
    C. Detection risk
    D. Correction risk

26. **Which of the following represents the risk that the controls will not prevent, correct, or detect errors in a timely manner?**
    A. Inherent risk
    B. Control risk
    C. Detection risk
    D. Correction risk

27. **What is the primary consideration when evaluating the acceptable level of risk?**
    A. The acceptance of risk by higher management
    B. That not all risks need to be addressed
    C. That all relevant risks must be recognized and documented for analysis
    D. The involvement of line management in risk analysis

28. **What is the best approach when focusing an audit on a high-risk area?**
    A. Perform the audit; the control failures will identify the areas of highest risk
    B. Perform the audit and then perform a risk assessment
    C. Perform a risk assessment first and then concentrate control tests in the high-risk areas
    D. Increase sampling rates in high-risk areas

29. **In a risk-based audit approach, which of the following is the least relevant to audit planning?**
    A. The adoption of a mature technology by the organization
    B. The risk culture and risk awareness of the organization
    C. The legal regulatory impact
    D. Previous audit findings

Types of audit and assessment

CISA candidates are expected to have a basic understanding of the various types of audits that can be performed, internally or externally, and the basic audit procedures associated with each of them. These are as follows:

Type of Audit	Description
IS audit	An IS audit is conducted to evaluate and determine whether an information system and any related infrastructure is adequately safeguarded and protected to maintain confidentiality, integrity, and availability.
Compliance audit	CA or more specifically, a compliance audit is conducted to evaluate and determine whether specific regulatory requirements are being complied with.
Financial audit	A financial audit is conducted to evaluate and determine the accuracy of financial reporting. A financial audit involves a detailed and substantive testing approach.
Operational audit	An operational audit is conducted to evaluate and determine the accuracy of an internal control system. It is designed to assess issues related to the efficiency of operational productivity within an organization.
Integrated audit	Here, different types of audit are integrated to combine financial, operational, and other types of audits to form a multi-faceted audit. An integrated audit is performed to assess the overall objectives to safeguard an asset's efficiency and compliance. It can be performed both by internal auditors or external auditors. An integrated audit includes compliance tests of internal controls.
Specialized audit	A specialized audit includes the following: • A third-party service audit • A fraud audit • A forensic audit

Computer forensic audit	A computer forensic audit includes the analysis of electronic devices. An IS auditor can help in performing forensic investigations and conduct an audit of the system to ensure compliance.
Functional audit	A functional audit is conducted to evaluate and determine the accuracy of software functionality. A functional audit is conducted prior to software implementation.

The following diagram shows various audits combined to form an integrated audit, giving an overall view of an organization's functioning:

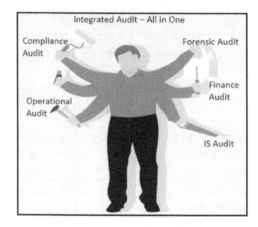

As you can see, integrated audit tests the internal controls of an organization. It can be performed either by the internal audit team or an external audit firm.

Self-evaluation questions

1. **Which audit is designed to collect and evaluate an information system and any related resources?**
   A. Compliance audit
   B. Operational audit
   C. IS audit
   D. Specialized audit

2. Which audit involves specific tests of controls to demonstrate adherence to specific regulatory or industry standards?
    A. Operational audit
    B. Compliance audit
    C. Integrated audit
    D. Financial audit

3. Which audit assesses the overall objectives within an organization in terms of safeguarding an asset's efficiency and compliance?
    A. Operational audit
    B. Compliance audit
    C. Integrated audit
    D. Financial audit

4. Which audit involves the independent evaluation of software products, verifying it's configuration items?
    A. Functional audit
    B. Integrated audit
    C. Specialized audit
    D. Compliance audit

5. In which audit can an IS auditor assist a forensic specialist in performing forensic investigations and conduct an audit of the system to ensure compliance?
    A. Specialized audit
    B. Integrated audit
    C. IS audit
    D. Computer forensic audit

6. Which audit is designed to assess issues related to the efficiency of operational productivity within an organization?
    A. Administrative audit
    B. Integrated audit
    C. Compliance audit
    D. Operational audit

Summary

In this chapter, we discussed various audit processes, standards, guidelines, practices, and techniques that an IS auditor is expected to use during audit assignments. We learned about risk-based audit planning and its advantages. The most important benefit of audit planning is that it helps the auditor to focus on high-risk areas. We also discussed the major risks associated with business applications.

In the next chapter, we will discuss and learn about audit execution, which includes project management techniques, sampling methodology, audit evidence collection techniques, and other aspects of conducting an audit.

Assessments

In this section, you will find the answers to the assessment questions.

Content of the audit charter

1. **Answer: A. Higher management**
   Explanation: Ideally, top management should approve the audit charter. The approved audit charter is the basis on which the chief audit officer carries out audit processes. The IS department and the IT steering committee should not be involved in the preparation of the audit charter.

2. **Answer: D. Outline the overall authority, scope, and responsibilities of the audit function.**
   Explanation: The overall scope, authority, and responsibility of the audit function is outlined in an audit charter. The charter should not be frequently modified. The audit charter will not cover procedural aspects such as the audit calendar and resource allocation. Business continuity arrangements should ideally be incorporated in the BCP document, and it should not form part of the audit charter.

3. **Answer: D. To prescribe the authority and responsibilities of the audit department**
   Explanation: The main purpose of the audit charter is to define the auditor's roles and responsibilities. The audit charter should empower auditors to perform their work. Procedural aspects such as audit procedure, resource allocation, and ethical standards should not be a part of the audit charter.

4. **Answer: B. The audit charter**
    The audit charter includes the overall scope, responsibility, and authority of the audit department. Audit planning is included in the audit calendar. The risk assessment and treatment plan should contain details of identified risks and their mitigating controls. The compendium of audit observations contains a summary of critical audit observations for top management.

5. **Answer: C. To understand the authority and responsibility of individuals**
    Explanation: An organization chart is used to derive details about the authority and responsibility of relevant functions in the organization. It will help to understand whether proper segregation of duties exists.

6. **Answer: A. The audit charter**
    Explanation: The overall scope, authority, and responsibility of the audit department is outlined in the audit charter. Primarily, the actions of the audit team will be influenced and guided by this charter.

7. **Answer. C. Security policy decisions**
    Explanation: On the basis of the outcome of the risk management process, the organization determines the security requirements. Other choices are not directly impacted by the results of the risk management process.

8. **Answer: B. The audit function's reporting structure**
    Explanation: The overall scope, authority, and responsibility of the audit department is outlined in the audit charter. It should also document the reporting matrix of the audit function. Generally, the head of the audit reports to an audit committee.

9. **Answer: A. The approved audit charter**
    Explanation: The overall scope, authority, and responsibility of the internal audit department is outlined in the audit charter. The audit charter should be approved by top management/members of the board. The other options are not correct.

10. **Answer: C. The internal audit function**
    Explanation: The overall scope, authority, and responsibility of the internal audit department is outlined in the audit charter. The authority, scope, and responsibilities of the external audit are governed by the engagement letter.

11. **Answer: C. The approved audit charter**
    Explanation: An internal audit charter is an official document that comprises the internal audit department's objectives, authority, responsibilities, and delegation of authority.

12. **Answer. B. The audit function must be independent of the business function and should have direct access to the board audit committee.**
Explanation: The audit function should be independent of influence and bias. Having direct and immediate access to the audit committee can enable auditors to raise major irregularities and concerns without any influence from business functions.

13. **Answer. D. To provide a clear mandate in terms of authority and responsibilities for performing the audit function**
Explanation: The charter's main purpose is to define the auditor's roles and responsibilities. The audit charter empowers the audit function to carry out their work. The other options are not relevant to this purpose.

Audit planning

1. **Answer: B. To identify high-risk processes in the organization**
Explanation: The identification of high-risk areas within the audit scope is the first step in the audit procedure. Audit planning can be done in accordance with the findings regarding the risk-prone areas.

2. **Answer: D. The optimal use of audit resources for high-risk processes**
Explanation: The identification of high-risk areas within the audit scope is the first step in the audit procedure. Audit planning can be done in accordance with the findings regarding the risk-prone areas. Risk-based audit planning is designed to ensure that enough audit resources are spent on the risk-prone areas.

3. **Answer: B. The evaluation of threats and vulnerabilities applicable to the data center**
Explanation: Getting information and an understanding of the processes being audited and evaluating the risks and various threats will help auditors to concentrate on high-risk areas, thereby making the audit more effective and relevant.

4. **Answer: A. To identify high-risk processes**
Explanation: The identification of high-risk areas within the audit scope is the first step in the audit procedure. Audit planning can be done in accordance with the findings regarding the risk-prone areas. Risk-based audit planning is designed to ensure that enough audit resources are spent on the risk-prone areas.

Business process applications and controls

1. **Answer: C. The contract for the trading partner is not entered**
   Explanation: Legal liability cannot be enforced in the absence of an agreement between trading partners. There may be uncertainty with respect to legal liability. This will be the area of most concern. A dedicated communication channel is considered a good control for EDI transactions.

2. **Answer: A. Ensuring the integrity and confidentiality of transactions**
   Explanation: Encryption is a technical control through which plaintext is converted into encrypted (non-readable) text. Encryption processes are implemented to ensure the integrity and confidentiality of transactions.

3. **Answer: B. Building a segment count total into transaction set trailer**
   Explanation: Building a segment count total ensures the completeness of inbound transactions in an EDI environment.

4. **Answer. B. Key verification**
   Explanation: In key verification, the same field is filled in twice and a machine compares the entries for verification and validation. A reasonableness check ensures the logical reasoning of an input transaction. The control total is a system-based control that ensures that all relevant data is captured. A sequence check ensures the continuity of serial numbers. Completeness controls ensure the presence input for all required fields.

5. **Answer: D. Non-repudiation**
   Explanation: Non-repudiation is a control that ensures that the sender cannot deny a transaction. It ensures that a transaction is enforceable.

Types of controls

1. **Answer: A. Preventive controls**
   Explanation: Preventive controls are incorporated in such a way that prevents a threat event and thus avoids its potential impact. Detective controls are implemented to detect threat events once they have occurred. Detective controls aim to reduce the impact of an event. Corrective controls are designed to minimize the impact of a threat event once it has occurred and help in restoring a business to its routine operations. Compensating controls are alternate measures that are employed to ensure that weaknesses in a system are not exploited. In many cases, a strong control in one area can compensate for a weakness in another area.

2. **Answer: B. Detective controls**

   Explanation: Preventive controls are incorporated in such a way that prevents a threat event and thus avoids its potential impact. Detective controls are implemented to detect threat events once they have occurred. Detective controls aim to reduce the impact of an event. Corrective controls are designed to minimize the impact of a threat event once it has occurred and help in restoring a business to its routine operations. Compensating controls are alternate measures that are employed to ensure that weaknesses in a system are not exploited. In many cases, a strong control in one area can compensate for a weakness in another area.

3. **Answer: A. Preventive controls**

   Explanation: Segregation of duties is an attempt to prevent fraud or irregularities by segregating duties such that no single employee can commit fraud or other irregularities.

4. **Answer: A. Preventive controls**

   Explanation: Well-designed documents are an attempt to prevent errors by implementing efficient and effective operational procedures in the organization.

5. **Answer: C. Corrective controls**

   Explanation: Corrective controls are designed to minimize the impact of a threat event once it has occurred and help in restoring the routine operations of the business.

6. **Answer: A. Preventive controls**

   Explanation: Employing only qualified personnel is an attempt to prevent errors or other irregularities.

7. **Answer: C. Corrective controls**

   Explanation: The check subroutine corrects the error. It modifies the processing system and minimizes the likelihood of future occurrences of the problem.

8. **Answer: D. Deterrent controls**

   Explanation: A deterrent control is anything intended to warn a potential attacker not to attack.

9. **Answer: B. Detective controls**

   Explanation: Detective controls use controls that detect and report the prevalence of an error, omission, or malicious act.

10. **Answer: B. Detective controls**
    Explanation: Detective controls detect and report the prevalence of an error, omission, or malicious act.

11. **Answer: C. Corrective controls**
    Explanation: Corrective controls are designed to minimize the impact of a threat event once it has occurred and help in restoring to the routine operations of a business.

12. **Answer: C. Corrective controls**
    Explanation: Corrective controls are designed to minimize the impact of a threat event once it has occurred and help in restoring to the routine operations of a business. They provide a remedy to problems discovered by detective controls.

13. **Answer: D. Compensating controls**
    Explanation: Compensating controls are an alternate measure that is employed to ensure that weaknesses in a system are not exploited. In many cases, a strong control in one area can compensate for weaknesses in other areas.

14. **Answer: A. Preventive controls**
    Explanation: Preventive controls detect problems before they arise. They prevent omissions, errors, or malicious acts from occurring.

15. **Answer: A. Preventive controls**
    Explanation: Access control aims to prevent access by unauthorized persons. It prevents omissions, errors, or malicious acts from occurring.

16. **Answer. C. Control risk**
    Explanation: Control risk is a term that signifies the possibility that a control will fail to prevent or detect unwanted actions.

17. **Answer. D. Detective controls are used to determine whether an error has occurred and corrective controls fix problems before losses occur.**
    Explanation: Detective controls are designed to detect or indicate that an error has occurred. Examples of detective controls include audits, hash totals, echo controls, and so on. Corrective controls are designed to correct a risk or deficiency to prevent losses. Examples of corrective controls include business continuity planning, backup procedures, and more.

18. **Answer. A. Give the auditor an overview of control testing.**
    Explanation: On the basis of control objectives, an auditor can plan control testing to evaluate the effectiveness and efficiency of implemented controls.

Risk-based audit planning

1. **Answer: C. Identifying vulnerabilities**
   Explanation: The identification of vulnerabilities is an important aspect of conducting a risk assessment. If a vulnerability is appropriately recognized, controls and audit planning may not be effective.

2. **Answer: B. Identifying high-risk processes of the organization**
   Explanation: The identification of high-risk processes is the first and most critical step in risk-based audit planning. Audit planning should be done in accordance with high-risk areas.

3. **Answer: B. Ensuring that critical vulnerabilities and threats have been recognized**
   Explanation: The identification of vulnerabilities and threats is critical in developing a risk-based audit strategy. This will help in the determination of the processes to be considered in the scope of audit. The audit team can concentrate on high-risk areas.

4. **Answer: D. Identifying and analyzing current controls**
   Explanation: Once the threats and vulnerabilities are identified, the auditor should evaluate existing controls to draw a conclusion about residual risk.

5. **Answer: D. Focusing on high-risk areas**
   Explanation: The main advantage of a risk-focused audit is that the auditor can focus on areas of high risk. This will help to plan an audit in such a way that means the audit team can concentrate on the high-risk processes.

6. **Answer: A. The criticality of IT assets**
   Explanation: Protecting an asset will involve costs. It is important to understand the criticality of assets when designing appropriate levels of protection.

7. **Answer: B. Detection**
   Explanation: Detection risk refers to the risk that an internal audit fails to prevent or detect. Inherent risk refers to risk that exists before applying any controls. Control risk refers to risk that internal controls fail to prevent or detect. Business risks are not impacted by inadequate audit procedure.

8. **Answer: C. Detection risk.**
   Explanation: Detection risk refers to risk that an internal audit fails to prevent or detect.

9. **Answer: A. The product of probability and impact**
   Explanation: Risk is the product of impact and product. Option A considers both probability and impact. Option B considers only the probability of occurrence. Option C considers only the quantum of the impact. Option D is not applicable to the structured and scientific process of risk assessment.

10. **Answer: D. Reviewing the threats and vulnerabilities applicable to the data center**
Explanation: The identification of vulnerabilities and threats is the first step in a risk assessment process. Once the threats and vulnerabilities are identified, the auditor should evaluate existing controls and their effectiveness to draw a conclusion about the residual risk. Continuous risk monitoring is implemented during the risk monitoring function.

11. **Answer: Evaluating the threats and vulnerabilities applicable to the data center**
Explanation: Out of the given options, the first step in evaluating the security controls of a data center is evaluating the threats to and vulnerabilities of the data center. Options A and D are followed once the vulnerabilities and threats are identified. Option C is not considered as a part of a security analysis.

12. **Answer: C. Information assets are subject to suitable levels of protection**
Explanation: Data classification helps in determining the appropriate level of protection for information assets. Having a specific level of information security is important when protecting data and other IT assets.

13. **Answer: A. Analyzing the inherent risk assessment**
Explanation: The inherent risk assessment is the assessment of risk at a gross level without considering the impact of controls. The first step in a risk-focused audit is to obtain relevant details about the industry and organization to consider the inherent risk level.

14. **(14) Answer: A. Determining high-risk processes**
Explanation: In risk-based planning, it is very important to determine high-risk areas. This will help to determine the areas to be audited.

15. **Answer: A. Subject-oriented**
Explanation: To determine risk, you need to calculate probability and impact. Probability is based on estimates and estimates are always subjective. Risk assessment is based on perception.

16. **Answer: C. Implementing relevant controls**
Explanation: The risk management process includes the assessment of risk and, on the basis of the outcome, the designing of various controls. The objective of the risk assessment process is to address the recognized risks by implementing appropriate controls.

17. **Answer: B. Senior business management**
Explanation: Top business management have the final authority and also the responsibility for the smooth operation of the organization. They should not further delegate their responsibility for risk management. The other options should help authorities in determining the risk appetite of the organization.

18. **Answer: A. Finding threats/vulnerabilities associated with current IT assets**
Explanation: The biggest factor in evaluating IT risk is finding and evaluating threats and vulnerabilities associated with IT assets. The other options, though very important factors for the risk assessment process, are not more important than option A.

19. **Answer: C. Identifying threats and their likelihood of occurrence**
Explanation: Once the critical assets are identified, the next step is to determine vulnerabilities and then to look at threats and their probability of occurrence.

20. **Answer: D. Vulnerability**
Explanation: A lack of security measures indicates a weakness or vulnerability. A vulnerability can be in the form of a lack of up-to-date anti-virus, weak software coding, poor access control, and more. It must be noted that vulnerabilities can be controlled by the organization.

21. **Answer: C. The identification of assets**
Explanation: The identification of critical assets is the first step in the development of a risk assessment process.

22. **Answer: B. Are created on the basis of risk analysis**
Explanation: In the bottom-up approach, risks related to processes are identified and considered. The approach starts by considering the process-level requirements and operational-level risk. The other options are the benefits of the top-down approach. In the top-down approach, policies are consistent across the organization and there is no conflict with overall corporate policy.

23. **Answer: A. Implementing controls**
Explanation: Risks are managed and reduced by incorporating proper security and relevant controls. Through insurance, risk is transferred. Auditing and certification help in providing assurance, while SLAs help in risk allocation.

24. **Answer: A. Addresses the risk**
Explanation: The most important factor for implementing controls is to ensure that the controls address the risk.

25. **Answer: A. Inherent risk**
Explanation: Gross risk or risk before controls is known as inherent risk.

26. **Answer: B. Control risk**
Explanation: Control risk refers to risk that internal controls fail to prevent or detect. Control risk refers to risk the internal control system of the organization will not able to detect, correct, or prevent.

27. **Answer: C. All relevant risks must be documented and analyzed.**
Explanation: It is most important that identified risks are properly documented. After proper documentation, other factors should be considered.

28. **Answer. C. Perform a risk assessment first and then concentrate control tests on high-risk areas**
Explanation: On the basis of risk assessment, the audit team should devote more testing resources to high-risk areas.

29. **Answer. A. The adoption of mature technology by the organization**
Explanation: Technology adoption may not have a huge impact while planning an audit as compared to other options. All the options are important, but the technology's maturity alone has the least influence on an organization's risk assessment.

Types of audit and assessment

1. **Answer. C. IS audit**
Explanation: An IS audit is designed to evaluate an information system and any related resources to determine the adequacy of the internal controls that provide the availability, integrity, and confidentiality of the IT assets of the system.

2. **Answer. B. Compliance audit**
Explanation: A compliance audit includes specific tests of controls to determine adherence to specific regulatory or legal requirements.

3. **Answer. C. Integrated audit**
Explanation: There are different types of integrated audits that may combine financial and operational audit steps to assess the overall objectives of an organization and safeguard the efficiency and compliance of assets.

4. **Answer. A. Functional audit**
Explanation: A functional audit provides an independent evaluation of software products. The audit comes either prior to software delivery or after implementation.

5. **Answer. D. Computer forensic audit**
Explanation: This is an investigation that includes the analysis of electronic devices. An IS auditor can support an IS manager or forensic specialist when conducting forensic analysis and auditing to ensure adherence to policy and procedure.

6. **Answer: A. Administrative audit**
Explanation: An administrative audit is designed to perform an operational audit and other aspects related to the effectiveness, efficiency, and productivity of an enterprise.

Audit Execution 2

In this chapter, we will learn about audit execution processes, such as project management techniques, sampling methodology, and audit evidence collection techniques. These topics are important because **Information System (IS)** auditors should be aware of audit execution process.

The following topics will be covered in this chapter:

- Audit project management
- Sampling methodology
- Audit evidence collection techniques
- Data analytics
- Reporting and communication techniques
- Quality assurance and improvement of the audit process

By the end of the chapter, you will have detailed knowledge of IS processes, business processes, and risk management processes to protect the assets of an organization.

Audit project management

Audit includes various activities, such as audit planning, resource allocation, determining audit scope and audit criteria, reviewing and evaluating audit evidence, forming audit conclusions, and reporting to management. All these activities are integral parts of audit, and project management techniques are equally applicable for audit projects.

The following are the basic steps for managing and monitoring audit projects:

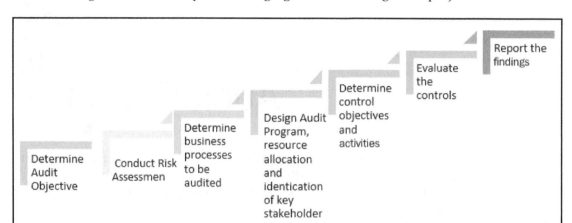

The activities mentioned in the preceding figure are performed to achieve some specific audit objectives. This is also discussed in the next topic.

Audit objectives

Audit objectives are the expected outcome of the audit activities. They refer to the intended goals that must be accomplished by the audit. Determining the audit objective is a very important step in planning the audit activity. Generally, audits are conducted to achieve the objectives mentioned here:

- To confirm that internal control exists
- To evaluate the effectiveness of internal controls
- To confirm compliance with the statutory and regulatory requirements

An audit also provides reasonable assurance about the coverage of material items.

Audit phases

The audit process has three phases. The first phase is about planning, the second phase is about execution, and the third phase is about reporting. An IS auditor should be aware of the phases of an audit process, as in the following figure:

Phase	Audit Steps	Descriptions
Planning Phase	Risk Assessment & Determine audit area	• First step is to conduct risk assessment and identify the function, process, system and physical location to be audited.
	Determine audit objective	• Primary goal during the planning stage of IS audit is to address the audit objective • Determine audit objective i.e. the audit purpose. • Audit may be conducted for regulatory or contractual requirements.
	Determine the audit scope	• Next step is to identify and determine the scope of audit. • Scope may be restricted to few applications or few processes only. • Defined scope will help auditor to determine resource requirement for conduct of the audit.
	Pre-audit Planning	• Pre audit planning includes understanding the business environment, relevant regulations. • It includes conducting risk assessments to determine area of high risk. • It also includes determining resource requirements and audit timings.
	Determine audit procedures	• On the basis of pre audit information, audit program is designed which includes resource allocation and audit procedures to be followed. • During this step, audit tools and methodology is developed to test and verify the controls.
Execution Phase	Gather data	• Next step is to gather relevant data and documents for the conduct of audit.
	Evaluate Controls	• Once the required information, data and documents are available, auditor is required to evaluate the controls to verify effectiveness and efficiency of the controls.
	Validate & Document the results	• Audit observations should be validated and documented along with relevant evidence.
Reporting Phase	Draft Report	• Draft report should be issued for obtaining comments from management on audit observations. • Before issuance of final report, draft report should be discussed with management.
	Issue Report	• Final report should contain audit finding, recommendation, management comment and expected date of closure of audit findings.
	Follow up	• Follow up should be done to determine whether audit findings are closed and follow up report should be issued.

For the CISA exam, please note down the following steps for the audit process:

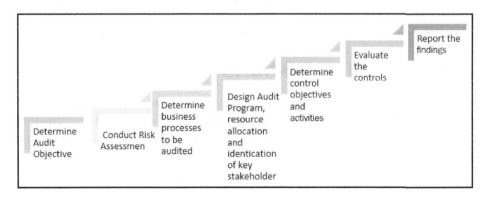

It should be noted that the steps should be followed in chronological sequence for the success of the audit project and to achieve the audit objective.

Fraud, irregularities, and illegal acts

The implementation of internal controls does not necessarily eliminate fraud. An IS auditor should be aware of the possibility, circumstances, and opportunities leading to fraud and other irregularities. The IS auditor should observe and exercise due professional care to ensure that internal controls are appropriate, effective, and efficient to prevent or detect fraud, irregularities, and illegal acts.

In the case of suspicious activity, the IS auditor may communicate the need for a detailed investigation. In the case of a major fraud being identified, audit management should consider reporting it to the audit committee board.

Key aspects from CISA exam perspective

The following table covers important aspects from the CISA exam perspective:

CISA questions	Possible answers
What does the information systems audit provide?	Reasonable assurance about coverage of material items.
What is the first step of an audit project?	To develop an audit plan.
What is the primary reason for a functional walkthrough?	To understand the business process.
What is the major concern in the absence of established audit objectives?	Not able to determine key business risks.
What is the primary objective for performing risk assessment prior to the audit?	Allocate audit resources to areas of high risks.
What is the step of the audit planning phase?	Conducting risk assessments to determine the area of high risk.

Self-assessment questions

1. **The first step to review a service-oriented application is:**
   - A. To understand services and their allocation to business processes
   - B. To review the coding process in accordance with service security standards
   - C. To review the service level agreement
   - D. To audit the application security procedure

2. **An information system audit provides:**
    A. Reasonable assurance about the coverage of material items
    B. Definite assurance about the coverage of material items
    C. Reasonable assurance about the coverage of all the items
    D. No assurance about the coverage of material items

3. **The best sampling method when an IS auditor is concerned about fraud is:**
    A. Stop-or-go sampling
    B. Discovery sampling
    C. Classical sampling
    D. Subjective sampling

4. **Which of the following is the first step in an audit project?**
    A. Prepare the audit schedule and monitor it
    B. Provide training to IS audit staff on the latest technology used in the organization
    C. Develop an audit plan on the basis of the risk assessment
    D. Monitor the progress of the audit

5. **What is the primary goal during the planning phase of an IS audit?**
    A. To address the audit's objectives
    B. To obtain evidence
    C. To determine the audit's test
    D. To minimize the audit's cost

6. **What is the primary reason for a functional walk-through?**
    A. To understand the business process
    B. To review control effectiveness
    C. To comply with auditing standards
    D. To determine the audit's fees

7. **An IS auditor has a strong suspicion of fraud during a preliminary investigation. What should they do next?**
    A. Collect more evidence for further investigation
    B. Report directly to the audit committee
    C. Report the probability of fraud to senior officials
    D. Obtain an external legal opinion

1. **Which of the following is the first activity to be performed when developing a risk management program?**
    A. A vulnerability assessment
    B. Data classification
    C. Inventory of assets
    D. Process walk-through

2. **An IS auditor has been assigned to audit a business continuity plan. The same auditor was involved in designing the business continuity plan. The IS auditor should:**
    A. Accept the assignment
    B. Provide a disclaimer of conflict of interest to audit management before accepting the audit
    C. Provide a disclaimer of conflict of interest to the business continuity team before accepting the audit
    D. Request audit management not to conduct the audit as the business continuity plan is well-designed

3. **Which of the following would be a major concern in the absence of established audit objectives?**
    A. Not being able to determine the audit's budget
    B. Not being able to identify key stakeholders
    C. Not being able to determine key business risks
    D. Not being able to determine previous audit findings

4. **Which of the following is the next step once the audit findings have been identified?**
    A. Discuss it with auditee management to find agreement on the findings
    B. Determine remedial measures for the findings
    C. Inform senior management about the findings
    D. Obtain assurance from management to close the findings

5. **The first step in developing an annual internal IS audit plan is to:**

    A. Identify the threats and vulnerabilities
    B. Determine the audit universe
    C. Determine the control environment
    D. Determine the sampling approach

13. **What will be the immediate step once the business process to be audited is identified?**
    A. To determine the audit universe
    B. To determine the audit resources
    C. To determine the key stakeholders
    D. To determine the control objectives and activities

14. **The prime consideration in determining the objective and scope of an audit is:**
    A. The statutory requirements applicable to the organization
    B. The policies and procedures of the organization
    C. The complexity of the business process
    D. The organization's structure

15. **Which of the following is the prime reason for performing a risk assessment?**
    A. To address management concerns
    B. To provide reasonable assurance about the audit coverage of material items
    C. To ensure budget adherence
    D. To allocate the audit resources

16. **The first step in the planning phase of an audit is:**
    A. Designing an audit program
    B. The allocation of audit resources
    C. Identification of key stakeholders
    D. Conducting a risk assessment

17. **What should be the next course of action for an IS auditor once the potential material findings are discovered?**
    A. Discuss the potential findings with the business unit
    B. Conduct additional testing
    C. Report the potential findings to the audit committee
    D. Recommend closure of the findings before the issuance of a report

18. **Which of the following is the best reason for a senior audit manager reviewing the work of an auditor?**
    A. Quality requirements
    B. SLA requirements
    C. Professional standards
    D. Client requirements

19. **Which of the following is the best course of action if it is not possible to cover the total audit scope due to resource constraints?**
    A. Concentrate on last year's audit findings
    B. Rely on the management assurance of internal controls
    C. Focus on high-risk areas
    D. Concentrate on the effectiveness of controls

20. **The most reliable source of information when designing a risk-based audit plan is:**
    A. Key controls identified by the process owner
    B. The key business process identified by senior management
    C. Vulnerabilities identified by the process owner
    D. The previous audit findings

Sampling methodology

Sampling is the process of the selection of data from a population. By analyzing the selected samples, characteristics of the full population can be concluded. Sampling is performed when it is not feasible to study the full population due to time and cost constraints. Samples are a subset of the population.

Sampling types

This is a very important topic for the CISA exam perspective. Two to three questions can be expected from this topic. A CISA candidate should have an understanding of the sampling techniques mentioned here:

Sampling Types	Description
Statistical sampling	• This is an objective sampling technique. • Also known as non-judgmental sampling. • It uses the laws of probability, where each unit has an equal chance of selection. • In statistical sampling, the probability of error can be objectively quantified, and hence the detection risk can be reduced.
Non-statistical sampling	• This is a subjective sampling technique. • Also known as judgmental sampling. • The auditor uses their experience and judgement to select the samples that are material and represent a higher risk.

Attribute sampling	• Attribute sampling is the simplest kind of sampling based on some attributes—that is, either complied or not complied. • It answers the question "how many?". • It is expressed in percentage form—for example, *90% complied*. • In compliance testing, attribute sampling is usually used.
Variable sampling	• Variable sampling contains more information than attribute data. • It answers the questions "how much?". • It is expressed in monetary value, weight, height, or some other measurement—for example, *an average profit of $25,000*. • Variable sampling is usually used in substantive testing.
Stop-or-go sampling	• Stop-or-go sampling is used where controls are strong and very few errors are expected. • It helps to prevent excess sampling by allowing the audit test to end at the earliest possible moment.
Discovery sampling	• Discovery sampling is used when the objective is to detect fraud or other irregularities. • If a single error is found, then the entire sample is believed to be fraudulent/irregular.

The following diagram will help you to understand the answers to specific CISA questions:

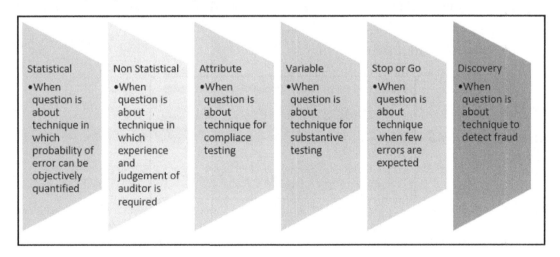

Also, remember the term **AC-VS—Attribute Sampling for Compliance Testing and Variable Sampling for Substantive Testing**.

Sampling risk

Sampling risk refers to a situation where a sample is not a true representation of the population. The conclusion drawn by analyzing the sample may be different from the conclusion that would have been drawn by analyzing the full population. Some of the other important sampling terms are discussed next.

Other sampling terms

A CISA candidate should be aware of the following terms related to sampling.

The confidence coefficient

A confidence coefficient, or confidence level, is a measure of the accuracy and confidence about the quality of a sample. The sample size and confidence correlation are directly related. A high sample size will give a high confidence coefficient.

Let's look at the following example:

Population	Sample Size	Confidence Co-relation
	95	95 %
100	50	50 %
	25	25 %

In the case of poor internal controls, the auditor may want to verify 95 samples out of a total population of 100. This indicates a 95% confidence co-relation.

In the case of strong internal controls, the auditor may want to limit the verification of only 25 samples out of the total population of 100. This indicates a 25% confidence co-relation.

Level of risk

The level of risk can be derived by deducting the confidence coefficient from 1. For example, if the confidence coefficient is 95%, then the level of risk is 5% (100% – 95%).

Expected error rate

This indicates the expected percentage of errors that may exist. When the expected error rate is higher, the auditor should select higher sample size.

Tolerable error rate

This indicates the maximum error that can exist without the audit result being materially misstated.

Sample mean

The sample mean is the average of all the samples selected. It is derived by adding all the samples and dividing it by the sample size.

Sample standard deviation

This indicates the variance of the sample value from the sample mean.

Compliance versus substantive testing

A CISA candidate should be able to differentiate between compliance testing and substantive testing. They should be able to determine which type of testing is to be performed under different scenarios.

The difference between compliance testing vis-à-vis substantive testing

The following table differentiates between compliance and substantive testing:

Compliance Testing	Substantive Testing
Involves verification of the process.	Involves the verification of data or transactions.
Compliance testing checks for the presence of controls.	Substantive testing checks for the completeness, accuracy, and validity of the data.
In compliance testing, attribute sampling is preferred.	In substantive testing, variable sampling is preferred.

Now, let's move on to study the examples of compliance testing and substantive testing.

Examples of compliance testing and substantive testing

The following examples will further help you to understand the difference between compliance testing and substantive testing:

Compliance Testing	Substantive Testing
To check for controls in router configuration	To count and confirm the physical inventory
To check for controls in the change management process	To confirm the validity of inventory valuation calculations
Verification of system access rights	To count and confirm cash balances
Verification of firewall settings	Examining the trial balance.
Review of compliance with the password policy	Examining other financial statements

In the next section, we will have a look at the relationship between substantive and compliance testing.

The relationship between compliance testing and substantive testing

A CISA candidate should understand the following relationship between compliance testing and substantive testing:

- Ideally, compliance testing should be performed first. Compliance testing should be followed by substantive testing.
- The outcome of compliance testing is used to plan for a substantive test. If the outcome of compliance testing indicates the existence of effective internal controls, then substantive testing may not be required or may be reduced. However, if the outcome of compliance testing indicates a poor internal control system, then more rigorous substantive testing is required. Thus, the design of substantive tests is often dependent on the result of compliance testing.
- The attribute sampling technique (which indicates that a control is either present or absent) is useful for compliance testing, whereas variable sampling will be useful for substantive testing.

Apart from the right sampling technique, another important aspect of the audit process is the right evidence gathering techniques. Audit evidence should be collected properly to establish its reliability. Details on the reliability of audit evidence and collection techniques is covered in the next section.

Key aspects from the CISA exam perspective

The following table covers important aspects from the CISA exam perspective:

CISA questions	Possible answers
Which sampling technique should be used when the probability of error must be objectively quantified?	Statistical sampling.
How can sampling risk be mitigated?	Statistical sampling.
Which sampling method is most useful when testing for compliance?	Attribute sampling.
In the case of a strong internal control, could the confidence coefficient/sample size be increased or lowered?	The confidence coefficient/sampling size may be lowered.
Which sampling method would best assist auditors when there is concerns of fraud?	Discovery sampling.
How can you differentiate between compliance testing and substantive testing?	The objective of compliance testing is to test the presence of controls, whereas the objective of substantive testing is to test individual transactions. Let's take the example of asset inventory: • To verify whether control exists for inward/outward of the assets is compliance testing • To verify the count of physical assets and comparing it with records is substantive testing
Give an example of compliance testing.	• To verify the configuration of a router for controls. • To verify the change management process to ensure controls are effective. • Review of system access rights. • Review of firewall settings. • Review of compliance with the password policy.
Give an example of substantive testing.	• Physical inventory of the tapes at the location of the offsite processing. • Confirm the validity of the inventory valuation calculations. • Conduct a bank confirmation to test the cash balances. • Examining the trial balance. • Examining other financial statements.
In what scenario can the substantive test procedure be reduced?	Internal control is strong/the control risk is within the acceptable limits.

Self-assessment questions

1. **Statistical sampling is preferred over non-statistical sampling:**
   A. To reduce the sampling error
   B. For an inexperienced auditor
   C. When the probability of error must be objectively quantified
   D. To reduce the audit error

2. **Which of the following risks can be mitigated by statistical sampling?**
   A. Audit risk
   B. Detection risk
   C. Inherent risk
   D. Sampling risk

3. **Which sampling method that will be MOST meaningful for compliance testing?**
   A. Attribute sampling
   B. Variable sampling
   C. Discovery sampling
   D. Stop-or-go sampling

4. **Which of the following is correct with respect to confidence correlation?**
   A. A small sample size gives a high correlation of confidence
   B. The confidence coefficient may be lowered if the auditor knows that internal controls are stringent
   C. A low correlation of confidence will lead to a high sample size
   D. A high sample size gives a low correlation of confidence

5. **To determine the correct processing of the last 5o new user requisitions, which of the following is best?**
   A. Discovery sampling
   B. Substantive testing
   C. Compliance testing
   D. Stop-or-go sampling

6. **The sampling method to be used when there is indication of fraud is**:
   A. Attribute sampling
   B. Variable sampling
   C. Discovery sampling
   D. Stop-or-go sampling

7. **Which sampling method will be best to ascertain the correctness of system access rights as per the approved authorization matrix?**
   A. Heterogeneous sampling
   B. Attribute sampling
   C. Homogeneous sampling
   D. Stop-or-go sampling

8. **In the case of a strong internal control, an auditor can adopt a**:
   A. High confidence coefficient and a selection of small samples
   B. Low confidence coefficient and a selection of large samples
   C. Higher confidence coefficient, which leads to a larger sample size
   D. Lower confidence coefficient, which leads to a lower sample size

9. **The best example of a substantive test is**:
   A. To ascertain compliance with firewall rules
   B. To ascertain compliance with a change management policy
   C. The use of a statistical sample to verify the inventory of a tape library
   D. To review the reports that capture the password history

10. **The difference between compliance testing and substantive testing is that**:
   A. While substantive testing tests the controls, compliance testing tests the details
   B. While substantive testing tests the details, compliance testing tests the controls
   C. While substantive testing verifies the correctness of trail balance, compliance testing tests the financial statements
   D. While substantive testing tests the internal controls, compliance testing tests the internal requirements

11. **To determine that only active users have access to a critical system, which of the following is best?**
    - A. A compliance test
    - B. A substantive test
    - C. A statistical sample
    - D. Judgment sampling

12. **The substantive test procedure can be reduced if, after a compliance test, it is concluded that:**
    - A. It would be too expensive for a substantive test
    - B. The organization has weak controls
    - C. The inherent risk is low
    - D. The risks of control are within acceptable norms

13. **An example of a substantive audit test includes:**
    - A. Ascertaining periodic management checks and controls
    - B. Ascertaining logical access controls
    - C. A review of reports detailing short shipments of the goods
    - D. A review of the accounts receivable for an aged trial balance

14. **Which of the following is the objective of a compliance test?**
    - A. To ascertain the adequacy, effectiveness, and efficiency of controls
    - B. To ascertain appropriate documentation
    - C. Users are granted access as specified
    - D. Data validation procedures are provided

15. **The use of a statistical sample to inventory the tape library is considered as:**
    - A. A substantive test
    - B. A compliance test
    - C. An integrated test
    - D. A continuous audit

16. **To determine whether the source and object versions are the same, what procedure is performed?**
    - A. A substantive test of the program library controls
    - B. A compliance test of the program library controls
    - C. A compliance test of the program compiler controls
    - D. A substantive test of the program compiler controls

17. **Evidence gathering to determine the accuracy of an individual transaction or data is:**
    A. Substantive testing
    B. Compliance testing
    C. Stop-or-go testing
    D. Discovery testing

Audit evidence collection techniques

Auditing is a process of providing an opinion about functions or processes under the scope of a audit. This audit opinion is based on the evidence obtained during the audit process. Audit evidence plays a critical role in the audit process. Evidence on which audit opinions are based should be reliable, competent, and objective. The objective and scope of an audit are the best factors to determine the extent of the data requirement.

Reliability of evidence

An IS auditor should consider the sufficiency, competency, and reliability of the audit evidence. Evidence can be considered as competent when it is valid and relevant. The following factors can be considered to determine the reliability of audit evidence.

Independence of the evidence provider

The source of the evidence determines the reliability of the evidence. External evidence (obtained from a source outside the organization) is more reliable than evidence obtained within the organization. A signed agreement with external parties is considered more reliable.

Qualifications of the evidence provider

The qualifications and experience of the evidence provider is a major factor when determining the reliability of audit evidence. Information gathered from someone without relevant qualifications or experience may not be reliable.

Objectivity of the evidence

Evidence based on judgement (involving subjectivity) is less reliable than objective evidence. Objective audit evidence does not have scope for different interpretation.

Timing of the evidence

Audit evidence that is dynamic in nature (such as logs, files, and documents that are updated on a frequent basis) should be considered on the basis of relevant timing.

The following figure highlights the evidence-related guidelines:

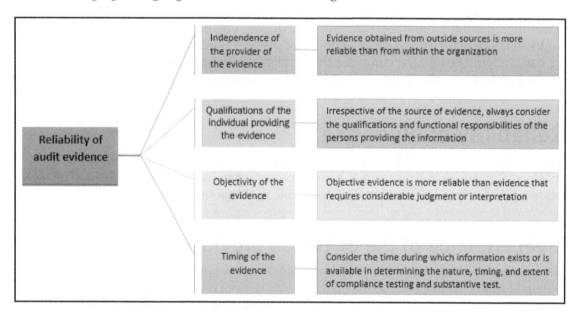

The rules shown in the preceding figure are very important from a CISA exam perspective. An IS auditor should also be aware about best practices and techniques to gather the evidence. This is discussed in the next topic.

Evidence gathering techniques

The following techniques are used by IS auditors to gather various evidence during the audit process:

Factors	Descriptions
Review organization structure	• The IS auditor should review the organization structure and governance model. • This will help the auditor to determine the control environment of the enterprise.
Review IS policies, processes, and standards	• The audit team should review the IS policies, procedures, and standards and determine the effectiveness of the controls implemented. • The audit team should also determine whether IS policies and procedures are reviewed periodically and approved by a competent authority.

Observations	• The IS auditor should observe the process to determine the following:
	  ○ The skill and experience of the staff
	  ○ The security awareness of the staff
	  ○ The existence of **segregation of duties (SoD)**

Interview technique	• The IS auditor should have the skill and competency to conduct interviews tactfully. • Interview questions should be designed in advance to ensure that all the topics are covered. • To the extent possible, interview questions should be open-ended to gain insight about the process. • The staff being interviewed should be made comfortable and encouraged to share information and area of concerns.
Re-performance	• In re-performance, the IS auditor themself performs the activity that is originally performed by the staff of the organization. • Re-performance provides better evidence than other techniques. • It should be used when other methods do not provide sufficient assurance about control effectiveness.
Process walkthrough	Process walkthrough is done to confirm the understanding of the policies and processes.

The evaluation of evidence is a subjective matter and the auditor needs to have the relevant skills, experience, and qualifications to judge the relevance, sufficiency, and appropriateness of the audit evidence. In the case of inconclusive evidence, it is recommended to perform an additional test to confirm the accuracy of the audit finding.

Evidence should be evaluated based on the business environment and complexity of the business processes. The following are some generic guidelines for evidence evaluation:

- In the case of the unavailability of evidence, the auditor should report the relevant risk in the audit report.
- Evidence obtained from a relevant third party is considered to be more reliable compared to internal evidence. An audit report by a qualified auditor is considered more reliable than a confirmation letter received from a third party.
- Evidence collected directly from the source by the audit team is considered more reliable compared to evidence provided by business units.
- **Computer-Assisted Audit Techniques** (CAATs) are the most effective auditing tools for computerized environments. The use of a CAAT ensures the reliability of audit evidence as data is directly collected, processed, and analyzed by the IS auditor.

Key aspects from the CISA exam perspective

The following table covers important aspects from CISA exam perspective:

CISA questions	Possible answers
What does the extent of the data requirements for the audit depend on?	Objective and scope of audit.
What should audit findings be supported by?	Sufficient and appropriate audit audience.
What is the most important reason to obtain sufficient audit evidence?	To provide reasonable basis of drawing conclusion.
What is the most effective tool for obtaining audit evidence through digital data?	Computer-assisted auditing techniques.
What is the most important advantage of using CAAT for gathering audit evidence?	CAAT provides assurance about data reliability.
What type of evidence is considered more reliable?	Evidence directly collected from the source by IS auditor is considered to be the most reliable. The Source of evidence should be independent.

Self-assessment questions

1. The most significant factor that impacts the extent of the data requirements for an audit is:
   - A. The extent of automation
   - B. The previous audit observations
   - C. The objective and scope of the audit
   - D. The auditor's expertise

2. While reviewing the implementation of an application, it is observed that the results of penetration are not yet declared and will not be finalized prior to implementation. What is the IS auditor's best option?
   - A. Publish the report and highlight the risk of implementation before considering the results of penetration testing
   - B. Publish the report without commenting on penetration testing as the results are inconclusive
   - C. Publish the report only when the penetration reports are made available
   - D. Conduct a penetration test and evaluate the test results

3. While reviewing a change management process, it is observed that the number of changes that are available for sampling does not give reasonable assurance. What is the best option for the IS auditor?
   - A. To design an alternative test procedure
   - B. To publish the report on the basis of the samples available
   - C. To conduct an interview with the staff associated with the process
   - D. To create a dummy sample for verification

4. Which of the following ascertains the extent of the data requirements for the audit?
   - A. The availability of information
   - B. The experience of the auditor
   - C. The nature of the business
   - D. The purpose, scope, and objective of the audit

5. **Which of the following can be considered most reliable evidence?**
    A. Confirmation letter from a relevant third party
    B. Information available on open source
    C. Assurance from management
    D. Ratio prepared by the auditor from data supplied by management

6. **The best evidence for the existence of the segregation of duties is:**
    A. Management assurance
    B. Information derived from an organization chart
    C. Observation and interview
    D. Review of user access

7. **Which of the following can be considered best evidence to determine system configuration settings?**
    A. A system configuration report extracted by the system administrator
    B. A configuration report extracted from the system directly by the audit team
    C. The documentation of configuration maintained by the IT team
    D. An approved configuration setting note

8. **Which of the following can be considered the most reliable information?**
    A. Oral declaration by management
    B. IS audit reports
    C. Data provided by management
    D. Confirmation letter received from a third party

9. **The best evidence to determine the effectiveness of control involving the review of system generated exceptional reports is:**
    A. A walkthrough of the control process
    B. Approved documented control process
    C. A sample exception report along with a follow-up action plan
    D. Management assurance

10. **The best evidence to determine the accuracy of system logic for transaction processing is:**
    A. A review of the source code
    B. The creation of simulated transactions for processing and comparing results for correctness
    C. An interview with the system developer
    D. An approved UAT report

11. **An IS auditor should use professional judgement primarily to ensure**:
    A. Appropriate audit evidence will be collected
    B. All deficiencies will be detected
    C. Significant risk will be corrected within a reasonable time
    D. An audit will be completed within the defined time frame

12. **An IS auditor should ensure that the audit findings are supported by**:
    A. The confirmation form auditee management.
    B. The audit program
    C. A closure recommendation
    D. Sufficient and appropriate audit evidence

13. **Sufficient audit evidence is obtained**:
    A. To comply with statutory requirements
    B. To provide reasonable basis of drawing a conclusion
    C. To justify audit coverage
    D. To justify cost of audit

14. **The most effective tool for obtaining audit evidence through digital data is**:
    A. Structured Query Language
    B. Extracted reports from applications
    C. Risk and control testing tools
    D. CAATs

15. **The use of a CAAT tool will impact which of the following attributes of evidence?**
    A. Appropriateness
    B. Sufficiency
    C. Reliability
    D. Relevance

16. **The prime advantage of an audit team directly extracting data from a general ledger system is**:
    A. No dependency on an auditee
    B. Quicker access to information
    C. More flexibility in the audit process
    D. More reliability of data

17. **The best evidence to determine the accuracy of system logic for transaction processing is**:
    A. Re-performance
    B. Interview
    C. Observation
    D. Review of documentation

Data analytics

Data analytics (DA) is the method of examining data or information. It helps you to understand the information by transforming raw data into usable and meaningful information.

Examples of the effective use of data analytics

The following are some examples of the use of data analytics:

- To determine the authorized user by combining logical access files with the human resources employee database.
- To determine authorized events by combining the file library settings with change management system data and the date of file changes.
- To identify tailgating by combining input with output records.
- To review system configuration settings.
- To review logs for unauthorized access.

CAATs

CAATs are extremely useful to IS auditors for gathering and analyzing large and complex data during an IS audit. CAATs help an IS auditor collect evidence from different hardware, software environments, and data formats.

The following figure pictorially represents CAAT tools:

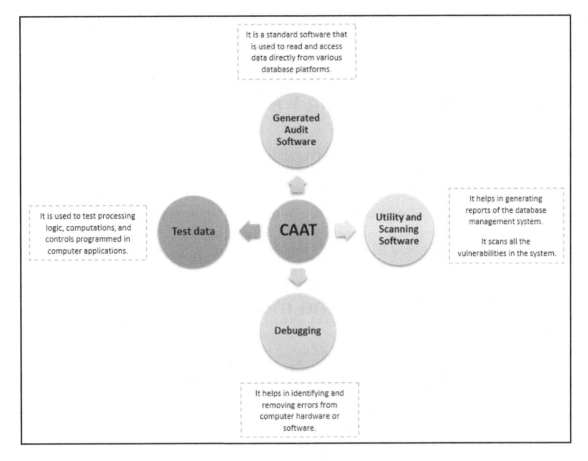

CAAT helps an IS auditor collect information independently. The source of information obtained through CAATs are considered as more reliable.

Examples of the effective use of CAAT tools

The following are some of the examples of the use of CAAT tools:

- CAAT tools are used to determine the accuracy of transactions and balances.
- CAAT tools are used for detailed analysis.
- CAAT tools are used to ascertain compliance with IS general controls.
- CAAT tools are used to ascertain compliance with IS application controls.

- CAAT tools are used for assessing network and operating system controls.
- CAAT tools are used for vulnerability and penetration testing.
- CAAT tools are used for the security scanning of source code and AppSec testing.

Precautions while using CAAT

An auditor should be aware of the following precautions for using CAAT tools:

- Ensure the integrity of imported data by safeguarding their authenticity, integrity, and confidentiality.
- Obtain approval for installing the CAAT software on the auditee servers.
- Obtain only read-only access when using CAAT on production data.
- Edits/modification should be applied to duplicate data and the integrity of the original data should be ensured.

Continuous auditing and monitoring

A CISA candidate should understand the difference between continuous auditing and continuous monitoring:

Continuous Auditing	Continuous Monitoring
In continuous auditing, an audit is conducted in a real-time or near-real-time environment. In continuous auditing, the gap between operations and an audit is much shorter than under a traditional audit approach.	In continuous monitoring, the relevant process of a system is observed on a continuous basis.
For example, high amount pay-outs are audited immediately after payment is made.	For example, antivirus or IDS may continuously monitor a system or a network for abnormalities.

Both continuous auditing and continuous monitoring are mutually exclusive. Continuous assurance can be ensured if both continuous monitoring and auditing are in place. Generally, the results of continuous auditing are the precursor for the introduction of a continuous monitoring process.

Continuous auditing techniques

For information system audits, continuous audit techniques are extremely important IS tools. The following are the five widely used continuous audit tools.

Integrated test facility

The following are the features of an **Integrated Test Facility (ITF)**:

In an ITF, a fictitious entity is created in the production environment:

- The auditor may enter test or dummy transactions and check the processing and results of these transactions for correctness.
- Processed results and expected results are evaluated to check the proper functioning of systems.
- For example, with the ITF technique, a test transaction is entered. The processing results of the test transaction are compared with the expected results to determine the accuracy of processing. If the processed results match the expected results then it determines that processing is happening correct. Once the verification is complete, test data is deleted from the system.

System control audit review file

The following are the features of a **System Control Audit Review File (SCARF)**:

- In this technique, an audit module is embedded (inbuilt) into the organization's host application to track transactions on an ongoing basis.
- A SCARF is used to obtain data or information for audit purposes.
- SCARFs record transactions above a specified limit or deviation-/exception-related transactions. These transactions are then reviewed by auditor.
- SCARFs are useful when regular processing cannot be interrupted.

Snapshot technique

The following are the features of the snapshot technique:

- This technique captures the snaps or pictures of the transaction as they are processed at different stages in the system.

- Details are captured both before execution and after the execution of the transaction. The correctness of the transaction is verified by validating the before-processing and after-processing snaps of the transactions.
- Snapshot is useful when an audit trail is required.
- The IS auditor should consider the following significant factors of this technique:
    - At what location snaps are captured
    - At what time snaps are captured
    - How the reporting of snapshot data is done

Audit hook

The following are the features of an audit hook:

- Audit hooks are embedded in application system to capture exceptions.
- The auditor can set different criteria to capture the exceptions or suspicious transactions
- For example, with the close monitoring of cash transactions, the auditor can set criteria to capture cash transactions exceeding $10,000. All these transactions are then reviewed by the auditor to identify fraud, if any.
- Audit hooks are helpful in the early identification of irregularities, such as fraud or error.
- Audit hooks are generally applied when only selected transactions need to be evaluated.

Continuous and Intermittent Simulation

The following are the features of **Continuous and Intermittent Simulation (CIS)**:

- CIS replicates or simulates the processing of the application system.
- In this technique, a simulator identifies transactions as per the predefined parameters. Identified transactions are then audited for further verification and review.
- CIS compares the results it produces with the result produced by application systems. If any discrepancies are noted, it is written to the exception log file.
- CIS is useful to identify the transactions as per the predefined criteria in a complex environment.

The following figure gives an example of continuous audit tools:

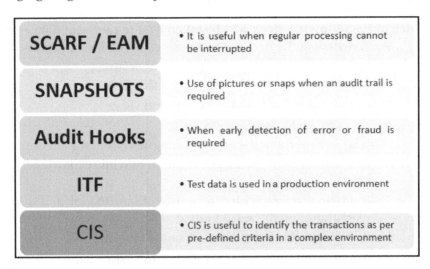

An IS auditor should be aware of the methods and procedure through which analysis and findings are placed to the audit committee and senior management. The effective reporting of audit findings and communicating the findings to all the stakeholders are very important parts of audit execution. More details on the reporting and communication of findings are covered in the next section.

Key aspects from the CISA exam perspective

The following table covers important aspects from CISA exam perspective:

CISA questions	Possible answers
What is the first step of conducting data analytics?	The first step will be determining the objective and scope of analytics.
Which is the most effective online audit technique when an audit trail is required?	Snapshot technique.
What is the advantage of the Integrated Test Facility (ITF)?	• Setting up a separate test environment/test process is not required. • ITF helps validate the accuracy of the system processing.
Which is the most effective online audit technique when the objective is to identify transactions as per predefined criteria?	CIS is most useful to identify transactions as per pre-defined criteria in a complex environment

Self-assessment questions

1. **Which of the following steps will be taken first to carry out data analytics?**
    A. A review of the results/conclusion by a qualified person
    B. Determining the data's adequacy and accuracy
    C. The requirement to capture and collect data
    D. Determining the analytics targets and range

2. **The prime benefit of the usage of CAAT is:**
    A. It is very useful in the case of a complex environment or processes
    B. It ensures the independence of auditors while capturing the relevant data
    C. It provides reliability for the source of information and thus reassurance on the audit findings
    D. It is a cost-effective method for audit activities

3. **Which of the following is a prime consideration when using CAAT?**
    A. To ensure the integrity of imported data by safeguarding its authenticity, integrity, and confidentiality
    B. To obtain approval for installing the CAAT software on the auditee servers
    C. To provide access to CAAT to trained and experienced auditors only
    D. To only use a licensed version of CAAT

4. **The best way to determine the proper functioning of the system calculation is:**
    A. To verify the existence of the segregation of duties
    B. Use of CAATs to perform substantive testing
    C. To interview the process owner
    D. To obtain post-change approval from management

5. **The best audit method when an audit trail is required is:**
    A. SCARF
    B. CIS
    C. Audit hooks
    D. Snapshots

6. **An important feature of ITF is**:
    A. Testing is done on live data
    B. Setting up a separate test environment/test process is not required
    C. As a continuous audit tool, ITF reviews the continuous operation of the system
    D. ITF does not require test data

7. **ITF is best used for**:
    A. The verification of system processing
    B. The verification of system integration
    C. The generation of test data
    D. The continuous auditing of system data

8. **The best continuous auditing technique for the early detection of errors or irregularities is**:
    A. SCARF
    B. ITF
    C. CIS
    D. Audit hooks

9. **The best auditing tool to capture transactions as per the predefined criteria is**:
    A. **Embedded Audit Modules (EAMs)**
    B. CIS
    C. SCARF
    D. Audit hooks

10. **An important feature of ITF is**:
    A. An ongoing review of the actual transactions
    B. The generation of test data
    C. The results of the test transaction are compared with the predetermined results to validate the system processing
    D. Analyzing a large range of information

11. **The best technique to identify excess inventory for the previous year is**:
    A. Analyzing the test data
    B. Generalized audit software
    C. CIS
    D. ITF

Reporting and communication techniques

Audit reporting and following up for the closure are the last steps of the audit process. The effectiveness of an audit largely depends on how the audit results are communicated and how follow-up is done for the closure of recommendation. Effective verbal and written communication skills are some of the attributes of a good auditor. A CISA candidate is expected to have an understanding of the elements of an exit interview, audit report objectives, the process and structure, and follow-up activities.

Exit interview

The general perception of an audit exit meeting is something like this:

However, auditing is not about finding faults. It is about adding value to the existing processes of an organization.

A formal exit interview is essential before the audit report is released. The following are the objectives of an exit interview:

- To ensure that the facts are appropriately and correctly presented in the report
- To discuss recommendations with auditee management
- To discuss an implementation date

The exit meeting ensures that the facts are not misunderstood or misinterpreted. Exit meetings help to align the audit team and auditee management on the findings that are presented, discussed, and agreed on.

Audit reporting

A CISA candidate should note following best practices with respect to audit reporting:

- The IS auditor's function is ultimately responsible for senior management and the final audit report should be sent to the **Audit Committee of Board** (**ACB**). If the IS auditor has no access to the top officials and the audit committee, it will impact the auditor's independence.
- Before the report is placed to the ACB, the IS auditor should discuss with auditee management to determine the accuracy of the audit observations and to understand the correction plan.
- Sometimes, auditee management may not agree with the audit findings and recommendations. In such cases, IS auditors should emphasize the significance of the audit findings and the risk of not taking any corrective action.
- If there is any control weakness that is not within the scope of the audit, it should be reported to management during the audit process. This should not be overlooked. Generally, accepted audit procedures require audit results to be reported even if the auditee takes corrective action prior to reporting.
- To support the audit results, IS auditors should have clear and accurate audit facts.

Audit report objectives

The following are the six objectives of audit reporting:

- The presentation of audit findings/results to all the stakeholders (that is, the auditees).
- The audit report serves as a formal closure to the audit committee.
- The audit report provides assurance to the organization. It identifies the areas that require corrective action and associated suggestions.
- The audit report serves as a reference for any party researching the auditee or audit topic.
- It helps in follow-ups of audit findings presented in the audit reports for closure.
- A well-defined audit report promotes audit credibility. This depends on the report being well-developed and well-written.

Audit report structure

An audit report includes the following content:

- An introduction to the report, which includes the scope of the audit, the limitations of the audit, a statement of the audit objective, the audit period, and so on.
- Audit findings and recommendations
- Opinion about the adequacy, effectiveness, and efficiency of the control environment.

Let's now have a rundown of the main objectives of follow-up activities.

Follow-up activities

The main objective of follow-up activities is to validate recommendations. An IS audit needs to determine whether management has acted on corrective actions to close the audit findings. It is essential to have a structured process to determine that corrective actions have been implemented.

Follow-up activities should be taken on the basis of the timeline agreed on by auditee management for the closure of audit findings. The status of compliance should be placed at the appropriate level of management.

Although audit follow-ups are primarily applicable to internal audit functions, external audit firms may be required to do the follow-up if it is included in the letter of engagement.

Key aspects from the CISA exam perspective

The following table covers important aspects from CISA exam perspective.:

CISA questions	Possible answers
What is the objective of an audit closure meeting?	To ensure that there have been no misunderstandings or misinterpretation of facts.
What is the objective of conducting a follow-up audit?	To validate remediation action.
What is the best way to schedule for the follow-up audit?	On the basis of due date agreed upon by auditee management.

Self-assessment questions

1. **Which of the following should an IS auditor do when an auditee has taken immediate corrective action of audit findings?**
    A. Exclude the finding from the final report without verifying the corrective action
    B. Report the observation and risk in the final report
    C. Verify the correction and if appropriately closed, it should be excluded from the report
    D. A call of the inclusion/exclusion should be taken after a discussion of the finding with auditee management

2. **The best course of action for an audit team if they find prior audit reports without work papers is:**
    A. To postpone the audit until work papers are available
    B. To continue the audit while relying on previous audit reports
    C. For the controls for the highest risk area to be retested
    D. To inform audit management and suggest retesting the controls

3. **An auditor should hold the closure meeting with the objective of:**
    A. Discussing audit observations
    B. Correcting deficiencies
    C. Assessing the audit staff performance
    D. Presenting the final audit report

4. **An IS auditor is responsible for the communication of audit results to:**
    A. Legal authorities
    B. Senior management and/or the audit committee
    C. The manager of the audited entity
    D. The compliance manager

5. **An auditor should hold the closure meeting with the objective of:**
    A. Allowing auditees to implement recommendations as soon as possible
    B. Enabling auditors to explain complicated findings before a written report is issued
    C. Allowing auditors to gain confidence in management
    D. Ensuring that there have been no misunderstandings or misinterpretations of facts

6. **Which of the following should be the first action in the case of non-agreement by the department manager over the audit findings?**
    A. Once again test controls to validate the audit finding
    B. Ask a third party to confirm the audit observation
    C. Report the findings with the auditee comments
    D. Revalidate the supporting evidence for the audit evidence

7. **The main reason for meeting with auditees before formally releasing the audit report is to**:
    A. Ensure all the important issues are covered
    B. Gain agreement on the findings
    C. Obtain feedback on the audit procedures
    D. Finalize the structure of the final audit report

8. **Which of the following should an IS auditor do when they find that a critical Disaster Recovery Plan (DRP) does not cover all of the systems?**
    A. Determine the impact of the non-inclusion of a critical system in the DRP
    B. Postpone the audit
    C. Continue an audit of the existing DRP
    D. Call for an explanation from management for not covering all the systems

9. **The main reason for meeting with auditees before formally releasing the audit report is to**:
    A. Seek management approval for the corrective action plan
    B. Validate the accuracy of the audit findings
    C. Assist in the management of the correction of the audit findings
    D. Prioritize the resolution of the audit findings

10. **Which of the following should an IS auditor do when they observe minor weaknesses in the database that are beyond the scope of the audit?**
    A. Include that database in the scope
    B. Note down the weakness for future review
    C. Work with database administrators to correct the weakness
    D. Report the weakness in the audit report

11. **Which of the following should an IS auditor do when they observe major weaknesses in the change management application supporting the finance application?**
    - A. Continue a review of the finance application and report deficiency of the change management application to the IT manager
    - B. Complete a review of the finance application and ignore the deficiency as it is not part of the audit scope
    - C. Formally report the deficiency in the audit report
    - D. Cease audit activity until the deficiency is corrected

12. **The prime objective of an audit team discussing the audit findings with the auditee is:**
    - A. Briefing about audit results
    - B. Finalizing timelines for corrective actions
    - C. Confirming audit findings and proposing a course of corrective action
    - D. Identifying compensating controls for the audit findings

13. **An IS auditor is reviewing a critical application that has not yet been implemented. Certain evidence is not yet available. The auditor should:**
    - A. Issue the audit report based on the available information, highlighting the potential security weaknesses and the requirement for follow-up audit testing
    - B. Issue the audit report, ignoring the areas where evidence is not available
    - C. Request for a delay of the implementation date until evidence is available
    - D. Cease the audit due to lack of evidence

14. **An IS auditor has observed inadequate controls of remote access for a critical application. The auditor should:**
    - A. Revise the finding, considering the management views
    - B. Withdraw the finding because the IDS controls are in place
    - C. Withdraw the finding because firewall rules are monitored
    - D. Document the audit findings in the audit report

15. **The audit team should ensure that the audit findings are supported by**:
     A. A response from auditee management
     B. A risk assessment document of the organization
     C. Audit evidence
     D. The work papers of other auditors

16. **Which of the following should an IS auditor do if an auditee does not agree with the audit findings?**
     A. Take a statement from the auditee accepting full legal responsibility
     B. Explain the impact of the findings and the risk of not correcting it
     C. Inform the audit committee of the disagreement for resolution
     D. Exclude the finding, considering the auditee's view

17. **The BEST way for an IS auditor to follow up on the closure activities is to**:
     A. Provide management with a remediation timeline and verify adherence
     B. Conduct a review of the controls after the projected remediation date
     C. Continue to audit the failed controls according to the audit schedule
     D. Review the progress of remediation regularly

18. **To review the adequacy of management's remediation action plan, the most important factor is**:
     A. The approval of the remediation action by senior management
     B. The man-days required for future audit work
     C. Potential cost savings
     D. The criticality of the audit findings

19. **The BEST way to schedule a follow-up for audit findings is to**:
     A. Schedule a follow-up audit based on closure due dates
     B. Schedule a follow-up audit only during the next audit cycle
     C. Schedule a follow-up audit on a surprise basis to determine whether remediation is in progress
     D. Schedule a follow-up audit when findings escalate to incidents

20. **Which of the following is the main objective of conducting follow-up audits?**
    A. To validate the correctness of the reported findings
    B. To validate the remediation action
    C. To validate the risk assessment
    D. To gather evidence for management reporting

Control self-assessment

Control Self Assessment (CSA), as the name suggests, is the self-assessment of controls by process owners. An employee understands the business process and evaluates the various risks and controls. It is the process wherein the process owner can have a realistic view of their own performance.

This ensures the involvement of the user group in a periodic and proactive review of risk and control.

Objectives of CSA

The following are the objectives of implementing a CSA program:

- To make functional staff responsible for control monitoring
- To enhance audit responsibilities (not to replace the audit's responsibilities)
- To concentrate on critical processes and areas of high risk

Benefits of CSA

Here are a few benefits of CSA:

- Risk detection at an early stage of the process and reduction in control cost.
- It helps in effective and stronger internal controls, which helps make an improved audit rating process.
- Helps the process owner to take the responsibility of control monitoring.
- It helps in increasing employee awareness of organizational goals. It also helps in understanding the risk and internal controls.

- Improves communication between senior officials and operational staff.
- It improves the motivational level of the employees.
- It provides assurance to all the stakeholders and customers.
- It provides assurance to top management about the adequacy, effectiveness, and efficiency of the control requirements.

Disadvantages of CSA

Due care should be taken when implementing the CSA function. It should not be considered as a replacement of the audit function. An audit is an independent function and should not be waived even if CSA is being implemented. It must be noted that both CSA and an audit are different functions, and one cannot replace the other.

An IS auditor's role in CSA

The IS auditor's role is to act as a facilitator for the implementation of CSA. It is their responsibility for the implementation of CSIS auditors should guide the process owners in assessing the risk and control of their environment. The IS auditor should provide insight into the objectives of CSA.

An audit is an independent function and should not be waived even if CSA is being implemented. It must be noted that both CSA and audit are different function and one cannot replace the other.

Key aspects from the CISA exam perspective

The following table covers important aspects from CISA exam perspective:

CISA questions	Possible answers
What is the primary objective of implementing the Control Self-assessment program?	• To monitor and control high-risk areas. • To enhance audit responsibilities.
What is the role of auditor in implementation of the Control self-assessment program?	To act as a facilitator for CSA program.
Which is the most significant requirement for a successful CSA?	Involvement of line management.

Self-assessment questions

1. **The prime objective of implementing the CSA structure is:**
    A. To replace audit responsibilities
    B. To enhance employees' capacity
    C. Compliance with regulatory requirements
    D. Concentration on critical processes and high-risk areas

2. **An IS auditor's role in implementing a CSA should be:**
    A. They're in charge
    B. They're a sponsor
    C. They're a reviewer
    D. They're a facilitator

3. **The most important factor for the successful implementation of a CSA program is:**
    A. To document a robust control policy
    B. To make auditors responsible for control monitoring
    C. To make line managers take charge of control monitoring
    D. To implement a robust control policy

4. **When implementing a CSA program, an IS auditor should participate primarily as a:**
    A. Program controller
    B. The auditor should not participate as it would create a potential conflict of interest.
    C. Program facilitator
    D. Program leader

5. **Which of the following is the CSA program's objective?**
    A. To replace audit responsibility
    B. To enhance audit responsibility
    C. To evaluate the risk management program
    D. To determine the audit scope

6. **The best period to conduct a CSA program involving all the concerned parties is:**
   A. After the issuance of the audit report
   B. During the preliminary survey
   C. After compliance testing
   D. After the completion of the risk assessment

7. **The primary purpose of a CSA structure is:**
   A. To substitute for the audit responsibilities
   B. To substitute for the risk management program
   C. To comply with regulatory requirements
   D. To enhance the audit responsibilities

8. **A PRIMARY advantage of the CSA program is that:**
   A. It identifies high-risk areas that may need to be reviewed in detail later
   B. IS auditors can independently assess the risks
   C. It replaces risk management activities
   D. It enables management to delegate responsibility for control

9. **The MOST significant element for a successful CSA is:**
   A. The capability of a workshop facilitator
   B. The documentation of the CSA program
   C. The design of the CSA program
   D. The involvement of line managers

10. **The main purpose of a CSA structure is:**
    A. To concentrate on critical processes and areas of high risk
    B. To arrange a training workshop
    C. To reduce the cost of control
    D. To replace the audit activities

11. **A PRIMARY advantage of the CSA program is that it:**
    A. Helps in the early detection of risks
    B. Helps in reducing audit activities
    C. Helps to reduce the cost of control
    D. Helps to reduce audit resources

Summary

An audit provides reasonable assurance about the coverage of material items. The initial step in designing an audit plan is to determine the audit universe for the organization. The audit universe is the list of all the processes and systems under the scope of the audit. Once the audit universe is identified, a risk assessment is to be conducted to identify the critical processes and systems.

In the next chapter, we will have a look at project management techniques, sampling methodology, and audit evidence collection techniques.

Assessments

You can find the answers to the previous assessment questions in this section.

Audit project management

1. **Answer: A. To understand services and their allocation to business processes**
   Explanation: Service-level architecture relies on the principle of multiple clients. The first step of the assignment is to understand how the services are allocated to different business units. Once this is done, the auditor will have a sufficient idea about the risk environment on the basis of which further audit procedures can be developed.

2. **Answer: A. Reasonable assurance about the coverage of material items**
   Explanation: The auditor does not provide absolute assurance but only reasonable assurance. Absolutes are not attainable due to the inherent limitation of audits, such as professional judgment, sampling, and the use of testing.

3. **Answer: B. Discovery sampling**
   Explanation: Discovery sampling is widely used to detect a fraudulent transaction. Even if only a single error is discovered, there is a possibility that the internal control system could be compromised. That one error may be sufficient to require an examination of the entire population or to formulate a new plan for further action. If one instance of fraud is found, the auditor is confident that fraud exists.

4. Answer: **C. Develop an audit plan on the basis of risk assessment**
   Explanation: Out of all the options given, the first step of the audit project is to develop the audit plan after considering the results of the risk assessment.

5. **Answer: A. To address the audit objectives**
   Explanation: The primary goal when planning for an IS audit is to address the audit objective. All the other options are secondary goals.

6. **Answer: A. To understand the business process**
   Explanation: The main reason for a functional walkthrough is to have a basic idea and knowledge about the business process. Once the business process is understood, an assessment can be carried out.

7. **Answer: A. Collect more evidence to determine whether an investigation is warranted**
   Explanation: An IS auditor should further evaluate the evidence to decide on the recommendation of a detailed examination.

8. **Answer: C. Inventory of assets**
   Explanation: The first step in the development of a risk management program is the identification of the assets to be protected. The others steps are to be followed later, once the inventory of assets is available.

9. **Answer: B. Provide a disclaimer of conflict of interest to audit management before accepting the audit**
   Explanation: It is the responsibility of the IS auditor to communicate any possible conflict of interest to audit management that can impact the IS auditor's independence. Audit management will make further calls on this aspect.

10. **Answer: C. Not being able to determine key business risks**
    Explanation: In the absence of audit objectives, an audit scope cannot be determined and hence a key business risk may not be identified. The auditor might not audit areas of highest risk for the organization. Other options are secondary concerns.

11. **Answer: A. Discuss it with auditee management to gain agreement on the findings**
    Explanation: After identifying the findings, the IS auditor should gain an agreement on the finding with auditee management. If the findings are not agreed upon, then there may be an issue at a later stage. When an agreement is obtained, it implies that the finding is understood and further action can be determined.

12. **Answer: B. Determine the audit universe**
    Explanation: The first step is to determine the audit universe for the organization. The audit universe is the list of all the processes and systems under the scope of the audit. Once the audit universe is identified, critical processes and systems are to be identified on the basis of their value to the organization. A risk assessment should be done of these critical systems and processes and accordingly, an audit plan should be designed.

13. **Answer: D. To determine the control objectives and activities**
    Explanation: Once the business process to be audited is identified, the next step is to identify the control objectives and activities associated with the business processes. The next step is to identify the audit resources. The audit universe is to be determined prior to the finalization of the audit scope.

14. **Answer: A. The statutory requirements applicable to the organization**
    Explanation: The prime consideration in determining the objective and scope of an audit is the statutory requirements applicable to the organization. The auditor cannot limit the scope relating to statutory requirements. Although the other factors are important, prime consideration should be given to the full coverage of statutory requirements.

15. **Answer: B. To provide reasonable assurance about the audit coverage of material items**
    Explanation: Risk assessment helps to identify the top risks of the organization and hence the auditor can focus the audit procedure on the highest risk areas. It helps to provide reasonable assurance about the coverage of material items.

16. **Answer: D. Conducting a risk assessment**
    Explanation: A risk assessment is the first step to be performed to allocate audit resources as per the high risks of the organization. The other options are to be followed once the risk assessment is prepared.

17. **Answer: B. Conduct additional testing**
    Explanation: The best course of action is to perform additional testing to confirm the correctness of the audit findings. Only on the basis of sufficient objective evidence should audit findings be reported. Findings should be confirmed through additional testing before they are discussed with the business unit or reported to the audit committee.

18. **Answer: C. Professional standards**
    Explanation: The professional standards issued by ISACA, IIA, and the International Federation of Accounts require the review of the work of an auditor by a senior audit manager to ensure that the audit objectives are met and the audit is conducted as per the accepted procedures.

19. **Answer: C. Focus on high-risk areas**
    Explanation: The best course of action is to reduce the audit scope and to focus on high-risk areas. The other options do not concentrate on areas where more audit focus is required.

20. **Answer: B. The key business process identified by senior management**
    Explanation: To design a risk-based audit plan, identification of the key business process is very important to determine the area of audit focus. Once the key business process is identified, the other options can be evaluated for further information.

Sampling methodology

1. **Answer: C. When the probability of error must be objectively quantified**
   Explanation: To objectively quantify the probability of error, there should not be any involvement of subjectivity. In all such scenarios, statistical sampling is preferred.

2. **Answer: B. Detection risk**
   Explanation: Detection risk can be minimized by statistical sampling. Detection risk is the risk that the auditor may fail to detect material control deficiency. As statistical sampling does not involve any subjectivity, the chance of failure is minimum. Thus, detection risk can be reduced by the use of statistical sampling. The other risks cannot be minimized using statistical sampling.

3. **Answer: A. Attribute sampling**
   Explanation: For compliance testing, attribute sampling will be most relevant.

4. **Answer: B. The confidence coefficient may be lowered if the auditor knows that internal controls are stringent**
   Explanation: The confidence coefficient, or confidence level, is a measure of the accuracy and confidence of the quality of the sample. Sample size and confidence correlation are directly related. A high sample size will give a high confidence coefficient. A confidence coefficient/sample size may be lowered if the auditor knows that the internal controls are stringent. When the internal control environment is strong, detail testing is not required and hence a small sample size will do.

5. **Answer: C. Compliance testing**
   Explanation: Compliance testing helps to determine the presence of controls. It indicates whether controls are being applied consistently. It helps to evaluate whether new accounts were appropriately authorized.

6. **Answer: C. Discovery sampling**
   Explanation: Discovery sampling is widely used to detect a fraudulent transaction. Even if only a single error is discovered, there is a possibility that the internal control system could be compromised. That one error may be sufficient to require an examination of the entire population or to formulate a new plan for further action. If one instance of fraud is found, the auditor is confident that fraud exists. Stop-or-go sampling is used when only a few errors are expected in a sample. Attribute sampling is used for compliance testing and variable sampling is used for substantive testing.

7. **Answer: B. Attribute sampling**
   Explanation: The attribute sampling method is often used to test whether or not a company's internal controls are being correctly followed. Attribute sampling is used for compliance testing and variable sampling is used for substantive testing.

8. **Answer: D. Lower confidence coefficient, which leads to a lower sample size**
   Explanation: The confidence coefficient, or confidence level, is a measure of the accuracy and confidence about quality of sample. Sample size and confidence correlation are directly related. A high sample size will give a high confidence coefficient. When there is a strong internal control, the confidence coefficient may be lowered and hence there will be review of only a few samples.

9. **Answer: C. The use of a statistical sample to verify the inventory of a tape library**
   Explanation: In substantive testing, the accuracy and integrity of the transaction and balances is verified. To verify the inventory, a substantive test is used.

10. **Answer: B. While substantive testing tests details, compliance testing tests the controls**
    Explanation: Compliance testing is used to evaluate the existence of the control. In substantive testing, the accuracy and integrity of the transaction and balances is verified.

11. **Answer: A. A compliance test**
    Explanation: Compliance testing is used to evaluate the existence of the control. In substantive testing, the accuracy and integrity of the transaction and balances is verified. In the given case, verifying that only active users have access to critical systems requires evaluating the existence of controls and hence a compliance test is used.

12. Answer: **D. The risks of control are within acceptable norms**
Explanation: It must be noted that the outcome of compliance testing is used to make a plan for a substantive test. If the outcome of compliance testing indicates the existence of effective internal control, then substantive testing may not be required or may be reduced. But if the outcome of compliance testing indicates a poor internal control system, then more rigorous substantive testing is required. Thus, a substantive test procedure can be reduced if the compliance test concludes that risks of control are within an acceptable level.

13. Answer: **D. A review of the accounts receivable for an aged trial balance**
Explanation: Compliance testing is used to evaluate the existence of the control. In substantive testing, the accuracy and integrity of the transaction and balances is verified.

14. Answer: **A. To ascertain the adequacy, effectiveness, and efficiency of controls**
Explanation: Compliance tests are conducted to ascertain the adequacy, effectiveness, and efficiency of controls.

15. Answer: **A. A substantive test**
Explanation: In substantive testing, evidence is gathered to evaluate the accuracy of the data or other information. The use of a statistical sample to inventory the tape library is a good example of a substantive test.

16. Answer: **B. A compliance test of program library controls**
Explanation: Compliance tests are conducted to ascertain the adequacy, effectiveness, and efficiency of controls. A compliance test will be used to determine whether the program library controls are working properly.

17. Answer: **A. Substantive testing**
Explanation: Compliance testing is used to evaluate the existence of the control. Compliance tests are conducted to ascertain the adequacy, effectiveness, and efficiency of controls. In substantive testing, the accuracy and integrity of the transaction and balances is verified.

Audit evidence collection

1. Answer: **C. The objective and scope of the audit**
Explanation: The objective and scope of the audit is the best factor to determine the extent of the data requirements. A limited scope may not require huge data collection. A wider scope may require more data for analysis and sample verification. The other options do not directly impact the extent of data collection.

2. **Answer. A. Publish the report and highlight the risk of implementation before considering the results of penetration testing.**
   Explanation: In the case of the unavailability of evidence, the auditor should report the relevant risk in the audit report. The auditor should not wait until the results are not made available. The auditor is not required to conduct a penetration test, which is beyond the scope of an audit.

3. **Answer. A. To design an alternative test procedure**
   Explanation: If the sample size is insufficient, the auditor should develop an alternative test procedure to evaluate the change management process.

4. **Answer. D. The purpose, scope, and objective of the audit**
   Explanation: The purpose, scope, and objective of the audit directly determine the extent of the data requirements. It should not be constrained by the availability of information, the experience of the auditor, or the nature of the business.

5. **Answer. A. Confirmation letter from a relevant third party**
   Explanation: Evidence obtained from a relevant third party is considered to be more reliable compared to the other options. *Option B* cannot be considered as independent. *Option C* cannot be considered as reliable.

6. **Answer. C. Observation and interview**
   Explanation: Observation and interview by an IS auditor can be considered the best evidence compared to the other options. A user access review does not provide complete information compared to an interview. Also, user access can be changed between audits. Management assurance and organization charts can be considered as additional evidence; however, observation and interview are considered as more reliable evidence.

7. **Answer. B. Configuration report protrude from the system by IS auditor**
   Explanation: Evidence collected directly from the source by the audit team is considered more reliable compared to the other options.

8. **Answer. B. IS audit reports**
   Explanation: *Option A* and *C* do not have the element of independence. An audit report by a qualified auditor is considered more reliable than a confirmation letter received from a third party.

9. **Answer. C. A sample exception report along with a follow-up action plan**
   Explanation: A review of the exception report along with a follow-up action represents the best possible evidence. It determines that the control process is in place and also follow-up actions are taken for exceptions.

10. **Answer. B. The creation of simulated transactions for processing and comparing results for correctness**
Explanation: The most effective evidence is to create simulated transactions for verification. The other options do give a good indication about the accuracy of logic; however, *Option B* can be considered as best evidence.

11. **Answer. A. Appropriate audit evidence will be collected**
Explanation: Primarily, an IS auditor's professional judgement is required to ensure that sufficient audit evidence is collected. An audit need not necessarily identify all the deficiencies. Auditee management is responsible for taking corrective action. Completing an audit within the defined timeline is an important element, but the primary objective of the audit procedure is to collect sufficient evidence.

12. **Answer: D. Sufficient and appropriate audit evidence**
Explanation: The audit team should ensure that their reporting is based on objective evidence. Evidence should be sufficient and appropriate to the audit findings.

13. **Answer: B. To provide reasonable basis of drawing a conclusion**
Explanation: Audit evidence helps the IS auditor to draw a conclusion about the subject under audit. Audit evidence can be used to trace back the audit finding.

14. **Answer: D. CAATs**
Explanation: CAATs are the most effective auditing tools for computerized environments.

15. **Answer: C. Reliability**
Explanation: The use of CAAT ensures the reliability of audit evidence as data is directly collected, processed, and analyzed by the IS auditor. The source of information is considered reliable. The use of CAAT does not have a direct impact on the other options.

16. **Answer: D. More reliability of data**
Explanation: CAAT provides assurance about the reliability of the data. This is a major advantage over all the other options.

17. **Answer: A. Re-performance**
Explanation: In re-performance, a transaction is processed again and results are compared to validate the transaction. This gives the strongest evidence among all the other options. When the same result is obtained after performance by an independent person, it provides assurance about the accuracy of the system logic.

Data analytics

1. **Answer: D. Determining the analytics targets and range**
   Explanation: The first step will be determining the objectives and the scope of analytics followed by *Option C*, *Option B*, and *Option A*.

2. **Answer: C. It provides reliability for the source of information and thus reassurance on the audit findings**
   Explanation: The most important aspect will be the reliability of the information. The other aspects are important but not as important as *Option C*.

3. **Answer: A. To ensure the integrity of imported data by safeguarding its authenticity, integrity, and confidentiality**
   Explanation: The most important aspect will be to ensure the authenticity, integrity, and confidentiality of the data. The others are important aspects but not as important as *Option A*.

4. **Answer: B. Use of CAATs to perform substantive testing**
   Explanation: Substantive testing using CAATs will be the best way to ensure that calculations are performed correctly by the system.

5. **Answer: D. Snapshots**
   Explanation: The snapshots technique captures snaps or pictures of the transaction as it is processed at different stages in the system. Details are captured both before the execution and after the execution of the transaction. The correctness of the transaction is verified by validating the before-processing and after-processing snaps of the transactions. Snapshot is useful when an audit trail is required.

6. **Answer: B. Setting up a separate test environment/test process is not required**
   Explanation: A fictitious entity is created in the *live* environment. There is no need to create separate test processes as a live environment is used.

7. **Answer: A. Technique to verify system processing**
   Explanation: In the ITF technique, a test transaction is entered. The processing results of the test transaction are compared with the expected results to determine the accuracy of the processing. If the processed results match the expected results, then it determines that processing is happening correctly.

8. **Answer: D. Audit hooks**
   Explanation: In the audit hook technique, a code is embedded into the application systems to review the selected transactions. The audit team can act at the earliest possible time before an error or an irregularity comes out of hand. They have low complexity in the design of criteria and are also very useful for the early identification of fraud or an error.

9. **Answer: B. CIS**

   Explanation: CIS is useful for identifying the transactions as per the predefined criteria in a complex environment. CIS replicates or simulates the processing of the application system. In this technique, the simulator identifies transactions as per the predefined parameters. Identified transactions are then audited for correctness. CIS decides whether any errors exist between the results it produces and those that the application system produces. If any discrepancies are noted, they are written to the exception log file. Audits hooks will not be able to concentrate on detailed criteria as they are of low complexity and focus only on specific conditions when identifying transactions for review. ITF is used to validate system processing by entering test data into the system.

10. **Answer: C. Pre-determined results are compared with processing output to determine the correctness of system processing**

    Explanation: In the ITF technique, a test transaction is entered. The processing results of the test transaction are compared with the expected results to determine the accuracy of the processing. If the processed results match the expected results, then it determines that the processing is happening correctly.

11. **Answer: B. Generalized audit software**

    Explanation: The IS auditor could design suitable tests to identify excess inventory using generalized audit software. The test information would not be relevant here as the actual data will need to be audited. ITF and EAM cannot identify errors for a previous period.

Reporting and communication techniques

1. **Answer: B. Report the observation and risk in the final report**

   Explanation: It is advisable to report the finding even if corrective action is taken by the auditee. For any action taken on the basis of audit observation, the audit report should identify the finding and describe the corrective action taken.

2. **Answer: D. To inform audit management and suggest retesting the controls**

   Explanation: The audit team should inform the management and suggest retesting the critical controls.

3. **Answer: A. Discussing audit observations**

   Explanation: The major purpose of the closure meeting is to discuss gaps, conclusions, and recommendations. This communication helps to address misunderstandings or the misinterpretation of facts.

4. **Answer: B. Senior management and/or the audit committee**
   Explanation: The audit team is finally responsible for the communication of audit results to the audit committee of the board and senior management. It is the board of directors who should report to legal authorities.

5. **Answer: D. Ensuring that there have been no misunderstandings or misinterpretations of facts**
   Explanation: Closing meeting helps to enhance the understanding between the auditor and the auditee in terms of what was presented, discussed, and agreed upon. *Choice A* is incorrect because the auditee does not need to implement controls immediately. The auditee will be given time to respond formally. *Choices B and C* are also not the objective of the audit closure meeting.

6. **Answer: D. Revalidate the supporting evidence for the finding**
   Explanation: It is advisable to revalidate the supporting evidence first to ensure that the auditor has sufficient objective evidence to support the conclusion drawn. Also, the auditor should consider compensating controls, if any. If even after revalidating some disagreement persists, then it should be included in the report.

7. **Answer: B. Gain agreement on the findings**
   Explanation: The goal of such a discussion is to confirm the relevance and accuracy of the audit observation and to discuss a course of correction.

8. **Answer: A. Determine the impact of the non-inclusion of a critical system in the DRP**
   Explanation: The audit should be continued as per the original plan. The IS auditor should evaluate the impact of not covering all the systems in the DRP. Also, they should inform management about the omissions.

9. **Answer: B. Validate the accuracy of the audit findings**
   Explanation: The goal of such a discussion is to confirm the relevance of the audit observation and to discuss the course of correction.

10. **Answer: D. Report the weakness in the audit report**
    Explanation: Even if the weakness is beyond the scope of the audit, it should be reported to management. It is not advisable to extend the scope of the audit to cover the full database. The IS auditor should report the weaknesses as an observation, rather than documenting it for a future audit. It is not suitable for the IS auditor to work with database administrators to correct the issue.

11. **Answer: C. Formally report the deficiency in the audit report**
    Explanation: It is the responsibility of the audit team to report on findings that could have a significant impact on the effectiveness of controls—whether they are within the scope of the audit or not.

12. **Answer: C. Confirming audit findings and proposing a course of corrective action**
    Explanation: The goal of such a discussion is to confirm the relevance of the audit observation and to discuss a course of correction.

13. **Answer: A. Issue the audit report based on the available information, highlighting the potential security weakness and the requirement for follow-up audit testing**
    Explanation: The lack of evidence should be highlighted in the audit report and follow-up testing should be scheduled for a later date.

14. **Answer: D. Document the audit findings in the audit report**
    Explanation: The IS auditor should take into account the management view; however, they should independently evaluate the risk related to the audit findings. Normally, an IS auditor would not automatically delete or revise the findings.

15. **Answer: C. Audit evidence**
    Explanation: The audit team should have sufficient and appropriate audit evidence to support the audit findings.

16. **Answer: B. Explain the impact of the findings and the risk of not correcting it**
    Explanation: It is important for an audit team to make management aware about the risk and possible impact of the findings.

17. **Answer: B. Conduct a review of the controls after the projected remediation date**
    Explanation: A confirmatory audit should be conducted as per the timelines agreed by management for corrective action. It is not advisable to dictate the timelines for remediation action. Also, a review of progress at frequent intervals may not be feasible. It will not make any sense to continue the audit of a failed control before remediation action.

18. **Answer: D. The criticality of the audit findings**
    Explanation: A remediation action plan should be in line with the criticality of the audit findings.

19. **Answer: A. Schedule a follow-up audit based on closure due dates**
    Explanation: It is always advised to schedule a follow-up audit based on closure due dates.

20. **Answer: B. To validate the remediation action**
    Explanation: The main objective of a follow-up audit is to ensure and validate the corrective action.

Control self-assessment

1. **Answer: D. To concentrate on a high-risk area**
   Explanation: The objective of CSA is to involve functional staff to monitor the high-risk processes. CSA aims to educate line management in the area of control responsibility and monitoring. The replacement of audit functions is not the objective of CSA.

2. **Answer: D. They're a facilitator**
   Explanation: An IS auditor is expected to facilitate the CSA program. The IS auditor should play the role of guide and mentor during a CSA workshop. Line managers should be trained for assessing underlying risks and implementing new controls. The other options are not the role of the IS auditor. Client staff should assume these roles.

3. **Answer: C. To make line managers take charge of control monitoring**
   Explanation: The involvement of line management in control monitoring is one of the success factors for an effective CSA program. The success of CSA depends on the level of involvement of the line managers in control monitoring.

4. **Answer: C. Program facilitator**
   Explanation: An IS auditor is expected to facilitatethe CSA program. The IS auditor should play the role of guide and mentor during a CSA workshop. Line managers should be trained for assessing underlying risks and implementing new controls. The other options are not the role of the IS auditor. Client staff should assume these roles.

5. **Answer: B. To enhance audit responsibility**
   Explanation: The following are some of the important objectives of the CSA program:
     - To focus on critical areas and processes
     - For the enhancement of the auditor's responsibility through the involvement of line management in monitoring the control effectiveness

   The other choices are methods for CSA of achieving the objectives

6. **Answer: B. During the preliminary survey**
   Explanation: The objective of CSA is to involve line management in assessing and monitoring the business risks and effectiveness of controls. Line management is required to understand the underlying risk of the business process and identify the relevant controls. The preliminary survey stage is the best time to conduct CSA. The other options may not be effective for conducting CSA.

7. **Answer: D. To enhance the audit responsibilities**
   Explanation: The following are some of the important objectives of the CSA program:
   - To focus on critical areas and processes
   - For the enhancement of the auditor's responsibility by the involvement of line management in monitoring the control effectiveness.

8. **Answer: A. It identifies high-risk areas that may need to be reviewed in detail later**
   Explanation: CSA assists in identifying high-risk areas that need to be reviewed and monitored. The risks need to be evaluated jointly with business staff. CSA enhances the audit responsibilities, and accountability for controls remains with management.

9. **Answer: D. The involvement of line managers**
   Explanation: One of the benefits of CSA is the involvement of functional staff in risk and control assessment. This helps in the early identification of the risk. Line management is required to understand the underlying risk of the business process and identify the relevant controls. The involvement of the line manager ensures that high-risk items are identified and addressed at the earliest opportunity. This process will help in the early identification of risks.

10. **Answer: A. To concentrate on areas of high risk**
    Explanation: The following are some of the important objectives of the CSA program:
    - To focus on critical areas and processes
    - For the enhancement of the auditor's responsibility through the involvement of line management in monitoring the control effectiveness

11. **Answer: A. Helps in the early detection of risks**
    Explanation: One of the benefits of CSA is the involvement of functional staff in risk and control assessment. This helps in the early identification of the risk. Line management is required to understand the underlying risk of the business process and identify the relevant controls. The involvement of the line manager ensures that high-risk items are identified and addressed at the earliest opportunity. This process will help in the early identification of risks.

2

Section 2: Governance and Management of IT

This part contains 17 percent of the CISA exam, approximately 26 questions.

This section contains the following chapters

- Chapter 3, *IT Governance*
- Chapter 4, *IT Management*

3
IT Governance

An Information System (IS) auditor needs to have knowledge of IT governance. IS auditors should be aware of aspects related to IT enterprise governance.

In this chapter, we will have a look at the following topics:

- IT enterprise governance (EGIT)
- IT-related frameworks
- IT standards, policies, and procedures
- Organizational structure
- Enterprise architecture
- Enterprise risk management
- Maturity models
- Laws, regulations, and industry standards affecting the organization

At the end of the chapter, you, as an IS auditor, will understand the concepts of IT governance and will be met with assessment questions with respect to IT governance.

IT enterprise governance (EGIT)

EGIT is a process used to monitor and control IT activities. IT governance ensures that information technology provides added value to business processes and also that IT risks are appropriately addressed. The purpose of EGIT is to ensure that IT activities are aligned with business objectives. The alignment of IT and business leads to the attainment of business value.

The **Board of Directors** is primarily responsible for EGIT. Governance is implemented through leadership, organizational structures, policies that are set out, and performance monitoring to ensure that business objectives are achieved.

The following diagram prescribes EGIT in a nutshell:

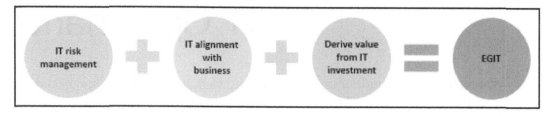

For the successful implementation of EGIT, it is essential to design and document well-structured processes. This is discussed in our next topic.

EGIT processes

The EGIT framework can be implemented by establishing and managing the following processes:

Processes	Description
IT resource management	• Aims to create and update the inventory of all IT resources. • Also aims to manage the risks associated with IT.
Performance measurement	• Aims to monitor the performance of IT resources on the basis of predetermined indicators. • Deviations are analyzed and appropriate action is taken to improve performance.
Compliance management	• Aims to implement processes with a view to managing legal, contractual, and regulatory requirements.

It is essential to govern and manage the preceding processes. A CISA aspirant should understand the difference between governance and management.

Difference between governance and management

The following table outlines the differences between governance and management:

Governance	Management
• Governance aims to provide direction for the attainment of business objectives. • This also involves the monitoring of performance and compliance with the agreed-upon direction and objectives.	• Management aims to implement policies and procedures to achieve the goals and direction set by the governance body.

EGIT good practices

CISA aspirants should be aware of the following EGIT good practices:

- Business and IT processes should be aligned to achieve the organization's overall objectives.
- It is important that the Board of Directors and senior officials are involved in IT governance.
- Enhanced control over outsourced IT activities.
- Performance monitoring vis-à-vis generally accepted standards and benchmarking with peers.
- A structured approach to monitoring compliance with legal, regulatory, and contractual requirements.

Effective information security governance

Information security governance is an integral part of overall IT governance. Information security governance addresses concerns regarding the safeguarding of information assets.

Like EGIT, accountability and responsibility for information security governance lies with the Board of Directors and senior management. The CEO is responsible for ensuring that appropriate policies and procedures are in place for the control of information assets.

Information security policy should be approved by management of the various functions within the enterprise to ensure that all the aspects have been covered regarding the protection of information assets.

The information security governance committee should comprise the following members:

- A board representative
- The CEO
- The CIO (Chief Information Officer)
- The CTO (Chief Technology Officer)
- The COO (Chief Operating Officer)
- The CFO (Chief Financial Officer)
- The CRO (Chief Risk Officer)
- The CAO (Chief Audit Officer)
- The CCO (Chief Compliance Officer)
- The CLO (Chief Legal Officer)
- The head of HR

EGIT – success factors

CISA aspirants should remember the factors mentioned in this section for the successful implementation of EGIT:

- IT governance is primarily the responsibility of directors and senior management. IT governance is designed to ensure the optimal use of IT resources to support business objectives.
- The effectiveness of an IT governance implementation can be determined most effectively by ensuring the involvement of all stakeholders.
- It is very important to define the accountability of each critical function.
- The IS auditor is required to review the organization's chart to understand the roles, responsibilities, and authority of various functionaries.
- IT can add value to the business only if IT strategies are aligned with the business strategy. The IS auditor should determine whether IT and business requirements are integrated and heading in the same direction. A strategic IT plan must contain a clear statement regarding the vision and mission of IT.

- The participation of senior officials is very important to ensure that the information security policy is in accordance with business objectives. Mediation between senior officials in terms of business and technology needs is the best option when it comes to improving strategic alignment.
- To achieve an organization's objective, the IT department should have long- and short-term plans. Plans should be consistent with the organization's business objectives.

Key aspects from the CISA exam perspective

The following table covers important aspects from CISA exam perspective:

CISA questions	Possible answers
What is the primary reason for reviewing the organizational chart?	To understand the structure of the organization
How to determine whether IT adds value to the organization?	Alignment of the IT strategy with the organizational strategy
Who has the final responsibility for IT governance?	Board of Directors
What is the main objective of IT governance?	Optimal use of technology resources
What is the prime purpose of corporate governance?	Provide strategic direction

Self-assessment questions

1. **The effectiveness of an IT governance implementation can be most effectively determined by:**
    - A. Ensuring that the objectives are defined
    - B. Ensuring the involvement of stakeholders
    - C. The identification of emerging risks
    - D. Ensuring that relevant enablers are determined

2. **The IS auditor noted that roles and responsibilities in terms of IT governance and management are not properly documented and defined. What is the most appropriate recommendation?**
    - A. To review the alignment of IT with business objectives
    - B. To define the accountability for each critical function
    - C. To conduct an IS audit on an ongoing basis
    - D. To create the role of CRO in the organization

3. **The primary reason for reviewing the organizational chart is as follows:**
   A. To understand the structure of the organization
   B. To understand various communication channels
   C. To understand the roles and responsibilities of individuals
   D. To understand the network and system architecture

4. **Which of the following is the prime consideration in determining whether IT adds value to the business?**
   A. The alignment of the IT strategy with the organizational strategy
   B. Defining organizational accountability
   C. Empowering IT with the latest technology
   D. Designing a risk management process for the IT department

5. **A major risk associated with a lack of top management support in terms of IT strategic planning is the following:**
   A. The absence of technical advancement
   B. The absence of IT processes, policies, and guidelines
   C. A lack of alignment between the technology and business objectives
   D. A lack of qualified IT staff

6. **The greatest concern with respect to an organization's governance model is the following:**
   A. Senior management does not review information security policy
   B. The patch management policy is not documented
   C. An IS audit is only conducted once every 2 years
   D. The IT risk management program only covers critical functions

7. **For sound IT governance, the IT plan should be consistent with the following:**
   A. The organization's business plan
   B. The organization's business continuity plan
   C. The organization's investment plan
   D. The organization's information security plan

8. **Who among the following is responsible for IT governance?**
   A. Directors
   B. Steering committee
   C. CEO
   D. CIO

9. **To achieve the organization's objective, the most important consideration for an IT department is to have which of the following:**
    A. A budget-oriented philosophy
    B. Long- and short-term strategies
    C. The latest technology
    D. Documented IT processes and guidelines

10. **While reviewing IT structures, a major concern revolves around which of the following:**
    A. The alignment of IT and business requirements
    B. A clear definition of the mission and vision
    C. The fact that an IT Balanced Scorecard is in place
    D. The availability of IT resources

11. **Which of the following is related to strategic planning?**
    A. Software testing methodology and results
    B. A short-term plan for a new system
    C. An approved supplier for the company's products
    D. Evaluation of project requirements

12. **The most important consideration when evaluating the IT strategy of an organization is:**
    A. The involvement of line management
    B. Adherence to budget
    C. The inclusion of a procurement process
    D. Support for the objectives of the business

13. **The most important method for ensuring alignment of the IT strategy with the organization's business objectives is:**
    A. To review the availability of all resources
    B. To review the compatibility of the IT plan and the business plan
    C. To review the effectiveness and efficiency of all resources
    D. To review the organizations' capacity management

14. **Strategic alignment can best be improved by:**
    A. Managing third-party service provider risk
    B. Updating the knowledge base on clients, the industry, and products
    C. Providing a platform to facilitate the sharing of business information
    D. Involvement of top management in aligning business and technology requirements

15. **Which of the following best ensures effective IT governance?**
    A. The management of risk to an acceptable level
    B. Deriving the business objective from the IT strategy
    C. The availability of effective IT resources
    D. Alignment of the IT strategy with the organization's strategies and objectives

16. **The most important factor regarding the effective implementation of IT governance is:**
    A. A documented IT Balanced Scorecard
    B. Identified organizational strategies
    C. Conducting risk assessments
    D. Documenting an IT policy

17. **An IT strategic plan should contain:**
    A. Technology requirements
    B. Control requirements
    C. A mission and vision
    D. Project management practices

18. **Which of the following is the main objective of IT governance?**
    A. The optimal use of technology resources
    B. A reduction in technology costs
    C. A review of technology processes and guidelines
    D. Centralized control of IT resources

19. **Which of the following is the primary purpose of corporate governance?**
    A. To provide strategic direction
    B. To control business functions
    C. To align IT and business needs
    D. To implement a reporting hierarchy

20. **Which of the following is a prime indicator in deciding the area of priority for IT governance?**
    A. Organization culture
    B. Process maturity
    C. Business risks
    D. Audit reports

21. **An IS auditor evaluating an IT governance framework will be more concerned about:**
    - A. The limited involvement of senior management
    - B. The ROI not being monitored
    - C. The IT Balanced Scorecard not being implemented
    - D. The IT risk management process not being documented

IT-related frameworks

IT-related processes should be defined and documented in a structured way. The adoption of IT-related frameworks helps an organization to add value to its stakeholders and also ensures confidentiality, integrity, and the availability of IT assets. The following are some of the EGIT frameworks:

Framework	Description
COBIT	• COBIT is developed by ISACA • Stands for *Control Objective for Information Technology.* • COBIT is an EGIT framework that ensures that IT is aligned with the business and delivers value for the business.
ISO 27000 series	• The ISO 27000 series is a set of best practices for information security programs. • ISO/IEC 27001 is a well-recognized standard for **ISMS (Information Security Management System)**.
ITIL	• Stands for *Information Technology Infrastructure Library.* • Developed by the UK **Office of Government Commerce** (OGC) in partnership with the IT Service Management Forum. • ITIL is a detailed framework for the operational service management of IT.
O-ISM3	• Stands for *Open Information Security Management Maturity Model.* • This is a process-based ISM maturity model for security.
ISO/IEC 38500:2015	• This standard relates to the governance of IT. • This provides guidance for the effective, efficient, and acceptable use of IT within an organization.
ISO/IEC 20000	• This standard relates to IT service management. • It is aligned with ITIL's service management framework.
ISO 31000:2018	• This standard relates to risk management. • It provides guidelines on risk management for organizations.

CISA aspirants should understand that there will not be any direct questions on any specific framework.

IT standards, policies, and procedures

EGIT is implemented through a specific set of standards, policies, and procedures. Let's understand how each one of these operates.

Standard

Here are a few significant aspects of IT standards:

- A standard is a mandatory requirement to be followed in order to comply with a given framework or certification.
- A standard helps to ensure an efficient and effective process resulting in reliable products or services.
- Standards are updated as and when required to be embedded within the current environment.

Policies

A policy is a set of ideas or strategies that are used as a basis for decision making. They are the high-level statements of direction by management.

- There can be multiple policies at the corporate level as well as the department level. It should be ensured that department-wise, policies are consistent and aligned with corporate-level policies.
- Policies should be reviewed at periodic intervals to incorporate new processes, technology, and regulatory requirements. The appropriate version history should be maintained. An IS auditor should check for currency.
- IS auditors should use policies to evaluate and verify compliance.
- The IS auditor should also consider the applicability of policies to third-party vendors and service providers and their adherence to said policies.

Procedures

Procedures are detailed steps and actions that help to support the policy objectives.

- A procedure is considered to be more dynamic as compared with a policy.
- A procedures' document should be made available to all users.
- An IS auditor should verify adherence to documented procedural aspects.

Guidelines

In some cases, guidelines are required to implement procedures.

- Guidelines should contain information such as examples, suggestions, requirements, and other details for executing procedures:

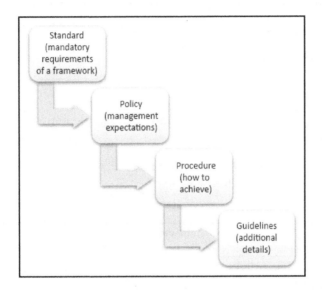

CISA aspirants are required to understand the difference between IT standards, policy, procedures, and guidelines.

Information security policy

The information security policy entails a commitment on the part of management and a plan of action to safeguard the information assets of the enterprise. An IS auditor should use information security policy as a reference document while conducting information system audits. An IS auditor should review and evaluate the following:

- Whether the information security policy is approved by senior management?
- Whether the information security policy is documented and communicated to relevant users and third-party suppliers?
- Whether the information security policy is adequate and appropriate to the functioning of the organization?

Content of the information security policy

An IS auditor should ensure that the information security policy includes the following elements:

- A statement of management commitment vis-à-vis information security
- A structure for conducting a risk assessment and risk management
- Information security policies, principles, and compliance requirements
- Information security awareness and training requirements for employees and third-party suppliers
- Roles and responsibilities relating to information security
- Business continuity arrangements
- Reference to other relevant documents that supplements the information security policy.

An organization may capture all these requirements in a single policy or different policies. These are documented in detail as follows:

Policy	Areas covered
Information security policy	This includes the management commitment vis-à-vis the safeguarding of information assets.
Data classification policy	This includes classification requirements and levels of control at each classification.
Acceptable use policy	This includes information relating to permissions and restrictions regarding the utilization of IT resources.
Access control policy	This includes a process for providing access in order to use information system assets.

Information security policy users

The policy should be disseminated to all end users. A relevant portion of information security requirements should also be made available to third-party suppliers.

Sign-off should be obtained from all employees and third parties having access to information assets regarding their readiness and preparedness to comply with the information security policy.

Information security policy audit

An IS auditor should consider the following aspects when evaluating the information security policy:

- The information security policy should be reviewed at least annually or when there are significant changes to the environment of the organization.
- Policy should have an owner responsible for updating the policy.
- A competent authority should review the policy.
- The policy implementation process.
- The process to impart awareness and training related to the policy.

Information security policy review

Management should consider the following aspects when reviewing the information security policy:

- Feedback from relevant parties
- Audit findings
- Significant changes to the environment of the organization
- Imminent threats and vulnerabilities
- Reported incidents
- Legal, contractual, and statutory requirements

The policy should be revised on account of the preceding factors to align information security requirements with business objectives.

Key aspects from CISA exam perspective

The following table covers important aspects from CISA exam perspective:

CISA questions	Possible answers
The most important action following the dismissal of an employee:	Disabling their rights of access
Information security policy should be approved by:	The Board of Directors
One advantage of developing operational policies by means of a top-down approach:	Consistency across the organization
One advantage of developing operational policies by means of a bottom-up approach:	Risk assessment is considered

Self-assessment questions

1. Which of the following is a first step for the auditor having observed that IT policies are not approved by management?
   - A. To ignore the requirement for management approval as the policy is being observed by all employees
   - B. To recommend that the policy should be approved immediately
   - C. To guide management regarding the importance of approval
   - D. To include this as non-compliance in an audit report

2. An area of most concern while reviewing HR policy is the absence of a:
   - A. Rotation process
   - B. Exit interview process
   - C. Termination process
   - D. Process of entering into an NDA with employees

3. The best reason for a policy that restricts a second employment is:
   - A. To protect against the misuse of an organization's assets
   - B. To prevent a conflict of interest
   - C. To ensure better productivity on the part of the employee
   - D. To restrict monetary benefits of employees

4. The greatest concern for an IS auditor reviewing an information security policy is the fact that:
   - A. The policy is not updated every year
   - B. The version control history is not maintained
   - C. The policy is not approved by senior management
   - D. The organization does not have an information security policy committee

5. Policy compliance can be ensured by:
   - A. An existing IT mechanism that supports compliance
   - B. The alignment of the policy with the business strategy
   - C. Technological initiatives
   - D. The compliance objective as defined in the policy

6. Which of the following is the most important action following the dismissal of an employee?
   - A. The handover of the job profile of the employee who has been dismissed to another employee
   - B. Taking backups of all the employee's files

C. Disabling access rights on the part of the employee

D. Settling the employee's outstanding payments

7. **A major risk of an unstructured policy regarding data and system ownership is the fact that:**

   A. The user management group cannot be ascertained

   B. A conflict of roles cannot be prevented

   C. Access can be granted to unauthorized users

   D. Recommendations from the audit committee may not be implemented.

8. **Which of the following is a major risk when employees are not aware of the information security policy?**

   A. The unintentional disclosure of sensitive information

   B. The change management procedure is not observed

   C. Information security training may not be effective

   D. The IS audit is not effective

9. **Information security policy should be approved by:**

   A. The IT department

   B. The Board of Directors

   C. The steering committee

   D. The audit committee

10. **Information security policy should include:**

    A. Details of critical assets to be protected

    B. The basis of access control authorization

    C. The SDLC methodology and procedure

    D. The identification of sensitive assets

11. **The most important factor for successful implementation of a security policy is:**

    A. The assimilation and intent of all users

    B. Approval from management

    C. Punitive action for violating the policy

    D. Stringent monitoring by the information security team

12. **Which of the following is most critical in terms of being addressed by an email policy?**

    A. Email ethics

    B. Email retention

    C. Email recovery

D. Email reuse

13. **Development of an information security program starts with:**
    A. The development of a corporate information security policy statement
    B. The development of an information security standard manual
    C. An IS audit of the security framework
    D. The development of access control software

14. **The risk of the unavailability of electronic evidence is reduced by:**
    A. An email ethics policy
    B. An email scanning policy
    C. An email archive policy
    D. An email usage policy

15. **The most important concern while reviewing information security policy is the fact that:**
    A. IT department objectives drive the policy
    B. Some users are not aware of the policy
    C. An information security procedure is not part of the policy
    D. The policy is not updated every 6 months

16. **The development of operational policies by means of a top-down approach helps:**
    A. To make them consistent across the organization
    B. To implement them as part of a risk assessment
    C. To comply with the policies
    D. To review them annually

17. **The most important factor while developing information security policy is:**
    A. Alignment with industry best practices
    B. Approval of the Board of Directors
    C. The consideration of business requirements
    D. An annual review of policy

18. **The most important factor in determining the appropriate level of protection is:**
    A. The outcome of a risk assessment
    B. The cost of assets
    C. The cost of control
    D. The outcome of a vulnerability assessment

19. **The first point of reference for an IS auditor conducting an audit is:**
    A. Existing procedures
    B. Approved policies
    C. Internal guidelines and standard documents
    D. The IT framework

20. **The most important factor in developing an information security policy is:**
    A. A vulnerability analysis
    B. A threat analysis
    C. Emerging risks
    D. The appetite for risk on the part of an enterprise

21. **The most important aspect in ensuring that an organization's policy complies with legal requirement is to:**
    A. Incorporate a blanket legal statement in each policy
    B. Have a periodic review of policy conducted by a subject matter expert
    C. Have policy approved by senior management
    D. Incorporate the most restrictive regulations

Organizational structure

A CISA candidate is expected to have an understanding of the organizational structure as well as the various roles and responsibilities of important IT functions.

The following table depicts the roles of IT-related functions:

Authority/committee	Description
Board of Directors	IT governance is mainly the responsibility of the Board of Directors.
Strategy committee	• Advises the board on IT initiatives. • This committee consists of members of the board and specialist members of the non-board.
Steering committee	• Ensures that the IS department is in line with the goals and priorities of the organization. • The committee must determine whether IS processes support business requirements in order to ensure this. • Monitors and encourages the implementation of IT services in support of business plans for specific projects.

Project steering committee	• This committee consists of a senior representative who will be affected by the new system for each feature. • Provides general feedback and monitors costs and timetables for the project. • Ultimately, the project steering committee is responsible for all project costs and schedules. • The steering committee's role is to ensure the project's progress. • If there are any issues that may impact the expected outcomes, these should be escalated by the steering committee.
User management	• User management takes over the project's ownership and the resulting framework. • They review and approve the findings as described and achieved.
System development management	• System development management provides technical support to the hardware and software environments through the production, implementation, and operation of the system requested.
Project sponsor	• The project sponsor is the person responsible for the business function, and is the data owner and the owner of the developing system • It is the project sponsor's responsibility to provide functional requirements to functional users.

Relationship between the IT strategy committee and the IT steering committee

The relationship between the IT strategy committee and the IT steering committee is shown in the following diagram:

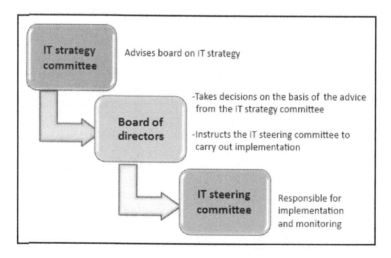

Differences between the IT strategy committee and the IT steering committee

A CISA aspirant should understand the functions of the IT strategy and IT steering committees. The following table outlines the differences between the two committees:

Strategy committee	Steering committee
Members include board members and specialist officers.	Members include the CEO, CIO, and other functionaries as required.
The strategy committee advises the board on IT strategies.	The steering committee focuses on the implementation and monitoring of IT projects.
Responsibilities include: • Aligning IT and business objectives • Identifying any exposure to IT risks • Providing direction to management regarding IT strategies	Responsibilities include: • Approving project plans and budgets • Setting priorities and milestones • Acquiring and assigning appropriate resources • Ensuring that the project meets business requirements and providing continuous monitoring • Ensuring the efficient use of IT resources
In a nutshell, the strategy committee sets out the IT roadmap.	In a nutshell, the steering committee drives IT-related projects.

Key aspects from the CISA exam perspective

The following table covers important aspects from CISA exam perspective:

CISA questions	Possible answers
The IS steering committee is primarily responsible for:	• Approving and monitoring major projects, the status of IS plans, and budgets • Monitoring project milestones and aligning project and business requirements • Prioritizing IT projects as per business requirements
Overall responsibility for system development projects is assumed by:	The steering committee
Ownership of a project should be assumed by:	User management
Accountability for ensuring relevant controls over IS resources rests with:	The resource owner (data owner/system owner)

Self-assessment questions

1. **Final responsibility for the development of an information security policy rests with:**
   A. The IS group
   B. The IS auditor
   C. The steering committee
   D. The Board of Directors

2. **Participation on the part of senior management is most important as regards the development of:**
   A. Strategic plans
   B. Information security standards
   C. The information security framework
   D. The system audit framework

3. **The IS steering committee is primarily responsible for:**
   A. Managing third-party service providers
   B. Maintaining the segregation of duties for critical functions
   C. Approving and monitoring major projects, the status of IS plans, and budgets
   D. Managing the IS audit

4. **Ultimate responsibility for IT governance rests with:**
   A. The IS auditor
   B. The Board of Directors
   C. The IS steering committee
   D. The CIO

5. **Overall responsibility for system development projects is assumed by:**
   A. The IS auditor
   B. The project steering committee
   C. The IS strategy committee
   D. The CIO

6. **Ownership of a project should be assumed by:**
   A. User management
   B. The steering committee
   C. The strategy committee
   D. Systems development management

7. **A request for proposal (RFP) to purchase a new system will most likely be approved by**:
   - A. The project steering committee
   - B. The person in charge of the project
   - C. The strategy committee
   - D. The system development manager

8. **The ultimate responsibility for internal control lies with**:
   - A. The finance department
   - B. Senior management
   - C. The IS auditor
   - D. The risk management department

9. **The ultimate responsibility for requirement specifications rests with**:
   - A. The CIO
   - B. The project sponsor
   - C. The project developer
   - D. The project strategy committee

10. **Which of the following is a function of the steering committee?**
   - A. To design requirement specifications
   - B. To escalate project issues
   - C. To design system controls
   - D. To document system architecture

11. **Who is accountable for ensuring relevant controls over IS resources?**
   - A. The system administrator
   - B. Resource owners
   - C. Network administration
   - D. The database administrator

12. **Ownership of a system development project and the system proposed is assumed by**:
   - A. User management
   - B. Database management
   - C. The project steering committee
   - D. The steering committee

13. **The role of the IT steering committee is:**
   A. To suggest a technology strategy
   B. To approve and control funds for IT initiatives
   C. To monitor the outsourcing of contracts
   D. To review IT frameworks

14. **Responsibility for monitoring project milestones and aligning a project with business requirements rests with:**
   A. The IT strategy committee
   B. The IT steering committee
   C. Business functions
   D. System developers

15. **The role of the IT steering committee is:**
   A. To issue advice to the IT department
   B. To provide technical support to the IT department
   C. To prioritize IT projects as per business requirements
   D. To advise the board on IT strategy

16. **The most suitable person to be appointed as chair of the steering committee is:**
   A. A member of the board
   B. Executive-level officer
   C. The CTO
   D. The CIO

17. **An IS steering committee comprises:**
   A. Members of the board
   B. User management
   C. Members of the IT department
   D. Key executive officers

18. **The primary role of the IT steering committee is:**
   A. To support user management
   B. To support the IT department
   C. To monitor the IT project's priorities and milestones
   D. To advise board members regarding IT strategy

19. **The IT steering committee is primarily required to determine:**
    A. That the IT processes are aligned with business requirements
    B. That capacity management processes are in place
    C. The architectural requirements of the new system
    D. The functionality of existing technology

20. **In a system development project, which of the following is considered a major control weakness?**
    A. The board is selective about approving recommendations from the IT strategy committee
    B. The project does not have a specified deadline
    C. The project does not have a project manager
    D. The organization does not have a project steering committee

Enterprise architecture

An **Enterprise Architecture (EA)** defines the structure and operations of the organization. The objective of EA is to determine how an organization can achieve its current as well as future objectives. It is important for the EA to include the entire future outcome. If a future-state description is not included in the EA, then it is not complete.

The EA's main focus is to ensure that technology initiatives are compatible with the IT framework. Hence, the EA's goal is to help the organization adopt the most successful technologies. The Zachman Framework is one of the first EAs created by John Zachman. It is a fundamental EA structure that provides a formal and structured way of viewing and defining an enterprise.

Enterprise security architecture

Enterprise security architecture is a subset of the overall enterprise architecture and includes security processes and procedures and how these are linked across the organization from a strategic, tactical, and operational perspective.

The first step in developing a security architecture is to establish a security policy for information and related technology. A security policy provides customers, administrators, and technical staff with a consistent security framework. An organization should carry out a risk assessment before implementing new technology.

Key aspects from CISA exam perspective

The following table covers important aspects from CISA exam perspective:

CISA questions	Possible answers
What is the main advantage of EA?	It facilitates technology selection and adoption
What is the best level of control when customized software is developed by a third-party vendor?	An escrow arrangement
What is the most important advantage of open system architecture?	Facilitates interoperability within different systems

Self-assessment questions

1. **An IS auditor finds that the organization has two separate EAs, in other words, one for current-state representation and a new project has been initiated to build a future-state representation. The IS auditor should:**
   A. Suggest finishing this separate project as early as possible
   B. Report this problem in the audit report as an observation
   C. Suggest implementation of the Zachman Framework
   D. Extend the scope of the audit to include the separate project as part of the current audit

2. **The main advantage of an EA initiative is to:**
   A. Allow the company to invest in the technology that is most suitable
   B. Ensure the application of appropriate controls on sensitive networks
   C. Ensure that development teams are more open to the needs of the business
   D. Provide independence for business units to choose approaches that meet their needs

3. **Which of the following is a major concern when IT is not involved in a system selection procedure?**
  A. The application's security checks do not meet requirements
  B. The program may not satisfy business users' requirements
  C. The application technologies may be incompatible with the architecture of the organization
  D. The program can result in unexpected IT support problems

4. **A vendor has been hired by a company to find a software solution for their electronic toll collection system (ETCS). As part of the solution, the vendor has developed their own application software. The contract will include:**
  A. The requirements for a backup system
  B. A requirement for the automatic updating of related files and data
  C. Training requirements for the organization's staff
  D. The inclusion of source code in escrow

5. **Which of the following factors is the most valuable on account of the technology transition rate?**
  A. IT functions
  B. Sound processes
  C. Skilled employees
  D. Auditors

6. **An enterprise is considering investing significantly in infrastructure improvements. Which of the following are the most critical options to consider?**
  A. A cost analysis
  B. The safety risks associated with the latest technology
  C. Compatibility with existing systems
  D. A risk analysis

7. **Which of the following is the most important advantage of open system architecture?**
  A. It facilitates interoperability within different systems
  B. It facilities the integration of proprietary components
  C. It will constitute a basis for discounts from equipment vendors
  D. It facilitates the attainment of further economics of scale for equipment

8. **Which of the following steps should be carried out first before designing a security architecture?**
   A. Document security guidelines
   B. Define a security policy
   C. Develop an access control matrix
   D. Define roles and responsibilities

9. **Compliance risk is not directly addressed by:**
   A. Risk acceptance
   B. Risk mitigation
   C. Risk avoidance
   D. Risk transfer

10. **Following the merger of two companies, a new common interface would replace several self-developed legacy applications. Which of the following options constitutes the biggest risk?**
   A. Project management and progress reporting is integrated in an external consultant-driven project management department
   B. The substitute plan consists of several independent projects without incorporating resource allocation in an approach to portfolio management
   C. Each organization's resources become inefficiently distributed as they become acquainted with the legacy systems of the other organization
   D. The new platform would push both company's business areas to adjust their job procedures, resulting in extensive training requirements

11. **The best recommendation for securing an organization's software investment is to:**
   A. Conduct due diligence on the development team
   B. Conduct a quarterly audit of the service provider
   C. Include a source code escrow arrangement in the service level agreement
   D. Include a penalty clause in the service level agreement

Enterprise risk management

Enterprise risk management (ERM) is the practices, methods, and processes adopted by organizations to manage and monitor risks. ERM is a structured process for managing various risks that can adversely impact business objectives. For effective risk management, it is important to determine an organization's appetite for risk.

Risk management process steps

Risk management is a process by means of which potential risks are identified, monitored, and managed. The following table depicts five risk management process steps:

Steps	Description
Asset identification	• The first step is the identification of assets that are critical to the organization and the need to be adequately protected. • Assets can be in the form of data, hardware, software, and people. • Once assets are identified, they should be classified in terms of criticality and sensitivity. • The purpose of classification is to prioritize the assets that need to be protected. Classification also helps in applying appropriate levels of protection in accordance with the critical nature of the assets. High-value assets may require more levels of control compared with other assets.
The identification of threats and vulnerabilities	• The next step involves the identification of threats and vulnerabilities applicable to critical assets. • Threats can include hackers, fraudsters, and natural calamities. • Vulnerabilities may take the form of weak security, unprotected networks, a lack of user awareness, or a lack of a business continuity arrangement.
Evaluation of impact	• Once the threats and vulnerabilities are identified, the next step is to determine their impact. • Impacts may take the form of financial losses, the loss of reputation, or the interruption of business activity.
Calculation of risk	• The next step is to calculate the overall risk for each threat. Risk is the product of probability and effect.
Risk response	• The final step is to evaluate each risk and prepare an appropriate risk response in accordance with the risk appetite of the organization. • Factors that may impact risk treatment include organizational processes and policies, the cost of control vis-à-vis benefits, and the organization's appetite for risk.

Risk analysis methods

A risk analysis method is a method of determining the level of risk in an organization. There are three types of method to determine the level – qualitative, semi-quantitative, and quantitative:

Methods	Description
Qualitative	• In qualitative risk analysis, descriptions such as high, medium, and low are used to define the impacts or likelihood. • This is a very simple and widely used method. • While often less complicated and less time-consuming than the other methods, this method is more subjective in nature and also lacks consistency when it comes to managerial decision making.
Semi-quantitative	• A semi-quantitative method includes a descriptive ranking along with a numerical rating. • This method is regarded as midway between the qualitative and quantitative methods and is generally employed when it is difficult to use the quantitative method and management is not in favor of the qualitative method. • For example, the qualitative measure of "high" may be given a quantitative weight of 5, "medium" may be given a quantitative weight of 3, and "low" may be given a quantitative weight of 1. • The total weight for the subject area that is evaluated may be the aggregate of the weights thus derived for the various factors under consideration.
Quantitative	• Quantitative analysis is a technique that seeks to understand risk behavior by using mathematical and statistical modeling, measurement, and research. Quantitative analysts aim to represent a risk ranking in terms of a numerical value. • For quantitative analysis, data is used from several sources, including historical records, predictive analysis, statistical records, and test results. • Measurable results are one of the important advantages associated with this method. • Military, nuclear, chemical, and financial entities, along with other areas, currently use many quantitative risk analysis methods. • In business impact analysis, a quantitative approach provides more accuracy in terms of selecting critical processes or assets. • However, it is important that there should be a standardized approach for conducting a quantitative analysis across the organization.

Risk treatment

Risk management includes the identification, analysis, evaluation, treatment, monitoring, and communication of risk impacts on IT processes. Four approaches are generally observed as regards the treatment of risk:

Risk treatment options	Description
Mitigate	This is also known as risk reduction. Risk can be mitigated or reduced by implementing necessary checks and controls. Out of all four options, risk mitigation is employed more frequently.
Accept	This option requires acceptance of the risk as it stands. This is generally applied to low risk situations, where the cost of control is higher than the impact of the risk.
Avoid	This option requires the avoidance of activity that would cause risk. This is generally applied in relation to high-risk scenarios, where the impact could be devastating.
Transfer	This is also known as the sharing of risk. Risk is transferred or shared by way of insurance or by entering into partnership and suchlike.

Therefore, risk can be avoided, reduced, transferred, or accepted. An organization can also choose to reject risk by ignoring it, which can be dangerous and should be considered a red flag by the IS auditor.

Key aspects from the CISA exam perspective

The following table covers important aspects from CISA exam perspective:

CISA questions	Possible answers
What is the first step in implementing a risk management program?	• Asset identification (first step) • Determine the threat, vulnerability, and risk profiles of the organization (if the asset identification option is not available)

Self-assessment questions

1. **Which of the following should be reviewed first while evaluating an organization's risk management procedure?**
    A. Existing controls
    B. The risk monitoring process
    C. The efficiency of controls
    D. Threats/vulnerabilities affecting the assets

2. **Which of the following treatments indicates the exchange of risk?**
   - A. To transfer risk
   - B. To accept risk
   - C. To avoid risk
   - D. To treat risk

3. **A team performing a risk analysis has difficulty anticipating the financial losses that might result from a risk. To evaluate the potential impact, the team should:**
   - A. Estimate the related cost amortization
   - B. Calculate an investment return
   - C. Apply a qualitative approach
   - D. Spend time defining the amount of loss precisely

4. **Establishing the level of acceptable risk is the responsibility of:**
   - A. Quality assurance management
   - B. Senior business management
   - C. The CIO
   - D. The CSO

5. **Performance of the process of risk management is an input for:**
   - A. Business plans
   - B. Audit charters
   - C. Security policy decisions
   - D. Software design decisions

6. **The first duty of the IS auditor is to review any current e-business program in search of vulnerabilities. What should the next task be?**
   - A. To report the risk immediately
   - B. To examine the technology framework of the e-business
   - C. To identify risks and the possibility of occurrence
   - D. To review the appropriate risk management budget

7. **An assessment of IT risk is best achieved by:**
   - A. Assessing the risks and vulnerabilities relevant to the current IT infrastructure and IT programs.
   - B. Using the post-actual experience of failure on the part of the company to assess current visibility
   - C. Studying reports released by similar organizations regarding losses
   - D. Reviewing the weak points of IT control identified in audit reports

8. **A poor choice of passwords and unencrypted data transmissions over unprotected communication lines are examples of:**
   - A. Vulnerabilities
   - B. Threats
   - C. Probabilities
   - D. Impacts

9. **The first step in implementing a risk management program is to:**
   - A. Determine the threat, vulnerability, and risk profiles of the organization
   - B. Determine overall risk exposures and impact analysis
   - C. Determine risk management priorities
   - D. Determine a risk treatment plan

10. **What is the best recommendation for a small-sized IT organization that does not have an independent risk management function and where the organization's operational risk reporting includes only a few forms of IT risk that are commonly defined?**
    - A. Develop an IT risk management team and set up an IT risk framework with the help of external risk management professionals
    - B. Use common industry standard guidelines to separate current risk reports into different risk categories that will be easier to manage
    - C. No guidance is needed as the current approach is suitable for a medium-sized company
    - D. Establish regular IT risk management meetings to define and assess risk and develop a contingency plan as an approach to controlling risk within the company

11. **Which of the following types of insurance cover a risk arising from employees' fraudulent actions?**
    - A. Disaster impact
    - B. Fidelity coverage
    - C. Errors and omissions
    - D. Business continuity

12. **Which of the following is of greatest interest to an IS auditor evaluating the risk strategy of an organization?**
    - A. All threats are successfully mitigated
    - B. Residual risk is zero following control implementation
    - C. All risks are identified and categorized
    - D. The organization uses a defined risk framework

13. **The most important consideration while reviewing a risk management program is:**
    A. The implementation of a cost benefit-based control
    B. The incorporation of an industry standard-based risk management framework
    C. The fact that a risk response approval process is in place
    D. The fact that IT risk is presented from a business perspective

14. **The risk appetite of an enterprise is best ascertained by:**
    A. The legal department
    B. The system department
    C. The audit department
    D. The steering committee

Maturity model

Implementing IT governance involves the ongoing performance measurement of the assets of an organization. Maintaining consistent process, productivity and efficiency requires the implementation of a process maturity framework. The system can be based on different models, for example, **Capability Maturity Model Integration (CMMI)** and the **Initiating, Diagnosing, Establishing, Acting, and Learning (IDEAL)** model. CISA aspirants should be aware that there will be no direct questions in the exam on any of the particular frameworks or models.

Laws, regulations, and industry standards affecting the organization

Laws and regulations are being enacted with the aim of protecting the interests of stakeholders. In the field of IT, the most common objectives of laws and regulations include the safeguarding of privacy and the confidentiality of personal data, the protection of intellectual property rights, and the integrity of financial information.

All these laws and regulations mandate various policies and procedures to protect the interests of stakeholders. CISA aspirants should be aware that there will be no direct questions in the exam on any of the particular laws or regulations.

An IS auditor's role in determining adherence to laws and regulations

An IS auditor should consider the following factors in determining the level of adherence to laws and regulations by an organization:

- Has an organization identified applicable laws and regulations pertaining to IT?
- How are the **Governance, Risk, and Compliance (GRC)** program implemented within the organization?
- Has the organization identified compliance- and legal-related risks and implemented appropriate controls to address these risks?
- Has an organization operating in multiple jurisdictions determined the legal and regulatory requirements for all areas where they operate?
- Has overall responsibility for adherence to regulatory requirements been assigned to an individual at senior management level?
- Is an appropriate monitoring, auditing, and reporting process in place in relation to legal and regulatory requirements?

The following guidelines (issued by IIA) need to be considered when auditing regulatory compliance:

- Standards and procedures: Employees and other entities should follow the provision of compliance requirements and procedures to reduce the risk of a regulatory violation.
- The assignment of responsibility to senior personnel: Individual(s) from senior management within the organization should have responsibility for compliance.
- Reliable staff background: Proper background checks need to be carried out before access or authority positions are established in order to ensure that such power is not assigned to people who have carried out illegal activities.
- Communication of procedures: Both staff and other stakeholders should be fully aware of policies and procedures.
- Compliance monitoring and auditing: Appropriate monitoring and reporting measures need to be taken to conform with requirements.
- Consistent enforcement: Organizations should ensure that compliance with effective disciplinary action against offenders is regularly applied throughout the organization.
- Appropriate response to an offense and mitigation of similar offenses: Once an offense is detected / has occurred, organizations need to disclose to the appropriate authorities and act in a timely basis to prevent future offenses.

Key aspects from the CISA exam perspective

The following table covers important aspects from CISA exam perspective:

CISA questions	Possible answers
Major factor to be considered in relation to offshore data storage/transfer:	Privacy laws
Concerns regarding the use of cloud services:	• Compliance with laws and regulations (first preference) • Data confidentiality

Self-assessment questions

1. **Which of the following is a determining factor in not maintaining customer data at an offshore location?**
    A. Time zone differences could prevent IT teams from interacting
    B. The high cost of telecommunications lines
    C. Privacy laws could prevent the flow of information across borders
    D. Differences in software development standards

2. **Which of the following is a major concern for an IS auditor when reviewing regulatory compliance of an organization?**
    A. A lack of documented processes for reporting offences
    B. A lack of staff training regarding regulatory requirements
    C. Junior staff are in charge of monitoring regulatory compliance
    D. No list of applicable laws and regulations is maintained

3. **The most important factor to consider in terms of the success of IT activities is:**
    A. To analyze the performance balance scorecard
    B. To analyze the IT budget spending ×
    C. To analyze IT support for compliance with regulatory requirements
    D. To analyze the utilization of manpower ×

4. **A major concern regarding the storage of sensitive data in the cloud is:**
    A. Inadequate storage capability
    B. Data confidentiality
    C. Inadequate disaster recovery arrangements
    D. The high cost of cloud services

5. **The most important concern regarding the use of cloud services is:**
    A. The high cost of maintenance
    B. Compliance with laws and regulations
    C. The data retrieval turnaround time
    D. Network bandwidth

Summary

EGIT is a process used to monitor and control IT activities. Information security governance is an integral part of overall IT governance. Information security governance addresses concerns regarding the protection of information assets, in other words, the confidentiality, integrity, and availability of the information.

In the next chapter, we will examine IT management with respect to the auditing of resource management processes, third-party suppliers, and performance monitoring processes.

Assessments

You will find answers to all your assessment questions here.

IT enterprise governance

1. **Answer: B. Ensuring the involvement of stakeholders**
   Explanation: The effectiveness of IT governance implementation can be determined most effectively by involving stakeholders and addressing their requirements. Considering the stakeholder's needs and involving them in the project drives its success.

2. **Answer: B. To define accountability for each critical function.**
   Explanation: The IS auditor should recommend defining accountability for each critical function of the organization. Undefined responsibilities constitute a major risk in attaining business objectives. Other options will not add value if accountability and responsibility are not defined.

3. **Answer: C. To understand the roles and responsibilities of individuals.**
   Explanation: The primary reason for reviewing the organizational chart is to understand the roles, responsibilities, and authority of the individual. This helps in determining whether there is proper segregation of functions. Options B and D can be determined with the use of a network diagram.

4. **Answer: A. Alignment of IT strategy with the organization's strategy**
   Explanation: IT can add value to the business only if IT strategies are aligned with business strategies. The other options are not as important as option A.

5. **Answer: C. A lack of alignment between technology and business objectives**
   Explanation: A major risk arising from the lack of involvement of senior management in supporting IT-related strategic planning is that IT activities are not aligned with business objectives. Investment in IT will be of no value if IT does not support the business objectives.

6. **Answer: A. Senior management does not review information security policy**
   Explanation: Participation by top management is critical in ensuring that information security policy complies with business requirements. The information security policy should be reviewed at least once a year to address new and emerging risks. An IT risk management program need not necessarily cover all the functions of the organization. Options B and C are not as critical as option A.

7. **Answer: A. An organization's business plan**
   Explanation: For effective and sound IT governance, IT and business plans should be aligned and should be moving in the same direction. IT should add value to the business.

8. **Answer: A. Directors**
   Explanation: IT governance is primarily the obligation of the Board of Directors. The Board of Directors is required to ensure that IT activities are moving in the desired direction and that IT is adding value to the business.

9. **Answer: B. Long- and short-term strategies**
   Explanation: To achieve an organization's objectives, the most important consideration for an IT department is to have long- and short-term plans. An organization's business objective and IT plan should correspond. This is most important consideration of all of the options.

10. **Answer: A. The alignment of IT and business requirements**
    Explanation: The most important consideration is determining whether IT and business requirements are integrated and heading in the same direction. The other options are important, but determining option A is more critical while reviewing the IT plan.

11. **Answer: C. An approved suppliers for the company's products**
Explanation: Selecting suppliers for the company's products constitutes strategic level planning. It aims to provide direction to the business function. The other options relate to short-term or tactical plans.

12. **Answer: D. Support the objectives of the business**
Explanation: The strategic plan of the IT department should be consistent with the organization's business objective. IT should add value to the business. The other options are not as important as option D.

13. **Answer: B. To review the compatibility of the IT plan and the business plan**
Explanation: The best way to determine whether the IT strategy supports the business objective is to review and ensure that the IT plan is consistent with the business strategy. The other options are important, but option B is the best approach.

14. **Answer: D. The involvement of top management in aligning business and technology**
Explanation: The involvement of top management in mediating between the imperatives of business and technology is the best option when it comes to improving strategic alignment.

15. **Answer: D. Alignment of the IT strategy with the organization's strategies and objectives**
Explanation: Effective IT governance can be best ensured by aligning the IT strategy with the organization's strategies and objectives. The Board of Directors is required to ensure that the IT strategy complies with the business strategy.

16. **Answer: B. Identified organizational strategies**
Explanation: The primary function of IT is to support the business functions. Therefore, identification of the business strategy is the most important factor as regards the effective implementation of IT governance.

17. **Answer: C. A mission and vision**
Explanation: The IT strategic plan must contain a clear statement regarding the mission and vision of IT. The other options may not need to be included in an IT strategic plan.

18. **Answer: A. The optimal use of IT resources**
Explanation: IT governance is intended to ensure the optimal use of IT resources and thereby support the business strategy. The other options are not the ultimate purpose of IT governance.

19. **Answer: A. To provide a strategic direction**
    Explanation: Corporate governance provides strategic direction to the organization as a whole and thereby aligns the efforts of all the functions in the same direction with a view to achieving a common business goal. Corporate governance is applicable to all functions, not just the IT function, and so option C is incorrect. Options B and D are not the main objectives of corporate governance.

20. **Answer: C. Business risks**
    Explanation: IT governance should concentrate on those areas with a high business risk. Other options may not provide an indication of a genuine risk to the business.

21. **Answer: A. Limited involvement on the part of senior management**
    Explanation: For an effective IT governance framework, the involvement of senior management is a must. It is essential to ensure that senior management is involved in the implementation of an IT governance framework. The other options are not as critical as option A.

IT standards, policies, and procedures

1. **Answer: D. To report the lack of approval by management**
   Explanation: The first step involves reporting the findings. The next step is to provide recommendations and guide management. Findings should be reported even if employees follow the policies. A policy that is not approved may not align with business objectives and thereby expose the organization to risk.

2. **Answer: C. The termination process**
   Explanation: A documented termination process is important in ensuring information security on the part of the organization. An employee who has been dismissed may take undue advantage of their previous privileges if their access is not deactivated on time. The other options are not as significant as the termination process.

3. **Answer: B. To prevent conflicts of interest**
   Explanation: The main reason for restricting second employment is to prevent conflicts of interest and thereby safeguard the organizations' sensitive information. Conflicts of interest may result in risks such as fraud, theft, or other irregular activities.

4. **Answer: C. Policy is not approved by senior management**
   Explanation: Senior management is responsible for developing, reviewing, approving, and evaluating security policy. The other options are critical, but not as critical as option C.

5. **Answer: A. Existing IT mechanisms that support compliance**
   Explanation: The most important factor is the ability of an organization to comply with a policy. Existing IT systems should be able to enable compliance. Other factors are important, but they do not enable compliance directly.

6. **Answer: C. Disabling access rights on the part of the employee**
   Explanation: For information security, it is very important to disable access rights of the dismissed employee immediately. This will help to prevent any misuse of access rights. The other options are not as critical as option C.

7. **Answer: C. Access can be granted to unauthorized users**
   Explanation: Without proper ownership of data and systems, there is an increased risk of providing access to individuals who are not otherwise authorized. User access provisions cannot be properly controlled without assigned owners.

8. **Answer: A. The unintentional disclosure of sensitive information**
   Explanation: All staff should be aware of the organization's information security policy. If employees are not aware, they may unintentionally disclose sensitive information pertaining to the organization. The other options are not as critical as option A.

9. **Answer: B. Board of Directors**
   Explanation: Generally, the approval of the information security policy is the responsibility of senior management, in other words, the Board of Directors. The IT department is responsible for the execution of the policy. The steering committee monitors IT projects. The audit committee oversees the audit function.

10. **Answer: B. The basis of access control authorization**
    Explanation: The security policy includes a broad framework of security arrangements as approved by top management. This includes an overall basis for access control authorization. Other options should form part of procedural documents.

11. **Answer: A. Assimilation and intent of all users**
    Explanation: Assimilation and intent of all users are very important in terms of the successful implementation of a security policy. The support of management is important but, for successful implementation, the educating and involvement of users is very important. Punitive action and stringent monitoring may not be effective.

12. **Answer: B. Email retention**
    Explanation: The email policy should address the issue of email retention as per business and legal requirements. The other options are not as critical as defining the policy and process of email retention.

13. **Answer: A. Development of a corporate information security policy statement**
Explanation: A policy statement is very important as an initial step as it reflects the intent and support of management in relation to security. Other options can only be implemented once the information security policy statement has been defined. A security program is determined by policy and standards can be derived on the basis of this security program.

14. **Answer: C. Email archive policy**
Explanation: The availability of an email archive policy helps to retain emails as per business and legal requirements. This, in turn, will help to retain electronic evidence as per the organization's requirements.

15. **Answer: A. IT department objectives drive IT policy**
Explanation: When the objectives of the IT department are not aligned with business objectives, then the IT policy may not support business processes. The fact that some users are not aware of the policy and that the policy has not been updated are areas of concern, but the primary concern relates to the policy being driven by business objectives.

16. **Answer: A. To make them consistent across the organization**
Explanation: In a top-down approach, all the policies are derived from corporate level policy. This ensures that all policies are consistent across the organization. The outcome of the risk assessment should influence policy. However, the primary reason for a top-down approach is to ensure consistency across the organization. A top-down approach does not necessarily guarantee compliance or an annual review.

17. **Answer: C. Consideration of business requirement**
Explanation: Information security policy must be in accordance with business objectives. This is the most important factor while developing information security policy. The other options are not as critical and important as option C.

18. **Answer: A. The outcome of a risk assessment**
Explanation: The outcome of a risk assessment determines the criticality of the assets. Appropriateness of control is considered on the basis of risk associated with assets. A risk assessment considers risk on the basis of probability and impact, while the other three options only consider one of them.

19. **Answer: B. Approved policies**
Explanation: Policies are high-level statements that indicate the mission and vision of an organization. Other options are derived from approved policies. The first point of reference for an IS auditor should be approved policies.

20. **Answer: D. The appetite for risk on the part of the organization**
    Explanation: Risk appetite is the level of risk that an enterprise is willing to accept in order to meet business objectives. The purpose of a security policy is to manage risk to an acceptable level. The IS auditor should ensure that the policy is primarily aligned with risk appetite.

21. **Answer: B. Have a periodic review of policy conducted by a subject matter expert**
    Explanation: A subject matter expert will help to ensure that an organization's policies are aligned with legal requirements. The other options do not help directly in achieving this objective.

Organizational structure

1. **Answer: D. Board of directors**
   Explanation: The primary responsibility and accountability for setting up the IS security policy resides with the Board of Directors.

2. **Answer: A. Strategic plans**
   Explanation: An organization's mission, vision, and goals can be achieved by creating and implementing strategic plans. Top management should be involved in developing strategic plans, ensuring that plans are aligned with business goals. The other options are derived and framed on the basis of strategic plans.

3. **Answer: C. Approving and monitoring major projects, the status of IS plans, and budgets**
   Explanation: One of the functions of the IS steering committee is to monitor and control information system projects. They are generally not involved in routine operations. The other options are not functions of the IS steering committee.

4. **Answer: B. Board of Directors**
   Explanation: Information technology governance is the primary responsibility of the Board of Directors. The function of the IT strategy committee is to advise the board. The function of the IS steering committee is to monitor and control IT projects in accordance with board-approved policy. Audit issues and risks are handled by the audit committee board.

5. **Answer: B. Project steering committee**
   Explanation: One of the functions of the IS steering committee is to monitor and control the information system projects. They provide overall direction to the project. Audit issues and risks are handled by the audit committee board. User management is involved in requirement specifications and is regarded as the owner of the project, but overall responsibility rests with the steering committee. User management conducts user acceptance testing and approves projects as they are defined and accomplished.

6. **Answer: A. User management**
   Explanation: User management is involved in requirement specifications and is regarded as the owner of the project. User management conducts user acceptance testing and approves projects as they are defined and accomplished. It is user management that assumes ownership of the project. The strategy committee advises the board on IT initiatives. The steering committee is responsible for providing overall direction and for monitoring project costs and schedules. System development management provides support in relation to technical aspects.

7. **Answer: A. Project steering committee**
   Explanation: The project steering committee includes top-level officers from each function, and so the steering committee is best suited to approving RFP. The project in-charge is responsible for executing the project. The strategy committee advises the board on IT initiatives. System development management provides support for technical aspects.

8. **Answer: B. Senior management**
   Explanation: The organization's senior management is responsible for effective internal control mechanisms. The other options are support functions through which management implements internal control policies.

9. **Answer: B. Project sponsor**
   Explanation: The project sponsor is generally regarded as being in charge of the business function for which a system is to be developed. They are responsible for finalizing the functional specifications for the new system under development.

10. **Answer: B. To escalate project issues**
    Explanation: The steering committee is responsible for the successful implementation of the project. In the case of any issues or concerns impacting anticipated results, the steering committee should escalate them.

11. **Answer: B. Resource owners**
    Explanation: Resource owners are responsible for maintaining appropriate security measures over information assets. Asset owners should make decisions relating to classification and access rights. System administrators, network administrators, and database administrators provide support in terms of asset security. However, resource owners remain accountable for maintaining appropriate security measures.

12. **Answer: A. User management**
    Explanation: User management assumes ownership of the project as regards system development.

13. **Answer: B. To approve and control funds for IT initiatives**
    Explanation: The IT steering committee is responsible for approving project plans and budgets, for setting priorities and milestones, and for ensuring that the project meets business requirements. It is the role of the IT strategy committee to advise the board on IT strategy. IT executives will review the outsourcing of contracts and the IT framework.

14. **Answer: B. IT steering committee**
    Explanation: The IT steering committee is responsible for approving project plans and budgets, for setting priorities and milestones, and for ensuring that the project meets business requirements. The IT strategy committee advises the board on IT strategy. It s not involved in implementation. System developers are involved in system development activities.

15. **Answer: C. To prioritize IT projects as per business requirements**
    Explanation: One of the functions of the IS steering committee is to monitor and control information system projects. It provides overall direction to the project. It approves project plans and budgets, sets priorities and milestones, and ensures that the project meets business requirements. One of the responsibilities of the IT steering committee includes the prioritization of IT projects as per business requirements.

16. **Answer: B. An executive-level officer**
    Explanation: The chairperson should be an executive-level officer who can have a significant impact on areas of the business area and who has the authority to make decisions. Board members generally are not expected to be involved in implementation. A CTO or CIO would not normally be the chair, although such individuals need to be members in order to provide input on IT strategy.

17. **Answer: D. Key executive officers**
Explanation: The steering committee should consist of key executives and representatives from user management. Only user management and IT members will not serve the aims of the committee. Board members are generally not expected to be involved in implementation.

18. **Answer: C. To monitor the IT project's priorities and milestones**
Explanation: One of the functions of the IS steering committee is to monitor and control information system projects. It provides overall direction to the project. One of the responsibilities of the IT steering committee includes the prioritization of IT projects as per business requirements.

19. **Answer: A. That IT processes are aligned with business requirements**
Explanation: The IT steering committee is required to determine the alignment of IT processes with business requirements. Other functions are not the prime objective of the steering committee.

20. **Answer. D. The organization does not have a project steering committee**
Explanation: One of the functions of the IS steering committee is to monitor and control information system projects. It provides overall direction to the project. It controls project costs and project schedules. The absence of a project steering committee can be considered a major weakness. The other options are not as critical as not having a project steering committee. It is not a requirement for the board to approve all the recommendations of the IT strategy committee.

Enterprise architecture

1. **Answer: B. Report this problem in the audit report as an observation**
Explanation: It is important for the EA to consider the entire future outcome because IT strategic and tactical plans will be determined by the difference between the present state and the future state. If a future-state description is not included in the EA, it is not complete and this problem should be identified as an observation.

2. **Answer: A. Allow the company to invest in the technology that is most suitable**
Explanation: The EA's primary focus is to ensure that the technology initiatives are compatible with the IT organization's framework, data, and implementation standards. Hence, the EA's goal is to help the organization adopt the most successful technologies.

3. **Answer: C. The application technologies may be incompatible with the architecture of the organization**
Explanation: The EA's primary focus is to ensure that innovation in infrastructure is compatible with the IT organization's structure, data, and quality requirements. For fields such as the use of common systems, repositories, or programming languages, the EA describes both a current and future state.

4. **Answer: D. The ETCS application's source code is put in escrow**
Explanation: The contract should provide for a source code escrow agreement whenever proprietary application software is purchased. This agreement means that the purchasing company will change the product if the vendor fails to function.

5. **Answer: B. Implementation and enforcement of sound processes**
Explanation: Change control includes the application and execution of good change management systems.

6. **Answer: D. A risk analysis**
Explanation: An organization should carry out a risk assessment before implementing new technology, which will then be presented to the management of the business unit for review and acceptance.

7. **Answer: A. Facilitates interoperability within different systems**
Explanation: An open system is a system in which the components and protocols conform to standards independent of a particular supplier. Open systems facilitate interoperability between systems made by different vendors.

8. **Answer: B. To define a security policy**
Explanation: The first step in developing a security architecture is to establish a security policy for information and related technology. A security policy provides customers, administrators, and technical staff with a consistent security framework.

9. **Answer: D. Risk transfer**
Explanation: Transferring risk usually covers financial risk. The purpose of an insurance policy is to transfer the financial risk; however, a compliance risk continues to exist.

10. **Answer: B. The substitute plan comprises several independent projects without combining resource allocation into an approach to portfolio management**
Explanation: The measures for maintaining compliance with the post-merger organization's overall strategy should be streamlined. When resource management is not distributed, there is a danger that independent initiatives may overestimate the availability of essential information tools for the legacy applications built in-house.

11. **Answer: C. Include a source code escrow arrangement in the service level agreement**
    Explanation: A source code escrow policy is primarily advised to help protect the company's tech investment as the source code will be accessed through a trusted third party and can be recovered if the start up developer leaves the operation.

Enterprise risk management

1. **Answer: D. Threats/vulnerabilities affecting the assets**
   Explanation: Threats and vulnerabilities affecting the assets should be reviewed first while evaluating the organization's risk management procedure The reliability of the infrastructure (the data) and the risks and weaknesses impacting the assets are among the main factors to be considered in evaluating the vulnerability of information systems.

2. **Answer: A. To transfer risk**
   Explanation: Risk transfer (for instance, when taking out an insurance policy) is a form of risk sharing.

3. **Answer: C. Apply a qualitative approach**
   Explanation: In qualitative risk analysis, descriptions such as "high", "medium", and "low" are used to define the impact or likely impact. It is a very simple and widely used method. This method is suitable when the impact cannot be quantified in numbers.

4. **AAnswer: B. Senior business management**
   Explanation: Top-level officials should be involved in determining the acceptable level of risk as they are accountable for the effective and efficient operation of the organization. This person can be the QA, CIO, or the CSO, but responsibility rests with the business manager.

5. **Answer: C. Security policy decisions**
   Explanation: The method of risk management involves making specific security-related choices, such as acceptable risk rates.

6. **Answer: C. Identify risks and the possibility of occurrence**
   Explanation: An IS auditor will classify the properties, search for vulnerabilities, and then assess the risks and the probability of occurrence to determine the risk associated with the e-business.

7. **Answer: A. An assessment of those risks and vulnerabilities relevant to current IT infrastructure and IT programs**
Explanation: To measure IT risk, it is important to analyze risks and weaknesses using qualitative or quantitative risk evaluation methods.

8. **Answer: A. Vulnerabilities**
Explanation: Vulnerability is a weakness of the information infrastructure that can be exposed through an attack. Because these are issues that the security specialist may fix, these are examples of vulnerabilities.

9. **Answer: A. Determine the threat, vulnerability, and risk profiles of the organization**
Explanation: The first step in implementing a risk management program is to determine the threat, vulnerability, and risk profiles of the organization. Once this is done, other options can be followed.

10. **Answer: D. Establish regular IT risk management meetings to define and assess the level of risk and develop a contingency plan as an approach to controlling risk within the company**
Explanation: Establishing regular IT risk management meetings in a medium-sized organization is the best way of identifying and evaluating IT-related risk, identifying responsibilities on the part of the respective management, and updating the risk register and mitigation plans.

11. **Answer: B. Fidelity coverage**
Explanation: Fidelity insurance is taken out by an employer against losses incurred as a result of dishonest actions by employees.

12. **Answer: C. All risks are identified and categorized**
Explanation: Risk that is likely to impact the organization should be identified and documented as part of the risk strategy. Without knowing the risk, there is no risk strategy.

13. **Answer: D. The fact that IT risk is presented from a business perspective**
Explanation: To be successful in managing risk, IT management must be matched with business objectives. This can be achieved by using appropriate terminology that is known by everyone, and the best way to do this is to present IT risks in business terms.

14. **Answer: D. The steering committee**
Explanation: The steering committee is well positioned to determine the risk level of the organization as it is represented by senior-level officials of different functions.

Laws, regulations, and industry standards affecting the organization

1. **Answer: C. Privacy laws could prevent the flow of information across borders**
   Explanation: Some privacy laws may restrict the movement of data outside the jurisdiction. This is a prime consideration. Differences in time zones and higher telecommunications costs are more manageable.

2. **Answer: D.No list of applicable laws and regulations is maintained**
   Explanation: In the absence of a list of all relevant laws and regulations, the level of compliance and consistency with specific laws and regulations cannot be monitored.

3. **Answer: C. To analyze IT support for compliance with regulatory requirements**
   Explanation: Compliance with regulatory requirements will be the most effective and necessary choice.

4. **Answer: B. Data confidentiality**
   Explanation: Considering various laws and regulations that require privacy/confidentiality of customer information, unauthorized access to information and data leakage are major concerns.

5. **Answer: B. Compliance with laws and regulations**
   Explanation: Legal requirements should be regarded as the most important elements in a contract undertaken with a cloud service provider.

4
IT Management

IT management refers to the monitoring, administration, and controlling of the IT assets of an organization. One objective of IT management is to ensure that IT assets operate effectively and efficiently. It aims to align the performance of those IT assets with the given business requirements. The following topics are covered in this chapter:

- IT resource management training scheduling and time-reporting terms and conditions of employment
- IT service provider acquisition and management
- IT performance monitoring and reporting
- Quality assurance and quality management in IT

In this chapter, CISA aspirants will learn and come to understand the practical aspects of IT resource management, including managing third-party risks, various aspects of the performance-monitoring process, and learning to identify opportunities for improvements.

IT resource management

One significant aspect of IT governance is to ensure the optimal utilization of IT resources. The resources used should be directed toward achieving business goals. An **Information Security (IS)** auditor should be aware of the management of different resources needed to deliver IT services. Control of IT services can be further split into the following domains:

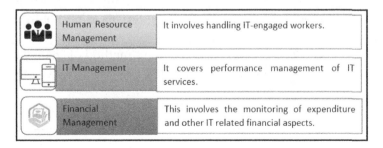

	Human Resource Management	It involves handling IT-engaged workers.
	IT Management	It covers performance management of IT services.
	Financial Management	This involves the monitoring of expenditure and other IT related financial aspects.

Let's understand each of the preceding IT resources in detail.

Human resource management

Human resource (HR) management refers to recruitment, preparation, task allocation, performance assessments, and other issues relevant to HR processes and procedures. The following are some of the important aspects of HR management.

Hiring

Hiring is one of the most important aspects of IT management. Here are some of the most important characteristics of IT management:

- To obtain a written and signed agreement from the employee to the employment terms and conditions
- To carry out a background check before the candidate is onboarded
- To establish a confidentiality or non-disclosure agreement and to receive a pledge from the employee to abide by the organization's security policy
- To distribute a rule book for employees that includes the following:
  - IS policies and procedures
  - The organization's acceptable usage policy
  - The employee code of conduct
  - The disciplinary procedure for non-compliance
  - Other relevant roles and responsibilities

Training

Another significant aspect of HR management is training.

- To give training to all the employees on the organization's IS requirements.
- This training should be offered at regular intervals as part of their induction and continuing throughout their employment.
- Training should also cover the organization's method of change management, crisis management, and business continuity structure.

- Any infrastructure changes should be accompanied by appropriate training.
- In the case of cross-training, it is important to consider the risk where a single employee has knowledge of the full system.

Scheduling and time reporting

Structured scheduling helps into efficient and effective organizational processes. Time monitoring helps management to track the organization's resource efficiency.

Detailed feedback is important for efficient planning and time reporting. Scheduling and time monitoring can be used to measure expenditure allocations, charges, invoices, and KPIs.

During employment

The following are some of the important HR controls during employment:

- Employee roles and responsibilities should be documented in a job description. Employees should be aware of their roles and responsibilities.
- Doing this will improve the employee's understanding of the responsibility that they have for their position and reduces the chance of human error.
- Administrative management processes of security violations should be reported and made accessible to all employees and related third-party vendors.
- Standards for the performance evaluation of employees should be structured and quantified as far as possible.
- Mandatory vacation policies should be implemented for each employee. During the absence of a dishonest employee, the majority of frauds are uncovered.
- Mandatory job rotation policies should also be implemented. This expands the possibilities for monitoring the risk of fraudulent or malicious acts.

Termination policies

The termination policies and procedures should be reported by the organization. This includes the appropriate procedure for terminating employees due to fraud or other illegal actions in order to protect the company's assets. Employees are required to obtain clearance from the departments involved to ensure that all belongings, access keys, ID cards, and so on are returned to the organization.

IT management practices

The following are some of the important aspects of IT management practices:

- IT administration requires rules and procedures for the design, delivery, control, and maintenance of the manner in which technology is used within an organization.
- IT management practices should be consistent with strategic business priorities.
- Senior management should authorize management policies and procedures to ensure that the IT management team properly manages the organization's activities in an efficient and effective manner.
- IT activities and procedures related to infrastructure need to be periodically updated to keep them in line with the new operating environment of the company.

Financial management practices

Sound financial management practices are essential for any company process to be effective. There are many ways of allocating IT-related expenditures to various functions/users.

- One form of managing and regulating IT expenditures is by introducing a user-pay system that is a form of chargeback. A standard structure is used in this system to distribute the costs of IT programs to end users. This method of redistribution of costs (also known as chargeback) increases the efficiency and effectiveness of the service provided by the information processing facility. At the same time, budget-based reporting is meant to predict and monitor IT costs.

Key aspects from CISA exam perspective

The following table covers the important aspects of the preceding topic from the CISA exam perspective:

CISA question	Possible answer
What is the objective of the software escrow agreement?	To address the risk of the closure of vendors of customized written software
What is the primary objective of mandatory holidays?	To detect fraud or illegal acts
What is the primary objective of job rotation?	To detect fraud or illegal acts
Primary compensating control for absence of segregation of duties	Transaction and log monitoring

First step when employee is terminated	To revoke the employee's access to all systems
What is the primary consideration when reviewing the IT priorities and coordination?	Alignment of the project with business objectives

Self-assessment questions

1. **Which of the following is the primary consideration when reviewing the IT priorities and co-ordination?**
    - A. Alignment of the project with business objectives
    - B. Management of project risk
    - C. Cost of project controls
    - D. IT project escalation process

2. **A software escrow agreement is intended primarily to address which of the following?**
    - A. Disaster recovery
    - B. System upgradation
    - C. The risk of business closure of a vendor of custom-written software
    - D. The requirements of the IS audit

3. **The prime objective of mandatory holidays for employees is which of the following?**
    - A. Improve the productivity of the employee
    - B. Reduce the opportunity for fraud or illegal acts
    - C. Provide training to other staff
    - D. Test the business continuity

4. **Which of the following roles, taken together, should not be trusted to a single individual?**
    - A. Network administrator and quality assurance
    - B. System administrator and application developer
    - C. Security administrator and end user
    - D. System analyst and database administrator

5. **The integrity of new staff can be determined by which of the following?**
    - A. Conducting background verification
    - B. Analyzing their family background
    - C. Analyzing prior experience
    - D. Reviewing the qualifications listed on a resume

6. **Which of the following dual roles is an area of major concern?**
   A. Quality assurance as the responsibility of network administrators
   B. System administrators as application programmers
   C. End users as security administrators for critical applications
   D. Database managers as system analysts

7. **The rate of change in technology increases the importance of which of the following?**
   A. Outsourcing IT functions
   B. Implementing and enforcing sound processes
   C. Hiring qualified personnel
   D. Meeting user requirements

8. **The most important consideration when planning to implement a new technology is which of the following?**
   A. A cost analysis
   B. The security risks of the current technology
   C. Compatibility with existing systems
   D. A risk analysis

9. **The best compensatory control for a lack of segregation of duties between IT staff and end users is which of the following?**
   A. Restricting physical access to computing equipment
   B. Reviewing transaction and application logs
   C. Conducting background checks before hiring IT staff
   D. Locking user sessions after a stated duration of inactivity

10. **Which of the following risks should be assessed by an IS auditor reviewing an organization that uses cross-training practices?**
    A. Dependence on a single person
    B. Inadequate succession planning
    C. All parts of a system being known to one person
    D. Disruption to operations

11. **The most important consideration when reviewing an approved software product list is which of the following?**
    A. Whether the risk associated with each product is reviewed periodically
    B. Whether the latest versions of products are listed
    C. Whether the list is approved every year
    D. Whether the list contains vendor support details

12. **The primary control objective of job rotations is to achieve which of the following?**
    - A. To provide cross-training
    - B. To motivate employees
    - C. To detect improper or illegal employee acts
    - D. To improve efficiency and productivity

13. **Which of the following should be done as a priority when an employee with access to highly confidential information resigns?**
    - A. Conducting a debriefing interview with the employee
    - B. Ensuring succession plans are in place
    - C. Revoking the employee's access to all systems
    - D. Reviewing the employee's job history

14. **The primary control objective of implementing a vacation policy is which of the following?**
    - A. To improve employee productivity
    - B. To increase the motivation level of employees
    - C. To identify potential errors or inconsistencies in business processes
    - D. To comply with regulatory requirements

IT service provider acquisition and management

Outsourcing services to a third-party vendor is a widely accepted practice in today's world for two major reasons. One of them is the tremendous savings in cost and the other is to avail the service of experts in the field.

CISA aspirants should be aware of the following important terms with respect to outsourcing:

- **Insourced**: Activities performed by the organization's own staff
- **Outsourced**: Activities performed by the vendor's staff
- **Hybrid**: Activities performed jointly by staff from both the organization and the vendor
- **Onsite**: Staff working onsite in the IT department
- **Offsite**: Staff working from remote locations in the same geographical area
- **Offshore**: Staff working from remote locations in different geographical areas

Evaluation criteria for outsourcing

CISA aspirants should understand the evaluation criteria for the outsourcing of any function. The following functions should not be outsourced:

- The core functions of the organization
- Roles that require specific expertise, procedures, and key resources that cannot be replicated externally or anywhere else
- Functions that cannot be outsourced due to contractual or regulatory constraints

Outsourcing of functions can be done if the following applies:

- Functions that can be carried out by another party to the same level of quality or better, at the same price or lower, without increasing risk
- The organization has sufficient experience in managing third parties working on its behalf

Steps for outsourcing

The following steps will help you to determine whether outsourcing will enable the company to achieve its desired goal considering the costs and risks involved:

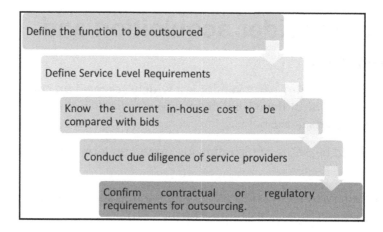

The following are detailed steps for the outsourcing of any function:

1. **Step 1: Define the function to be outsourced**: The organization should first define and determine the functions that need to be outsourced.
2. **Step 2: Define a Service-Level Agreement (SLA)**: Defining an SLA is a very important aspect of outsourcing. SLAs should be approved by the legal, risk management, and compliance teams.
3. **Step 3: Determine the cost**: Here, you need to determine the cost of outsourcing.
4. **Step 4: Conduct due diligence**: Due diligence includes verifying the profile of the service provider, their market credibility, financial stability, capability to serve on a long-term basis, and other relevant details.
5. **Step 5: Confirm contractual or regulatory requirements for outsourcing**: It is also of utmost importance to determine any regulatory and contractual requirements when outsourcing any activity.

Outsourcing – risk reduction options

The following are important aspects for reducing the risk related to outsourcing:

- A requirement for achievable output should be included in the SLA.
- The use of an escrow arrangement for software assets.
- The use of multiple suppliers helps to lower the risk of dependence.
- Periodic reviews of performance.
- Building a cross-functional contract management team.
- Setting up appropriate controls for any anticipated contingencies.

Provisions for outsourcing contracts

SLAs will serve as a monitoring tool for the outsourcing process. They should contain, at the least, the following clauses:

- Requirements for achievable output
- **Confidentiality, Integrity, and Availability (CIA)** requirements for resources/systems/data
- Confidentiality agreements to protect both parties
- A right-to-audit clause
- Business continuity and disaster recovery provisions
- Intellectual property rights

Role of IS auditors in monitoring outsourced activities

The following are some of the important functions of the IS auditor in monitoring outsourced activities:

- To review contracts at the service level at periodic intervals
- To review documented procedures and outcomes of the outsourcer's quality assurance programs
- Periodic checks to ensure that the processes and procedures comply with outsourcer's quality standards

Globalization of IT functions

CISA aspirants should understand the following aspects with respect to the globalization of IT functions:

- Globalization includes remote or offshore setups of IT systems.
- Outsourcing may or may not require globalization.
- For outsourcing reasons, many companies are globalizing their IT functions.
- To promote the smooth functioning of IT functions from offsite locations, certain problems need to be addressed, including the following:
    - Legal and regulatory issues
    - Continuity of operations
    - Telecommunication issues
    - Cross-border and cross-cultural issues

Outsourcing and third-party audit reports

Monitoring third-party performance and compliance with the SLA and other statutory requirements is important. Obtaining an independent third-party audit report will provide clarity regarding the state of affairs of service providers.

An audit report should cover any confidentiality, integrity, data, and system availability issues. Regulatory bodies mandate some third-party audits. One example is reporting by the **Service Organization Control (SOC)**, covering the following details:

Report	Description
SOC 1	This is based on the SSAE 18 standard that focuses on program controls for financial reporting by the service organization.
SOC 2	Security, availability, processing integrity, confidentiality, and privacy are aspects of the audit (that is, the trust service principles). SOC 2 reports are restricted to the use of the service organization's management, customers, and other related parties.
SOC 3	Similar to SOC 2 reports, these reports however are for general use and can be distributed freely.

IS auditors should review reports of penetration testing activities, vulnerability assessments, and other compliance reviews in accordance with the service's criticality.

Monitoring and review of third-party services

Critical services managed by third parties can increase the organization's risk of business continuity, and ultimately, reputational damage. Poor third-party system controls increase the risk of data leakage. Continuous monitoring and control of third-party risks and performance is therefore important.

The monitoring and analysis of third-party providers described so far in this section will ensure compliance with the SLA and other legal requirements. IS auditors should ensure proper monitoring covering the following details:

- That the risk management and legal teams will review the SLA and ensure that the applicable provisions are included
- The implementation of a documented process to track compliance with the agreements
- Management analysis of results of the work of third parties at regular intervals
- Auditing of third parties to analyze their IS policies at least annually

Key aspects from CISA exam perspective

The following table covers the important aspects of the preceding from the perspective of the CISA examination:

CISA questions	Possible answers
What is the primary objective of outsourcing?	To obtain services of expert firms and to save on costs
What is the primary concern about outsourcing to offshore locations?	Privacy laws and regulatory requirements
What is the primary function of IT management when a service has been outsourced?	To monitor the outsourcing provider's performance
What is the best way to determine whether the terms of the contract are adhered to in accordance with the SLA?	An independent audit
What is the primary requirement for the development of software by a vendor?	An escrow arrangement for source code
What is the primary risk of subcontracting?	The requirement to protect information may be compromised

Self-evaluation questions

1. **Which of the following clauses in an outsourcing contract helps improve the level of service and reduce costs?**
    A. The use of the latest operating system and hardware
    B. Gain-sharing performance bonuses
    C. A penalty levy on errors
    D. Provision of training to outsourced staff

2. **What is the most important function that IS management performs in such situations where an organization has outsourced some of its IS processes?**
    A. Ensuring that charges for outsourcing are paid in compliance with the SLA
    B. Providing training to the staff of outsourcing vendors
    C. Levying a penalty for non-compliance
    D. Monitoring the outsourcing provider's performance

3. **Which of the following will IS auditors recommend when it is noticed that outsourcing vendors were appointed without formal written agreements?**
   - A. Obtaining feedback about the service provider from the wider industry
   - B. Setting up a framework for monitoring and controlling the service provided by the vendor
   - C. Ensuring that formal contracts are in place
   - D. Revoking the service provider's contract

4. **Which of the following is the primary benefit of outsourcing a business function?**
   - A. Reliance can be placed on the expertise of outsourcing vendors.
   - B. More control can be exercised over the IT process.
   - C. Organizations can pass on their responsibilities with respect to data protection laws.
   - D. Employee satisfaction will improve.

5. **Which of the following cannot be outsourced?**
   - A. IT security policy accountability
   - B. Benchmarking security policies with other organizations in the industry
   - C. IT security policy implementation
   - D. Developing IT security policy awareness among users

6. **A major concern when outsourcing IT support services to a provider in another country is which of the following?**
   - A. Legal jurisdictions
   - B. An increase in cost
   - C. A delay in service delivery due to time differences
   - D. The fact that it is difficult to monitor the outsourcing vendor's output due to the geographic distance

7. **Which of the following is the most important clause to be included in an SLA?**
   - A. The types of hardware to be used
   - B. The software configuration to be used
   - C. The ownership of intellectual property
   - D. Employee training policies to be implemented

8. Another major concern when outsourcing IT support services to a provider in another country is which of the following?
    A. Communication issues
    B. Scope creep
    (C) Privacy laws preventing the flow of information across borders
    D. The high cost of maintenance

9. Inclusion of which of the following clauses is the most important when reviewing and floating a Request for Proposal (RFP)?
    A. Maintenance plan details ✗
    B. **Proof of Concept (POC)** details
    (C.) References from other customers ✗
    D. Details about the **Business Continuity Plan (BCP)**

10. The most important parameter by which to evaluate the performance of the IT support service provider is which of the following?
    A. The number of support staff ✗
    (B.) The number of incidents solved in the first call
    C. Support timing window ✗
    D. The qualifications of support staff ✗

11. Which of the following should occur first when an organization is going through the process of entering into an agreement with an outsourced vendor?
    A. Deciding on the periodicity of the contract ✗
    B. Getting approval from the compliance team
    C. Deciding the levels of penalties ✗
    (D.) Finalizing the service-level requirements

12. Which of the following documents will serve the purpose of vendor performance reviews by an IS auditor?
    A. The vender's customer testimonials ✗
    (B.) The SLA
    C. Penalty-levied reports ✗
    D. Performance reports submitted by vendor

13. **The best way to control the creation of access rights for the service provider is which of the following?**
    A. Including a penalty clause in the SLA
    B. Creating user accounts on a need-to-know basis with expiration dates
    C. Providing full access to the system for a limited period
    D. Providing rights to the service provider to delete IDs when work is completed

14. **Which of the following is the major concern when reviewing a system development approach?**
    A. The user manages acceptance testing
    B. A quality plan is not part of the contracted deliverables
    C. The application development process will be carried out in three phases
    D. Business requirements are compiled by prototyping

15. **The most important factor when reviewing the process of application software acquisition is which of the following?**
    A. The availability of a documented operating procedure
    B. The availability of a backup server with all the relevant software and data
    C. Providing training to staff
    D. An escrow arrangement for source code

16. **The most important role of IT management when a service has been outsourced is which of the following?**
    A. Ensuring a timely payout to the provider
    B. Participating in systems design with the provider
    C. Interviewing the provider's resource
    D. Monitoring the provider's performance

17. **The best control to ensure the continuity of an application acquired from a newly established vendor is which of the following?**
    A. Obtaining vendor feedback from the industry
    B. Arranging a software escrow agreement
    C. Evaluating the financial stability of the vendor
    D. Entering an SLA

18. **The most important factor that should be clearly clarified in an outsourcing contract is which of the following?**
    A. Software configuration requirements
    B. Access control requirements
    C. Intellectual property ownership
    D. The system development methodology

19. **Which of the following is the major risk present when a third-party service provider further outsources work to a fourth-party service provider?**
    A. The requirement to protect information may be compromised
    B. The contract can be terminated because prior authorization has not been received from the organization
    C. Fourth-party service providers are not subject to audit
    D. It increases the turnaround time for support

20. **The best control to monitor the service provision of a third-party service provider is which of the following?**
    A. To obtain periodic reports from the service provider
    B. To conduct periodic meetings with the manager of the service provider
    C. To conduct periodic audit reviews of the service provider
    D. To include performance parameters in the service level agreement

21. **The most important consideration when outsourcing an IT support function is which of the following?**
    A. Whether outsourcing has resulted in a decrease in cost
    B. Whether the service provided is as per the contract
    C. Whether the training needs of the employees of service provider are identified
    D. Whether the service provider submits invoices on a timely basis

22. **The most important factor to be considered when setting up a customer data warehouse on an offshore location is which of the following?**
    A. The impact of the time zone difference
    B. The impact of telecommunications costs
    C. The impact of privacy laws
    D. The impact of the data retrieval procedure

23. The first factor to be considered when reviewing the SLA is which of the following?

    A. The inclusion of an audit clause in the SLA ×

    B. The inclusion of performance metrics in the SLA

    C. Contractual warranties that support the company's business requirements

    D. The inclusion of a no-subcontracting clause ×

24. The greatest concern regarding the outsourcing of IT support service is which of the following?

    A. The outsourcing of core activities

    B. Weak negotiation power in outsourcing cost negotiations

    C. An agreement does not include all the business requirements

    D. More than one service provider having been engaged

25. The most important clause to be included in an SLA for the outsourcing of an IT support service is which of the following?

    A. The training requirements of support staff

    B. An uptime guarantee

    C. An indemnification clause

    D. Payout release terms

26. The most important clause to be included in an SLA for the outsourcing of an IT support service is which of the following?

    A. Provisions for staff background checks

    B. Provisions for the right to audit

    C. Provisions for year-to-year incremental cost reductions

    D. Provisions for staff training

27. The most important factor to be reviewed for an outsourced credit monitoring program is which of the following?

    A. Whether the program's claims are within the industry benchmarks

    B. Whether the service provider is conducting external security reviews

    C. Whether the service provider has a good market reputation ×

    D. Whether the service provider conducts business continuity tests every six months ×

28. **The most important factor to be reviewed for an outsourced cloud hosting service is which of the following?**
   - A. Whether the vendor agrees to provide an internal audit report every year ×
   - B. Whether the vendor agrees to provide an internal audit completion certificate every year ×
   - C. Whether the vendor agrees to provide management certifications of compliance to the organization as a policy every year ×
   - D. Whether the vendor agrees to provide an external independent audit report every year

29. **Which of the following is the best way to ensure that the service provider adheres to the security requirements of the organization?**
   - A. By obtaining a sign-off from all the users of the service provider ×
   - B. By including an indemnity clause in the SLA with the service provider
   - C. By providing annual security awareness training for all users
   - D. By easing the security requirements ×

IT performance monitoring and reporting

One of the important elements of IT governance is the monitoring of IT performance. It provides management with a level of comfort from the knowledge that IT operations are moving in the desired direction. It is extremely important to develop performance metrics for monitoring performance. Let's have a look at these metrics.

Steps for the development of performance metrics

Developing performance metrics usually involves three steps:

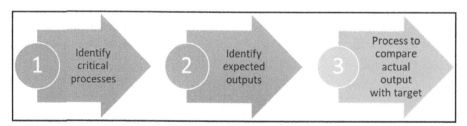

Let us have a quick rundown of these steps.

1. **Step 1: Identify the critical process**: The first step is to identify the critical process that needs to be monitored.
2. **Step 2: Identify the expected output**: The second step is to define the expected output or target for each process that needs to be monitored.
3. **Step 3: Compare the actual output with the target**: On a periodic basis, compare the actual output with the target. If the target is not achieved, conduct a root cause analysis to determine areas of improvement.

Effectiveness of performance metrics

The effectiveness and reliability of the metrics can be enhanced by considering the best practices listed here:

- Metrics should be regularly assessed.
- Data should be readily available to be used for metric measurements.
- The data should be complete, accurate, and correct.
- Quantified and comparable data should be available.
- Targets should be set from the top down and should be aligned with business goals.
- Metrics should be set from the bottom up and should attempt to cover the fulfillment of the target at all levels to allow progress to be monitored.
- All key IT processes should have proper metrics.
- Targets should be approved by stakeholders, and accountability and responsibility for achieving targets should be clearly defined.

Tools and techniques

The following table outlines some of the industry-recognized tools and techniques for performance measurement:

Tools	Description
Six Sigma	• Six Sigma is a quantitative process analysis methodology for process improvement and reduction of defects. • Anything outside the customer specification is defined as a Six Sigma defect.
Lean Six Sigma	• Lean Six Sigma has a similar approach to Six Sigma. It seeks to remove unnecessary steps that do not add value.

An IT **Balanced Scorecard (BSC)**	• An IT BSC is one of the most effective IT governance tools, and shows the efficiency and value creation of the IT team and assesses IT performance, risks, and capabilities. • BSC helps to align IT with business needs. • An IT BSC assesses measures relating to customer satisfaction, internal (operational) processes, and innovation abilities. An IT BSC looks at four aspects: • The mission • Strategies • Measures • Sources
KPIs	• A **Key Performance Indicator** (**KPI**) is a measurable attribute related to the organization's key business goals. • KPIs are used for measuring performance against predetermined goals. • KPIs are a key indicator of goal achievement. They also show abilities, practices, and skills.
Benchmarking	• Benchmarking includes evaluating and comparing the business processes and performance metrics with other organizations ' best practices. • Benchmarking helps us to learn the best ways to implement processes.
BPR	• **Business process reengineering** (**BPR**) is the process of redesigning the performance improvement and cost reduction processes. • Processes are synchronized across BPR and are responsive to the customer base and market needs.
Root cause analysis	• This means finding the basic cause of something in order to understand the cause of a given incident. • Once the root cause analysis has been performed, effective corrective action is taken to prevent a system failure or deficiency. • It helps us to learn from errors and issues, and to ensure that the given incident does not occur again.
Life cycle cost-benefit analysis	• Life cycle cost-benefit analysis is used to determine the strategic direction for the IT team and IT portfolio management overall. • It covers the various phases of IT development, along with life cycle cost estimates such as the maintenance and upgrade of IT infrastructure.

Key aspects from CISA exam perspective

The following table covers important aspects of the preceding from the CISA exam perspective:

CISA questions	Possible answers
What is the pre-requisite for implementation of balanced score card?	Availability of key performance indicators
What is the primary objective of an IT performance measurement process?	To optimize the performance
Which is the best method to understand the effectiveness of an organization's IT asset planning and management?	To analyze the IT balanced scorecard

What is the risk of a lack of measurable performance indicators?	In the absence of measurable performance indicators, misleading indications of IT performance could be presented to management

Self-evaluation questions

1. **Which of the following is a prerequisite for implementing an IT BSC?**
    A. Providing efficient services.
    B. Defining KPIs.
    C. Projects should be profitable.
    D. IT expenses are within budget.

2. **An IS auditor noted that the performance indicators of key processes are not measurable. Which of the following is a major risk?**
    A. In the absence of measurable performance indicators, a BSC cannot be used for evaluation by management.
    B. In the absence of measurable performance indicators, IT projects can fail due to excessive costs. ✗
    C. In the absence of measurable performance indicators, misleading indications of IT performance could be presented to management.
    D. In the absence of measurable performance indicators, IT SLAs might not be accurate.

3. **The most significant function of IT management with respect to an outsourced service is which of the following?**
    A. The timely release of payment to the provider
    B. Training the employees of the provider
    C. Renegotiating the provider's fees ✗
    D. Monitoring and controlling the provider's performance

4. **The main objective of measuring IT performance is which of the following?**
    A. To reduce the error
    B. To analyze the performance data
    C. To determine baselines
    D. To optimize performance

5. **Where is the most important factor to determine the effectiveness of an organization's IT asset planning and management?**
   A. To analyze the data models
   B. To analyze the IT BSC
   C. To analyze the enterprise structure
   D. To analyze financial trends

6. **An IS auditor is reviewing an organization's project portfolio. Which of the following is the most important consideration?**
   A. Total cost should exceed the IT budget
   B. The project portfolio should be managed by a senior official
   C. The project portfolio has been approved by a steering committee
   D. The project portfolio is aligned with the business plan

7. **The best enabler for strategic alignment between business and IT is which of the following?**
   A. A capacity maturity model
   B. The organization's goals and metrics
   C. The organization's security objectives
   D. The organization's profit trends

Quality assurance and quality management in IT

Let's have a look at quality assurance and quality management processes in IT in detail. According to **CISA Review Manual (CRM)**, the IS auditor must understand the concepts, processes, roles, and responsibilities of quality assurance and quality management within the company.

Quality assurance

Quality assurance (QA) is a process that aims to provide adequate confidence that an item or product conforms to the requirements developed. QA staff verify that changes to the system are approved, checked, and implemented in a controlled manner. **Quality control (QC)** is a method for performing tests or reviews to verify that the product is free of defects and meets the user's requirements.

Generally, QA personnel perform two distinct tasks:

- **QA**: Provides assurance that an object or product meets the requirements as lain down
- **QC**: Observation strategies or exercises to ensure that quality-related criteria are fulfilled

The following table differentiates between QA and QC:

QA	QC
Proactive	Reactive
Prevent defects	Find defects
More focused on process	More focused on products

Let us understand this in more detail.

- The QC team is responsible for ensuring that the program meets consumer standards and is free from defects.
- Before the programs are moved into development, QC must be completed.
- It is recommended that the QA department be autonomous within the company in order to achieve successful QA output.
- The role of QC should not be performed by an individual whose position would create a **Segregation of Duties (SoD)**. An individual should not, under any circumstances, review their own work. For example, a database administrator should not carry out a quality assessment of processes that would affect the database, because they work on the system themselves.

Quality management

Quality management is all about monitoring, tracking, and enhancing quality management processes. Some quality management areas include the following:

- Software development, maintenance, and implementation
- Purchase of hardware and software
- Operational activities
- Service management
- Security
- HR management

Key aspects from CISA exam perspective

The following figure covers important aspects from the perspective of the CISA exam:

CISA question	Possible answer
What is the primary objective of implementing a quality management system?	Continuous improvement

Self-evaluation questions

1. **Which of the following is an area of major concern with respect to QA processes?**
    A. QA processes have not been documented
    B. The outcome of quality checks is not presented to senior management
    C. QA is performed by a staff member nominated by a business manager
    D. QA parameters are not benchmarked to industry standards

2. **An IS auditor is reviewing the QC processes of a software development company. Which of the following would be an area of major concern?**
    A. QC parameters are not documented
    B. QC activity is outsourced
    C. QC parameters are not benchmarked to industry standards
    D. QC is carried out 3 months after the program has been moved to production

3. **The prime objective of implementing a quality management system is which of the following?**
    A. To comply with best practice
    B. To monitor continuous improvement targets
    C. To document and update standard operating procedures
    D. To document and update KPIs

Summary

In this chapter, we learned about various aspects of IT resource management, the different criteria and risks associated with outsourcing, IT monitoring and reporting structures, and aspects of QA and quality management. IS auditors should first focus on ensuring IT alignment with the business.

In the next chapter, we will discuss project governance and management aspects, the importance of the business case and feasibility analysis, and various system development methodologies.

Assessment answers

Here are the answers to the self-evaluation questions.

IT resource management

1. **Answer: A. Alignment of the project with the business objectives**
   Explanation: The main goal of IT projects is to add value to business processes. An IS auditor should first focus on ensuring that IT initiatives are aligned with business objective. The other answers are not as critical as option A.

2. **Answer: C. The risk of business closure of a vendor of custom-written software**
   Explanation: An escrow agreement is entered into between a service provider and a client to ensure the permanent availability of the client's source code. The source code is held by some third party. In the event of the vendor going out of business, the client can claim back the source code from the third party.

3. **Answer: B. It reduces the opportunity for fraud or illegal acts**
   Explanation: Mandatary holidays aim to hand over the processes that employee was responsible for to another employee, thereby unearthing any fraud or process lapses committed by the employee on holiday. The other answers are secondary advantages.

4. **Answer: B. System administrator and application developer**
   Explanation: Ideally, all of the roles listed as answer options should be segregated, but the major concern is about the system administrator and application developer. This person can do almost anything, including creating the back door. System administration and developer roles should therefore be segregated.

5. **Answer: A. Conducting background verification**
   Explanation: A background verification process is the main tool to ensure the integrity of a prospective employee. This may include criminal history checks, financial status checks, verification education, and so on.

6. **Answer: B. System administrators and application programmers**
Explanation: It is extremely important to ensure SoD for functions that are prone to risk if a single individual is handling them both. The roles of system administrator and application programmer need to be split between different individuals. A single employee with both roles can misuse their privileges and do almost anything on a system, including creating a back door. The other options are not as critical as the same individual handling administration as well as programming.

7. **Answer: B. Implementing and enforcing sound processes**
Explanation: It is essential to implement sound IT process and policies to cope with frequent and rapid IT changes.

8. **Answer**: D. A risk analysis
Explanation: Before introducing new technologies, an organization will carry out a risk evaluation, which is then submitted for review and acceptance to the business management unit.

9. **Answer: B. Reviewing transaction and application logs**
Explanation: When it is not possible to implement SoD, an appropriate compensating control should be in place. Monitoring and reviewing logs acts as the best compensating control in this scenario. This will act as both a preventive and detective control as employees will be deterred from misuse of power as they are aware of the possibility of being caught.

10. **Answer: C. All parts of a system are known to one person**
Explanation: In cross-training, individuals are trained on other aspects of the jobs in addition to their routing function. It is important to ensure that cross-training does not lead to potential exposures related to abuse of privilege. If an individual knows all parts of the system, they may abuse their knowledge and privilege.

11. **Answer: A. The risk associated with the use of the products is periodically assessed**
Explanation: IT products should be assessed on a periodic basis to ensure that any new and emerging risks are appropriately addressed. This should be incorporated as a part of the IT risk management process.

12. **Answer: C. Detect improper or illegal employee acts**
Explanation: Job rotation is a well-planned practice to reduce the chances of irregularities and fraud by an employee handling a given function for a long time and who is well versed in all the processes and ways to bypass control mechanisms.

13. **Answer: C. Revoke the employee's access to all systems**
    Explanation: If an employee has dealt with highly classified information, the first step is to remove their access to all systems to prevent the exfiltration of data and restrict access to sensitive information.

14. **Answer: C. To identify potential errors or inconsistencies in business processes**
    Explanation: Mandatory vacation policies require employees to take time away from their job. These policies help to reduce fraud and uncover malicious activities by employees. These policies help to prevent employees from continuing with fraudulent activities.

IT service provider acquisition and management

1. **Answer: Gain-sharing performance bonuses**
   Explanation: Performance bonuses will help to improve the level of service and reduce costs, as a service provider will have a financial incentive to provide the best service, even in excess of what was agreed to in the SLA. Other options may not be as effective as a gain-sharing performance bonus.

2. **Answer: D. Monitoring the outsourcing provider's performance**
   Explanation: It is most important that IT management should control and monitor the activities of the service provider and ensure that the service delivered is as per the agreement. Other functions are not as critical as monitoring the performance of the service provider.

3. **Answer: C. Requires formal contracts are in effect**
   Explanation: It is difficult to enforce the terms of a contract in the absence of a formal written agreement. Written agreements will assist management in ensuring compliance with contractual requirements.

4. **Answer. A. The expertise of outsourcing vendors can be reliable**
   Explanation: Through outsourcing arrangements, the services of an expert can be obtained in the absence of in-house expertise. No organization can transfer their accountability through outsourcing.

5. **Answer: A. IT security policy accountability**
   Explanation: In no circumstance can accountability be transferred to external parties. No matter what function is outsourced, it is ultimate responsibility of the organization to be accountable to the relevant stakeholders.

6. **Answer: A. Legal jurisdiction**
   Explanation: Here, the main concern is legal jurisdiction. In absence of proper clarification, there may be compliance-related and legal issues. The other choices aren't as relevant as the issue of legal jurisdiction. Also, even though a service provider is in a different country, that doesn't necessarily indicate a delay or difficulty in monitoring. Generally, outsourcing to other countries is done to save costs.

7. **Answer: C. Ownership of intellectual property**
   Explanation: A clause with respect to ownership of intellectual property is a must in an outsourcing contract. The contract specifies who owns the intellectual property. Other choices, though important, are not as significant as an intellectual property clause.

8. **Answer: C. Privacy laws may prevent the flow of information across borders**
   Explanation: The most important factor to be considered is legal and regulatory issues that may restrict the flow of information across borders.

9. **Answer: C. References from other customers**
   Explanation: References from other customers will help the IT department to deduce the performance level of a prospective service provider. Checking references may be a means of obtaining independent verification of the fact that the service provider can perform the services it says it can. Other options are important and should also be understood before awarding contracts. However, the most significant option here is references from other customers.

10. **Answer: B. The number of incidents solved in the first call**
    Explanation: The number of incidents solved in the first call indicates the efficiency and effectiveness of the service provider. It helps to manage the performance of the service provider. The other options may not be that effective.

11. **Answer: D. Finalize the service level requirements**
    Explanation: The very first step, out of the options provided, should be to finalize the service level requirements. These requirements then form part of the SLA. Once service level requirements are finalized, other solutions are implemented.

12. **Answer: B. SLA**
    Explanation: SLA is an independent document that can be used to monitor the performance of the vendor.

13. **Answer: B. To create user accounts on the need-to-know basis with expiration dates**
    Explanation: The most efficient control under the specified scenario and options would be the development of a need-based user ID and the automatic revocation of IDs via the use of expiry dates. The SLA penalty clause may function as a deterrent, but the automatic revocation of IDs is a more effective control tool. Full exposure will be risky.

14. **Answer: B. The quality plan is not part of the contracted deliverables**
    Explanation: The quality plan is a key component that must be included in the deliverables contracted. Other options are not the area of concern.

15. **Answer: D. An escrow arrangement for source code**
    Explanation: An escrow arrangement for source code is the placing of software source code with a third-party escrow agent. The source code of the program will be released to the licensee if the licensor files for bankruptcy or otherwise does not maintain and upgrade the program as agreed in the license agreement. In these cases, management of escrow is very important. Escrow arrangement ensures that purchasing company will be able to change the program in case the vendor ceases to be in business.

16. **Answer: D. Monitoring the outsourcing provider's performance**
    Explanation: It is most important that IT management should control and monitor the activities of the service provider and ensure that the service delivered is as per the agreement. Other functions are not as critical as monitoring the performance of the service provider.

17. **Answer: B. A software escrow agreement**
    Explanation: An escrow agreement is a contract that defines an arrangement between parties where the service provider deposits the source code with a reliable third party. This third party then returns the asset to the organization in case the service provider is not in a position to support the organization. This addresses the risk of the service provider's financial stability or exposure, and the provider's risk of leaving the company.

18. **Answer: C. Intellectual property ownership**
    Explanation: The clause with respect to ownership of intellectual property is a must in an outsourcing contract. The contract specifies who owns the intellectual property. Other choices, though important, are not that significant compared to the intellectual property clause.

19. **Answer: A. The requirement to protect information may be compromised**
    Explanation: A subcontract increases the risk of data leakage, and requirements to protect information may be compromised. Other options are not as significant as data compromise.

20. **Answer: C. Conducting periodic audit reviews of the service provider**
Explanation: The best control to monitor the services of third-party service providers is to conduct periodic audit reviews of the given service provider. The other options will not be as effective as conducting an audit. An audit will help to determine the level of actual compliance with the security requirements.

21. **Answer: B. Whether the service provided is as per the contract**
Explanation: The most important consideration for the outsourcing of IT support functions is to determine whether the service provider is working as per the SLA. Then other options are not as critical as adherence to the SLA.

22. **Answer: C. The impact of privacy laws**
Explanation: The most important factor to be considered when setting up a customer data warehouse in an offshore location is to determine the impact of privacy laws. Privacy law may restrict the movement of data to an offshore location. Other factors are not as significant as legal or regulatory requirements.

23. **Answer: C. Contractual warranties support the company's business requirements**
Explanation: The first factor to be considered when reviewing the SLA is whether the contractual warranties support the requirements of the organization. This is the prime consideration. IS auditor should ensure that objective of outsourcing is achieved.

24. **Answer: A. The outsourcing of core activities**
Explanation: The core activities of an organization should not necessarily be outsourced, since they are what the company does best; an IS auditor should be concerned with this situation.

25. **Answer: B. Uptime guarantees**
Explanation: The most significant aspect of an SLA is the measurable compliance requirements, such as uptime agreements.

26. **Answer: B. Including provisions for the right to audit**
Explanation: When an IT department's functions are outsourced, an IS auditor should ensure that independent audit reports covering all main areas are provided, or that the outsourcer has complete access to the audit.

27. **Answer: B. Whether the service provider is conducting external security reviews**
Explanation: It is important that an independent security analysis of the outsourcing provider be obtained, as the provider will hold customer credit details if chosen.

28. **Answer: D. Whether the vendor agrees to provide an external independent audit report every year**
Explanation: The best way to ensure that any possible risk is mitigated is to have an independent audit carried out by an external auditor on a periodic basis.

29. **Answer: B. To include an indemnity clause in the agreement with the service provider**
Explanation: An indemnity clause is a contractual transfer of risk between two contractual parties, generally to prevent loss or compensate for a loss that may occur as a result of a specified event. Once the service provider signs the indemnity agreement, the provider will be liable for a penalty in the case of any violations of security requirements, which will make the service provider more conscious about their security arrangements.

IT performance monitoring and reporting

1. **Answer: B. Defining KPIs**
Explanation: It is essential to have defined and documented KPIs since a BSC is more a means of measuring efficiency. Other options are not necessarily prerequisites for setting up a BSC.

2. **Answer: C. In the absence of measurable performance indicators, misleading indications of IT performance could be presented to management**
Explanation: It is essential to have defined and documented KPIs since a BSC is more a means of measuring efficiency. In the absence of measurable performance, subjectivity may impact what is reported to management. Any misleading reporting may lead to unsound management decisions

3. **Answer: D. To monitor and control the provider's performance**
Explanation: The most important function of IT management is to ensure that the service provider adheres to the requirements of the agreement. The performance of the service provider should be constantly monitored and controlled. Other options are not as significant as monitoring the provider's performance.

4. Answer: D. To optimize performance
Explanation: The main objective of measuring IT performance is to optimize performance. The other options are secondary objectives. IT performance is used for decision-making to maximize efficiency and effectiveness.

5. **Answer: B. To analyze the IT BSC**
Explanation: The most important factor to determine the effectiveness of an organization's IT asset planning and management is to analyze the IT BSC. The BSC is a management system that clarifies the strategy and vision of an organization, translating them into actions that can be tracked. It helps to monitor and determine customer satisfaction, organizational processes, and innovation capacity.

6. **Answer: D. The project portfolio is aligned with the business plan**
Explanation: The most important consideration should be the alignment of the project portfolio with business objectives. The project should be in accordance with the requirements of the business. Other options are not as significant as the alignment of the project portfolio and business plan.

7. **Answer: B. The organization's goals and metrics**
Explanation: Priorities and indicators ensure IT priorities are set based on company objectives and are the best enablers of strategic alignment.

Quality assurance and quality management in IT

1. **Answer: C. QA is performed by a staff member nominated by the business manager**
Explanation: It is recommended to have a separate QA department within the company for successful quality assurance. A person whose position would create a conflict with SoD should not perform the QA function. A person should not under any circumstances review their own work.

2. **Answer: D. QC is done after 3 months after the program has been moved to production**
Explanation: QC is responsible for ensuring that the program meets consumer standards and is free from defects. Before the program is put into development, QC must be completed. There is nothing wrong with outsourcing QC if sufficient outsourcing controls are in place.

3. **Answer: B. To monitor continuous improvement targets**
Explanation: Continuous and observable quality enhancement is the primary prerequisite for achieving business targets for the **Quality Management System (QMS)**.

3

Section 3: Information Systems Acquisition, Development, and Implementation

This part contains 12 percent of the CISA exam, approximately 18 questions.

This section contains the following chapters:

5
Information Systems Acquisition and Development

A CISA aspirant should have a sound understanding of the information systems acquisition, development and implementation

process. You should able to understand how an organization evaluates, develops, implements, maintains and disposes of its information systems and related components.

The following topics will be covered in this chapter:

- Project management structure
- Business case and feasibility analysis
- System development methodologies
- Control identification and design

Let's have a look at each of these in detail.

Project management structure

Project management structure can be primarily classified into the following three categories:

Functional Structured	Project Structured	Matrix Structured
• No authority for project manager • Project manager only advises peers on project activities.	• Project manager has formal authority on budget, schedules, and team members of the project.	• Authority is shared between project management and department heads.

In all the preceding project structures, the project should be approved and prioritized by the IT steering committee. A person in charge of the project must be appointed and should be made responsible for project execution. The project manager should be given the relevant resources and infrastructure to ensure the smooth completion of the project.

Project roles and responsibilities

IS auditors should have a basic understanding of the generic roles and responsibilities of individuals involved in the project management process. An understanding of the project's organizational structure is very important when conducting an audit. In this section, we'll look at some of the responsibilities of important stakeholders.

Board of Directors

The **Board of Directors (BoD)** has ultimate responsibility and accountability for IT governance.

IT strategy committee

The IT strategy committee guides and recommends the BoD on IT initiatives. It comprises board members and other experts in the field of IT.

Project steering committee

The project steering committee is responsible for project prioritization, monitoring, and control, and approving project budgets. It comprises senior representatives from different business functions.

Project sponsor

Project sponsors are the owners of the resultant systems under development. Project expenditure cost is assigned and allocated to the project sponsor.

The project sponsor is responsible for providing system specifications and other requirements.

They assume ownership of the project and are responsible for UAT and system approvals.

System development management

System development management is responsible for providing technical support to the project.

Project cost estimation methods

Four widely used methodologies to estimate the cost of system development projects are the following:

- **Analogous estimate**: The cost of a new project is estimated on the basis of experience of prior projects. This is the quickest estimation method.
- **Parametric estimate**: Past data is used to leverage statistical data (such as estimated hours and technological requirements) to estimate cost. It is considered more accurate than analogous estimates.
- **Bottom-up estimate**: Detailed cost estimates of each activity are drawn up and the sum of all activities are considered to produce a cost estimate for the project. This is the most accurate estimate, but it is a time-consuming activity.
- **Actual costs**: This is the same as analogous estimation, where the actual cost of past projects is extrapolated to estimate costs.

Software size estimation methods

Accurate estimates for the size of software development efforts are important for the allocation of resources and time and for the monitoring of the project. Some widely used methodologies to estimate the size of system development are as follows:

- **Source Lines of Code (SLOC)**: SLOC is a traditional way of estimating software size on the basis of a single parameter, such as the number of lines of code. However, this may not be effective in the case of complex systems with functionality other than code. Such functionality could include diagrams, objects, database queries, or graphical user interfaces.

- **Function Point Analysis (FPA)**: FPA is an indirect technique to estimate the size of software. Function points are a unit of measurement for software size, just like time is measured in hours or distance in miles. To arrive at a function point, different factors are considered, such as the complexity of the design, input, processing, outputs, and modules and their interactions. FPA is more consistent and appropriate than SLOC.

- **COCOMO**: COCOMO stands for **Constructive Cost Model**. It can be considered as an advanced version of SLOC. In COCOMO, apart from the number of lines of code, the complexity of the system is also considered in drawing up the estimation.

Project evaluation methods

Monitoring the progress of the project and the project duration is a very critical process in project management. Some widely used methodologies for project evaluation are as follows:

Critical path methodology

The **Critical Path Method** (CPM) is used to estimate the duration of the project. Any project will have a minimum of one critical path:

- A critical path is determined by identifying the longest path of dependent activities. The time required to finish the critical path is the shortest possible time required for finishing the project.
- No slack time will be available for the activities on the critical path.
- Slack time is the time that acts as a buffer or extra time, and an activity can be delayed up to the limit of the slack time without impacting the overall project completion date.
- Project managers concentrate on activities with zero slack time (that is, those on the critical path), and if the critical path duration can be reduced then it will help to minimize the overall project duration.

Program Evaluation Review Technique (PERT)

Like CPM, **PERT** is also a technique used to estimate project duration:

- The difference between PERT and CPM is that while CPM considers only a single scenario, PERT considers three different scenarios (optimistic (best), pessimistic (worst), and normal (most likely)) and on the basis of those three scenarios, a single critical path is arrived at.
- PERT is considered more accurate and appropriate than CPM for calculating estimates of project duration.

The following diagram will help you to understand PERT:

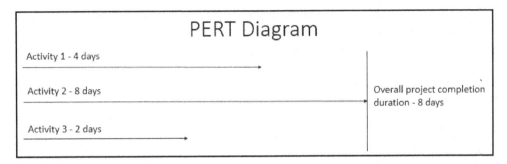

In the preceding diagram, the critical path is activity If more resources are allocated to activity 2, the overall project duration can be reduced.

Providing more resources to activity 1 and activity 3 would not make any sense. The emphasis should be on activity 2.

Activity 2 has zero slack time. The critical path will always have zero slack time. Activity 1 has a slack time of 4 days (8 minus 4), whereas activity 3 has a slack time of 6 days (8 minus 2).

The following diagram will help you to understand the Gantt chart:

Gantt Chart

Activity	Planned Duration (in weeks)	Actual Spent (in weeks)	Completion %	Status
Activity 1	4	4	90%	Delayed
Activity 2	5	3	100%	Before Schedule
Activity 3	4	2	50%	On Schedule
Activity 4	4	1	25%	On Schedule

Let's now have a look at Earned Value Analysis.

Earned Value Analysis

The objective of **Earned Value Analysis (EVA)** is to measure the progress of the project at any given point in time, to forecast the completion date and the final cost, and to analyze any variance in the budget.

EVA determines and evaluates the following factors on a periodic basis:

- What is the actual spending up to the present date, compared to the budget?
- What is the estimated completion time?
- What is the estimated total expenditure?

EVA helps to forecast the schedule date and expected cost and to determine the variance of cost and schedule at any given point during the project.

In EVA, it is assumed that a project can reasonably be completed within the original schedule. For example, a development team has spent eight hours of activity on the first day against a budget of 24 hours (over three days). The projected time to complete the remainder of the activity is 20 hours, so according to EVA, the analysis is as follows:

Particular	Day 1	Day 2	Day 3	Total
Budget	8	8	8	24
Completed	4 (Total Budget - Work Pending, for example, 24 - 20)	-	-	-
Delay	4	-	-	-

This indicates a delay of 4 hours.

Timebox management

The benefit of timebox management is that it ensures the timely completion of the project and thus prevents project cost overruns.

Timebox management is heavily applied in prototyping and **rapid application development (RAD)** where time management is very critical.

It helps to save time by integrating system and user acceptance testing. However, a quality assurance process will still need to be carried out.

Project objectives, OBS, and WBS

The main goal for the implementation of any project is to achieve the project objectives. Project objectives should be specific,

attainable, and measurable. **Object Breakdown Structure (OBS)** is one of the commonly accepted approaches for defining the project objectives. OBS is a combination of separate components and their interaction with each other.

The next step is to design a **Work Breakdown Structure (WBS)**. WBS provides individual components of work to be done. It helps with cost and resource planning. OBS includes solutions, whereas WBS includes individual processes.

Role of the IS auditor in project management

An IS auditor is expected to play a vital role in the project management process. This role may take place during the project implementation stage or upon completion of the project. Its tasks include the following:

- To determine system objectives and requirements and to identify areas of control
- To determine major risks associated with the project and the relevant controls to be implemented to mitigate these
- To determine the appropriateness of the approach/methodology adopted for the SDLC
- To determine whether quality assurance and UATs are conducted before deployment of the system
- To determine the controls to be implemented to ensure the integrity of the production resources
- To determine the adequacy of the post-implementation review process

Key aspects from the CISA exam perspective

The following table shows important aspects from the perspective of the CISA exam:

CISA questions	Possible answers
Techniques to prioritize project activities and determine project timelines:	• PERT • CPM PERT is considered to be more effective than CPM
The technique to monitor the progress of the project	• Gannt chart
The technique for software size estimation	• Function Point Analysis (FPA) • Source Code of Line (SLOC) FPA is more reliable when the system is more complex in terms of complexity of inputs, outputs, files, graphical interfaces, linked modules and their interactions, diagrams and queries. Source Line of Code (SLOC) is a traditional may of estimating software size on the basis of a single parameter that is, number of lines of code.
The objective of time box management	To prevent project cost overruns and delays from scheduled delivery without impacting quality.

For early completion of the project, which activity should be addressed first?	The activity with zero slack time
The technique for projecting estimates at completion	• Earned Value Analysis (EVA) (EVA helps to forecast the closure date and cost and to analyze the variance at any given point during the project.)

Self-assessments questions

1. **The best technique to prioritize project activities and to determine the timeline for each activity is which of the following?**
   A. SLOC
   B. FPA
   C. Gantt charts
   D. Program evaluation and review techniques

2. **The prime objective of evaluating a project using the capability maturity model is which of the following?**
   A. To ensure the reliability of the product
   B. To improve the programmers' efficiency
   C. To design security requirements
   D. To ensure a stable software development process

3. **The best technique to estimate the duration of the project is which of the following?**
   A. The program evaluation review technique
   B. Component-based development
   C. RAD
   D. FPA

4. **To determine project priorities and implementation, the IS auditor should review which of the following?**
   A. Portfolio management
   B. Change management
   C. Patch management
   D. The capability maturity model

5. **The phases and deliverables of a new system should be determined when?**
    A. Once the sign-off has been obtained from user management
    B. During the initial planning stage of the project
    C. Once clearance has been obtained from the risk management team
    D. Continuously throughout the project

6. **Which of the following techniques is used to estimate the size of software having many linked modules and different attribute fields?**
    A. SLOC
    B. PERT
    C. FPA
    D. Gantt charts

7. **Which of the following should be revalidated first when planning to add more personnel to the project to reduce the completion time?**
    A. The project budget
    B. The project manager's performance
    C. The critical path of the project
    D. The number of existing resources

8. **Which of the following is true for timebox management?**
    A. It is not appropriate for RAD
    B. It aims to prevent excess cost and time overruns that affect project completion
    C. It does not encourage UAT
    D. It does not encourage quality assurance processes

9. **To reduce the overall cost of the project, quality management techniques should be applied when?**
    A. Upon initiation of the project
    B. Continuously throughout the project
    C. Before handing over the project for UAT
    D. After implementation of the project

10. **For early completion of the project, emphasis on which of the following activities will be helpful?**
    A. An activity with zero slack time
    B. An activity with the highest time
    C. An activity with the highest slack time
    D. An activity with the highest level of resource allocation

11. **The technique to evaluate project progression in terms of time, cost, and schedule, and to determine estimates of these by completion, is which of the following?**
    - A. EVA
    - B. FPA
    - C. PERT
    - D. CPM

12. **An IS auditor noted that a project, which is expected to be completed in 2 years, has utilized only 25% of the budget after completion of the first year. The auditor should first determine which of the following?**
    - A. Work completed compared against the completion schedule
    - B. Whether the project budget can be reduced
    - C. The process for estimating project duration
    - D. The process for estimating project cost

13. **To obtain reasonable assurance about the completion of the project within the timeline, the best method is which of the following?**
    - A. To compare the estimated end date and estimated time for completion of the project
    - B. To extrapolate the end date on the basis of completed work and resource availability at this point
    - C. To obtain confirmation from the project manager about the project completion date
    - D. To calculate the end date on the basis of the remaining budget

14. **The most appropriate technique to evaluate the progress of a project is which of the following?**
    - A. Gantt charts
    - B. PERT
    - C. CPM
    - D. SLOC

15. **On the evaluation of a 4-day project of 32 hours (8 hours per day), the IS auditor noted that at the end of day 1, 28 hours of work is still pending. The IS auditor should report which of the following?**
    - A. That the project is in accordance with the schedule
    - B. That the project is ahead of schedule
    - C. That the project is behind schedule
    - D. That the project will be difficult to be completed

16. **In which of the following phases should a proper plan and strategy for new systems be developed?**
    A. The testing phase
    B. The development phase
    C. C. The design phase
    D. The implementation phase

Business cases and feasibility analysis

It is very important to consider the business case and feasibility analysis before undertaking any new project. The IS auditor should have a basic understanding of the business case as well as the feasibility study.

Business cases

A business case is a justification for a proposed project. The business case is prepared to justify the effort and investment in a proposed project. It captures the reasoning for initiating a project or task. Generally, the business case is the precursor to the start of the project. The business case is a key element in decision-making for any project. Development of the business case is the responsibility of the project sponsor.

The proposed ROIs, along with any other expected benefits, are the most important consideration for decision-making in any new project.

Feasibility analysis

A feasibility study is an analysis that takes various factors into account, including economic, technical, and legal factors, to ascertain the likelihood of completing the project successfully. The feasibility study should consider how the project will impact the organization in terms of risk, costs, and benefits. It helps to assess whether a solution is practical and achievable within the established budgets and schedule requirements.

A feasibility study report generally includes the following elements:

Elements	Description
Scope	Report should include a detailed project plan, expected benefits and associated risks.
Current Process	Report to include analysis of current process and strength and justification for upgrade.
Requirements	Report should include the needs and requirements of stakeholders from the proposed project.
Approach	Report should include a detailed approach for execution of the project.
Evaluation	Alternatives to be evaluated for the most effective solution Feasibility report should include: • Resource requirements • Vendors and third-party contractors' costs • Project schedule start and end dates
Review	Sign off to be taken from all the stakeholders for decisions taken on the basis of the feasibility report. If the project is rejected, details need to be documented for future reference.

Apart from the parameters mentioned in the preceding table, an organization may consider other parameters as per the need and requirements of the project.

The IS auditor's role in business case development

The IS auditor should have a good understanding of business case development for information systems. They play an important role in reviewing and evaluating the business case and feasibility study. They are required to ensure that the business case and feasibility study are evaluated in an effective and unbiased manner. Generally, the following tasks are performed by the IS auditor while reviewing the feasibility study:

- Reviewing the approval process for initiation of the project
- Reviewing the process followed for the development of the business case and feasibility study
- Reviewing the process followed for the evaluation of various alternatives
- Reviewing the appropriateness of the cost justification/benefits projected
- Determining whether the business case and feasibility analysis are aligned with the business objectives

Self-assessment questions

1. **The main concern for the implementation of a new project is which of the following?**
   - A. The business case has not been prepared
   - B. Security standards have not been considered
   - C. Users are not involved in the implementation
   - D. UAT is not documented

2. **The most important consideration in a business case is which of the following?**
   - A. The cost of the project
   - B. The resource requirements for the project
   - C. The ROI of the project
   - D. The security requirements of the project

3. **An auditor reviewing the outsourcing process of an organization should be primarily concerned about which of the following?**
   - A. The non-inclusion of the right to audit clause in the SLA
   - B. The business case not having been prepared
   - C. The unavailability of a source code escrow arrangement
   - D. The non-inclusion of a business continuity clause in the SLA

4. **An inadequate software baseline can result in which of the following?**
   - A. Scope creep
   - B. Inadequate security
   - C. High resource requirements
   - D. Inadequate UAT

5. **The prime objective of assigning process ownership in a system development project is to do which of the following?**
   - A. Help in keeping an eye on the completion of the project
   - B. Help in efficient and effective UAT
   - C. Ensure that project requirements are aligned with business needs
   - D. Minimize the impact of scope creep

6. **The most important factor for whether a business case helps management in decision-making is which of the following?**
   - (A.) The feasibility study
   - B. Security considerations
   - C. Resource constraints
   - D. Effective implementation

7. **Business case documentation needs to be preserved until which of the following?**
   - (A.) The end of the project life cycle
   - B. The end of the project approval stage
   - C. The end of the post-implementation review stage
   - D. The end of UAT

8. **The IS auditor noted that a project that is more than 75% complete has already overrun by 20%, with costs increasing by 30%. Which of the following is the first course of action for the IS auditor?**
   - A. Recommend the adoption of effective project management practices
   - B. Recommend reviewing the capability of the project manager
   - C. Determine the complexity of the project
   - (D.) Review the business case and project management

9. **What should an auditor recommend when a business case is no longer valid due to an increase in cost and a reduction in the expected benefits?**
   - A. To discontinue the project
   - (B.) To update the business case to determine the relevance of the project
   - C. To complete the project at the earliest
   - D. To obtain reapproval for budget excess

10. **An auditor reviewing a feasibility study of a new project should be mainly concerned about which of the following?**
    - (A.) The project impact on the organization not having been evaluated
    - B. The project manager not having been identified
    - C. Inputs from all IT teams not having been considered
    - D. The project completion period not having been determined

System development methodologies

A system development methodology is a structure that organizations use for the design, development, and implementation of new systems. Different methodologies are available, with each of them having different characteristics. In this section, we will understand the following concepts:

- SDLC models
- SDLC phases
- Software development methods

SDLC models

Three widely used SDLC models are the traditional waterfall, the V-shaped model, and the iterative model. Let's have a look at each of them in detail.

Traditional waterfall

This model aims to ensure that mistakes are identified at an early stage and not during final acceptance testing. The significant points of this method are given below:

- The waterfall method is the most commonly adopted approach for developing business applications.
- It works well when requirements are well defined and do not undergo frequent changes.
- This approach is useful when prototypes are required to understand the design and requirements of the proposed system.

V-shaped

V-model stands for verification and validation model. The importance of this method is as follows:

- In this method, unit tests are conducted immediately once the program is written.
- The system test is carried out to evaluate architectural specification, and a final UAT phase is carried out to validate the requirements of the proposed system.

Iterative

The significant aspects of this model are as follows:

- Requirements are developed and tested in iterations until the entire application is built and tested.
- Each development process goes through a cycle from requirement gathering to testing.

SDLC phases

A CISA aspirant should have a basic understanding of the following phases of the SDLC.

Phase 1 – Feasibility study

This phase is as follows:

- The first phase in the SDLC.
- In the feasibility study, the expected benefits are outlined against the cost of implementation of the system.
- The feasibility study provides justification for the implementation of the project.

Phase 2 – Requirements

In this phase, we have the following:

- The requirements of the new systems are detailed and documented.
- Users of the system should be involved during the requirement identification process.

Phase 3 – Software selection and acquisition

Based on the requirements gathered, a baseline needs to be defined for the new system. In phase 3, we have the following:

- The design should include the architectural and technical specifications of the new system. Security requirements should also be considered during this phase.
- If an on-the-shelf system is to be purchased from the vendor, detailed requirements should be included in the request for proposal.

Phase 4 – Development

In this phase, we have the following:

- Developmental activity takes place.
- In the case of a ready-made system, the configuration is conducted in this phase.

Phase 5 – Testing and implementation

In phase 5, the following significant testing is conducted:

- Different testing is conducted at this phase to verify and validate the developed system against the requirements.
- Unit testing, system testing, and UAT are conducted.

Phase 6 – Post-implementation

In the last SDLC phase, the following points should be taken care of:

- During this phase, post-implementation reviews are conducted and **Return on Investment (ROI)** is assessed.
- Lessons learned and improvement plans for future projects are documented.

Software development methods

In this section, we will study some of the important system development methodologies.

Agile development

Agile means "the ability to move quickly and easily". In the Agile method, programmers do not spend much time on documentation. They can write a program straight away. Here are the objectives of the Agile approach:

- The objective of the Agile approach is to produces releasable software in short iterations without giving much importance to formal paper-based deliverables.
- Once each iteration is completed, the emphasis is placed on what went well and where there was scope for improvement in the following iterations.
- Agile is one of the most preferable approaches for programmers as it saves them from a lot of planning, paperwork, and approval processes.

Let's now have a quick rundown on prototyping.

Prototyping

In the prototyping approach, the system is developed through trial-and-error methods. A prototype is basically a preliminary version of a system to test a concept or process or assumptions about functionality, design, or internal logic. A prototype model helps to save a considerable amount of time and cost for the organization. Given here are a few risks of the prototyping approach:

- One of the potential risks of a prototype approach is that the finished system may not have adequate controls compared to traditional system development approaches. The prototype approach provides more emphasis on user requirements.
- In prototyping, design and requirements change too often and they are hardly documented or approved.
- The change control process is very weak in the prototype environment.
- The most effective testing method for the initial phase of prototyping is a top-down approach. In the top-down approach, testing begins with a system's major functionality and gradually moves to other functionality.
- In prototyping, more emphasis is given to major functionality, such as screens and reports, thus shaping most of the proposed system's features in a short period.

Rapid Application Development

The following elements are used in **Rapid Application Development (RAD)**:

- A well-trained team of developers
- Prototypes
- Sophisticated tools and software for modeling, prototyping, and component reusability
- A central repository

With the use of the preceding techniques, RAD aims for the quick development of the system while reducing cost and ensuring quality.

RAD relies on the prototype, which can be frequently updated to address the ever-changing user or business requirements.

Object-Oriented System Development

Object-Oriented System Development (OOSD) is a programming technique with an objective to make program code that is reusable and maintainable.

- An *object* is basically a small piece of code in a program. The system is developed via the use and combination of different objects. OOSD uses a technique known as *encapsulation*, in which objects interact with each other. Encapsulation provides enhanced security for data.
- The ability of two or more objects to interpret a message is termed as *polymorphism*.

Component-based development

In component-based development, ready-made components (objects) are assembled together to design and develop a specific application.

- As developers are not required to write programming code, they can concentrate on business functionality.
- Component-based development supports multiple development environments. Components can interact with each other irrespective of their programming language.
- As components are already available, it saves considerable time and cost in the development of the system. Also, it ensures quality, as components are already tested.
- Component-based development promotes modularity that is different components can be used independently.

Software engineering and reverse engineering

It is important to understand these two terms from a system development perspective:

- **Software reengineering**: Reengineering is the process of updating a system to enhance the system functionality to make the system better and more efficient. Software reengineering helps to support the major changes of the organization's processes.
- **Reverse engineering**: Reverse engineering is the process of the detailed analysis and study of a system with the objective to develop a similar system.

Key aspects from the CISA exam perspective

The following table covers important aspects from CISA exam perspective:

CISA questions	Possible answers
The major risk associated with the Agile approach	Lack of documentation
Characteristics of the Agile approach	• Systematic review after completion of each iteration to identify areas of improvement • Quick and easy without much emphasis on paper documentation
Characteristics of the Waterfall approach	• The most common method of software development • Suitable when requirements are well defined and do not undergo frequent changes • After completion of each stage, testing is done before moving to the next stage
Characteristics of a Prototype approach	• Save a considerable amount of time and cost • Risk of inadequate controls • Effective testing methods for the initial phase of prototyping is a top-down approach.
Which technique uses a prototype that can be frequently updated to address the ever-changing user or business requirements?	Rapid Application Development (RAD)
Difference between reengineering and reverse engineering	• Reengineering is the process of updating a system to enhance the system's functionality to make it better and more efficient. • Reverse engineering, also called back engineering, is the process of understanding and extracting the design, architecture, components, and knowledge of a system with the objective of producing a similar system.
Benefit of OOSD	Ability to reuse the modules
The benefit of component-based development	Ability to support multiple development environments

Self-assessment questions

1. **A major risk in the Agile development process is which of the following?**
   - A. Inadequate documentation
   - B. Inadequate testing
   - C. Inadequate requirement gathering
   - D. Inadequate user involvement

2. **One of the important characteristics of the Agile approach is which of the following?**
   A. A systematic review after the completion of each iteration to identify areas of improvement
   B. Systematic and detailed planning before writing a program
   C. The use of software development tools to improve productivity
   D. Detailed documentation

3. **A major limitation of the Agile software development methodology is which of the following?**
   A. A limited budget may impact the quality of the system.
   B. The lack of a requirements gathering process.
   C. The lack of a review process to identify areas of improvement.
   D. A lack of proper documentation due to time management.

4. **A major benefit of using prototyping for system development is which of the following?**
   A. More emphasis on system controls
   B. More emphasis on stringent change management processes
   C. A reduction in deployment time
   D. More emphasis on stringent approval processes

5. **The most effective testing method for the initial phase of prototyping is which of the following?**
   A. Bottom-up testing
   B. Top-down testing
   C. Interface testing
   D. Unit testing

6. **The technique that relies on a prototype that can be frequently updated to address ever-changing user or business requirements is which of the following?**
   A. Business process reengineering
   B. RAD
   C. Software reengineering
   D. Object-oriented system development

7. **The major benefit of the prototype approach is which of the following?**
    A. Significant time and cost savings
    B. A stringent approval process
    C. Strong change controls
    D. Proper documentation

8. **In the prototyping method, change control can be impacted by which of the following?**
    A. User participation
    B. Frequent changes in requirements and design
    C. The trial-and-error method
    D. Limited budgets

9. **The methodology for quick development at a reduced cost while ensuring high quality is which of the following?**
    A. The Waterfall method
    B. PERT
    C. RAD
    D. FPA

10. **RAD has which of the following advantages over the traditional SDLC?**
    A. User involvement in system development
    B. UAT
    C. A reduction in the development time frame
    D. Enhanced technical support

11. **A benefit of object-oriented development technique is which of the following?**
    A. Object modules can be reused
    B. The use of a prototype that can be frequently updated to address the ever-changing user or business requirements
    C. Enhanced control compared to the traditional SDLC
    D. There is no need for the developer to design the system

12. **A characteristic of the OOSD method that enables greater security over data is which of the following?**
    A. Encapsulation
    B. Polymorphism
    C. Prototyping
    D. Modulation

13. **The waterfall life cycle approach is more suitable for which of the following?**
    A. Well-defined requirements with no expected changes
    B. Well-defined requirements in a context where the project is to be competed in a short time frame
    C. Open requirements that are subject to frequent changes
    D. Users do not want to spend much time on testing

14. **A technique to study and analyze an application or a system, and to use that information to develop a similar system, is known as which of the following?**
    A. Business process reengineering
    B. Agile development
    C. Software reengineering
    D. Reverse engineering

15. **Which of the following is a technique to enhance the system by extracting and reusing design and program components?**
    A. Regression
    B. Agile development
    C. Software reengineering
    D. Reverse engineering

16. **Which of the following is a major concern of an IS auditor reviewing the system development approach?**
    A. The process owner is responsible for signing off on UAT
    B. The absence of a quality plan for system development
    C. Old modules are discontinued in phases
    D. The use of prototypes to test system functionalities

17. **A major benefit of component-based system development is which of the following?**
    A. It supports multiple data types
    B. It supports complex relationships
    C. It supports the demands of a changing environment
    D. It supports multiple development environments

18. **The greatest concern for an IS auditor reviewing the business process reengineering process is which of the following?**
    A. The unavailability of key controls to protect assets and information resources
    B. The unavailability of appropriate documentation
    C. Non-adherence to time and resource budgets
    D. The unavailability of documented roles and responsibilities

19. **Business process reengineering aims to achieve which of the following?**
    A. Keep the business processes stable
    B. Train the new employees
    C. Improve the performance of products and services
    D. Reduce the resource demands

20. **The first step in business process reengineering is to do which of the following?**
    A. Finalize the scope and areas to be reviewed
    B. Develop a project plan
    C. Analyze the process under review
    D. Conduct reengineering for the process under review

21. **The prototyping approach is used to design which of the following?**
    A. Screens, interactive edits, and sample reports
    B. Screens, interactive edits, and program logic
    C. Sample reports and program logic
    D. Program logic and interactive edits

Control identification and design

An IS auditor needs to have sufficient understanding of the various control techniques used while designing the applications. In the next few sub-sections, we will go through some of the important controls built into in an application system.

Check digits

A check digit is an extra digit used for error detection. A check digit is arrived at by a mathematical algorithm. It is added to the original data to ensure that data is not altered.

It helps to ensure that the original data is not tampered or altered. Check digits help to prevent transposition and transcription errors. The most famous example for use of a check digit is the bank account numbers assigned to customers.

For instance, a bank account number is 63000024145The last digit is the check digit, 3, and if the other numbers are correct then the check digit calculation must produce 3:

1. Add the numbers placed in odd digit positions: 6+0+0+2+1+5 = 14.
2. Add the numbers placed in even digit positions: 3+0+0+4+4 = 11.
3. Deduct the result of *step 2* from *step 1*: 14 - 11 = 3.

Therefore, the check digit value is 3.

Here we have given a simple calculation for easy understanding. In real scenarios, calculations are more complicated. Please note that the preceding calculation is only for the purposes of your learning and understanding. In the CISA exam, such a calculation will not be tested.

Parity bits

Parity bits are used to verify complete and accurate data transmission. Parity bits are used as the simplest form of error-detecting code when data is transferred from one computer to another:

- An extra bit is added to the data in such a way that the total number of 1 bits in the data string is either even or odd. This extra bit is called a parity bit.
- This parity is then verified by the receiving computer to validate the data accuracy and completeness during transmission.

The following diagram will help you understand about parity bits:

Parity Bits				
Character	Sender	Parity Bit	Receiver	Parity
E	1000101	1	10001011	Even
A	1000001	0	10000010	Even
C	1000011	1	10000111	Even
q	1110001	0	11100000	Odd

Indicates error in data transmission

In the preceding diagram, even parity is being used at the sender's end. Similarly, odd parity can also be used.

 Note: This diagram is only for learning purposes. In the CISA exam, such calculations will not be tested.

Checksums

Checksums work on the same principle as parity bits but they have the capability to recognize complex errors through advanced mathematical formulas.

Cyclic Redundancy Checksums (CRC)/Redundancy Checksums are a more advanced version of checksums that work by increasing the complexity of the arithmetic.

Forward error control

Forward error control works on the same principle as redundancy checksum. In addition to detecting the error, they have capability to correct the error. It helps the receiving computer to correct the error.

Data integrity principles

The data integrity principles of atomicity, completeness, isolation, and durability are described as follows:

- **Atomicity**: The principle of atomicity prescribes that a transaction is either processed completely or should not be processed at all. In the case of an error or interruption, partial processing, if any, should be rolled back.
- **Consistency**: The principle of consistency prescribes that all integrity conditions must be applied to each transaction of the database.
- **Isolation**: The principle of isolation prescribes that each transaction should be separated from other transactions.
- **Durability**: The principle of durability prescribes that the database should be resilient enough to survive any system failures.

Limit checks

Limit checks restrict the data input up to a certain predefined limit. Data is checked for one limit, either upper or lower, as in, data should not be greater than 100.

Limit checks are input control. These are a form of preventive control to restrict invalid input into the system. It ensures that only data within the predefined limit can enter the system.

Automated systems balancing

Automated systems balancing reconciles the total input with the total output.

Any difference will be shown as an error for further investigation and correction.

Automated system balancing helps to determine whether any transactions are lost during processing as any mismatch in input and output will be highlighted for further investigation.

Sequence checks

Sequence checks involve testing a list of items or files of records for correct ascending or descending sequences based on predefined requirements.

For example, it checks whether vouchers are in sequence and thus prevents the duplication of the vouchers.

Decision support systems

A **Decision Support System (DSS)** is a semi-structured interactive decision-making framework. DSS collects data from a variety of sources and gives managers useful information.

The characteristics of DSS are as follows:

- DSS supports semi-structured or less structured decisions.
- DSS uses traditional data access and restoration techniques.
- DSS is flexible and user-friendly in changing environments and user responses to the decisions made.

The following diagram explains the characteristics of DSS:

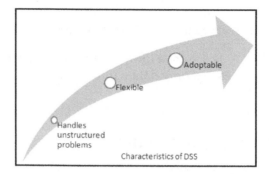

These characteristics will help us to understand the efficiency and effectiveness of DSS, as described next.

Efficiency versus effectiveness

A DSS design principle is to concentrate less on productivity (that is, performing tasks quickly and reducing costs) and more on effectiveness (that is, performing the right task).

Design and development

The most popular approach to DSS design and development is prototyping.

Risk factors

DSS has the following inherent risks that need to be considered while designing the system:

- Users might not be willing to use the system.
- The purpose or objective of DSS may not be clear to the users.
- A lack of expertise in how to use the system.

Decision trees

Decision trees are a simple way to create a visualization based on clearly defined criteria of the paths toward decision-making. A decision tree can be of significant help in making the correct choice. It is used as a questionnaire to direct a client through a series of choices before coming to a conclusion.

Decision trees are a framework that can be used to better advantage in the audit department when identifying opportunities and risks. It helps in the decision-making process but also allows a clear identification of the causes. Decision trees are one way of making reasonable and effective use of this data in auditing.

Key aspects from the CISA exam perspective

The following table covers important aspects from CISA exam perspective:

CISA questions	Possible answers
What is the best control to ensure that no transactions are lost during processing?	Automated Systems Balancing
What is the best technique to detect the transposition and transcription error?	Check Digit
Which of the data integrity principle requires that transactions are either processed completely or should not be processed at all? In case of an error or interruption, partial processing. if any, should be rolled back.	Atomicity
Which technique is best to prevent the duplication of the vouchers during data entry?	Sequence Check
What are the techniques to ensure data completeness and data integrity during transmission?	• Cyclic Redundancy Checksum (first preference) • Checksum (second best) • Parity Bits (third best)
Which technique is used to detect as well as correct the errors by transmitting redundant information with each character?	Forward Error Control (Please note that parity bit/checksums/CRC do not have ability to correct the error. Forward Error Control has ability to detect as well as correct the error)
What are the characteristics of DSS?	• DSS supports semi-structured or less structured decisions. • DSS uses traditional data access and restoration techniques. • DSS is flexible and user-friendly in changing environment and user response to decision-making
Questionnaires to lead the user through a series of choices to reach a conclusion is known as	Decision Tree

Let's now have a look at the self-assessment questions.

Self-assessment questions

1. **Which of the following is the best control to address input errors?**
    - A. The hash total
    - B. The run-to-run total
    - C. Limit checks
    - D. Daily reconciliation

2. **Which of the following is the best control to ensure that no transactions are lost during processing?**
    - A. Limit checks
    - B. Check digits
    - C. Automated system balancing
    - D. Validation control

3. **To detect transposition and transcription errors, which of the following controls is the most effective?**
    - A. Limit checks
    - B. Check digits
    - C. Automated system balancing
    - D. Range checks

4. **The data integrity principle, which prescribes that a transaction is either processed completely or not processed at all, falls under which of the following principles?**
    - A. Consistency
    - B. Atomicity
    - C. Isolation
    - D. Durability

5. **The technique to prevent duplication of a voucher during data entry is which of the following?**
    - A. Limit checks
    - B. Check digits
    - C. Sequence checks
    - D. Range checks

6. The technique to control the completeness of data transmission is which of the following?
    A. Limit checks
    B. Parity bits
    C. Sequence checks
    D. Range checks

7. The technique used by banks for the prevention of transposition and transcription mistakes, thus ensuring the integrity of bank account numbers allotted to customers, is which of the following?
    A. Limit checks
    B. Parity bits
    C. Check digits
    D. Range checks

8. Which of the following is the purpose of the checksum control?
    A. To ensure confidentiality
    B. To ensure availability
    C. To ensure integrity
    D. To ensure non-repudiation

9. Parity bits are implemented to validate which of the following?
    A. Data confidentiality
    B. The data source
    C. Data availability
    D. Data completeness

10. The best method to find transmission mistakes by adding an extra bit at the end of segment is which of the following?
    A. Parity bits
    B. Checksums
    C. Validation control
    D. Redundancy checks

11. Which of the following techniques helps to detect errors in a network transmission?
    A. Parity bits
    B. Checksums
    C. Validation control
    D. Redundancy checks

12. **Which of the following techniques helps to detect as well as correct the errors by transmitting redundant information with each character?**
    A. Parity bits
    B. Forward error control
    C. Checksums
    D. Redundancy checks

13. **The data integrity principle of atomicity ensures which of the following?**
    A. That a database survives a hardware or software failure
    B. That a transaction is completed in its entirety
    C. That database consistency is maintained
    D. That each transaction is separated from other transactions

14. **Which of the following is a feature of DSS?**
    A. DSS enables flexibility in the user's approach to decision-making
    B. DSS only supports structured tasks related to decision-making
    C. DSS is designed to solve highly structured problems
    D. DSS uses non-traditional data access and restoration techniques

15. **The knowledge domain of an expert system, which uses questionnaires to guide the user through a series of choices before coming to a conclusion, is known as which of the following?**
    A. Diagram trees
    B. Decision trees
    C. Semantic nets
    D. Networks trees

16. **The main risk of using a DSS is which of the following?**
    A. It does not support semi-structured problems
    B. The cost of implementing the system
    C. The inability to specify purpose and usage patterns
    D. The constant change in decision-making processes

17. **Questionnaires to guide the user through a set of choices to arrive at a conclusion is used by which of the following?**
    - A. Audit checklists
    - B. Decision trees
    - C. Logical analysis
    - D. Budget checklists

18. **A DSS does which of the following?**
    - A. Focuses on the highly structured problems
    - B. Supports only the top management requirements
    - C. Emphasizes flexibility in the user's approach to decision-making
    - D. Fails to support unstructured problems

19. **The business information system that provides answers to semi-structured issues and validates business decisions is which of the following?**
    - A. A DSS
    - B. An executive support system
    - C. A transaction processing system
    - D. A vendor support system

20. **When reviewing the decision support system, an IS auditor should be most concerned with which of the following?**
    - A. Input data quality
    - B. The level of skills and experience contained in the knowledge base
    - C. The system's logical access control
    - D. The processing controls implemented in the system

Summary

In this chapter we broadly discussed project management structure and methodologies. We also learnt about importance of business case and feasibility studies. We discussed about some of the important system related controls like check digits, parity bits, checksums and principles of data integrity.

In the next chapter, we will discuss the testing and implementation phases of project development.

Assessments

Here are the answers to the self-evaluation questions.

Project management structure

1. **1. Answer: D. PERT**
   Explanation: PERT is a technique for estimating project duration. PERT is considered more accurate and appropriate compared to CPM for estimations of project duration. Gantt charts are primarily used to monitor the progress of the project. SLOC and FPA are techniques to estimate software size.

2. **Answer: D. To ensure a stable software development process**
   Explanation: CMM enables an auditor to determine whether the organization follows a stable process of software development. CMM does not support the other options.

3. **Answer: A. PERT**
   Explanation: PERT is considered the best technique to estimate the duration of the project. Component-based development and RAD are software development methodologies. FPA is a technique for the estimation of software size.

4. **Answer: A. Portfolio management**
   Explanation: The objective of a portfolio management is to manage the various projects of an organization. It includes prioritization, budgeting, approvals, and monitoring the implementation. It helps to align the projects in accordance with the business objective.

5. **Answer: B. During the initial planning stage of the project**
   Explanation: It is very critical to have proper planning for system phases and deliverable user requirements for effective and efficient program management. It should be planned during the initial stage of the project to enable project tracking and resource management.

6. **Answer: C. FPA**

   Explanation: FPA is an indirect technique to estimate the size of software. Function points are a unit of measurement for software size, just as time is measured in hours and distance is measured in miles. To arrive at the function point, different factors are considered, such as the complication of the design, input, processing, outputs, modules, and their interactions. FPA is more consistent and reliable than SLOC.

   SLOC is a traditional way of estimating software size on the basis of a single parameter, such as the number of lines of code. However, this may not be effective in the case of complex systems with functionality other than codes. Such functionality could include diagrams, objects, database queries, or graphical user interfaces.

   PERT and Gantt charts are techniques for determining and monitoring project duration.

7. **Answer: C. The critical path of the project**

   Explanation: CPM is used to estimate the duration of the project. Any project will have a minimum of one critical path. A critical path is determined by identifying the longest path of the dependent activities. The time required to finish the critical path is the shortest possible time required for finishing the project. No slack time will be available for the activities on the critical path. If the addition of new resources is unable to shorten the critical path, new resources will have no impact on the overall project duration. Other paths may be shortened, but this will result in slack time and the overall project duration will not be shortened. Hence it is necessary to revalidate the critical path of the project first.

8. **Answer: B. It aims to prevent excess cost and time for project completion.**

   Explanation: The major advantage of this approach is that it prevents project cost overruns and delays to the scheduled time frame for delivery. It is used for prototyping or RAD where a project needs to be completed within a given time frame. It integrates system and user acceptance testing, but does not eliminate the need for a quality process.

9. **Answer: B. Continuously throughout the project**

   Explanation: It is important to establish quality management processes throughout the life cycle of the project. It helps to reduce the overall cost of the project by identifying quality gaps and ensuring early rectification.

10. **Answer: A. An activity with zero slack time**
    Explanation: Slack time is the buffer or extra time before the project completion deadline, and an activity can be delayed up to the slack time without impacting the overall project completion date.
    Project managers concentrate on activities with zero slack time (that is, the critical path) and if the critical path can be reduced, then it will help to minimize the overall project duration.

11. **Answer: A. EVA**
    Explanation: EVA is a method of measuring a project's progress at any given point in time, forecasting its completion date and final cost, and analyzing variances in the schedule and budget as the project proceeds. EVA determines and evaluates the following factors on a periodic basis:
    - How does the actual spending up to the current date compare to the budget?
    - What will the estimated completion time be?
    - What will the estimated total expenditure be?

    PERT and CPM will help to determine the project time but lacks projection for estimates as completio

12. **Answer: A. Work completed compared to the schedule for completion**
    Explanation: The auditor needs to determine what percentage of work has been completed before making any recommendation. Costs cannot be assessed only on the basis of a time schedule. It may be possible that major expenses are expected in a later part of the project.

13. **Answer: B. To extrapolate the end date on the basis of completed work and resource availability**
    Explanation: It is also advisable to rely on direct observations of results on the basis of factual data. Relying on estimates and interviews with the project manager may not give correct information.

14. **Answer: A. Gantt charts**
    Explanation: Gantt charts are a technique to monitor the progress of a project. Gantt charts are used to determine the status of the project, such as whether the project is delayed, ahead of schedule, or on schedule. Gantt charts are used for tracking and monitoring achievements of milestones.
    PERT and CPM are techniques for determining the duration of the project. SLOC is a technique for software size estimation.

15. **Answer: C. The project is behind schedule**
    Explanation: EVA is based on the assumption that a project can
    reasonably be completed within the time frame allotted. So if a project is allotted
    32 hours (4 days with 8 hours per day) and at the end of the day, 28 hours of
    work is still is pending, then the work completed is only 4 hours on the first day,
    against the schedule of 8 hours. Hence, the project is behind schedule.

Particular	Day 1	Day 2	Day 3	Day 4	Total
Budget	8	8	8	8	32
Completed	4 (Total Budget - Work Pending, for example, 32 - 28)	-	-	-	-
Delay	4	-	-	-	-

Thus, it indicates a deviation of 4 hours from the schedule.

16. **Answer: C. The design phase**
    Explanation: The implementation process affects the design of the system. Hence
    it is recommended to consider and plan for implementation during the design
    phase itself.

The business case and feasibility analysis

1. **1.Answer: A. The business case is not prepared**
   Explanation: The business case is a justification for the proposed project. The
   business case is prepared to justify efforts and investment in a proposed project.
   The business case is a precursor to the start of the project. The first concern of an
   IS auditor is whether the new project meets the needs of the business. This
   should be established by an approved business case. Other options are not as
   important as the availability of a business case.

2. **Answer: C. ROI of the project**
   Explanation: The business case is a justification for the proposed project. The
   business case is prepared to justify efforts and investment in a proposed
   project. The proposed ROIs along with the expected benefits are the most
   important considerations for decision-making in any new project.

3. **Answer: B. The business case is not prepared**
   Explanation: The business case is a justification for why the proposed project should be undertaken. The business case helps to determine the efforts and investment in a proposed project against the expected benefit. Generally, the business case is a precursor to the start of the project and is the key element in decision making for any project. Development of the business case is the responsibility of the project sponsor.

4. **Answer: A. Scope creep**
   Explanation: A software baseline is the agreed-upon features of the software to be designed and developed. Any additional requirement must go through the formal change management procedure. An inadequate baseline will result in scope creep. Scope creep refers to an uncontrolled project scope due to continuous changes in project requirements. Scope creep is one of the major factors in the failure of a project.

5. **Answer: C. Ensure that project's requirements are aligned with business needs**
   Explanation: The involvement of the process owner in the system development project is to ensure that the requirements of the project are aligned with business needs. It is very important to have the sign-off from the process owner before the implementation of the project. Other options are not the prime objective.

6. **Answer: A. A feasibility study**
   Explanation: A feasibility study is an analysis that takes various factors into account, such as economic, technical, and legal factors, to ascertain the likelihood of completing the project successfully. It helps to assess whether a solution is practical and achievable within the established budgets and schedule requirements.

7. **Answer: A. The end-of-project life cycle**
   Explanation: A business case is prepared to justify efforts and investment in a proposed project. The business case is the precursor to the start of the project. Documentation of the business case should be retained throughout the life cycle of the project. It provides focus and valuable insight for the success of the project throughout its life cycle. It provides valuable input about expectations versus actual outcomes. It also serves as a reference document for the new personnel involved in the project.

8. **Answer: D. Review the business case and project management**
   Explanation: The first step of an IS auditor is to review the business case to determine the expected benefits of the project and review the factors that contributed to schedule overruns and excess budget expenditure. On the basis of this review, the auditor should make relevant recommendations.

9. **Answer: B. To update the business case to determine the relevance of the project**
Explanation: It is important to update the business case per the current scenario and to determine whether the project is still viable.

10. **Answer: A. The project's impact on the organization has not been evaluated.**
Explanation: A feasibility study is an analysis that takes various factors into account, such as economic, technical, and legal factors, to ascertain the likelihood of completing the project successfully. A feasibility study should consider how the project will impact the organization in terms of risk, costs, and benefits. Other options are not as significant as non-evaluation of the impact of the project on the organization.

System development methodologies

1. **Answer: A. Inadequate documentation**
Explanation: The dictionary definition of agile is "able to move quickly and easily." In the Agile method, the programmer does not spend much time on documentation. They are allowed to write their program straight away. Hence inadequate documentation is considered one of the major risks of the Agile approach.

2. **Answer: D. Reviews at the end of each iteration to identify lessons learned for use in future projects**
Explanation: As we are aware, the dictionary definition of agile is 'able to move quickly and easily.' In the Agile method, the programmer does not spend much time on documentation. They are allowed to write their program straight away. The objective of the Agile approach is to produce releasable software in short iterations without giving much importance to formal, paper-based deliverables. Once each iteration is completed, emphasis is placed on what went well and where there is scope for improvement in the following iterations. Agile is one of the most preferable approaches for programmers as it saves them from a lot of planning, paperwork, and approvals.

3. **Answer: D. A lack of proper documentation due to time management**
Explanation: A major limitation of the agile development approach is the lack of documentation. The other options here are not correct.

4. **Answer: C. A reduction in deployment time**
   Explanation: In the prototyping approach, the system is developed through the trial-and-error method. A prototype is basically a preliminary version of a system to test a concept, process, or any assumptions about functionality, design, or the internal logic. A prototype model helps to save a considerable amount of time and expenditure for the organization. One of the potential risks of the prototype approach is that the finished system may not have adequate controls compared to the traditional system development approach. The prototype approach provides more emphasis on user requirements. In prototyping, there are frequent changes made to the designs and requirements and hence they are seldom documented or approved.

5. **Answer: B. Top-down testing**
   Explanation: The most effective testing method for the initial phase of prototyping is the top-down approach. Top-down testing begins with the system's major functionality and gradually moves to other functionality. In prototyping, more emphasis is given to major functionality such as screens and reports, thereby covering most of the proposed system's features in a short period.

6. **Answer: B. RAD**
   Explanation: The objective of RAD is the quick development of a system while reducing cost and ensuring quality. RAD relies on a prototype, which can be frequently updated to address the ever-changing user or business requirements.

7. **Answer: A. Significant time and cost savings**
   Explanation: In the prototyping approach, the system is developed through the trial-and-error method. A prototype is basically a preliminary version of a system to test a concept, process, or any assumptions about functionality, design, or the internal logic. A prototype model helps to save a considerable amount of time and expenditure for the organization. One of the potential risks of the prototype approach is that the finished system may not have adequate controls compared to the traditional system development approach. In prototyping, the design and requirements change too often and are hardly documented or approved.

8. **Answer: B. Frequent changes in requirements and design**
   Explanation: In prototyping, there are frequent changes in the designs and requirements and hence they are seldom documented or approved. Change control becomes more complicated with prototyped systems. Other options do not have an adverse effect on change control.

9. **Answer: B. RAD**
   Explanation: The objective of RAD is the quick development of a system while reducing costs and ensuring quality. RAD relies on a prototype that can be frequently updated to address the ever-changing user or business requirements. The waterfall method is a traditional method that is comparatively costly and time-consuming. PERT and FPA are not the system development methodology. PERT is a system development evaluation tool while FPA is a software estimation method.

10. **Answer: C. A reduction in the development time frame**
    Explanation: The objective of RAD is the quick development of a system while reducing costs and ensuring quality. The major benefit of RAD is the reduction of the time required for the development of a system. Other options are true for both RAD and the traditional SDLC.

11. **Answer: A. Object modules can be reused.**
    Explanation: OOSD is a programming technique with the objective to make program code that can be reusable and maintainable. *Object* here refers to a small piece of the program that can be used individually or in combination with other objects. The other options here are not normally benefits of the object-oriented technique.

12. **Answer: A. Encapsulation**
    Explanation: OOSD is a programming technique with an objective to make program code that is reusable and maintainable. An *object* is basically a small piece of code in a program. The system is developed via the use and combination of different objects. OOSD uses a technique known as *encapsulation*, in which objects interact with each other. Encapsulation provides enhanced security for data. The ability of two or more objects to interpret a message is termed as *polymorphism*.

13. **Answer: A. Well-defined requirements with no expected changes**
    Explanation: The waterfall method is the most commonly adopted approach for developing business applications. It works well when requirements are well defined and do not undergo frequent changes. This model aims to ensure that mistakes are identified at early stages and not during final acceptance testing. In the waterfall approach, UAT is done after the completion of each stage before moving on to the next stage.

14. **Answer: D. Reverse engineering**
    Explanation: Reverse engineering is the process of detailed analysis and study of a system with the objective of developing a similar system. Software reengineering and business process reengineering are the processes of updating a system or process to enhance the system functionality to make the system or processes better and more efficient.

15. **Answer: C. Software reengineering**
    Explanation: Software reengineering and business process reengineering are the processes of updating a system or process to enhance the system functionality to make the system or processes better and more efficient. Reverse engineering is the process of detailed analysis and study of a system with the objective of developing a similar system.

16. **Answer: B. The absence of a quality assurance plan for system development**
    Explanation: It is very important to have a quality assurance plan in order to get better outcomes for the final system. The quality assurance plan should be documented and consider various aspects of the SDLC to maintain the agreed-upon quality.
    UAT is normally managed by the process owner. It is reasonable to discontinue the old system in phases, especially when the system is large. Prototyping is a valid method to test system functionality.

17. **Answer: D. It supports multiple development environments**
    Explanation: In component-based development, ready-made components (objects) are assembled together to design and develop a specific application. As developers are not required to write programming code, they can concentrate on business functionality. Component-based development supports multiple development environments. Components can interact with each other irrespective of their programming language.

18. **Answer: A. The unavailability of key controls to protect assets and information resources**
    Explanation: The main concern of an IS auditor is the unavailability of key controls to protect assets and information resources. The other options are not as significant as the unavailability of key controls.

19. **Answer: C. It aims to improve the performance of products and services**
    Explanation: Reengineering is the process of updating a system to enhance the system functionality to make the system better and more efficient. A reduction of resource requirements may be the outcome of business process reengineering, but the ultimate objective is to improve the performance of the product and service.

20. **Answer: A. Defining the scope and the areas to be reviewed**
    Explanation: The first step in business process reengineering is to finalize the scope and areas to be reviewed. The next step is to develop the project plan.

21. **Answer A. Screens, interactive edits, and sample reports**
Explanation: It must be noted that program logics are not developed by a prototyping tool. In the prototyping approach, the system is developed through the trial-and-error method. The prototype is basically a preliminary version of a system to test a concept, process, or any assumptions about the functionality, design, or internal logic. In prototyping, more emphasis is given to major functionality such as screens, and the report thus shapes most of the proposed system's features in a short period.

Control identification and design

1. **Answer: C. Limit checks**
Explanation: Limit checks restrict the data input up to certain predefined limits. Data is checked for certain limits, either upper or lower, as in, the number entered should not be greater than 100. A limit check is an input control. It is a preventive control to restrict invalid input into the system. It ensures that only data within the predefined limit can enter the system. All other options are controls that address the output.

2. **Answer: C. Automated system balancing**
Explanation: Automated system balancing reconciles the total input and total output. Any difference will be shown as an error for further investigation and correction. Automated system balancing helps to determine whether any transactions are lost during the processing as any mismatch in input and output will be highlighted for further investigation.

3. **Answer: B. Check digits**
Explanation: A check digit is a form of redundancy check used for error detection on identification numbers. It helps to ensure that the original data is not tampered with or altered. Check digits help to prevent transposition and transcription errors.

4. **Answer: B. Atomicity**
Explanation: The data integrity principles of **ACID (Atomicity, Completeness, Isolation, and Durability)** are as follows:
    - **Atomicity**: The principle of atomicity prescribes that a transaction is either processed completely or should not be processed at all. In the case of an error or interruption, partial processing, if any, should be rolled back.
    - **Consistency**: The principle of consistency prescribes that all integrity conditions must be applied to each transaction of the database.

- **Isolation**: The principle of isolation prescribes that each transaction should be separated from other transactions.
- **Durability**: The principle of durability prescribes that the database should be resilient enough to survive any system failures.

5. **Answer: C. Sequence checks**
Explanation: Sequence checks involve testing a list of items or files of records for the correct ascending or descending sequence based on predefined requirements. It checks whether vouchers are in sequence and thus prevents the duplication of the vouchers.

6. **Answer: B. Parity bits**
Explanation: Parity bits are used to verify complete and accurate data transmission. Parity bits are used as the simplest form of error-detecting code when data is transferred from one computer to another. An extra bit is added to the data in such a way that the total number of 1 bits in the data string is either even or odd. This extra bit is called a parity bit. This parity is then verified by the receiving computer to validate the data accuracy and completeness during transmission.

7. **Answer: C. Check digits**
Explanation: A check digit is a form of redundancy check used for error detection on identification numbers. It helps to ensure that the original data is not tampered with or altered. Check digits help to prevent transposition and transcription errors. A check digit is a mathematically calculated value that is added to data to ensure that the original data has not been altered.

8. **Answer: C. To ensure integrity**
Explanation: The purpose of a checksum is to ensure data integrity and data completeness. It requires adding an extra bit to the data in such a way that the total number of 1 bits in the data string is either even or odd. This parity is verified by the receiving computer to ensure data completeness and data integrity during transmission.

9. **Answer: D. Data completeness**
Explanation: Parity bits are used to verify complete and accurate data transmission. Parity bits are used as the simplest form of error-detecting code when data is transferred from one computer to another. An extra bit is added to the data in such a way that the total number of 1 bits in the data string is either even or odd. This extra bit is called a parity bit. This parity is then verified by the receiving computer to validate the data accuracy and completeness during transmission.

10. **Answer: D. Redundancy checks**

    Explanation: Parity checks, checksums, and cyclic redundancy are used to verify and validate complete and accurate data transmission. However, CRCs/redundancy checks involve applying complex mathematical calculations and are more accurate than parity bits and checksums.

11. **Answer: D. Redundancy checks**

    Explanation: Parity checks, checksums, and cyclic redundancy are used to verify and validate complete and accurate data transmission. However, CRCs/redundancy checks involve applying complex mathematical calculations and are more accurate than parity bits and checksums. CRCs can check for a block of transmitted data. The sending computer generates the CRC and transmits it with the data. The receiving machine again generates a CRC and compares it to the transmitted CRC. If both of them are equal, then the block is assumed error-free.

12. **Answer: B. Forward error control**

    Explanation: Forward error control works on same principle as redundancy checksums. In addition to detecting errors, they have the capability to correct the errors found. It helps the receiver computer to correct the error.

13. **Answer: D. A transaction is completed in its entirety.**

    Explanation: Data integrity principles of ACID (atomicity, completeness, isolation, and durability) are as follow:
    - **Atomicity**: The principle of atomicity prescribes that a transaction is either processed completely or should not be processed at all. In the case of an error or interruption, partial processing, if any, should be rolled back.
    - **Consistency**: The principle of consistency prescribes that all integrity conditions must be applied to each transaction of the database.
    - **Isolation**: The principle of isolation prescribes that each transaction should be separated from other transactions.
    - **Durability**: The principle of durability prescribes that the database should be resilient enough to survive any system failures.

14. **Answer: A. It enables flexibility in the user's approach to decision-making**

    Explanation: The characteristics of DSS are as follows:
    - It supports decisions that are either semi-organized or less organized.
    - It uses standard data access and retrieval techniques.
    - It is flexible and user-friendly when it comes to changing environments and user decision-making.

15. **Answer: B. Decision trees**
    Explanation: A decision tree uses a set of questions to guide the user through a set of choices to arrive at a conclusion.

16. **Answer: C. The inability to specify the purpose and usage patterns**
    Explanation: The inability to define objective and usage patterns is a risk to be expected by developers when implementing a DSS.

17. **Answer: B. Decision trees**
    Explanation: A decision tree uses a set of questions to guide the user through a set of choices to arrive at a conclusion.

18. **Answer: C. It emphasizes flexibility in the user's approach to decision-making**
    Explanation: DSS puts emphasis on flexibility in the users' approach to decision-making. The characteristics of DSS are given as follows:
    - It supports decisions that are semi-organized or less organized.
    - It uses methods that include traditional data access and retrieval functions.
    - It is flexible and functional in terms of changing environments and the user's approach to decision making.

19. **Answer: A. A DSS**
    Explanation: A DSS is a semi-structured interactive decision-making framework. A DSS collects data from a variety of sources and gives managers useful information. A DSS supports semi-structured or less structured decisions. A DSS is flexible and user-friendly when it comes to changing environments and with regard to the user's approach to decision making. Executive support systems are more focused on strategic problems.

20. **Answer: B. The level of skills and experience contained in the knowledge base**
    Explanation: A primary issue for the IS auditor is the level of expertise or competence in the knowledge base, as errors in decision-making based on a lack of information may have a significant effect on the organization.

6

Information Systems Implementation

It is very important for an IS auditor to understand the implementation process of information systems. They need to determine, evaluate, and address various risks associated with the implementation process. Implementation is the process of ensuring that a system is operational. It involves either the creation of a new system from scratch or the migration of an old system to a new system.

The following topics will be covered in this chapter:

- Testing methodology
- System migration
- Post-implementation review

By the end of the chapter, you, as an IS auditor, will understand the concepts of information system implementation, and you will be given some assessment questions to test you.

Testing methodology

Testing is one of the critical elements of the **System Development Life Cycle (SDLC)**. The objective of testing is to ensure that the system is capable of providing its intended objective. For the CISA exam, we need to understand the following kinds of testing.

Unit testing

The following are some of the important aspects of unit tests:

- Unit tests include tests of each separate program or module.
- Testing is generally conducted by developers themselves. It is conducted as and when a program or module is ready and it does not need to wait until the completion of the entire system.
- Unit testing is done via a white box approach wherein internal program logic is tested.

Integrated testing

An integrated test examines the integration or connection between two or more system components. The purpose of the integration test is to validate accurate and correct information flow between the systems.

The following figure will help us to understand the difference between unit testing and integrated testing:

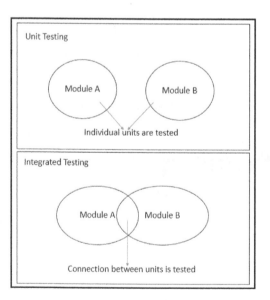

Thus in unit testing, between modules is tested.

System testing

System testing tests the entire system's capabilities. It covers end-to-end system specifications. It covers functionality tests, recoverability tests, security tests, load tests, volume tests, stress tests, and performance tests.

Final acceptance testing

Final acceptance testing consists of two tests, a **Quality Assurance Test (QAT)** and a **User Acceptance Test (UAT)**.

Regression testing

The meaning of regression is to return to an earlier stage.

The objective of a regression test is to confirm that a recent change has not introduced any new faults and other existing features are working correctly.

It must be ensured that the same data (which was used in earlier tests) is used for the regression test. This will help to confirm that there are no new errors or malfunctions.

Sociability test

Sociability is the quality of being able to merge with others:

- The objective of the sociability test is to ensure that the new system works as expected in the existing infrastructure without any adverse impact on other existing systems.
- The application works as expected in the specified environment where other applications run concurrently.

Pilot testing

A few characteristics of pilot testing are as follows:

- A pilot test is a small-scale preliminary study to understand and evaluate system functionality and other aspects.
- A pilot test is conducted for only a few units or a few locations to evaluate the feasibility.
- The objective of the pilot test is to determine the feasibility of the new system before full-fledged implementation.

Parallel testing

Parallel testing involves the testing of a new system and comparing the results of a new system with that of an old system. The objective of parallel testing is to ensure that the new system meets the requirements of the user.

White box testing

In white box testing, program logic is verified:

- To conduct a white box test, appropriate knowledge of the relevant programming language is a must.
- Unit testing usually entails white box testing.

Black box testing

In black box testing, the emphasis is on the functionality of the system:

- To conduct a black box test, knowledge of the relevant programming language is not mandatory.
- Black box testing is generally a feature of user acceptance tests and interface tests.

The following diagram helps us to understand white box testing and black box testing:

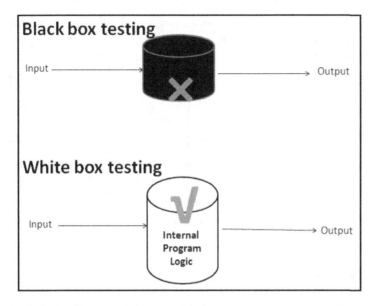

For white box testing, a tester is required to have sufficient knowledge about programming because they need to evaluate and test the program.

Alpha testing

Alpha testing is conducted by an internal user:

- Alpha testing is conducted before beta testing.
- Alpha testing may or may not include a full functionality test.

Beta testing

Beta testing is conducted by an external user:

- Beta testing is conducted after alpha testing.
- Beta testing is generally conducted to test the full functionality of the program.

Testing approach

Generally, there are two approaches for conducting a test: a bottom-up approach and a top-down approach. Let's look at the difference between them. The following figure explains the difference between the bottom-up and top-down approaches:

Bottom-up approach	Top-down approach
In a bottom-up approach, the test starts from a separate program or module and gradually, the complete system is tested.	In a top-down approach, the test starts at a broad system level and moves toward a separate program and modules.
• The benefit of a bottom-up approach is that the test can begin before the full system is completed. • Also, it has the advantage of early detection of faults in critical modules.	• The benefit of a top-down approach is the early detection of interface errors. • A top-down approach is more relevant for prototype-based system development.

Let's now have a look at various testing phases in the life cycle of system development.

Testing phases

Generally, in the system development life cycle, unit testing is conducted first. It is followed by integrated testing, system testing, and final acceptance testing.

The following diagram depicts the phases of software development testing:

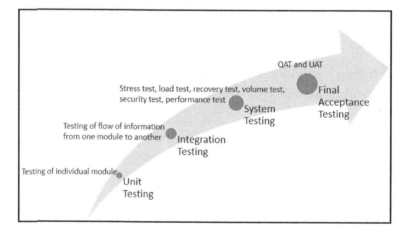

Generally, unit tests are the first tests. Unit tests are followed by integration tests, system tests, and the final acceptance test.

Let's now have a look at key aspects from the exam perspective.

Key aspects from the CISA exam perspective

The following table covers important aspects from the CISA exam perspective:

CISA questions	Possible answers
What is the testing that is performed at the final stage by users outside the development team – that is, external users?	Beta testing
What is the test in which the testing of architectural design is conducted?	Integration testing
What is the testing for linked and connected modules?	Integration testing
In which of the tests does failure in testing have the greatest impact?	Acceptance testing
What is the testing that is performed to determine the ability of a new system to operate in the existing environment without having an adverse impact on other systems?	Sociability testing
What is top-down testing approach?	Major functions are tested earlier and also ensures that interface errors are detected early
What is bottom-up testing approach?	Starts with individual modules and programs and gradually covers the full system
What is the most suitable approach for prototype-based development?	The top-down approach
What is the advantage of white box testing?	Determines the accuracy of program logics
What is the best approach for unit testing?	White box testing
What is the testing that is performed to evaluate the performance of the system during normal and peak conditions?	Load testing
What is an effective method for conducting stress test?	Use of live data in a test environment: • Test data should be designed as per the live workload for accurate test results • In any given scenario, test environment should always be used (that is, test should not be conducted in a live/production environment).
What is the most important factor for test data selection?	Data must be designed as per expected live processing
What is the objective of a system test?	To evaluate full system functionality
What is the objective of a parallel test?	To validate device functionality with user specifications
What kind of data be used while conducting regression test?	Same data set of previous tests

Let's now have a look at some self-assessment questions.

Self-assessment questions

1. **A test that is conducted when a system is in the development phase is:**
   - A. A sociability test
   - B. A functionality test
   - C. A load test
   - D. A unit test

2. **The approach to unit testing is:**
   - A. Top-down
   - B. Black box
   - C. Bottom-up
   - D. White box

3. **Testing the network between two or more systems for accurate data flow is:**
   - A. Stress testing
   - B. Interface testing
   - C. Functionality test
   - D. Security testing

4. **In some instances, system interface failures occur when corrections are re-submitted to previously observed errors. This might indicate the absence of which of the following kinds of testing?**
   - A. Stress testing
   - B. Integration testing
   - C. Unit testing
   - D. Security testing

5. **Unit testing shows that individual modules function correctly. The IS auditor should:**
   - A. Conclude that the system as a whole can produce the results stated
   - B. Report the test result as a symbol of the functionality of the program
   - C. Review integrated test findings
   - D. Carry out the test again to validate the results

6. **The purpose of regression testing is to decide whether:**
   A. A new or modified system will operate without having an impact on the existing system
   B. The flow of data between two or more systems is accurate and correct
   C. It meets new requirements
   D. No new errors were introduced within the unchanged code

7. **Which of the following data elements should be used while conducting a regression test?**
   A. The same dataset as previous tests
   B. Randomly generated data
   C. A completely different dataset from the previous tests
   D. Data produced by a test generator

8. **The test that verifies that changes in Windows Registry have not adversely affected the performance of any other features is:**
   A. Regression testing
   B. Unit testing
   C. Integrated testing
   D. Sociability testing

9. **Which of the following type of test would be relevant when an organization needs to determine whether a replacement or modified system is capable of functioning in its target environment without affecting other existing systems?**
   A. Regression testing
   B. Sociability testing
   C. Interface/integration testing
   D. Pilot testing

10. **What feature of white box testing differentiates it from black box testing?**
    A. Testing is conducted by an IS auditor
    B. Testing includes the verification of internal program logic
    C. Testing is conducted via a bottom-up approach
    D. Testing does not include verification of internal program logic

11. **Which of the following is the PRIMARY purpose of conducting parallel testing?**
    A. To determine the budget versus the actual cost
    B. To record the functionalities of the program
    C. To highlight errors in the program logic
    D. To validate device functionality with user specifications

12. **An advantage of using a bottom-up approach as opposed to a top-down approach is:**
    A. Errors can be found early on in critical modules
    B. Testing will only take place after all the systems have been completed
    C. Interface errors can be noticed early
    D. Confidence is earlier achieved in the method

13. **Which of the following is the greatest concern about acceptance testing?**
    A. The objective of the test is not documented
    B. The result of the test is not documented
    C. Test data is not reviewed
    D. There may be major unsolved issues

14. **An unsuccessful result of which of the following tests has a major impact on budgeted time and cost?**
    A. Load testing
    B. Interface testing
    C. Parallel testing
    D. Acceptance testing

15. **Which of the following is the main objective for conducting a system test?**
    A. To determine security controls
    B. To document the system's functionality
    C. To evaluate the functioning of the system
    D. To determine the cost of the system versus the approved budget

16. **An IS auditor noted a system vulnerability. To address all the undetected vulnerabilities, which of the following tests is recommended?**
    A. Integration testing
    B. Stress testing
    C. System testing
    D. Security testing

17. **For prototype-based system development, the most effective test approach is:**
    A. Bottom-up
    B. Load
    C. Stress
    D. Top-down

18. **The most effective method for conducting stress tests is:**
    A. Using test data within the test environment
    B. Using live data within the production environment
    C. Using live data within the test environment
    D. Using test data within the production environment

19. **The greatest risk in a combined QAT and UAT during the final acceptance test is:**
    A. High cost of the test
    B. Insufficient documentation
    C. Insufficient functional testing
    D. The report may be delayed

20. **The most important factor for test data selection is:**
    A. The extent and size of the data
    B. Data designed as per expected live processing
    C. Random data selection
    D. Different data for each test

System migration

A system migration is the process of transferring IT resources (mostly data) to a new hardware or software platform with the purpose of gaining better business value.

IS auditors should ensure the following aspects for efficient, effective, and accurate system and data migration:

- Processes should be in place to preserve the format, coding, structure, and integrity of data to be migrated.
- Processes should be in place to test the migrated data for its integrity and completeness.
- Data conversion processes must have audit trails and logs to verify the accuracy and completeness of the converted data.

The migration process should ensure the following:

- There is no disruption of routine operations.
- There is appropriate security control over data, ensuring confidentiality, integrity, and availability.

The migration process should also ensure the availability of fall-back arrangements. Tools and applications should be available to reverse the migration if there is an error.

The last copy of the old data and the first copy of the converted data should be archived for future reference.

Changeover is the process of shifting to a new system and stopping the use of the old systems. It is also known as the go live technique or the cutover technique. In the next sections, we look at some of the ways to change over to a new system.

Parallel changeover

In this method, the new and old systems are operated in parallel for some time. Once the users are confident about the new system, the old system may be discontinued. This helps to minimize the risk of consequences of defects in the new system. A major challenge in this method is the requirement of more resources to maintain both systems.

It provides assurance that the new system meets the requirements before the old system is discontinued.

Parallel changeover provides the greatest redundancy.

Phased changeover

In this method, changes are implemented in a phased manner. The system is broken into different phases. Each old phase is gradually replaced by a new phase. This changeover from the old system to the new system takes effect in a pre-planned phased manner.

Abrupt changeover

In this method, a new system is implemented from a cut-off date and the old system is completely discontinued once the new system is implemented. This process is also known as direct cutover. This is considered the riskiest approach with no scope for rollback if the new system fails.

It is very important to obtain sign-off from a user department before changeover. It is the user department who should assume the ownership of the project and should provide sign-off for completion and implementation of the system with regard to the agreed deliverables.

Key aspects from the CISA exam perspective

The following table covers important aspects from the CISA exam perspective:

CISA questions	Possible answers
What is the benefit of parallel cutover?	Assurance that the new system is working as required before the old system is discarded
Which system migration method is the riskiest?	Direct cutover, or abrupt cutover
Which system migration method has the greatest redundancy?	Parallel changeover
Who is responsible for signing off on the accuracy and completeness of the data migration to the new system?	Data owner/user
What is the greatest concern about direct cutover?	Lack of backup plan

Self-assessment questions

1. **Who should approve the completion and implementation of a new system application?**
   - A. Board members
   - B. User management
   - C. Quality assurance team
   - D. Project steering committee

2. **The greatest advantage of a parallel changeover is:**
   - A. It provides significant cost savings
   - B. It provides assurance that the new system meets the requirements before the old system is discontinued
   - C. It provides hands-on training to employees for using the new system before the old system is discontinued
   - D. It provides the opportunity to integrate the new and old systems

3. **Which of the following is the prime objective of parallel testing?**
   - A. To determine the cost effectiveness of the system
   - B. To ensure the new system meets the user requirements
   - C. To enhance the system's capabilities
   - D. To evaluate the results of unit testing

4. **Which of the following is the greatest risk in system migration procedures?**
    A. The new system will be rolled out in a phased manner
    B. A quality plan is not available for system migration
    C. Users are involved in acceptance testing
    D. Using the prototyping approach to confirm user requirement

5. **Which of the following is the greatest concern for a system migration project?**
    A. A planned migration window is too short for completing all tasks
    B. An abrupt changeover is planned, immediately disposing of the legacy system
    C. Employees have been handed over to the new system without adequate training
    D. Printing functionality of the new system is tested after the changeover

6. **To determine the functionality of the new system without adversely affecting other existing systems, the most appropriate test is a:**
    A. Unit test
    B. Pilot test
    C. Sociability test
    D. Integration test

7. **Which of the following changeovers comes with the greatest risk?**
    A. Parallel
    B. Pilot
    C. Phased
    D. Direct cutover

8. **Which of the following changes has the greatest redundancy?**
    A. Parallel
    B. Pilot
    C. Phased
    D. Direct cutover

9. **Who has the prime responsibility for signing off on the accuracy and completeness of the data migration of a new system?**
    A. Steering committee
    B. IS auditor
    C. Data owner
    D. Project manager

10. **Which of the following is the greatest concern for an immediate cutover to the new system?**
     A. The lack of a backup plan
     B. User acceptance testing has not been properly documented
     C. The project deadline is extended
     D. Users are not trained properly to use the new system

Post-implementation review

A post-implementation review is the process of determining and evaluating the performance of the system against the requirement and objective defined in the business case. The post-implementation review is conducted once the project is implemented and completed. These are the objectives of conducting a post-implementation review:

- To determine the extent to which a project met its objectives and addressed the originally defined requirements
- To determine the cost-benefit analysis and return on investment
- To determine the lessons learned from the project to improve future projects

The project development team and business users should jointly conduct a post-implementation review. From the IS audit perspective, the post-implementation review is conducted to determine the adequacy and effectiveness of the system. The IS auditors' prime focus is to determine the controls built into the new system.

Key aspects from the CISA exam perspective

The following table covers the important aspects from the CISA exam perspective:

CISA questions	Possible answers
What is the objective of the post-implementation review?	• To determine the extent to which the project met its objective and addressed the originally defined requirements • To conduct a cost-benefit analysis and work out the return on investment • To determine the lessons learned from this project for the improvement of future projects
What should be the area of focus of the IS auditor during the post-implementation review?	To determine the adequacy and effectiveness of the security controls

Self-assessment questions

1. **The post-implementation review includes:**
   A. Interface testing
   B. An analysis of the return on investment
   C. A review of the audit trails
   D. A review of enterprise architecture diagrams

2. **The IS auditor's primary focus during the post-implementation review is:**
   A. To determine appropriate documentation of user feedback
   B. To determine whether the return on investment is being measured
   C. To determine the operating effectiveness of the controls built into the system
   D. To review change management procedures

3. **An IS auditor is conducting a post-implementation review of an ERM system. They are most likely to review:**
   A. Access control settings
   B. The procedure for unit testing
   C. The procedure for system testing
   D. Detailed design documentation

4. **A post-implementation review should cover:**
   A. An assessment of the downtime risk
   B. The lessons learned in order to improve future projects
   C. A verification of the controls built into the system
   D. The deletion of test data

5. **A post-implementation review is conducted primarily to:**
   A. Ensure that the project meets the intended business requirements
   B. Determine the adequacy of information security
   C. Determine the project's compliance with regulatory requirements
   D. Evaluate the project's expenses against the budget

6. **Which of the following is the main objective of a post-implementation review?**
   A. Documentation of lessons learned
   B. Identification of future enhancements
   C. To determine timely delivery of the project
   D. To determine whether the project objectives have been met

Summary

In this chapter, we discussed various testing methodologies, different approaches to system migration and cutover techniques, and the objectives of post-implementation reviews. We also discussed how to conduct post-implementation reviews of systems to determine whether project deliverables, controls, and requirements have been met.

A system migration is the process of transferring IT resources (mostly data) to a new hardware or a software platform with the objective of gaining better business value.

Changeover is the process of shifting to a new system and stopping using old systems. It is also known as the go live technique or the cutover technique. Parallel changeover, phased changeover, and abrupt changeover are some of ways to change to a new system.

A post-implementation review is conducted to determine the extent to which the project met its objectives and addressed the originally defined requirements, perform a cost-benefit analysis, determine the return on investment, and determine lessons learned from the project for the improvement of future projects.

In the next chapter, we will discuss various aspects of information system operations, such as technology components, asset management, incident management, and database management.

Assessments

Here you will find the answers to assessment questions.

Testing methodology

1. **Answer: D. A unit test**
   Explanation: Unit tests include tests of each separate program or module. Testing is generally conducted by developers themselves. They are conducted as and when a program or module is ready, and it is not necessary to wait until the entire system is completed. Unit testing is done through a white box approach wherein internal program logic is tested.

2. **Answer: D. White box**
   Explanation: In white box testing, program logic is verified. To conduct white box testing, appropriate knowledge of programming language is a must. White box testing is generally conducted during unit testing.

3. **Answer: B. Interface testing**
   Explanation: Integration testing comprises a test of the integration of or connection between two or more system components. The purpose of the integration test is to validate the accurate and correct information flow between the systems.

4. **Answer: B. Integration testing**
   Explanation: Integration testing is performed to ensure correct and accurate data flow between two or more systems. Integration testing aims to ensure the accuracy of the device interface's most critical components. To evaluate the results, pilot testing takes place first at a single location.

5. **Answer: C. Review integrated test findings**
   Explanation: After the unit test, the next phase is the interface or integration test. Integration testing tests the integration of or connection between two or more system components. The purpose of the integration test is to validate the accurate and correct information flow between the systems.

6. **Answer: D. No new errors were introduced within the unchanged code.**
   Explanation: Regression testing is performed to ensure no errors have been introduced in improvements or corrections. Sociability testing is performed to ensure the new or changed system will operate without affecting the existing system.

7. **Answer: A. The same dataset as previous tests**
   Explanation: The objective of a regression test is to confirm that a recent change has not introduced any new faults and other existing features are working correctly.
   It must be ensured that the same data that was used in earlier tests is used for the regression test. This will help to confirm that there are no new errors or malfunctions.

8. **Answer: D. Sociability testing**
   Explanation: Sociability is the quality of being able to merge with others. The objective of sociability testing is to ensure that the new system works as expected in the existing infrastructure without any adverse impact on other existing systems.

9. **Answer: B. Sociability testing**
   Explanation: Sociability is the quality of being able to merge with others. The objective of sociability testing is to ensure that the new system works as expected in existing infrastructure without any adverse impact on other existing systems.

10. **Answer: B. Testing includes the verification of internal program logic**
Explanation: In white box testing, the program logic is verified. To conduct white box testing, appropriate knowledge of relevant programming language is a must. White box testing is generally conducted during unit testing. In black box testing, the emphasis is on the functionality of the system. To conduct black box testing, knowledge of relevant programming language is not mandatory.

11. **Answer: D. To validate device functionality with user specifications**
Explanation: Parallel testing involves the testing of a new system and comparing the results of the new system with that of the old system. The objective of parallel testing is to ensure that the new system meets the requirements of the user.

12. **Answer: Errors can be found early on in critical modules.**
Explanation: In the bottom-up approach, the test starts from an individual program or module and gradually the entire system is tested. One benefit of the bottom-up approach is that tests can begin before the full system is completed. Also, it has the advantage that it can detect faults in critical modules early. In the top-down approach, the test starts at the broad system-level and moves toward individual programs and modules. One benefit of the top-down approach is the early detection of interface errors. The top-down approach is best suited for prototype-based system development.

13. **Answer: D. There may be major unsolved issues.**
Explanation: The main concern will be major issues that have not yet been addressed. The other options are not as critical as major unsolved issues.

14. **Answer: D. Acceptance testing**
Explanation: Generally, in a system development life cycle, unit testing is conducted first. It is followed by integrated testing, system testing, and final acceptance testing. Acceptance tests include QAT and UAT. It is usually the final step before implementation of the system. If the acceptance test indicates a system failure, then this may lead to major schedule delays and cost overruns. The effect of failure in other tests, such as unit, interface, and system tests, is less than with acceptance testing.

15. **Answer: C. To evaluate the functioning of the system**
Explanation: System testing tests the complete and full system capabilities. It covers end-to-end system specifications. It covers functionality test, recoverability test, security test, load test, volume test, stress test and performance test. Objective of the system test is to evaluate the reliability of the complete software.

16. **Answer: C. System testing**
    Explanation: System testing tests the entire system's capabilities. It covers end-to-end system specifications. It covers functionality tests, recoverability tests, security tests, load tests, volume tests, stress tests, and performance tests. The objective of the system test is to evaluate the reliability of the entire software.

17. **Answer: D. Top-down**
    Explanation: In the top-down approach, the test starts at the broad system level and moves toward separate programs and modules. One benefit of the top-down approach is early detection of interface errors. The top-down approach is best suited for prototype-based system development. A prototype is a sample model of an actual system to be implemented. The objective of the prototype is to create major functionality such as system screens and in a short period of time. The top-down design approach is most successful for the development of prototypes.

18. **Answer: C. Using live data within the test environment**
    Explanation: It is always advisable to use live data in a test environment. Test data should be designed so that it is as similar as possible to the live workload for accurate test results. In any given scenario, the test environment should always be used (that is, tests should not be conducted in a live/production environment).

19. **Answer: C. Insufficient functional testing**
    Explanation: The greatest risk in a combined QAT and UAT during the final acceptance test is insufficient functional testing. Combining the tests may result in skipping some of the functional requirements. Other options are not as significant as insufficient functional tests.

20. **Answer: B. Data designed as per expected live processing.**
    Explanation: It is always advisable to use live data in a test environment. Test data should be designed to be as similar as possible to the live workload for accurate test results. This will provide accurate test results.

System migration

1. **Answer: B. User management**
   Explanation: It is the user management that assumes ownership of the project and should provide sign-off for completion and implementation of the system with regard to the agreed deliverables.

2. **Answer: B. It provides assurance that the new system meets the requirements before the old system is discontinued.**
Explanation: In a parallel changeover, the new and the old systems are operated in parallel for some time. This helps to minimize the risk of consequences of defects in the new system.

3. **Answer: B. To ensure the new system meets the user requirements**
Explanation: The objective of parallel testing is to ensure that user requirements are met. Parallel testing involves comparing the results of the new system with the old system to determine the correct processing of the new system.

4. **Answer: B. A quality plan is not available for system migration**
Explanation: It is very important to have a quality plan for any project. Quality plans should be comprehensive and should address the issue of data integrity during migration. Other options cannot be considered risks.

5. **Answer: B. An abrupt changeover is planned, immediately disposing of the legacy system**
Explanation: Changeover should be phased or parallel to address the risk of implementing a new system. Disposing of the old system will complicate the fall-back strategy. Abrupt changeover has its own risks and consequences. Other options are not as significant as abrupt changeover without a backup plan.

6. **Answer: C. Sociability test**
Explanation: The objective of the sociability test is to determine whether a new system can operate effectively without adversely affecting other existing systems. Integration tests verify the connection and information between two or more systems. Pilot testing consists of testing in different phases, that is, first at one location and then extended to other locations. Unit testing is the test of individual functions, modules, or units.

7. **Answer: D. Direct cutover**
Explanation: In direct cutover, a new system is implemented from a cut-off date and the old system is completely discontinued once the new system is implemented. This process is also known as abrupt changeover. This is considered the riskiest approach as there is no scope for rollback if the new system fails.

8. **Answer: A. Parallel**
Explanation: In this method, the new and old systems are operated in parallel for some time. Once the users are confident about the new system, the old system may be discontinued. This helps to minimize the risk of consequences of defects in the new system. The main challenge in this method is the requirement of more resources to maintain both systems. It provides assurance that the new system meets the requirements before the old system is discontinued. Parallel changeover provides greatest redundancy.

9. **Answer: C. Data owner**
   Explanation: The data owner assumes the responsibility for reviewing the completeness and accuracy of data migration and provides sign-off for it.

10. **Answer: A. The lack of a backup plan**
    Explanation: In an immediate cutover scenario, the absence of a backup plan is a major concern as it takes considerable time, effort, and cost to restore the old systems. It is advisable to have a parallel or phased changeover strategy. Other options are not as critical as the lack of backup plan.

Post-implementation review

1. **Answer: B. An analysis of the return on investment**
   Explanation: One of the purposes of conducting a post-implementation review is to do a cost-benefit analysis and check the return on investment to determine that the original business case requirements are met.

2. **Answer: C. To determine the operating effectiveness of the controls built into the system**
   Explanation: From the IS audit perspective, an IS auditor's prime focus should be on determining the adequacy and effectiveness of the controls built into the system. Other options are important but a more significant area of focus should be the effectiveness of the controls built into the system.

3. **Answer: A. Access control settings**
   Explanation: An IS auditor is most likely to review whether security parameters have been appropriately mapped in the new system. One of the parameters is to review access control configuration. The post-implementation review is done after user acceptance testing. User acceptance testing already covers other aspects such as unit testing, system testing, and design documentation. Hence, the auditor may not like going into the details of unit testing, system testing, or design documentation.

4. **Answer: B. The lessons learned in order to improve future projects**
   Explanation: One of the reasons for conducting a post-implementation review is to identify the lessons learned and use them to improve future projects.

5. **Answer: A. Ensure that the project meets the intended business requirements**
   Explanation: A post-implementation review is conducted primarily to ensure that the project is implemented in accordance with the business requirements. The other options are not the primary objective.

6. **Answer: D. To determine whether the project objectives have been met**
   Explanation: The main objective of performing a post-implementation review is to determine the project's overall success and its impact on the business. If the project's objectives have been successfully achieved, it indicates success of the project. Although the other options are important, it is more important to determine whether the project's objectives have been met.

4

Section 4: Information System Operations and Business Resilience

This part contains 23 percent of the CISA exam, approximately 34 questions.

This section contains the following chapters:

Information System Operations

7

The objective of a well-managed information system is to ensure the effectiveness and efficiency of IT processes and procedures through the optimal use of information system assets.

The following topics will be covered in the chapter:

- Common technology components
- IT asset management
- Job scheduling
- End user computing
- System performance management
- Problem and incident management
- Change management, configuration management, and patch management
- IT service level agreements
- Database management

Let's have a detailed look at each of these topics.

Understanding common technology components

The following are some of the important technologies that a CISA aspirant should understand:

- The types of server
- **Universal Serial Bus (USB)**
- **Radio frequency identification (RFID)**

Let's understand each of these in detail.

The types of server

From the perspective of the CISA exam, it is important that you understand the basic workings of the following servers:

- **Print server**: For multiple users, a network printer is configured. Printing materials are captured in the print server and sent to the printer in a queue.
- **File server**: Document repositories can be centralized with the help of a file server. It should be controlled with access restrictions. The file server makes group collaboration and document management easy.
- **Application or program server**: An application server hosts software programs. It also includes application business logic and communication with the application's database.
- **Web server**: A web server provides information and services through web pages. They are accessed through their URLs.
- **Proxy server**: A proxy service provides a connection between users and resources. It prevents direct access to the network and other resources.
- **Database server**: A database server stores data and information. It acts as a repository. Data is used by application servers and web servers for processing.

USB

A USB is a device that can be connected to different peripherals through a single standardized interface socket. It improves plug-and-play capabilities and can be connected or disconnected without rebooting the computer. Examples of the use of USBs include memory sticks, **secure digital (SD)** cards, and flash drives.

USBs – Risks

The following are some of the risks related to USBs:

- There is a risk of malware being transmitted during data transfer. It is advisable to use USB drives in read-only mode when transferring files from unknown sources. This will prevent the installation of software to the machine.
- There is a risk of data theft. It is advisable to disable the ports of machines as much as possible.

- There is a risk of sensitive data that's stored on USB drives being lost or stolen. It is advisable to encrypt the contents of USB drives to prevent unauthorized access to it.
- There is a risk of data corruption when a USB device is removed improperly from a machine.

USBs – Security controls

The following are some of the important controls that can be used to reduce the risks related to the use of USB drives:

- Encryption is a very important security control to prevent unauthorized data access in the case of loss or theft of USB drives. A system should be enabled to access only encrypted devices.
- Hardening a system through centralized management is very important. It is advisable to disable all the USB ports for all the users. Approval for an active USB port should be provided on a need-to-know basis.
- The physical movement of USBs should be restricted. Security personnel should be aware of USB drives and the risks related to them.
- Anti-virus should be enabled to automatically scan all removable media.
- It is advisable to stick information such as contact details to USB drives, which can help in device retrieval if devices are lost. However, details about the company or data should not be disclosed in these details. Legal disclaimers about data usage may help to some extent.

RFID

RFID is used to identify and locate assets within a limited radius. It uses radio waves to identify tagged objects. A tag includes a microchip and an antenna. The microchip in a tag is used to store the information and the antenna is used to transmit information to an RFID reader.

RFID – Applications

The following are some of the applications of RFID:

- RFID is widely used in asset management. RFID can manage any assets that can be tagged. RFID helps in enabling smoother asset management as compared to paper-based or barcode-based systems.
- RFID helps to identify and locate any asset or inventory that is tagged.
- RFID helps to match and reconcile two tagged items. A trigger is generated in the case of an incorrect match.
- RFID helps in enabling more effective and efficient business processes. It eliminates the need for manual processes.
- Through RFID, access control can be managed more effectively. It automatically checks whether an individual is authorized to physically access a facility.
- RFID helps in supply chain management by way of asset management, proper tracking, controlling movement, and updating payment systems.

RFID – Risks

The following are some of the risks associated with RFID:

- Unauthorized access to RFID-generated information may harm the business of the organization.
- There is a risk of non-adherence to regulations, if the RFID system uses personal information without the appropriate consent of the customer.
- Any attacks on RFID systems may impact business processes adversely.

RFID – Security controls

The following are some of the security controls for RFID:

- Implementing physical and logical security controls for access to RFID systems and RFID-generated data. Access should be provided on a need-to-know basis.
- Implementing technical controls such as encrypting data on tag and wireless communication, enabling tags to self-destruct on some events, and so on.
- Ensuring management oversight for RFID systems and processes.
- Existing policies being updated to address risks and control RFID systems and processes.

Self-assessment questions

1. **Which of the following risks is applicable to active RFID?**
   A. The risk of social engineering
   B. The risk of phishing
   C. The risk of eavesdropping
   D. The risk of malicious code

2. **Which of the following reports should an IS auditor verify to determine compliance with the uptime requirement defined in the SLA?**
   A. The availability report
   B. The utilization report
   C. The hardware error report
   D. The asset management report

3. **Which of the following is of great help when determining the efficiency of preventive maintenance programs?**
   A. The system downtime report
   B. The service provider's report
   C. The maintenance log
   D. The preventive maintenance schedule

4. **Which of the following activities should not be conducted during peak production hours to avoid unexpected downtime?**
   A. Data migration
   B. Tape back-up
   C. Preventive maintenance
   D. Configuration of the standby router

5. **Which is these is the best method of determining the availability of updated security patches for critical servers?**
   A. Verify the patch update process
   B. Manually verify each critical server
   C. Review the change management log
   D. An automated tool to verify the availability of updated patches

IT asset management

IT assets include systems, data, networking components, and IT-related processes and procedures. An IS auditor should be able to determine and evaluate how effectively and efficiently IT assets are managed and controlled. The following are some of the important concepts of IT asset management:

- IT assets include people, information, infrastructure, and reputation.
- The first step in IT asset management is to identify and create an inventory of IT assets.
- The inventory of an IT asset should include details such as the following:
    - Owner
    - Custodian
    - Asset identification
    - Location
    - Security classification
- IT asset management is a very important element in designing and developing an effective security strategy.
- IT asset management includes both hardware and software.
- The IT department should have a list of approved software that can be installed and used. The installation of unapproved software is a serious violation that carries major legal, financial, and security risks. Processes should be in place to ensure that only standard approved software is installed.
- The synchronization of production source code and objects can be best controlled by date-and-time stamping source and object code. Date-and-time stamping helps here to ensure that both the source and the object code are in sync.
- The first step of the implementation of an access control rule is creating a list of IT assets as an inventory. This is followed by categorization and grouping.

Self-assessment questions

1. **The synchronization of production source code and object code is best controlled by which of the following?**
    A. Comparing version releases of source code and object code
    B. Restricting any changes to source code
    C. Restricting any access to source code and object code
    D. Date-and-time stamping for source and object code

2. **What is the first step after the replacement of hardware?**
    A. Sync the hardware with the hot site
    B. Updating the IT asset inventory
    C. Identify and assess the vulnerability
    D. Conduct risk assessment

3. **What is the first step in the implementation of access control?**
    A. Group IT assets
    B. Categorize IT assets
    C. Implement an access control list
    D. Creating an inventory of IT assets

4. **What is the first step in developing a risk management program?**
    A. Assess vulnerability
    B. Assess control
    C. The identification of assets
    D. Map risk owners

5. **Which of the following is the major concern for an IS auditor reviewing desktop software compliance?**
    A. Installed software not being updated in IT department records
    B. Users not being trained in the usage of the software
    C. The installed software not being approved
    D. The license renewal process not being centralized

Job scheduling

A job schedule is a program that is used to run various processes automatically. Apart from scheduling batch jobs, it is also used to automate tape backups and other maintenance. While scheduling jobs, it is important to give optimum resource availability to high-priority jobs. As far as possible, maintenance functions should be performed during non-peak times.

The following are some of the advantages of using job scheduling software:

- It reduces the probability of error as manual intervention is eliminated.
- Increases the availability of records for job executions thereby making it easier to take subsequent action on failure reports effectively.
- It provides a more secure environment as compared to manual processes.

An IS auditor should consider the following aspects while reviewing the job scheduling process.

- Whether procedures for collecting and reporting key performance indicators are defined and implemented
- Whether the priority of each job has been identified and scheduled correctly
- Whether an audit trail is captured for each job
- Whether job completion status is monitored and appropriate action is taken on failed jobs
- Whether approval roles are defined for scheduling, changing, or prioritizing jobs

Self-assessment questions

1. **Which of the following is a major concern for an auditor reviewing the job scheduling process?**
    - A. High instances of emergency changes
    - B. A few jobs not having completed on time
    - C. A few jobs having been overridden by the operator
    - D. A job failure analysis being done by the IT manager

2. **Which of the following is the best compensating control for tape management system where some parameters are set to bypass or ignore tape header records?**
    - A. A review of logs
    - B. Staging and job setup
    - C. A full back-up of tapes
    - D. Storage of tapes at an offsite location

3. **Which of the following is most important for an IS audit reviewing the preventive maintenance activity processes of a data center by a third-party service provider?**
    - A. Background verification of service personnel
    - B. Escorting service personnel during maintenance activities
    - C. Maintenance activities being conducted during non-peak hours
    - D. A review of maintenance activities by the IT manager

End user computing

Here we will look at some of the important aspects of end user computing.

End user computing refers to a system wherein a non-programmer can create their own application. Various products are available to aid end users in designing and implementing systems according to their requirements without the help of programmers. From a user perspective, end user computing is a quick way to build and deploy applications without relying on an IT department. These applications are generally flexible and have the ability to quickly address any new requirements or modifications.

This also reduces pressure on the IT department, who can concentrate on more critical and complex applications.

The following are some of the inherent risks of end computing:

- Applications, so developed, may not be subject to various tests and therefore carry a risk to information security in terms of data integrity, confidentiality, and availability.
- Users may not adhere to change management and release management procedures.
- System controls in terms of authorization, authentication, audit trails and logs, encryption, and non-repudiation may not be given due importance.
- An appropriate redundancy and backup arrangement may not be addressed for business continuity.

To address the preceding risks, a documented policy of **End User Computing (EUC)** should be available. Also, the auditor should ensure that an inventory of all such applications exists and that sensitive and critical applications are subject to the appropriate controls.

Self-assessment question

1. **Which of the following is the greatest concern for an IS auditor reviewing the end user computing process?**
    A. The lack of a documented end user computing policy
    B. The lack of training for the end user
    C. No involvement of the IT department in the development of applications
    D. Applications not being subject to audit

System performance management

It is important to understand the system architecture and features of each function that supports and manages a system's performance. In this section, we will discuss some of the prominent functions.

Nucleus (kernel) functions

The nucleus is responsible for basic processes associated with the operating system. It manages process creation, interrupt handling support for input and output process, allocation, the release of memory, and so on. The nucleus is a highly sensitive area where access is restricted to only authorized users. Above the nucleus are other operating system processes to support users. These processes are known as system software. System software ensures the integrity of a system and controls the system interfaces. Examples of system software include access control software, tape and disk management software, job scheduling software, and more.

Utility programs

Utility programs help to manage and control computer resources. These programs support the operating system. Examples include disk tools, backup software, and data dictionaries. Many of these programs can function by bypassing the security system and function without producing an audit trail. It is very important to restrict and control the activities of utility programs.

Parameter setting for the operating system

Parameter setting is an important factor that determines how a system will function. Software control parameters handle data management, resource management, job management, and priority setting. A review of parameter setting is the most effective method to determine the functioning of controls within an operating system.

Registry

System settings and parameters are set in configuration files known as a registry. Control of the registry is an important aspect of IS auditing. Protecting the registry is important for ensuring the integrity, confidentiality, and availability of systems.

Activity logging

It is very important to log activities for future analysis. Also, these logs should be appropriately protected as an intruder may attempt to alter logs to hide their activities. The best way to protect logs is to capture them in a centralized secure server using **security information and event management (SIEM)** software.

Software licensing issues

An IS auditor should ensure that software copyright laws are followed by the organization. Any violation may lead to regulatory consequences, reputational loss, and financial loss by way of penalties.

Even if an organization is using open source software, it is bound to abide by the terms and conditions of it usage.

The best way to determine the use of unauthorized software is to scan the entire network using automated tools and capture a list of installed software. Then, review that list by comparing it with the approved software list.

Some free software licensing types are as follows:

Type	Description
Open source	This software can be listed, modified and redistributed as required. However, this should be done in accordance with terms and conditions mentioned in the software license.
Freeware	Software is free but source code cannot be redistributed. For example: Adobe Reader.
Shareware	Some softwares are available for free for some trial period and has limited functionality as compared to the full version.

An organization is bound to abide by the terms and conditions of the usage of all software. Let's now have a look at source code management.

Source code management

Source code is a computer program that is created by a programmer. It is human-readable code. Humans can read and understand source code. Source code is converted into object code by assemblers and compilers. Computers are able to understand object code but not source code. If an application is developed by a third-party vendor, it is essential to have access to the source code. If the source code is not supplied, it is important to arrange for escrow agreement. Access to the source code should be restricted. Any update to the source code should be managed by using a **version control system** (**VCS**). Also, appropriate backups of source code should be maintained.

Capacity management

Capacity management is the process of planning and monitoring IT resources for their effective and efficient utilization. It ensures the smooth expansion or reduction of resources as per business requirements. It is necessary to obtain inputs from business users in order to manage capacity. Capacity management should be reviewed and updated on at least an annual basis.

The following are the advantages of capacity management:

- It ensures the availability of required resources at the optimal price.
- It aligns IT resources as per the requirements of the business.
- It reduces the risk of performance problems or failure through the constant monitoring of utilization thresholds.

Key aspects from a CISA exam perspective

The following table covers the important aspects from a CISA exam perspective:

CISA questions	Possible answers
What is the major concern about use of open source software?	Non adherence to terms and conditions for use of open source software
Best audit process to determine use of unlicensed software	Use of automated tools
Most important factor to examine security configuration of an operating system	Review of parameter setting

Self-assessment questions

1. **An auditor sees certain indications that an organization is using unlicensed software. What should be the auditor's first step?**
   A. Report the indications in the audit report
   B. Verifying the software through testing
   C. Discuss the issue with auditee management
   D. Recommend the immediate uninstallation of the software

2. **Which of the following is the greatest concern for the use of open source software?**
   A. No payment is made to acquire open source software.
   B. An organization must comply with open source software license terms.
   C. Open source software is vulnerable.
   D. Open source software is not reliable.

3. **How can the optimal configuration of a server be ensured?**
   A. Benchmarking with industry standards
   B. Log capturing
   C. Server utilization reports
   D. Network protocol reports

4. **An IS auditor notes that some users have installed personal software on their PCs. There is no restriction by security policy. What is the best recommendation for the auditor to make?**
   A. Implement necessary controls to restrict the installation of unauthorized software
   B. To include a clause related to the restriction of unauthorized software in the security policy
   C. Restrict the downloading of unauthorized software
   D. Allow users to install software only after IT manager approval

5. **Which of the following is the most important consideration when reviewing a hardware maintenance program?**
   A. The schedule is maintained
   B. Approval for the steering committee
   C. The maintenance program covers vendor-provided specification
   D. Reports are submitted to the vendor

6. **Which of the following is most useful for examining the security configuration of an operating system?**
    A. Reviewing transaction logs
    B. Reviewing parameter settings
    C. Reviewing network encryption settings
    D. Reviewing firewall settings

7. **An IS auditor notes that storage resources are continuously added. What should they review?**
    A. The adequacy of offsite storage
    B. The capacity management process
    C. The data compression process
    D. The incident management process

8. **An IS auditor notes that it takes a significant amount of time to log on to the system during peak business hours as compared to other times. What should the recommendation of the auditor be?**
    A. Improve the network bandwidth
    B. Increase the number of PCs
    C. To establish performance measurement criteria
    D. Increase the number of users

Problem and incident management

As a CISA aspirant, you must be aware of the ways in which you can manage problems and incidents. Here are some of the most important concepts regarding this topic:

- The objective of problem management is to prevent the recurrence of an incident by identifying the root cause of the incident and taking appropriate preventive action.
- The elements of problem management are investigation, in-depth analysis, root cause analysis, and addressing the issues identified during the root cause analysis.
- Some widely accepted methodologies include fishbone analysis, Ishikawa cause and effect diagrams, 5 whys, and brainstorming. To prevent the reoccurrence of an incident, it is important to conduct a root cause analysis and address the issues.

- It is important to note the difference between problem management and incident management. The objective of problem management is reducing the number of incidents, whereas the objective of incident management is achieving a return to a normal state as quickly as possible after an incident and thus minimizing the impact on the business.
- The primary risk of a lack of attention to problem management is the interruption of business operations.
- An IS auditor should review problem reports and logs to ensure that problems are addressed in a time-bound manner.
- For effective incident management, it is very important to design and implement a support model in an efficient manner. Ineffective support models will not be able to prevent and react to potential outages.
- The best performance indicator for an outsourced helpdesk function is how quickly and effectively a solution is provided to users. It is vital to ensure that the end user is told about the resolution and that consent for the resolution is obtained.

Network management tools

There are some widely used tools to manage networks. You need to understand these tools for the exam:

Tools	Description
Response time reports	To determine the response time taken by host system to address the query of the user.
Downtime reports	To determine and track the unavailability of telecommunication lines and circuits.
Help desk reports	To determine help desk activities like nature of queries, no. of open calls, turnaround time, problems and their resolution.
Online monitors	To determine data transmission error and accuracy.
Network monitor	To provide real time information and network nodes and status.
Network protocol analyzers	They are network diagnostic tool to determine and monitor packets flowing along the link. They produce network usage reports.
Simple Network Management Protocol (SNMP)	A TCP/IP based protocol to monitor, control and manage configuration. It collects statistics on performance and security.

Next, let's have a look at some questions from the perspective of the CISA exam, and then there will be a few self-assessment questions for you to review.

Key aspects from a CISA exam perspective

The following table covers the important aspects from a CISA exam perspective:

CISA questions	Possible answer
Which tool is used to monitor and record network information?	Network Protocol Analyzer
What is the first step in the implementation of problem management?	Reporting an exception
What is the best method to prevent reoccurrence of the incident?	Root cause analysis

Self-assessment questions

1. **Which of the following network diagnostics tools monitors and records network information?**
    A. Response time report
    B. Online monitor
    C. Help desk report
    D. Network protocol analyzers

2. **An IS auditor is reviewing help desk activities. Which of the following is an area of major concern?**
    A. The help desk team not being able to close a few calls
    B. End users not being informed about the closure of resolved incidents
    C. The help desk team not operating 24 hours a day
    D. The help desk team not having been provided with dedicated phone lines

3. **Which of the following does the use of network performance monitoring tools directly affect?**
    A. The confidentiality of a system
    B. The integrity of a system
    C. The accuracy of the system
    D. The availability of a system

4. **Which of the following performance indicators is best to include in an SLA for an outsourced help desk function?**
    A. The number of users to be supported
    B. The percentage of resolution in the first call
    C. The number of incidents to be supported
    D. The number of help desk agents to be deployed

5. An IS auditor notes that several incidents were assigned the wrong priorities and hence were not able to achieve the defined SLA. Which of the following is the most important concern?

    A. The support model was not documented.

    B. The support model was not approved.

    C. The support model was not properly designed and executed.

    D. The SLA contains an unrealistic resolution time.

6. Which of the following is the first step in the implementation of a problem management mechanism?

    A. Reporting an exception

    B. Root cause analysis

    C. Risk analysis

    D. Ranking exceptions

7. What is the best method to prevent the recurrence of IT system failure?

    A. Availability of redundant systems

    B. Capacity management planning

    C. Performance monitoring

    D. Performing the root cause analysis

Change management, configuration management, and patch management

CISA aspirants should be aware of the following aspect of change, configuration, and patch management for the exam.

Change management process

A change management process is used to change hardware, install software, and configure various network devices. A change management process includes approval, testing, scheduling, and rollback arrangements.

While implementing a change, all relevant personnel should be kept informed and specific approval should be obtained from the relevant information asset owners.

To carry out changes, it is always advisable to use individual IDs rather than generic or shared IDs. Individual IDs help to establish accountability for any transaction.

For every change, transaction logs should be maintained. A transaction log is used as an audit trail for further investigation. A log should contain details such as date, time, user ID, terminal, and other relevant details of the transaction.

One of the most important aspects of change management control is code signing. Code signing provides assurance that software has been generated from a reputable source and that the code has not been modified after having been signed. The process employs the use of a hash function to determine the integrity and authenticity of code.

Patch management

It is important to test a patch before its implementation because patches may impact other systems and operations. Impact analysis is a very important aspect of patch management. Patch deployment without appropriate testing may result in system failure or disruption.

Configuration management

Configuration management is considered one of the key components of network management. It determines network functionality both internally and externally. It ensures that the setup and management of a network is done appropriately.

Configuration management determines a base software release. The baseline is used to identify the software and hardware components that make specific versions of a system. In the case of the failure of a new release, the baseline will be considered as a point to which to return.

Emergency change management

In some scenarios, there are business requirement changes that need to be implemented to which normal change management processes cannot be applied. These changes have a significant impact on business operations and delay cannot be tolerated. Such changes should be carried out through an emergency change process. Emergency changes should be logged, and post facto approval should be obtained on the next working day.

Backout process

It is advisable that the risk of a change having an adverse impact is reviewed and that a rollback plan is available to back out of changes, in case that becomes necessary. There should be a process by which you can back out completely and restore the system to its previous state. This is known as a backout procedure.

The effectiveness of a change management process

Compliance testing will help to ensure that a change management process is applied consistently and that changes are appropriately approved.

The best method to determine the effectiveness of a control process is to first review a sample of conducted changes and then ask for relevant approvals for these changes. The process of identifying changes and then tracing back to their records will provide the best evidence of unauthorized changes.

Key aspects from a CISA exam perspective

The following table covers the important aspects from a CISA exam perspective:

CISA questions	Possible answers
What is the most important factor for patch management?	To test and conduct impact analysis before installation of patch
Procedure to restore a system to its prior state is known as:	Backout procedure
Objective of code signing	To ensure that software has not subsequently modified
Objective of library control software	To prevent unauthorized changes or access
What is the best control for emergency changes?	Subsequent review and approval of all emergency changes
A key component of a network management is	Configuration management
Best method to determine the effectiveness of change management process	Select a few samples of changes and then trace back to their records

Self-assessment questions

1. **Which of the following is the most important consideration when ensuring system availability during the change management process?**
    A. A documented procedure for sound change management
    B. The change management procedure being followed consistently
    C. Change only being authorized by the IT manager
    D. User acceptance testing being properly documented

2. **Which of the following is the best option for patch management to ensure that a new patch will not impact system processing?**
    A. A patch should be tested prior to updating.
    B. A user should be trained in the patch updating process.
    C. A patch should be applied immediately and post-implementation testing should be carried out.
    D. A documented patch management process should be available.

3. **What is the best way to find evidence of unauthorized changes in a production system?**
    A. Log reviews
    B. Compliance testing
    C. Forensic reviews
    D. Utilization reports

4. **A review of the change management process indicates that the process is not fully documented and also that some migration processes failed. What should the next step for the IS auditor be?**
    A. Trying to get further information about the findings through root cause analysis.
    B. Report the findings to the audit committee of the board.
    C. Recommend reframing the change management process.
    D. Recommend discontinuing the migration process until the change management process is documented.

5. **Which of the following procedures is used to restore a system to its prior state?**
    A. Incident management
    B. Capacity management
    C. Backout procedure
    D. Software development life cycle

6. **Which of the following is considered a critical component in network management?**
    A. Proxy troubleshooting
    B. Topological structure
    C. Change and configuration management
    D. Network monitoring tools

7. **Which of the following is an important aspect of patch management?**
    A. Conducting an impact analysis before the installation of a patch
    B. The selection of a well-established vendor for patch management
    C. The availability of a documented patch management process
    D. The immediate installation of security patches

8. **Which of the following provides the best evidence regarding the effectiveness of a change control procedure?**
    A. Reviewing system-generated logs for the change made
    B. Verifying the approvals for the changes conducted
    C. Verifying the approvals for the change management policy
    D. Verifying the approvals for the creation of privilege rights

9. **An IS auditor reviewing a change management procedure notes that some code that was missed during the production release was subsequently included in production without following the normal change management process. Which of the following is the area of most concern?**
    A. The code was not released during the initial implementation
    B. The code was subsequently included without change management approval
    C. The error was not noted during user acceptance testing
    D. The error was not noted during final system testing

10. **What is the most effective way to gauge the design effectiveness of a change management process?**
    A. A sample test of change requests
    B. A sample test of change authorization
    C. Interviewing the staff
    D. Conducting an end-to-end walk-through of the change management process

11. **The IS auditor notes that the system malfunctioned after the installation of a security patch. Which of the following is the best control for such an incident?**
    A. Patch installation should be conducted only by the system administrator
    B. The change management procedure should be followed for patch installation
    C. The patch management process should be outsourced to third-party service providers
    D. The approval of the business manager should be obtained for patch installation

12. **What is the objective of code signing?**
    A. Ensuring that software has not subsequently modified
    B. Ensuring smooth integration with other code-signed systems
    C. Ensuring the integrity of the private key
    D. Ensuring the availability of the system

13. **What is the objective of library control software?**
    A. Providing assurance that program changes are authorized
    B. Providing assurance that program changes are tested
    C. Providing assurance that areas are automatically moved to production
    D. Providing assurance that only developers can access a program

14. **Data is copied from a backup server to the production server. Which of the following is the best way to ensure that no unauthorized software moves to the production server?**
    A. Reviewing changes in software version control
    B. Conducting a full backup
    C. Carrying out a backup process manually
    D. Reviewing the backup server log

15. **Which of the following is the best compensatory control where developers themselves release emergency changes directly to production?**
    A. Changes should be logged and approved on the next business day
    B. Developers should only be allowed to do changes during office hours
    C. Second-level approval is required before a change is released
    D. Changes should be deployed only in the presence of the user

16. **An organization has changed the vendor maintaining critical applications. In the new contract, the incident resolution time has been modified. Which of the following is a major concern?**
    A. The impact of the modification is not considered in the disaster recovery document
    B. The impact of the modification is not considered when determining the recovery point objective
    C. The application owners are not aware of the modification
    D. The old service provider does not agree with the new resolution time

17. **Which of the following is the best control for configuration changes?**
    A. An adequate audit trail
    B. Adequate training of personnel
    C. Adequate documentation for configuration management
    D. An adequate process of approval and review for critical changes

18. **Which of the following is a major concern in a change management process?**
    A. Different configurations for the test and production systems
    B. The non-availability of manual change management records
    C. The non-availability of a configuration management database
    D. Inadequate training of the personnel involved

19. **Which of the following is a major concern for an in-house-developed application?**
    A. A delay in implementation due to user acceptance testing
    B. An inadequate budget estimate
    C. A delay in implementation due to unit testing
    D. A change request being initiated and approved by the same employee

20. **Which of the following is the best process to use to test program changes?**
    A. Reviewing samples of change authorization first and then analyzing the relevant modified programs
    B. Conducting a walk-through of the program changes from beginning to end
    C. Reviewing samples of change authorization first and then analyzing the supporting change authorization
    D. Using automated tools to analyze change authorization for missing fields

21. **Which of the following is the best control for emergency changes that bypass the normal change process?**
    A. Subsequent review and approval of all emergency changes
    B. Capturing the logs of all emergency changes
    C. A documented process for emergency change management
    D. Emergency changes being pre-approved

22. **What is the most important aspect for patch updating for an operating system?**
    A. Post-update regression testing
    B. Approval from the owner of the information system asset
    C. Approval from the information security team
    D. Adequate training for the system administrator

23. **An IS auditor notes that IT personnel have not yet installed the patches that were released 2 months ago. What should the IS auditor do?**
    A. Review the patch management policy and analyze the risks associated with delayed updates
    B. Recommend the immediate installation of the patch
    C. Report the findings to the audit committee of the board
    D. Determine the competency of the system administrator

24. **What is the most likely reason for adopting emergency change procedure?**
    A. The implementation of new functionality
    B. User acceptance testing not being required for minor changes
    C. A change having a significant impact on business operation
    D. A change being released by a third-party service provider

25. **Which of the following best establishes accountability for personnel when it comes to emergency change?**
    A. Granting production access to individual IDs as and when required
    B. The use of a generic firefighter ID for emergency changes
    C. The use of dedicated personnel to carry out emergency changes
    D. Pre-authorization for emergency changes

26. **An IS auditor notes that the IT department has not updated a new patch for an application because other security controls are in place. What should the recommendation of the auditor be?**
    A. The overall risk should be analyzed before any recommendation is made.
    B. Implement firewall rules.
    C. Implement an intrusion detection system.
    D. Provide adequate training to the system administrator.

27. **An IS auditor notes that users are granted occasional authority to change a system. What should the IS auditor's first step be?**
    A. Determine whether this process is allowed by policy
    B. Determine whether the training of the users is adequate
    C. Determine whether logs are captured for these changes
    D. Determine the availability of compensatory controls for this process

28. **An employee is granted authority to change the parameters of a critical file. Which of the following is the most effective control on that employee's activities?**
    A. Changes should be approved by supervisor.
    B. Changes should be logged.
    C. Changes should be approved by peers.
    D. Changes should be approved by the employee themselves.

29. **Which of the following is the fastest technique for determining data-file change management controls?**
    A. One-to-one file checking
    B. Access confidentiality
    C. Transaction logs
    D. Backup files

IT service level management

In this section, we will first have a look at IT service management practices, followed by a look at some assessment questions, the answers to which are given at the end of the chapter.

The following are some of the important aspects of service level management:

- An SLA defines the nature, expectations, escalations, and other relevant information for the services being offered.
- The SLA should be documented in non-technical terms and serve as the basis for measuring and monitoring services.
- Service level management is the process of defining, documenting, and managing service requirements.
- The following characteristics should be considered to define an SLA:
    - Accuracy
    - Completeness
    - Timeliness
    - Security
- It is very important to monitor service levels at regular intervals to ensure that the objective of the service is achieved.
- It must be noted that when service delivery is outsourced, the accountability of a service still rests with the service receiver.
- It is the responsibility of the organization to ensure that the service provider uses data for correct and agreed-upon purposes only. It should also ensure that service providers have appropriate controls in place to protect sensitive and critical data.
- An independent third-party audit report is the best assurance of the effectiveness of service provider controls.

Key aspects from the CISA exam perspective

The following table covers the important aspects from the CISA exam perspective:

CISA questions	Possible answers
What is the major concern about use of open source software?	Non adherence to terms and conditions for use of open source software
Best audit process to determine use of unlicensed software	Use of automated tools
Most important factor to examine security configuration of an operating system	Review of parameter setting

Self evaluation questions

1. Which of the following is a major concern for an IS auditor reviewing a third-party SLA?

   A. A transition clause on the expiry of the contract not being included

   B. An escalation matrix for service deficiency not being included

   C. A late payment clause not being included

   D. Details of the service provider's **Single Point of Contact (SPOC)** not being defined

2. Which of the following is a major concern for an IS auditor reviewing a third-party agreement?

   A. A "right to audit" clause not being included

   B. A penalty clause for adverse performance not being included

   C. The agreement with no mention of poor performance for negative performance

   D. The service provider's liability limitation clause not being included

3. Which of the following is a major concern for an IS auditor reviewing an SLA for storing sensitive customer data with a third-party cloud provider?

   A. The service level escalation matrix not being documented

   B. The cloud provider reserving the right to access data for certain processes

   C. The bulk data upload process not being defined

   D. Backup responsibility being with the customer organization

4. Which of the following is a major concern to an IS auditor reviewing an SLA with a third party?

   A. The service parameters not being included in the SLA

   B. The last review of the SLA having been done more than a year ago

   C. The data sharing process not being included in the SLA

   D. Late payment charges not being defined

5. Which of the following provides the greatest assurance about the control effectiveness of a third-party service provider?

   A. The clauses in the SLA

   B. An independent audit report

   C. The **Business Continuity Plan (BCP)** document of the service provider

   D. The number of employees in the information security team of the service provider

6. **Which of the following is the main objective of service level management?**
    A. Documenting, monitoring, and managing agreed-upon service parameters
    B. Complying with regulatory requirements
    C. Minimizing the cost of a service
    D. Timely technology upgrades

7. **During an IS audit, the auditor is informed about a verbal agreement between the IT and user departments about IT service parameters. What should the IS auditor do first?**
    A. Report the findings to senior management.
    B. Get confirmation from the departments about the content of the agreement.
    C. Stop the audit until the agreement is documented.
    D. Refer the best available agreement template.

8. **What is the most reliable source of evidence for verifying an ISP's compliance with an SLA?**
    A. The downtime report produced by the ISP
    B. The downtime report maintained by the organization
    C. The availability report produced by the ISP
    D. The utilization report maintained by the organization

Evaluating the database management process

A **database management system (DBMS)** helps in organizing, controlling, and managing data. It aims to reduce data redundancy and improve access time. It also aims to provide appropriate security for sensitive data.

Advantages of database management

The following are some of the advantages of using DBMS:

- Centralized data management reduces the cost, time, and effort it takes to manage data.
- It helps in improving database performance by reducing data redundancy.

- It helps in improving the efficiency of transaction processing.
- It ensures data consistency.
- It provides security for sensitive data.
- Various checks and controls in DBMSes ensure data integrity.
- A DBMS provides a structured way to manage user access.

Database structures

It is important to understand various database structures to evaluate database risks. CISA aspirants should understand the following database models.

Hierarchical database model

Let's try to understand the hierarchical model using the following diagram:

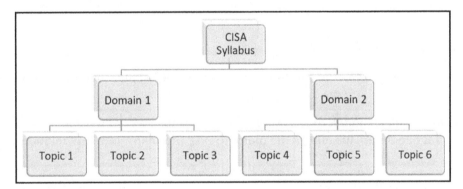

From the preceding figure, you can observe that:

- This model is arranged logically in an inverted tree pattern.
- In this model, records are logically organized into a hierarchy of relationships.
- All records in the hierarchy are called nodes.
- Each node is related to the others in a parent-child relationship. The top parent record in the hierarchy is called the root record.
- Each parent record may have one or more child records, but no child record may have more than one parent record.
- The hierarchical data structure implements one-to-one and one-to-many relationships.

Network database model

In the network database model, each set is made up of an owner record and one or more member records.

Let's try to understand the network database model using the following diagram:

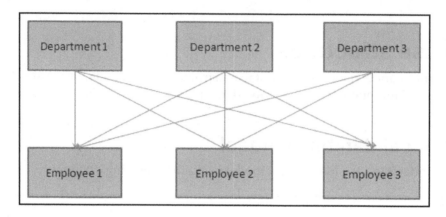

This model keeps all records in sets.

The network model can show redundancy in data more efficiently than the hierarchical model.

Unlike the hierarchical model, the network model permits a record to be a member of more than one set at one time. This allows the many-to-one and many-to-many relationship types.

Network databases directly address the location of a record on disk. This gives excellent retrieval performance.

Relational database model

The following are some of the important elements of relational database models:

- In a relational database, all the tables are related through one or more fields.
- Through these common fields, it is possible to connect all the tables in a database.

- For each table, one of the fields is identified as a primary key, which is the unique identifier for each record in the table. The primary key is used to join or combine data from two or more tables.
- Referential integrity refers to the integrity and correctness of data within a related table.
- The data in primary or master tables should be consistent with the data in related tables (also known as foreign tables).
- Any changes to the primary key must be applied to associated foreign keys.
- Referential integrity will prevent users from adding records in a foreign table, if records are not available in the primary table.
- At the same time, users cannot delete primary keys, if related records are available in the foreign table.

The following diagram will help you to understand referential integrity:

	Primary Table			Foreign Table	
Primary Key ⟶	Employee No.	Employee Name	Foreign Key ⟶	Employee No.	Salary
	1	David		1	1000 $
	3	Molly		3	800 $
	4	Jia		4	950 $
	5	Thabo		5	750 $
	6	Smith			

Let's understand the preceding table in detail:

- Foreign tables are also known as related tables. Foreign keys are also known as related keys.
- Referential integrity will restrict adding anything to a foreign table for which there is no primary key. In the preceding table, employee number 2 cannot be entered in the foreign table as they do not exist in the primary table.
- Referential integrity will restrict deletion from the primary table as long as there is an associated foreign key. In the preceding table, employee number 1 cannot be deleted as it also exists in foreign tables. However, employee number 6 can be deleted from the primary table as they do not exist in any foreign tables.

Object-oriented database model

The following are some of the important elements of the **object-oriented database model (OODM)**:

- An object-oriented database is a set of objects. Each object is an independently functioning application or program, assigned a specific task to perform.
- The OODM is designed to manage all these independent programs to quickly process large and complex requests.
- An object-oriented database provides a mechanism to store complex data such as images, audio, and video.

Database normalization

The following are some of the important aspects of database normalization:

- Normalization is the process of reducing duplicate data and thus reducing data redundancy.
- Redundancy is considered as a negative thing in a database environment as it means more effort and storage being necessary to handle data.
- Denormalizing increases data redundancy.
- Disabling normalization will result in more redundant data, which may impact the consistency and integrity of data.
- When an IS auditor observes that some tables in a database are not normalized, they should review justification and compensatory control for denormalization.

Database checks and controls

The following are some of the important checks and controls for the effective and efficient management of databases:

- **Concurrency control**: To prevent integrity issues during simultaneous updates by multiple users.
- **Table link/table reference check**: To identify table linking errors such as incomplete or inaccurate content in a database.
- **Integrity constraint**: To allow only valid predefined data to enter the database, and to prevent out-of-range data in the database. It is a preventive control.

- **Atomicity**: To ensure that either the entire transaction is processed or none of it is processed. This will ensure that partially executed transactions are rolled back and not processed.
- **SQL**: This helps to determine the portability of an application for connecting to a database.
- **Referential integrity**: This will prevent the deletion of a primary table as long as it has associated foreign keys.
- **Normalization**: This is the process of removing duplicate data elements from a database and thus improving the database's performance.
- **Commitment and rollback controls**: This ensures that a transaction is completed in its entirety or not at all. It ensures integrity.
- **Tracing and tagging**: This is used to test applications, systems, and controls.
- **User spool and database limit control**: This helps to control space utilization and thus improve database query performance.
- **Restore procedure**: In the case of corruption in a database, the database can be restored to its last archived version. This is a connective control.
- **Column- and row-level restrictions**: This helps to restrict particular sensitive columns or rows of a database to only a few authorized users. This means there is no need to have a separate database for such sensitive information.

Segregation of duties

An IS auditor should understand the various roles and responsibilities of **database administrators (DBAs)** to ensure that an appropriate segregation of duties exists.

The following are some of the routine activities of a DBA:

- Conducting changes in the database table
- Conducting backup and recovery procedures
- Consulting on database interfaces
- Using tools and techniques to optimize database performance

It is very important to ensure that the DBA conducts the preceding activities using their named account (and not a shared account) to establish accountability. Logs should be captured for all database activities. Logs should be restricted for modification and DBAs should not be provided with access to the log server.

From the perspective of control, DBAs should not be allowed to perform the following activities:

- Activities related to log capturing and the monitoring of DBA functions
- End user activities
- Security patch updates for the operating system

Key aspects from a CISA exam perspective

The following table covers some important aspects from a CISA exam perspective:

CISA questions	Possible answers
Which key provides the assurance of database referential integrity?	Foreign key
Denormalizing the tables in database will increase the risk of	Redundancy risk/integrity risk
Objective of concurrency control	To prevent integrity issues during simultaneous updates by multiple users
Objective of table link check	Assurance about integrity of database
Objective of integrity constraint	Preventive control that checks for out of range data and restrict this from being entered into database
Feature ensures that partially executed transactions are rolled back and not processed	Atomicity
Objective of commit and rol back control	Commit features ensure that data is saved and updated in database once transaction processing is completed. Rollback features ensures that partially completed transaction (due to interruption) are reversed back and not saved. Thus commit and rollback control ensures that only entire transaction is saved in database.
Accountability of updating database is best ensured by	Log capturing and reviewing
Responsibility for authorizing access to data	Data owner

Self-assessment questions

1. **Which of the following provides assurance of database referential integrity?**
   A. Foreign key
   B. Secondary key
   C. Table definition
   D. Domain key

2. **What is the most important consideration for database hardening?**
    A. That the default settings are modified
    B. The denormalization of the database table
    C. The encryption of the database table
    D. Two-factor authentication for database access

3. **Which of the following functions should not be performed by the DBA?**
    A. Conducting changes in the database table
    B. Performing update patches for the operating system
    C. Conducting backup and recovery processes
    D. Consulting on database interfaces

4. **What does an IS auditor refer to a data flow diagram for?**
    A. Understanding the data flow and storage
    B. Identification of key controls
    C. Understanding the data classification scheme
    D. Understanding the data definitions

5. **What will denormalizing the tables in a database result in?**
    A. Increased risk to confidentiality
    B. Increased risk to availability
    C. Increased risk to redundancy
    D. Increased risk to access

6. **Which of the following is the primary concern for changing the database vendor?**
    A. Data integrity
    B. Data availability
    C. Data normalization
    D. Data confidentiality

7. **What does concurrency control help to do in a database?**
    A. Prevent unauthorized access to data
    B. Prevent integrity issues during simultaneous updates by multiple users
    C. Ensure the confidentiality of data
    D. Prevent unauthorized modification of data

8. **How is existing database integrity best assured?**
   - A. Log monitoring
   - B. Table link checks
   - C. Query time checks
   - D. Rollback features

9. **What account should DBAs use for database changes?**
   - A. Their named account
   - B. A shared DBA account
   - C. A user's account
   - D. A server administrator's account

10. **Which of the following is the best control against unauthorized changes to a database after office hours?**
    - A. Changes only being made with DBA user accounts
    - B. Changes only being made with application owner accounts
    - C. Using the DBA account to make changes and then reviewing the logs for the change the next day
    - D. Using the application owner account to make changes and then reviewing the logs for the change the next day

11. **Which of the following is the best control to use to protect logs related to DBA activities?**
    - A. A document log retention policy.
    - B. DBAs should not have access to the log server.
    - C. Changes to the database should be approved.
    - D. Taking a backup of the database on tape.

12. **Which of the following additional functions should not be performed by DBAs?**
    - A. Maintenance of the database activity log
    - B. Conducting table link error test
    - C. Implementing backup and recovery procedures
    - D. Using database optimization tools

13. **Which of the following controls will prevent out-of-range data in a database server?**
    - A. Reviewing logs for data updates
    - B. Incorporating integrity constraints in the database
    - C. Incorporating before-and-after image capture
    - D. Reviewing user access rights

14. **Which of the following features ensures that partially executed transactions are rolled back and not processed?**
    - A. Atomicity
    - B. Consistency
    - C. Isolation
    - D. Durability

15. **How is the portability of an application with a database ensured?**
    - A. Atomicity
    - B. Structured Query Language
    - C. Table link error checks
    - D. Tracing and tagging

16. **What does the corruption of some values of the foreign key result in?**
    - A. An error, as corrupted data may not be available on the master database when these transactions are processed
    - B. An error, as re-indexing is not possible
    - C. An error, as data may be denormalized
    - D. An error, as the integrity constraint will stop functioning

17. **In the case of referential integrity, which of the following keys will prevent the deletion of a row as long as its value is stored in another table?**
    - A. Private key
    - B. Public key
    - C. Primary key
    - D. Foreign key

18. **Which of the following is the next action to take when an IS auditor observes that some tables in a database are not normalized?**
    - A. Analyze the justification
    - B. Recommend normalization
    - C. Analyze the table link check report
    - D. Analyze the data flow diagram

19. **Which of the following constitutes a major compromise for the security of database servers?**
    - A. DBA activity logs not being reviewed
    - B. Default security settings not being changed
    - C. Table link checks not being performed
    - D. The purging policy not being documented

20. **What does the denormalization of a database table increase risk to?**
    A. Confidentiality
    B. Integrity
    C. Security
    D. Non-repudiation

21. **For an online transaction processing system's database, what is the integrity of transactions maintained by?**
    A. Tagging and tracking control
    B. Commitment and rollback control
    C. Access review control
    D. Log monitoring control

22. **Which of the following controls is implemented to decrease the warehouse query performance?**
    A. Rollback controls
    B. Tagging and tracking control
    C. Access review control
    D. User spool and database limit control

23. **Restoration of the database using before-image dumps will begin from:**
    A. The first transaction of the batch
    B. Immediately prior to the last transaction
    C. Immediately after the last transaction
    D. Immediately after the last checkpoint

24. **How can the integrity of transaction processing for an interrupted online transaction be ensured?**
    A. Referential integrity control
    B. Input integrity checks
    C. Output integrity checks
    D. Commit and rollback control

25. **Which of the following is the best corrective control for problems related to corrupted data in a database?**
    A. Stringent access control
    B. Concurrency control
    C. Restore procedure
    D. System audit

26. **What will the use of segmentation for critical databases do?**
    - A. Minimize exposure
    - B. Minimize threat
    - C. Minimize cost
    - D. Minimize criticality

27. **How is accountability for updating databases best ensured?**
    - A. Log capturing and reviewing
    - B. Need-to-know access
    - C. User access review
    - D. Segregation of duties

28. **What is the most important factor for the quality of data in a database?**
    - A. The integrity of source data
    - B. The credibility of data source
    - C. The data extraction process
    - D. The data transformation process

29. **How is out-of-range data in a database best prevented?**
    - A. Integrity constraint
    - B. Log review
    - C. Table link error check
    - D. Tracing and tagging control

30. **How should you determine the correctness of individual transaction balances that are migrated from one database to another?**
    - A. A hash total should be compared before and after migration.
    - B. You should verify the migrated individual account balance on a sample basis.
    - C. You should compare the number of records before and after migration.
    - D. The control total should be compared before and after migration.

31. **Who should be responsible for authorizing access to data?**
    - A. The owner of the data
    - B. The custodian of the data
    - C. The security administrator
    - D. The steering committee

32. **What should be the next step of an IS auditor who finds that the DBA has read and write access to production data?**
    A. Recommend for the immediate revocation of rights
    B. Analyze the justification of the DBA's rights
    C. Review the logs related to the DBA's activities
    D. Accept the current process as a common practice

33. **What is the best method for protecting sensitive information in a data warehouse?**
    A. Incorporating column- and row-level restrictions
    B. Incorporating two-factor authentication
    C. Creating a different database for each subject
    D. Capturing logs to review user activities

34. **What is the best method for establishing accountability among users accessing a sensitive database?**
    A. Capturing and reviewing the logs
    B. Incorporating two-factor authentication
    C. Using different application and database servers
    D. Incorporating column- and row-level restrictions

35. **Which of these is a major concern when storing critical client details in a web server?**
    A. The integrity of client data
    B. The confidentiality of client data
    C. High storage requirements
    D. The non-availability of data

Summary

Information system operations are the core of the IS cycle, and depending on the size of the enterprise and its business context, the nature of information system operations can vary.

In this chapter, we discussed and learned about various technology components and how to identify risks related to IT assets. We also discussed IT operations and IT management practices. IT asset management is a very important element in designing and developing an effective security strategy.

In the next chapter, we will learn about various risks, controls, and practices related to business resilience.

Assessment

Here are the answers to the self-assessment questions.

Common technology components

1. **Answer: C. The risk of eavesdropping**
   Explanation: RFID tags are exposed to the risk of eavesdropping. It is the same as a wireless device. RFID, by its nature, is not subject to other exposure, such as social engineering, phishing, or malicious code.

2. **Answer: A. The availability report**
   Explanation: An availability report indicates the time period during which the system is up and available for use. An IS auditor can determine downtime with the help of availability reports. Utilization reports determine the level of use of systems. A utilization report is used to predict resource requirements. Asset management reports include an inventory of assets. Hardware error reports identify system failures and other issues.

3. **Answer: A. The system downtime report**
   Explanation: The system downtime log indicates the effectiveness of preventive maintenance programs. High downtime indicates that preventive maintenance is not effective. Effective preventive maintenance should result in zero or very minimal downtime. Other options will not directly indicate the efficiency of preventive maintenance programs.

4. **Answer: C. Preventive maintenance**
   Explanation: Preventive maintenance should be conducted during non-peak times to avoid any downtime. Other activities may not directly impact system availability.

5. **Answer: D. An automated tool to verify the availability of update patches**
   Explanation: An automated tool can be used to generate reports for the availability of security update patches in each of the critical servers. The other options may not be as efficient and effective as automated tools.

IT asset management

1. **Answer: D. Date-and-time stamping for source and object code**
   Explanation: Date-and-time stamping for both the source code and the object code will help to ensure that the code is in sync. The other options are good practice, but they will not ensure that the source code and object code are of the same version.

2. **Answer: B. Updating the IT asset inventory**
   Explanation: Updating the IT assets should be the first step. Once the inventory is updated, the other options can be followed.

3. **Answer: D. Creating an inventory of IT assets**
   Explanation: The first step for the implementation of an access control rule is to create a list of IT assets as an inventory. This will be followed by categorization and grouping.

4. **Answer: C. The identification of assets**
   Explanation: CISA aspirants should understand the following sequential activities for the development of a risk management program: the identification of assets, the identification of vulnerabilities and threats, impact analysis, risk prioritization, control evaluation, and the implementation of appropriate controls.

5. **Answer: C. The installed software is not approved**
   Explanation: The installation of unapproved software is a serious violation that carries major legal, financial, and security risks. Processes should be in place to install only standard approved software. The other options are not as significant as option C.

Job scheduling

1. **Answer: C. A few jobs having been overridden by the operator**
   Explanation: The overriding of scheduled jobs should be restricted as this can lead to unauthorized changes to programs or data. This is a major area of concern as overriding a scheduled job is only to be done by following the appropriate approval process. The other options are not as significant as overriding the schedule.

2. **Answer: B. Staging and job setup**
   Explanation: Bypassing or ignoring tape header records may result in loading the wrong tape and deleting a loaded time. Staging and job setup is useful in compensating for weaknesses in tape label control. Through staging, data is stored in an intermediate place (between the data source and the data target) and processing is done. This ensures data integrity and effective operations.

3. **Answer: C. Maintenance activities being conducted during non-peak hours**
   Explanation: As far as possible, maintenance functions should be performed during non-peak times. Mishaps or incidents during maintenance activities can interrupt business processes if maintenance is carried out during peak hours. It is prudent to conduct any maintenance activity during non-peak hours only.

End user computing

1. **Answer: A. The lack of a documented end user computing policy**
   Explanation: End user computing refers to a system wherein a non-programmer can create their own application. This also reduces pressure on the IT department, who can concentrate on more critical and complex applications. End user computing is subject to some inherent risks. It is important that the documented policy of end user computing should be available to address the risks. The other options are not as significant as a lack of documented policy.

System performance management

1. **Answer: B. Verifying the software through testing**
   Explanation: By gathering additional evidence, you first need to confirm if the software is unlicensed. Without appropriate audit evidence, the other options may not be feasible.

2. **Answer: B. An organization must comply with open source software license terms**
   Explanation: It is very important for organizations to understand the terms of use of open source licenses and to adhere to them. An IS auditor should be more concerned about licensing compliance to avoid any legal consequences.

3. **Answer: C. Server utilization reports**
Explanation: Server utilization reports identify underutilized servers and help to monitor overall server utilization. Thus, through server utilization reports, IT personnel can take appropriate measures to raise the effectiveness of server utilization. The other options will not directly impact the optimal configuration of the server.

4. **Answer: B. To include a clause related to the restriction of unauthorized software in the security policy**
Explanation: The most important thing is to address the issue by inserting a clause related to unauthorized software in the IS policy. When the policy is specific about unauthorized software, the IT department can implement controls using various options.

5. **Answer: C. The maintenance program covers vendor-provided specification**
Explanation: It is very important to ensure that hardware maintenance schedules are validated against the vendor-provided specification. A maintenance schedule is not required to be approved by the steering committee. The other options are not as significant as coverage of the vendor-provided specification.

6. **Answer: B. Reviewing parameter settings**
Explanation: Parameter settings will indicate the security configuration of the system. Reviewing the parameter settings helps to identify access controls, system usage, and other operating system-related securities. The other options would not provide an indication of the operating system.

7. **Answer: B. The capacity management process**
Explanation: Capacity management helps to ensure that IT resources are used effectively and efficiently. Effective capacity management processes help in planning and purchasing additional resources.

8. **Answer: C. To establish performance measurement criteria**
Explanation: Establishing performance criteria for authentication servers would help to monitor performance, and remedial action can be taken where performance is not acceptable.

Problem and incident management

1. **Answer: D. Network protocol analyzers**
   Explanation: Protocol analyzers are network diagnostic tools used to monitor the packets flowing along a network. They operate at the data link or network layer. Response time reports state the time taken by a system to respond to queries. Online monitors check for data transmission errors. Help desk reports provide analysis for IT support.

2. **Answer: B. End users not being informed about the closure of resolved incidents**
   Explanation: It is very important that end users are advised about the resolution of a logged incident. Incidents should be regarded as closed only when this is confirmed by the end user. The help desk is not expected to operate 24 hours a day. The other options are not as significant as option B.

3. **Answer: D. The availability of the system**
   Explanation: Network performance tools monitor network performance and problems. They help the administrator to take corrective action in the case of network-related issues. As such, they ensure availability. The other options are not directly impacted by network performance monitoring tools.

4. **Answer: B. The percentage of resolution in the first call**
   Explanation: The best performance indicator is the percentage of calls that are resolved the first time. This will indicate the effectiveness of help desk service providers; the other options are not as significant as this one.

5. **Answer: C. The support model was not properly designed and executed**
   Explanation: For effective incident management, it is critical to design and execute a support model in an efficient way. Ineffective support models will not be able to prevent or react to potential incidents. The other options are not as significant as the design and execution of the support model.

6. **Answer: A. Reporting an exception**
   Explanation: Reporting an exception is generally considered as the first step in handling a problem. The other options will be followed once the exception is reported.

7. **Answer: D. Performing the root cause analysis**
   Explanation: To prevent the recurrence of an incident, it is important to conduct a root cause analysis of the incident. The root cause analysis determines the key reason why an incident happened. It allows appropriate action to be taken to prevent the incident from recurring. The other options will not directly be able to prevent the recurrence of the incident.

Change management, configuration management, and patch management

1. **Answer: B. The change management procedure is followed consistently**
   Explanation: The most important control for ensuring system availability is a sound change management procedure that is followed consistently. Changes are required to be authorized by business managers also, not only by IT managers. User acceptance testing will not have any direct impact on system availability.

2. **Answer: A. A patch should be tested prior to updating**
   Explanation: It is very important to test a patch before its implementation because patches may impact other systems and operations.

3. **Answer: B. Compliance testing**
   Explanation: Compliance testing will help to determine whether a change management process is applied consistently and whether changes are appropriately approved. A forensic review is a specialized investigation for criminal cases. Logs would help identify the changes; however, to determine authorization, compliance testing of the change management process should be conducted.

4. **Answer: A. Trying to get further assurance about the findings using root cause analysis**
   Explanation: Before recommending any action, an IS auditor should gain assurance that the deficiencies noted can be attributed to the failure of the change management process rather than some other process failure.

5. **Answer: C. Backout procedure**
   Explanation: The backout procedure is one of the elements of the change management process. The backout procedure is used to restore a system to an earlier state, prior to the state of upgrade. This process is used when upgrades are not successfully implemented and, as a result, some issues arise in the system's functioning.

6. **Answer: C. Change and configuration management**
   Explanation: Configuration management is considered one of the key components in network management. It determines the network functionality both internally and externally. It ensures that the setup and management of the network are done properly. The other options, though important, are not as critical as change and configuration management.

7. **Answer: A. Conducting an impact analysis before the installation of a patch**
   Explanation: It is very important to test a patch and conduct an impact analysis before the installation of a patch. This is the most important aspect.

8. **Answer: B. Verifying the approvals for the changes conducted**
Explanation: The most effective method of determining the effectiveness of a change control procedure is to determine what changes have been made and ask for the approvals for such changes. The other options may not indicate consistent implementation of the change control process.

9. **Answer: B. The code was subsequently included without change management approval**
Explanation: The most important area of concern is the inclusion of code without following the change management process. Unauthorized changes might impact system performance. The other options are significant; however, the most critical area of concern is option B.

10. **Answer: D. Conducting an end-to-end walk-through of the change management process**
Explanation: To determine design effectiveness most effectively, you should understand the end-to-end process of change control management. This observation is the best way to ensure that the process is effectively designed. The other options are not as effective as having a process walk-through.

11. **Answer: B. The change management procedure should be followed for patch installation**
Explanation: The change management process includes approvals, testing, scheduling, and rollback arrangements. It will help to prevent the system from malfunctioning due to an unorganized process of patch installation; the other options may not directly address the concern.

12. **Answer: A. Ensuring that software has not subsequently modified**
Explanation: The objective of code signing is to provide assurance that code is generated from a reputable source and that the code has not been modified after being signed. Code signing will not provide assurance with respect to any other options. The process employs the use of a hash function to determine the integrity and authenticity of the code.

13. **Answer: A. Providing assurance that the program changes are authorized**
Explanation: A program stored in a library can be accessed only by authorized users. Also, it has provisions for reviewing and approving software changes. Library control software ensures that only authorized changes are allowed.

14. **Answer: A. Reviewing changes in software version control**
Explanation: Software version control will help to address this issue. An IS auditor should review the version of the software that is moved to production. This will help to determine that only the updated version is transferred to the production server.

15. **Answer: A. Changes should be logged and approved on the next business day**
Explanation: Options B, C, and D are not feasible for releasing emergency changes. The best compensatory control is to log all such changes and subsequently approve those changes.

16. **Answer: C. The application owners not being aware of the modification**
Explanation: The major risk in this scenario is that application owners are not aware of the modification. This can have serious repercussions on critical business processes. Options A and B are important but not as critical as option C.

17. **Answer: D. An adequate process of approval and review for critical changes**
Explanation: It is very important to follow the process of approval and review for changes. It ensures proper authorization for critical changes and also enforces separation of duties. It prevents unauthorized changes by any single employee. The other options serve as good controls, but option D is considered the best for processing configuration changes.

18. **Answer: C. The non-availability of a configuration management database**
Explanation: The configuration management database is used to monitor configuration assets and their dependencies. Its absence may result in incorrect approvals and configuration. Also, dependencies may be ignored during configuration. The other options are not as significant as option C.

19. **Answer: D. A change request being initiated and approved by the same employee**
Explanation: The major concern here is change requests being initiated and approved by the same employee. This violates the principle of segregation of duties. An employee should not be able to approve their own request. The other options are not as significant as option D.

20. **Answer: C. Reviewing samples of change authorization first and then analyzing the supporting change authorization**
Explanation: Reviewing a sample of modified programs and then tracing back to relevant supporting change authorization is the best way to test change management control. The other options will not able to identify changes without supporting authorization.

21. **Answer: A. Subsequent review and approval of all emergency changes**
Explanation: The best control is to review and approve such changes on the next working day. Only capturing the logs will not serve the purpose. Logs should be reviewed and approved for better control. Pre-approved changes are against best practices. It is good to have documented processes of emergency change management, but the best control is the subsequent review and approval of all changes.

22. **Answer: B. Approval from the owner of the information system asset**
Explanation: It is important to have the approval of the asset owner to avoid serious business disruption due to patch updates. The other options are not as significant as option B.

23. **Answer: A. Review the patch management policy and analyze the risks associated with delayed updates**
Explanation: An IS auditor should determine whether policies are appropriate and examine the risks associated with a delayed update. There may be a scenario where the risk of system instability is greater than the risk of having a delayed patch update. So, before reporting, the IS auditor should determine the overall risk associated with a delayed update.

24. **Answer: C. A change can have a significant impact on business operation**
Explanation: In some scenarios, a change is required to be implemented as soon as possible, for which normal change management procedures cannot be applied. Such changes have a significant impact on business operations.

25. **Answer: A. Granting production access to individual IDs as and when required**
Explanation: The best process to use to establish accountability is the use of individual IDs. When a change is complete, access can be removed. Generic IDs do not establish accountability. It is not cost-effective to employ dedicated resources for only emergency changes. Emergency changes require immediate action and obtaining prior authorization may not be feasible.

26. **Answer: A. The overall risk should be analyzed before any recommendation is made.**
Explanation: The first step is to analyze the overall risk, and then appropriate steps can be taken to address the risk.

27. **Answer: A. Determine whether this process is allowed by policy**
Explanations: In a few scenarios, users are granted the authority to change a system. However, the process should be followed as required by policy. If there is no policy of granting access, then such a policy should be designed to ensure that there are no unauthorized changes.

28. **Answer: A. Changes should be approved by supervisor**
Explanation: The best method is having approval by the supervisor as a requirement. This will prevent unauthorized changes to critical files.

29. **Answer: C. Transaction logs**
Explanation: Transaction logs are used as an audit trail, which contains a detailed list of events with information such as the date and time of the event, the user ID, and the terminal location. This will help to investigate exceptions in the shortest possible time.

IT service level management

1. **Answer: A. A transition clause on the expiry of the contract not being included**
Explanation: In the absence of a transition clause, service providers may not provide appropriate support upon the expiry or termination of the contract. They may not make relevant data or applications available to the organization. This may impact the continuity of the outsourced process. This would be the greatest risk as compared to the other options.

2. **Answer: A. A "right to audit" clause not being included**
Explanation: The absence of a "right to audit" clause would prevent the organization from determining the security arrangement of the service provider. The organization would not have any assurance about contractual and legal compliance from the service provider. The other options are not as significant as this one. Option D, in fact, exposes the service provider's liability to an unlimited extent and that is not a concern for the service receiver.

3. **Answer: B. The cloud provider reserving the right to access data for certain processes**
Explanation: The organization must review regulations as there may be regulatory restrictions on accessing and utilizing sensitive customer data with the consent of the customer. Also, the organization must determine that appropriate controls are applied to protect customer data.

4. **Answer: A. The service parameters not being included in the SLA**
Explanation: The absence of service parameters will make it difficult to determine the efficiency and effectiveness of a third-party service provider.

5. **Answer: B. An independent audit report**
Explanations: Independent audit reports will provide the greatest assurance about the control effectiveness of service providers. The other options are good indicators but do not provide reasonable assurance.

6. **Answer: A. Documenting, monitoring, and managing agreed-upon service parameters**
Explanation: The main objective of service level management is to document and monitor the service parameters. Service level management does not necessarily support other objectives.

7. **Answer: B. Get confirmation from both the departments about the content of the agreement**
Explanation: The first step will be to understand the current practice being followed. Also, make sure that both parties are on the same page and that there is no disagreement regarding the service parameters.

8. **Answer: B. The downtime report maintained by the organization**
   Explanation: Data maintained by the organization is more reliable. Downtime reports maintained by organizations should be used to validate compliance with the SLA. The utilization report does not provide evidence to monitor the ISP; it indicates the resource utilization of the organization.

Database management

1. **Answer: A. Foreign key**
   Explanation: Referential integrity refers to the integrity and correctness of data within a related table. The primary key and its associated foreign key must be consistent. Changes to the primary key must be applied to associated foreign keys. Referential integrity will prevent users from adding records in a foreign table. At the same time, users cannot delete primary keys if related records are available in foreign tables.

2. **Answer: A. That the default settings are modified**
   Explanation: Keeping the default database server settings is a major risk that needs to be addressed immediately. Default password settings can be easily exploited by malicious code or by intruders. The other options are not as critical as option A.

3. **Answer: B. Update patches for the operating system**
   Explanation: Patch updating is the function of the system administrator and should not be performed by a DBA to avoid the risks associated with the inappropriate segregation of duties. The other functions are normally performed by a DBA.

4. **Answer: A. Understanding the data flow and storage**
   Explanation: A data flow diagram is ideally used to understand how data is flowing and where data is stored. It helps an IS auditor to understand the input, processing, and output of data. A classification policy helps to understand data classification schemes. A data dictionary is used to understand data definitions.

5. **Answer: C. Increased risk to redundancy**
   Explanation: Normalization is a process of reducing duplicate data and thus reducing data redundancy. Redundancy is considered negative in a database environment as it requires more effort and storage to handle the data. Denormalizing increases data redundancy.

6. **Answer: A. Data integrity**
   Explanation: The major concern when it comes to data migration from one vendor to another vendor is the integrity of data and ensuring that the data is migrated completely, correctly, and accurately. The other options may not be directly impacted by data migration.

7. **Answer: B. Prevent integrity issues during simultaneous updates by multiple users**
   Explanation: Concurrency control manages simultaneous operations in DBMSes and ensures that there are no conflicts. Concurrency control ensures that the integrity of data remains intact. It will not directly impact other options.

8. **Answer: B. Table link checks**
   Explanation: A table link check helps to identify table linking errors, such as incomplete or inaccurate content in a database. It provides assurance about the integrity of a database. Log monitoring may indicate some events; however, table link checks provide reliable assurance about integrity. Query time checks help to improve database performance. Rollback and roll forward help in recovering from disruption but do not help to check the integrity of existing database content.

9. **Answer: A. Their named account**
   Explanation: The use of a DBA's named account will provide accountability for the changes made. A shared account makes it difficult to establish the identity of the person making the change. Server administrative accounts are generally shared by administrators. Users should not have the privilege to make database changes.

10. **Answer: C. Using the DBA account from making the change and reviewing logs for that change the next day**
    Explanation: A database should only be changed using a DBA account. Furthermore, any changes made after office hours should be appropriately reviewed and approved the next day.

11. **Answer: B. DBAs should not have access to the log server**
    Explanation: To protect the integrity and availability of the database, it is required to store the logs in a separate server to which the DBA does not have any access. The other options do not directly help to protect the integrity of the database logs.

12. **Answer: A. Maintenance of the database activity logs**
    Explanation: Maintenance of the database activity logs should be done by a separate team. This will help to protect logs related to DBA activities. This will ensure the appropriate segregation of duties. The other options are generally performed by the DBA as part of their normal job function.

13. **Answer: B. Incorporating integrity constraints in the database**
Explanation: Integrity constraints are preventive controls that check for out-of-range data and prevent that data from being entered into the database. The other options are detective controls and will not prevent out-of-range data.

14. **Answer: A. Atomicity**
Explanation: Atomicity ensures that either a complete transaction is executed or none of it is processed. Consistency ensures that the transaction has not violated any integrity rules. Isolation ensures that each transaction is isolated from other transactions. Durability ensures that once a transaction is completely processed, it will not be impacted by subsequent hardware or software failure.

15. **Answer: B. Structured Query Language**
Explanation: Structured Query Language is an industry-accepted language that helps to ensure the portability of an application for connecting to a database. Atomicity is a feature of DBMSes that ensures that either an entire transaction is processed or none of it. Table link checks check for any table linking errors. Tracing and tagging are used to test application systems and controls.

16. **Answer: A. An error, as corrupted data may not be available on the master database when these transactions are processed**
Explanation: When a foreign key is corrupted, a new transaction will not be able to effectively look for relevant data in the master database. As such, this will result in an error while updating the database. It is possible to correct this error by re-indexing. This will not have any impact on the normalization and integrity constraints of the database.

17. **Answer: D. Foreign key**
Explanation: Referential integrity will prevent the deletion of a row in the primary table as long as it has an associated foreign key.

18. **Answer: A. Analyze the justification**
Explanation: The next step should be a review of the justification for denormalization. In many cases, denormalization is considered the best option for improving database performance.

19. **Answer: B. Default security settings not being changed**
Explanation: The default security settings are known to everyone and if not changed, they can be exposed by intruders. The other options are not as serious as this one.

20. **Answer: B. Integrity**
Explanation: Normalization is the process of the removal of duplicate data elements from a database. Disabling normalization will result in more redundant data, which may impact the consistency and integrity of data.

21. **Answer: B. Commitment and rollback control**
Explanation: Commitment and rollback control ensures that a transaction is completed entirely or not at all. In the case of disruption, if a transaction cannot be fully completed, then partial updates are rolled back so that the database returns to its prior state. This ensures the integrity of a transaction.

22. **Answer: D. User spool and database limit control**
Explanation: A user spool limit control limits the space available for executing user queries. This will help to prevent poorly formed queries from utilizing excess system resources and thereby impacting general query performance. The other options would not directly impact query performance.

23. **Answer: B. Immediate prior to the last transaction**
Explanation: For before-image dumps, restoration will begin from before the last transaction, as the last transaction would not have been entered during the interruption.

24. **Answer: D. Commit and rollback control**
Explanation: Commit features ensure that data is saved and updated in the database once transaction processing is completed. Rollback features ensure that partially completed transactions (due to interruption) are reversed and not saved. Thus, commit and rollback controls ensure that only entire transactions are saved in the database.

25. **Answer: C. Restore procedure**
Explanation: The restore procedure is the corrective control of all the options here. The restore procedure helps to restore databases to their latest archived version. All other options are either preventive or detective controls.

26. **Answer: A. Minimize exposure**
Explanation: Segmentation for critical data will minimize exposure to particular threats. The threat may remain the same but overall exposure will be minimized. Segmentation will not have an impact on cost and criticality.

27. **Answer: A. Log capturing and reviewing**
Explanation: Capturing detailed audit logs and reviewing them will establish accountability for database changes. If logs are not captured, other options will not help to establish accountability.

28. **Answer: A. The integrity of source data**
Explanation: Correct, complete, and accurate source data is the most important factor for the quality of data. If source data is questionable, then other options will not help in capturing quality data.

29. **Answer: A. Integrity constraints**
    Explanation: The use of integrity constraints is a preventive control for out-of-range data. Integrity constraints allow only predefined tables or rules and thus prevent undefined data from being entered. Logs are a detective control and will not prevent out-of-range data. Table links are also detective controls for finding linkage errors. Tracing and tagging is a type of test to test application systems and controls.

30. **Answer: B. You should verify the migrated individual account balance on a sample basis.**
    Explanation: Verifying the individual account balances on a sample basis is the correct option here. The other options will provide assurance about the batch level but not about the correctness of an individual balance.

31. **Answer: A. The owner of the data**
    Explanation: The data owner is responsible for authorizing access to data.

32. **Answer: B. Analyze the justification of the DBA's rights**
    Explanation: The first step will be to analyze the justification and review the relevant controls for DBA activities.

33. **Answer: A. Incorporate column- and row-level restrictions**
    Explanation: Column- and row-level restrictions control user access. A particularly sensitive column or row can be restricted to only a few authorized users. Creating a separate database for each subject is not feasible. Options B and D should apply to all users and do not specifically address the protection of specific sensitive data.

34. **Answer: A. Capturing and reviewing the logs**
    Explanation: Accountability means the acknowledgment of responsibility for actions. To enforce accountability, a log management process is required. Logs should be able to capture relevant details, such as usernames, timing, transactions, and other details that can be traced back to a particular user.

35. **Answer: B. The confidentiality of client data**
    Explanation: Storing client data in a web server increases the risk to data confidentiality as data is exposed to the internet. This is a major concern.

8
Business Resilience

In this chapter, we will discuss and learn about some important aspects of building a resilient business environment. Business resilience is the mechanism by which prevention and recovery mechanisms are developed to deal with possible threats to a company. It is the ability to adapt quickly to disruptions while maintaining ongoing business operations and safeguarding people, assets, and brand equity overall. Business resilience goes one step beyond recovering from disasters by providing post-disaster solutions to prevent expensive disruption, strengthen vulnerabilities, and sustain company operations in the face of new, unforeseen breaches.

The following topics will be covered in the chapter:

- **Business impact analysis (BIA)**
- Data backup and restoration
- System resiliency
- **Business continuity plan (BCP)**
- **Disaster recovery plan (DRP)**
- DRP – test methods
- **Recovery Time Objective (RTO)** and **Recovery Point Objective (RPO)**
- Alternate recovery site

Business impact analysis

An IS auditor should have a thorough understanding of the objectives of the BIA. The BIA is a process to determine and evaluate the impact of disruption on business processes and so prepare to deal with such disruptive events.

The following are some of the important aspects of a BIA:

- A BIA is a process to determine critical processes that have a considerable impact on business processes. It determines processes to be recovered as a priority so as to ensure an organization's survival.

- In order to conduct a successful BIA, it is necessary to obtain an understanding of the organization and key business processes and its dependency on IT and other resources. This can be obtained from the outcome of the risk assessment.

- The involvement of senior management, the IT department, and end users is critical in terms of conducting a BIA successfully.

- The following are some of the approaches when it comes to performing a BIA:

  - A questionnaire approach involves developing a detailed set of questions and circulating it to key users. The information obtained is then tabulated and analyzed to develop a BIA.

  - An interview approach involves interviewing key users. The information obtained is tabulated and analyzed to develop a BIA.

  - A meeting approach involves holding meetings with key users to ascertain the potential business impact of various disruptions.

- As far as is possible, the BIA team should also consider past transaction history to determine possible impacts if systems are not available as a result of a particular incident.

- To determine the business impact, two independent cost factors need to be considered. The first one is downtime cost. Examples of downtime cost include a drop in sales, the cost of idle resources, and interest costs. Another cost element relates to alternative collection measures, such as the activation of a BCP and other recovery costs.

- Once the BIA is available for each process, it is important to prioritize the processes that need to be recovered first. This criticality analysis should be performed in co-ordination with IT and business users.

- The business process owner possesses the most relevant information relating to processes, and so they are regarded as the best source for determining process criticality.

- Once the critical assets have been determined through the BIA, the next step is to develop a recovery strategy that ensures that critical assets are recovered as soon as possible to minimize the impact of the disaster. A recovery strategy is primarily influenced by the BIA.

- The BIA and risk assessment have almost the same elements, except for a downtime analysis, which is an additional component in a BIA. A downtime analysis determines the acceptable system downtime. This is only conducted in a BIA.
- The primary criterion for determining the severity of service disruption is the period during which the system will remain down. The higher the system downtime, the higher the disruption severity.

Key aspects from the perspective of the CISA exam

The following table covers the key aspects from the perspective of the CISA exam:

CISA questions	Possible answers
Who can provide best information to determine the criticality of the system?	Business Process Owner
Objective of BIA	To determine critical processes that have considerable impact on business processes. It determines processes to be recovered on priority to ensure organization's survival.
What is the primary criteria to determine severity of service disruption?	Period of downtime
Recovery strategy is primarily influenced by	BIA

Self-assessment questions

1. **As regards the BIA, which of the following is the best source for determining system criticality?**
    A. IT senior management
    B. Industry practices
    C. Business process owner
    D. Audit reports

2. **Which of the following is the best method for determining the criticality of application systems?**
    A. To conduct a BIA
    B. To interview developers
    C. To perform an audit
    D. To conduct a gap analysis

3. **Which of the following is the next step once the BIA has been completed?**
    A. To develop a business continuity strategy
    B. To develop testing procedures
    C. To develop a user training schedule
    D. To develop a BCP

4. **Which of the following factors differentiates a BIA from a risk assessment?**
    A. The availability of an asset inventory
    B. A vulnerability analysis
    C. A threat analysis
    D. A system downtime analysis

5. **Which of the following is the primary criterion for determining the severity of service disruption?**
    A. The amount of recovery
    B. The period of downtime
    C. The nature of the disruption
    D. Negative market impact

6. **Which of the following is primarily influenced by the BIA?**
    A. A recovery strategy
    B. An alternate site
    C. The responsibilities of the crisis management team
    D. The responsibilities of the disaster recovery team

7. **Which of the following is the main objective of the BIA?**
    A. To define a recovery strategy
    B. To identify an alternate site
    C. To define a testing methodology
    D. To determine loss expectancy

8. **The BIA determines:**
    A. processes that generate the most financial value
    B. processes that should be recovered as a priority to ensure an organization's survival
    C. processes that are aligned with the business strategy
    D. processes that have a direct impact on customer service

9. **The priority in terms of the recovery of IT assets during a disaster can be determined by:**
    A. a crisis management plan
    B. an incident management plan
    C. BIA
    D. a vulnerability analysis

10. **As part of a BIA, which of the following is identified first?**
    A. The risk applicable to critical business processes
    B. The critical business processes to prioritize recovery
    C. The resources required for recovery
    D. Threats applicable to critical business processes

Data backup and restoration

In information technology, a backup, or data backup, is a copy of computer data taken and generally stored in a remote location so that it may be used to restore the original after a data loss event. Data loss can be the result of any number of internal or external factors, including computer viruses, hardware failure, file corruption caused by fire, natural calamities, and hacking attacks.

An organization should have a documented backup policy in place that clearly identifies the type of data and information for which making a backup is mandatory.

Let's now have a look at the different types of backup strategies.

Types of backup strategy

The backup policy should be approved by senior management. It should have clear and specific instructions regarding the organization's backup and retention procedure. The **CISA Review Manual (CRM)** covers the following types of backup strategy:

- Backup of the full database
- Backup of new data
- Differential backup
- Incremental backup

In a full backup, the entire database is backed up every time, regardless of previous backups. However, a full backup consumes a lot of time and space. To avoid this, many organizations resort to either a differential backup or an incremental backup. Let's understand the difference between differential and incremental backups:

Differential Backup	Incremental Backup
Backup is taken only of the new data created since last full backup (last backup to be a full backup only).	Backup is taken only of the new data created since last backup (last backup can be either full backup or incremental backup).

Let's understand this with the help of the following example:

Day	Differential Backup	Incremental Backup
Monday	Full backup is taken on Monday	Full backup is taken on Monday
Tuesday	On Tuesday backup taken for new data created after Monday's backup	On Tuesday, backup is taken for new data created after Monday's backup
Wednesday	On Wednesday backup taken for new data created after Monday's backup (ignoring Tuesday's backup)	On Wednesday, backup is taken for new data created after Tuesday's backup
Thursday	On Thursday backup taken for new data created after Monday's backup (ignoring Tuesday's and Wednesday's backups)	On Thursday, backup is taken for new data created after Wednesday's backup
Friday	On Friday backup taken for new data created after Monday's backup (ignoring Tuesday's, Wednesday's and Thursday's backups)	On Friday, backup taken for new data created after Thursday's backup

Storage capacity for each backup scheme

Let's understand the requirements in terms of time and media capacity for various data storage schemes:

- **Full backup**: Requires more time and storage capacity compared with the other two schemes
- **Differential**: Requires less time and storage capacity compared with a full backup, but more than an incremental backup
- **Incremental**: Requires less time and storage capacity compared with the other two schemes

Restoration capability for each backup scheme

Let's understand the effectiveness of the various schemes in the case of data restoration:

- **Full backup**: The fastest of all three schemes
- **Differential**: Slower than a full backup, but faster than an incremental backup
- **Incremental**: The slowest of all three schemes

Advantages and disadvantages of each scheme

The IS auditor should understand the following advantages and disadvantages of each backup strategy:

Full Backup	Incremental Backup	Differential Backup
• Advantage-Unique Repository in case of restoration • Disadvantage-Requires more time and capacity	• Advantage-Faster backup and less media capacity is required. • Disadvantage-Restoration requires more time.	• As compared to full backup, faster backup and requires less capacity. However more times requires for restoration. • As compared to incremental backup, more media capacity is required. However restoration is quicker.

Each method has its own advantages and disadvantages, as mentioned in the preceding diagram.

Key aspects from the perspective of the CISA exam

The following table covers the key aspects from the perspective of the CISA exam:

CISA Questions	Possible Answer
A backup is taken of the full database irrespective of earlier backup:	Full backup
A backup is taken only for new data created after last full backup:	Differential backup
A backup of data is taken only for new data created either after last backup	Incremental backup
A backup strategy that demands highest media capacity for backup storage	Full backup
The most effective and faster backup strategy for data restoration	Full backup

Self-assessment questions

1. In which of the following backup strategies is a backup taken of the full database irrespective of the previous backup?
    A. A full backup
    B. A differential backup
    C. A day's end backup
    D. An incremental backup

2. In which of the following backup strategies is a backup only taken of new data created after either a full backup or an incremental backup?
    A. A full backup
    B. A differential backup
    C. A grandfather-father-son rotation backup
    D. An incremental backup

3. In which of the following backup strategies is a backup only taken of new data created after a full backup (an incremental backup is ignored)?
    A. A full backup
    B. A differential backup
    C. A grandfather-father-son rotation backup
    D. An incremental backup

4. The backup strategy that demands the highest media capacity for backup storage is:

    A. a full backup

    B. a differential backup

    C. a grandfather-father-son rotation backup

    D. an incremental backup

5. The most effective and fastest backup strategy for data restoration is:

    A. a full backup

    B. a differential backup

    C. a grandfather-father-son rotation backup

    D. an incremental backup

System resiliency

System resilience is the ability of a system to withstand a disaster and to recover within an acceptable timeframe. In this section, we will have a detailed discussion on application resiliency and telecommunications resiliency.

Application resiliency – clustering

Clustering helps to protect an application against a disaster. The aim of clustering is to provide for the high availability of the system. A cluster is a software that is installed on every server where the application runs. An application that is clustered is protected against a single point of failure.

Application clusters can be either active-passive or active-active. In an active-passive setup, an application runs only on one node, while other passive nodes are used only if an application fails on the active node.

In an active-active cluster setup, the application runs on every cluster. An active-active setup, though more expensive than an active-passive setup, provides quick application recovery, load balancing, and scalability.

Telecommunication network resiliency

In today's business scenario, it is very important to arrange for redundant telecommunication and network devices in order to ensure the continuity of business operations. The following are network protection methods:

- **Alternative routing:**
  - Last-mile circuit protection
  - Long-haul network diversity
- **Diverse routing**

Alternative routing

Alternative routing can be further bifurcated into two types:

Last mile circuit protection	Long haul network diversity
Last mile circuit protection is used to have redundancy for local communication.	It is used to have redundancy for long distance communication.
Backup is taken only for new data created after last full backup	Differential Backup
backup of data is taken only for new data created either after last backup	Incremental Backup
Backup strategy which demand highest media capacity for backup storage	Full backup
Most effective and faster backup strategy for data restoration	Full backup

This is a method for routing the information through alternative cables, including copper or fiber optics cables.

Diverse routing

This is a method for routing information through split or duplicate cables:

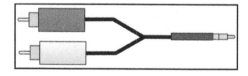

In diverse routing, a single cable is split into two parts, whereas in alternative routing, two entirely different cables are used.

Self-assessment questions

1. An arrangement for routing information through split or duplicate cables is known as:
    - A. a bridge
    - B. diverse routing
    - C. alternative routing
    - D. a gateway

2. In which of the following approaches are redundant cables, such as local carrier lines, microwaves and/or coaxial cables, used to access local communication?
    - A. Long-haul network diversity
    - B. Last-mile circuit protection
    - C. Diverse routing
    - D. Bridge routing

3. An arrangement for routing information via an alternative medium, such as copper or fiber optics coaxial cables, is known as:
    - A. a bridge
    - B. diverse routing
    - C. alternative routing
    - D. a gateway

Business continuity plan

The objective of a BCP process is to manage and mitigate the risk of disaster so that the continuity of business operations can be ensured. It is very important that the BCP is reviewed and approved by senior management. This will ensure that the BCP is aligned with the goals of the business.

Steps of the BCP life cycle

The first step in preparing a BCP is to identify the processes of strategic importance for attaining business objectives.

The following are the steps of the BCP life cycle:

1. Project and scope planning
2. Risk assessment and analysis
3. BIA
4. Business continuity strategy development
5. BCP development
6. Business continuity awareness training
7. BCP testing
8. BCP monitoring, maintenance, and updating

Content of the BCP

The plan should be well documented and written in simple language that should be understandable to all. Interviewing the key personnel to determine their understanding of the BCP will help the auditor to evaluate the clarity and simplicity of the BCP. The plan should clearly document the responsibilities and accountability of each individual responsible for specific tasks in the event of a disaster.

Responsibility for declaring the disaster

It is very important to make a key employee responsible for declaring a disaster. If a disaster is not declared by anyone, the BCP would not be invoked and thereby threaten the continuity of the business.

A Single Plan

It is recommended to have a single continuity plan for the whole organization. In cases where the BCP is maintained unit-wise, it should be ensured that all the plans have a uniform approach and are linked to one another, wherever required. It is very important that each plan has a uniform structure and language and that plans are consistent with one another.

IT plans and procedures must be consistent with, and support, the BCP. A copy of the BCP should be kept at an offsite location.

Backup procedure for critical operations

A BCP should also consider the type and requirement of the backup procedure. Generally, for critical and time-sensitive data, shadow file processing is recommended. In shadow file processing, exact duplicates of files are maintained, preferably at a remote site. Both the files are processed concurrently. Shadow file processing can be implemented as a recovery mechanism for extremely time-sensitive transaction processing. It is important to ensure that the offsite location is not subject to the same risks as the primary site. If both the primary site and the offsite location operate from the same place, a disaster may put both of them out of action, which could have an adverse impact on business continuity.

The involvement of process owners in the BCP

As regards successful development of the BCP, one important aspect is input from the process owners. The involvement of process owners is very important in identifying critical processes, their dependencies, and the required level of the RTO.

The protection of human life is a critical factor in any business continuity procedure. This takes precedence over all other elements.

BCP and risk assessment

It is recommended to review the BCP in terms of its adequacy every time a risk assessment is conducted in order to ensure that the BCP is aligned with the latest risk assessment of the organization.

It is important that the BCP contains the level of information security that is required when a business recovery process is in place. The information security level may be the same, or lower or higher compared with what is required during normal business operations. On the basis of the risk assessment, the worst case scenarios and corresponding strategies can be incorporated in the BCP.

Testing the BCP

The adequacy of the BCP can be evaluated by performing a number of tests. A few important tests are explained here. The following are some of the tests to be performed in order to evaluate the adequacy of the BCP:

- **Paper test/desk-based evaluation**: In this type of test, concerned staff have a walkthrough of the BCP and discuss what might happen if service disruption of a particular type occurs.

- **Preparedness test**: In this type of test, with the help of a simulated system crash, preparedness is verified in a localized environment. This is a cost-effective way to determine the adequacy of the plan. It also provides an opportunity to improve the plan in increments. This is regarded as a localized version of a full test, wherein resources are expended in the simulation of a system crash. A preparedness test includes phase-wise simulation of the entire environment at a very reasonable cost and helps the recovery team to understand the various challenges associated with the actual test scenario.

- **Full operational test**: In this type of test, the BCP is implemented in consideration of actual service disruptions involving a complete shutdown of operations. A full operational test is to be conducted only after a paper test and preparedness test have been carried out. A full operational test is a costly and time-consuming affair and involves many challenges.

It must be noted that the results of the preceding test should be properly documented and evaluated. It is not possible to evaluate the effectiveness of the BCP if test results are not properly documented and analyzed. Testing the BCP will help to determine the effectiveness of the plan and to identify any gaps therein. This provides an opportunity to improve the plan.

The following diagram summarizes the BCP requirements from the perspective of an IS audit:

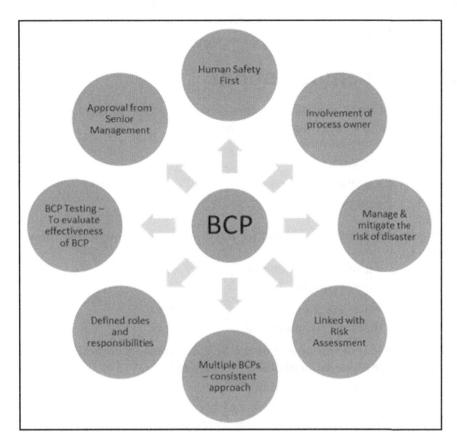

A CISA aspirant should be familiar with the aforementioned key aspects of the BCP.

Key aspects from the perspective of the CISA exam

The following table covers the key aspects from the perspective of the CISA exam:

CISA questions	Possible answers
Which kind of test simulates a system crash and is performed on different aspects of plan in a cost- effective way?	Preparedness test
The objective of testing BCP	To identify limitations of BCP

Critical factor in any business continuity procedure	Protection of human life
Best way to determine the effectiveness of a BCP	BCP test results
Factor to be considered for activation of an organization's BCP	Period of outage
BCP should be aligned with	Risk assessment

Self-assessment questions

1. **A BCP test that simulates a system crash and is performed on different aspects of the plan in a cost-effective manner is:**
   - A. a full operational test
   - B. a paper test
   - C. a walkthrough test
   - D. a preparedness test

2. **The most appropriate method for backing up an airline reservation system's data is:**
   - A. warm site provisioning
   - B. hot site provisioning
   - C. hard-disk mirroring in the same server
   - D. shadow file processing

3. **For successful development of the BCP, the most important aspect is:**
   - A. the involvement of the process owner
   - B. the involvement of the DBA
   - C. the involvement of the head of IT
   - D. the involvement of the Board of Directors

4. **The aim of integrating the testing aspect of non-critical systems in the DRP with the BCP is:**
   - A. to ensure that the DRP is well drafted
   - B. to ensure that the services of the subject matter expert are acquired for testing
   - C. to integrate the BCP's assumptions regarding the existence of capabilities with DRP testing
   - D. to train business executives on aspects of disaster recovery capabilities

5. **Which of the following is considered a major weakness with respect to management of the BCP?**
    A. The plan is approved by the CEO
    B. A call tree is not reviewed for more than 6 months
    C. Test results are not documented and evaluated
    D. A training schedule for the recovery team is not included

6. **Which of the following is the main reason for testing a BCP?**
    A. To make employees aware of the plan
    B. To ensure that all risks are eliminated
    C. To consider all possible disaster scenarios
    D. To identify limitations in the BCP

7. **The most important aspect to be considered in a business continuity audit is:**
    A. the backup procedure
    B. recovery site availability
    C. human safety procedures
    D. the extent of insurance coverage

8. **The effectiveness of a BCP can be evaluated by reviewing:**
    A. the involvement of various stakeholders
    B. plan test results
    C. employee awareness regarding the plan
    D. offsite controls

9. **The aim of an IS auditor in interviewing key stakeholders to determine their understanding of the BCP is:**
    A. to determine the simplicity of the BCP
    B. to determine the effectiveness of the BCP
    C. to determine the adequacy of the BCP
    D. to determine the organization's ability to respond in the event of a disaster

10. **A BCP does not define a situation in which a crisis can be declared. Which of the following is of the greatest concern?**
    A. A delay in assessing the situation
    B. The impact arising from the execution of the DRP
    C. A delay in notifying the recovery team
    D. A delay in potential crisis recognition

11. **What is recommended as the next step once the annual risk assessment has been completed?**
    A. To review the existing BCP for adequacy
    B. To conduct a full operational test on the existing BCP
    C. To improve BCP awareness among employees
    D. To update the call tree in the BCP

12. **With respect to information security, the most important inclusion in the BCP is:**
    A. the level of information security requirements during a business recovery process
    B. the requirement for information security resources
    C. the change management structure for information security
    D. the information security budget

13. **The most important consideration when establishing an offsite facility is the fact that:**
    A. the offsite facility is located at a different geographical location and is not subject to the same risks as the primary site
    B. the offsite facility is provided with the same level of protection as the primary site
    C. the offsite facility is managed by a reliable third party
    D. the offsite facility is approved by the Board of Directors

14. **The prime objective of integrating the BCP into IT project management is:**
    A. to test the requirements of business continuity
    B. to develop more comprehensive requirements
    C. to minimize the BCP budget
    D. to minimize project timelines

15. **While reviewing BCP test results, the IS auditor noted that notification systems may not be available during a severe disaster. What should the IS auditor recommend?**
    A. That a salvage team should recover notification systems as a priority
    B. That the notification system should be tested at frequent intervals
    C. The use of a resilient notification system along with redundancy
    D. The use of a vault for notification system storage

16. **Which of the following should be considered before activating an organization's BCP?**
    - A. A period of outage
    - B. The source of the outage
    - C. The cause of the outage
    - D. The type of outage

17. **The effectiveness of the BCP can be reviewed by:**
    - A. the adoption of industry good practices
    - B. the results of the business continuity test
    - C. the availability of an offsite facility
    - D. comparing the BCP budget with actual costs

18. **To keep the BCP updated, it is recommended:**
    - A. to perform a walkthrough of different scenarios of the plan from beginning to end
    - B. to ensure that critical systems are resilient
    - C. to perform a full interruption test procedure
    - D. to make key employees aware of the BCP

19. **The appropriate method for testing a BCP is:**
    - A. an interface test
    - B. a paper test
    - C. a system test
    - D. a unit test

20. **An effective BCP can be ensured by:**
    - A. circulating the plan to all concerned parties
    - B. the involvement of all user departments
    - C. the approval of senior management
    - D. a regular audit of the BCP

21. **The prime objective of the BCP and DRP is to:**
    - A. protect critical assets
    - B. minimize impact during a disaster
    - C. provide for the continuity of operations
    - D. protect human life

22. **In case an organization has a department-wise BCP, it is essential that:**
    A. each plan is consistent with the others
    B. all plans are approved by senior management
    C. a single plan is available that merges all other plans
    D. each plan has an implementation sequence

23. **Which of the following documents will help the most in developing a BCP?**
    A. An external audit report
    B. A risk assessment
    C. A resource analysis
    D. A gap analysis

24. **Which of the following areas is of most concern to an IS auditor?**
    A. The responsibility for declaring a disaster is not defined
    B. The disaster level is considered on the basis of damaged functions and not on the basis of duration
    C. A BCP document was reviewed and approved more than 1 year ago
    D. The difference between a disaster and an incident is not documented

25. **In the case of a separate BCP for each department, which of the following areas should be reconciled first?**
    A. A version control
    B. An evacuation plan
    C. An approval authority
    D. An offsite facility

26. **For effective implementation of the BCP, it should be:**
    A. stored in a secure offsite facility
    B. communicated to the appropriate personnel
    C. approved by senior management
    D. hosted on an organization's intranet

27. The **prime objective of the BCP is:**
    A. to provide assurances to stakeholders regarding business continuity
    B. to comply with regulatory requirements
    C. to arrange for an alternate site to meet the RTO
    D. to manage risk while recovering from a disaster

28. **The most efficient test for evaluating the effectiveness of the DRP is:**
    - A. a preparedness test
    - B. a unit test
    - C. a full operational test
    - D. a paper test

Disaster recovery plan

A DRP is a set of documented processes to recover and protect a business's IT infrastructure in the event of a disaster. It involves various plans for actions to be taken before, during, and after a disaster.

A DRP is like insurance; you will only realize its importance when a disaster occurs.

The BCP versus the DRP

A CISA aspirant should able to understand the difference between the BCP and the DRP. The objective of the BCP is to keep business operations functioning either from an alternate location or by means of alternative tools and processes. The objective of the DRP is to restore normal business operations and to recover from a disaster. The BCP is the overall architecture for business continuity, whereas the DRP is regarded as a technological aspect of the BCP with more focus on IT systems and operations.

Relationship between the DRP and the BIA

The first step in preparing any DRP is to conduct a BIA. A BIA is used to determine critical business processes and systems that need to be recovered as a priority in order for the organization to survive. Priorities are set on the basis of assigned RTOs and RPOs (discussed later in the chapter) for various processes.

If the results of the BIA are not used to design a DRP, all the required critical assets may not be covered in the DRP and, as a result, the DRP may not be adequate in helping an organization recover from a disaster.

Furthermore, an IS auditor should ensure that process owners are being involved in preparation of the BIA. The BIA and DRP may not be reliable if inputs from the process owner are not considered.

Costs associated with disaster recovery

Disaster recovery entails costs. Basically, two types of cost are associated with disaster recovery: downtime costs and recovery costs. Downtime costs include a loss of sales, idle resources, salaries, and when production or service is at a standstill due to a disaster, and these costs tend to increase over time. The earlier the recovery, the lower the downtime costs:

- Recovery costs are the costs associated with recovery procedures, such as additional costs related to the activation of the alternate site, and the costs related to the reparation of damaged assets.
- The objective of a structured DRP is to minimize both downtime and recovery costs during a disaster.
- However, to maintain a DRP, additional costs in the form of resources, the recovery site, testing, and other maintenance will result in additional costs.

Data backup

Data backup is an extremely important element of a DRP. Without access to backup data, all other efforts are in vain and it becomes very difficult to recover data following a disaster.

Considering the disaster recovery requirement, backup intervals should be aligned with the RPO. The RPO determines the maximum loss an organization can tolerate. Backup data should be taken in such a way that the latest backup supports the RPO. If the RPO is zero, then there should be real-time, online backups to ensure zero data loss.

DRP of a third-party service provider

Whenever an application or database is managed by a third-party service provider, an IS auditor should ensure the following requirements:

- DRP requirements should be incorporated in the service level agreement with the third-party service provider. It is essential that the service provider should have a contractual obligation (through an agreement) regarding the DRP arrangement. Without contractual obligations, it is difficult to enforce DRP requirements.
- The service level agreement should also include a right-to-audit clause, and the DRP arrangement should be audited at least once a year, either by the recipient of the service an or independent auditor of a service provider.

Resilient information assets

It is very important to first identify the assets that can be made more resilient to disaster. Resilient assets can withstand the effects of a disaster and prevent problems. Preventive control is always better than corrective control.

Service delivery objective

The service delivery objective is the level of service and operational capability to be maintained from an alternate site. The service delivery objective is directly related to business needs and is the level of service to be attained during disaster recovery. This is influenced by business requirements.

Key aspects from the CISA exam perspective

The following table covers the key aspects from the CISA exam perspective:

CISA questions	Possible answers
What is the Recovery Time Objective (RTO)?	Extent of acceptable system downtime
What is the Recovery Point Objective (RPO)?	Extent of acceptable data loss
Backup intervals should be best aligned with	RPO
Service delivery objective is primarily influenced by	Acceptable operational capability during disaster recovery phase
Disaster recovery prioritization is primarily influenced by	The BIA

Self-assessment questions

1. **With respect to disaster recovery costs, which of the following statements is correct?**
   A. Downtime costs decrease over time
   B. Downtime costs increase over time
   C. Downtime costs are time-neutral
   D. Downtime costs are related to the RPO

2. **Which of the following is the most important factor as regards the execution of a DRP?**
   - A. Data backup at an offsite location
   - B. An updated list of key disaster recovery team members
   - C. A well-documented RPO
   - D. A well-documented RTO

3. **Which of the following is regarded as a major risk as regards implementation of the DRP?**
   - A. The plan has not been tested
   - B. A hot site has not been identified as a recovery strategy
   - C. The results of the BIA are not considered in determining the DRP
   - D. The DRP was approved more than a year ago

4. **Which of the following is the most critical for the IS auditor when reviewing the DRP of an organization having limited IT resources?**
   - A. A test has not been conducted to ensure the adequacy of resources to recover from a disaster
   - B. The DRP was approved more than a year ago
   - C. Security requirements are not included in the DRP
   - D. A test has not been conducted for backup restoration

5. **The most important aspect for an IS auditor reviewing an organization's DRP is the fact that:**
   - A. the DRP should be tested every 6 months
   - B. the DRP should be regularly reviewed and updated
   - C. the DRP should be approved by the CEO
   - D. the DRP should be made available to every employee in the organization

6. **To determine the DRP of an application hosted in a third-party cloud, the first step of an IS auditor is:**
   - A. to conduct an audit of the third-party cloud service provider
   - B. to review the SLA with the cloud service provider
   - C. to review the DRP of the cloud service provider
   - D. to request a copy of the independent auditor's report of the cloud service provider

7. **Which of the following is a major concern for an IS auditor reviewing a disaster recovery hot site?**
    A. The use of shared accounts by system administrators at the hot site
    B. Disk space availability at the hot site is not aligned with data utilization at the primary site
    C. Physical security controls at the hot site are not audited
    D. Server security controls at the hot site are not reviewed

8. **The prime objective of the DRP is to:**
    A. decrease the length of recovery time and the associated costs
    B. increase the length of the recovery time and associated costs
    C. comply with contractual obligations
    D. decrease the length of recovery time and increase the costs of recovery

9. **The most reliable evidence with respect to disaster recovery preparedness of an organization is:**
    A. the availability of a DRP
    B. the availability of an alternate site for disaster recovery
    C. the results of DRP tests and exercises
    D. the approval of senior management in relation to the DRP

10. **The most important consideration when auditing a DRP is:**
    A. the availability of a hot site for disaster recovery
    B. the availability of approval from senior management in relation to the DRP
    C. adequate insurance coverage
    D. timely data backups and offsite storage

11. **The area of most concern for an IS auditor reviewing a DRP is:**
    A. the lack of process owner involvement
    B. the lack of documented test criteria
    C. the lack of a disaster recovery facility
    D. the lack of a data classification policy

12. **To determine acceptable downtimes in relation to the DRP, the most important criterion is:**
    A. expected annual losses
    B. the maximum tolerable outage
    C. the service delivery objective
    D. the type of disaster recovery site

13. **An organization's DRP has been modified due to a change in IT processes. However, the new plan has not been tested. Which of the following is the primary risk?**

    A. The inability to recover from catastrophic service disruption

    B. The plan may require further recovery resources

    C. The plan may be difficult to implement

    D. Downtime costs may increase

14. **Which of the following is the first approach in developing a disaster recovery strategy?**

    A. To assess whether all threats can be completely removed

    B. To assess whether resiliency can be established for critical information assets

    C. To assess whether the RTO can be minimized

    D. To assess whether the costs of recovery can be minimized

15. **The test results of the DRP indicate that server performance at the recovery site is slow. What should be the next course of action for an IS auditor?**

    A. A review log that captures processes at the recovery site

    B. A review process for conducting tests and documenting results

    C. Reviewing the DRP from the point of view of adequacy

    D. Reviewing the server setting configurations and comparing these with the primary site

16. **Which of the following DRP test results should be the greatest concern for an IS auditor?**

    A. The scope of the test only includes critical systems

    B. Backup systems were found to be defective during testing

    C. The time taken to restore the system is more than what is specified in the DRP

    D. The test procedure is not documented

17. **Which of the following should be frequently updated for continued effectiveness of the DRP?**

    A. The contact details of key staff members

    B. Asset inventory

    C. The roles and responsibilities of key staff members

    D. Procedures for conducting tests

18. **Considering the disaster recovery requirement, backup intervals should be aligned with:**
    A. the maximum tolerable period of disruption
    B. the RPO
    C. the RTO
    D. the maximum acceptable outage

19. **The disaster recovery strategy is primary influenced by:**
    A. the quantum of the data handled
    B. the nature of the data handled
    C. the maximum tolerable downtime
    D. network redundancy

20. **The service delivery objective is primarily influenced by:**
    A. acceptable operational capabilities during the disaster recovery phase
    B. downtime costs during the disaster recovery phase
    C. recovery costs during the disaster recovery phase
    D. the RTO

21. **For data synchronization between the primary site and the recovery site, which of the following is the most important objective?**
    A. The RPO
    B. The RTO
    C. The service delivery objective
    D. The maximum tolerable downtime

22. **Disaster recovery prioritization is primarily influenced by:**
    A. a vulnerability analysis
    B. a BIA
    C. the crisis management team structure
    D. the RTO

23. **Which of the following is the best evidence in terms of determining that disaster recovery procedures satisfy requirements?**
    A. Benchmarking with industry good practices
    B. Approval from senior management
    C. Tabletop exercises involving the procedures
    D. Documented responsibilities of recovery team members

24. **The most reliable method for determining the success of a disaster recovery effort is:**
    A. a tabletop test
    B. a data restoration test
    C. a paper test
    D. a unit test

25. **A DRP should primarily cover:**
    A. recovery site information
    B. crisis management team information
    C. test procedures
    D. the prioritization of processes and assets

26. **A DRP is:**
    A. not related to the BCP
    B. an operational aspect of the BCP
    C. a technological aspect of the BCP
    D. the same as the BCP

27. **The cost of normal business operations when a DRP is in place will most likely:**
    A. reduce
    B. increase
    C. not be affected
    D. fluctuate

28. **The first task in preparing a DRP is:**
    A. to design a recovery strategy
    B. to conduct a BIA
    C. to make arrangements for an alternate site
    D. to test a DRP

DRP – test methods

Regular DRP testing and exercises are very important in determining the continued adequacy and effectiveness of the DRP. It helps to validate the compatibility of the offsite facility to support the organization in case of a disaster. The following are some of the important methods for testing the DRP.

Checklist review

This test is performed prior to a real test. A checklist is provided to all members of the recovery team for review. This checklist is updated.

Structured walkthrough

This includes a review of the DRP on paper. Team members review each step to evaluate the effectiveness of the DRP. Identified gaps, deficiencies, and constraints are addressed to improve the plan.

Tabletop test

A tabletop test is conducted with the aim of practicing coordination efforts and communication methodology among the relevant members of the recovery team.

Simulation test

In this type of test, roleplay is prepared for a disaster scenario and the adequacy of the DRP is determined. This does not include activation of the recovery site.

Parallel test

In this type of test, the recovery site is activated and, at the same time, the primary site continues to operate normally.

Full interruption test

This type of test is the most expensive and potentially disruptive. The primary site is completely shut down and operations are carried out from the recovery site as per the DRP.

It is advisable that testing should start with a simple exercise and once confidence is established, it should gradually expand to a full restoration test. The following table shows how tests can be performed gradually. Tests should be scheduled in such a way that will minimize disruptions to normal operations. Key recovery team members should be actively involved in test procedures. It is recommended to conduct full interruption tests on an annual basis once the individual test is performed satisfactorily.

Test results should be recorded and evaluated to determine the adequacy and effectiveness of the DRP.

Key aspects from the CISA exam perspective

The following table covers the key aspects from the CISA exam perspective:

CISA questions	Possible answer
Primary objective of testing offsite disaster recovery facility	To validate compatibility of offsite facility
Test that involves participation of key members to practice coordination efforts	Tabletop test
Test that involves roleplay of the disaster scenario	Simulation test
Test that involves review each step of plan to evaluate the effectiveness of DRP	Structured walkthrough
Most disruptive kind of test	Full operational test

Self-assessment questions

1. **Which of the following is the primary objective of testing an offsite disaster recovery facility?**
   A. To ensure the data integrity of the offsite database
   B. To rule out the need for a detailed disaster plan
   C. To ensure continued compatibility of the offsite facility
   D. To provide training to the recovery team

2. **To ensure an effective DRP, it is most important that:**
   A. the recovery plan is stored at an alternate site
   B. the recovery plan is communicated to all users
   C. the recovery plan is tested regularly
   D. the recovery plan is approved by senior management

3. **A test that involves the participation of key members to practice coordination efforts is:**
   A. a full operational test
   B. a tabletop test
   C. a functional test
   D. a preparedness test

4. **In which of the following tests is a roleplay for the disaster scenario prepared and the adequacy of the plan determined accordingly?**
   A. Parallel test
   B. Simulation test
   C. Full interruption test
   D. Structured walkthrough

5. **In which of the following tests does a team member review each step of the plan to evaluate the effectiveness of the DRP?**
   A. Parallel test
   B. Simulation test
   C. Full interruption test
   D. Structured walkthrough

6. **Which of the following tests is the most expensive and potentially disruptive?**
   A. Checklist review
   B. Simulation test
   C. Full interruption test
   D. Structured walkthrough

Recovery Time Objective (RTO) and Recovery Point Objective (RPO)

The RTO and RPO are two very important aspects to understand from the perspective of the exam as they are very important concepts in the designing of a disaster recovery strategy.

RTO

The RTO is a measure of the user's tolerance to system downtime. In other words, the RTO is the extent of acceptable system downtime. For example, an RTO of 2 hours indicates that an organization will not be overly impacted if its system is down for up to 2 hours.

RPO

The RPO is a measure of the user's tolerance to data loss. In other words, the RPO is the extent of acceptable data loss. For example, an RPO of 2 hours indicates that an organization will not be overly impacted if it loses data for up to 2 hours.

Let's understand each of them by way of the following diagram:

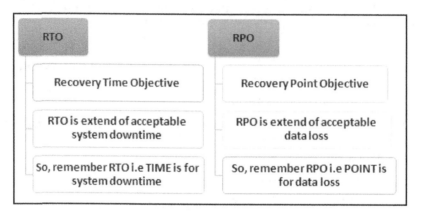

Let's understand the preceding diagram with the aid of some practical examples:

Example 1: An organization can accept data loss for up to 4 hours. However, it cannot afford to have any downtime.

Solution:

RTO – 0 hours

RPO – 4 hours

Example 2: An organization takes a data backup twice daily; that is, at 12 a.m. and then at 12 p.m. What is the RPO?

Solution: Here, a data backup is done every 12 hours, and so the maximum data loss is 12 hours. Hence, the RPO is 12 hours.

Example 3: An organization takes a data backup three times a day. The first backup is at 8 a.m., the second at 4 p.m., and the third at 12 a.m. What is the RPO?

Solution: Here, data backup is done every 8 hours, and so the maximum data loss is 8 hours. Hence, the RPO is 8 hours.

Example 4: Following an incident, systems at the primary site went down at 3 p.m. and systems then resumed from the alternate site at 6 p.m., as per the defined RTO. What is the RTO?

Solution: The system was down for 3 hours, and so the RTO is 3 hours.

Example 5: Identify the RTO and RPO in an instance where the BCP for an organization's critical system specifies that there should not be any data loss and service should be resumed within 36 hours.

Solution: Here, the organization is accepting a system downtime of up to 36 hours, and so the RTO is 36 hours. However, the organization cannot afford to have any data loss, and so the RPO is 0 hours.

RTO – 36 hours

RPO – 0 hours

RTO and RPO for critical systems

The RTO indicates a user's tolerance for system downtime. Similarly, the RPO indicates a user's tolerance for data loss. In the case of critical systems and critical data, an organization cannot afford to have much downtime or data loss. Hence, in the case of critical systems, generally, the RTO and RPO is zero, or near zero. A low RTO indicates that a system should be resumed at the earliest possible juncture. A low RPO indicates that data loss should be at a minimum.

Put another way, if the RTO and RPO are low (that is, zero or near zero), then systems and data will be critical for the organization.

RTO and RPO and maintenance costs

A low RTO indicates that systems are critical and need to be resumed as soon as possible. To achieve this objective, organizations need to invest heavily in redundancy. A hot site is ideal where the RTO is lower. This will be a costly affair.

On the other hand, if the RTO is high, this indicates that systems are not that critical, and that an organization can afford downtime to some extent. An organization need not invest in redundancy for systems with a high RTO. A cold site is ideal where the RTO is higher.

A low RPO indicates that data is critical, and it should not be lost. For example, an organization having an RPO of 0 hours needs to ensure that there should not be any data loss at all. They should invest heavily in data backup management. Data mirroring or data synchronization is an ideal technique where the RPO is zero or very low. Hence, for a low RPO, data maintenance costs will be higher compared with a high RPO.

Thus, if the RTO and RPO are low (that is, zero or near zero), then the cost of maintaining the environment is high.

RTO, RPO, and disaster tolerance

Disaster tolerance indicates the tolerance level of the organization to accept the non-availability of IT facilities. A low RTO/RPO indicates that disaster tolerance is low, that is, the organization cannot tolerate system downtime. A high RTO/RPO indicates that disaster tolerance is high, that is, the organization can tolerate system downtime up to a certain level.

Key aspects from the CISA exam perspective

The following table covers the key aspects from the CISA exam perspective:

CISA questions	Possible answer
What is Recovery Time Objective (RTO)?	The extent of acceptable system downtime.
What is Recovery Point Objective (RPO)?	The extent of acceptable data loss.
What does low RPO/RTO indicates that the system/data is?	It indicates that the system/data is critical.

Self-assessment questions

1. **Which of the following indicates an RTO?**
   A. The extent of acceptable system downtime
   B. The extent of minimum business objectives
   C. The extent of acceptable data loss
   D. The extent of crisis management insurance

2. **An organization will generally have what following level of RTO for its critical monitoring system?**
   A. A higher RTO
   B. A lower RTO
   C. Critical systems do not have an RTO
   D. A medium level of RTO, close to 50%

3. **Which of the following is indicated by the RPO?**
   A. The extent of acceptable system downtime
   B. The extent of minimum business objectives
   C. The extent of acceptable data loss
   D. The extent of crisis management insurance

4. **An organization will generally have what following level of RPO for its critical data?**
   A. A higher RPO
   B. A lower RPO
   C. Medium
   D. Above the industry standard

5. **What will be the cost of maintaining the recovery environment if the RPO is close to zero?**
   A. Lower
   B. Higher
   C. Medium
   D. The RPO and the cost of the recovery environment are independent

6. **Which of the following is ideal for implementing a hot site as a recovery strategy?**
   A. When the RTO is higher
   B. When the RPO is higher
   C. When the RTO is lower
   D. When disaster tolerance is higher

7. **Which of the following is ideal for implementing data mirroring as a recovery strategy?**
    A. When disaster tolerance is higher
    B. When the RTO is higher
    C. When the RPO is lower
    D. When the RPO is higher

8. **The most cost-effective solution for an RTO of 72 hours and an RPO of 0 hours will be:**
    A. implementation of a hot site that can be operational within 4 hours and where a data backup is performed every hour
    B. entering a reciprocal agreement for an alternate site where data backup is performed every 4 hours
    C. implementation of a hot site that can be operational within 4 hours and where data is backed up synchronously
    D. implementation of a warm site that can be operational within 60 hours and where data is backed up synchronously

9. **Which of the following is ideal for implementing a hot site as a recovery strategy?**
    A. A low disaster tolerance
    B. A high RTO
    C. A high RPO
    D. A high disaster tolerance

Alternate recovery site

In the case of an incident, a primary site may not be available for business operations. To address such similar scenarios, an organization should have an arrangement for the resumption of services from an alternate site so as to ensure the continuity of business operations. Many business organizations cannot afford the discontinuity of business processes even for a single day and so they need to invest heavily in an alternate recovery site. These arrangements can vary according to the needs of the business organization.

From the perspective of the CISA exam, candidates should have an understanding of the following alternate recovery sites:

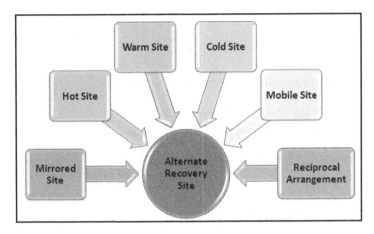

Let's look at each of the preceding alternate sites in detail.

Mirrored site

A mirrored site is regarded as an exact replica of the primary site. When arranging a mirrored site, the following components are already factored in:

- The availability of space and basic infrastructure
- The availability of all business applications
- The availability of an updated data backup

A mirrored site can be made available for business operations in the shortest possible timeframe as everything (in terms of systems and data) is already being considered and made available. It must be noted that the cost of maintaining a mirrored site is very high compared to the alternatives.

Hot site

A hot site is the second best alternative after a mirrored site. The following components are already factored in while arranging a hot site:

- The availability of space and basic infrastructure
- The availability of all business applications

However, for a hot site to function, it also requires the following components:

- An updated data backup

Warm site

The following components are already factored in while arranging a warm site:

- The availability of space and basic infrastructure
- The availability of a few business applications

However, for a warm site to function, it also requires the following components:

- An arrangement regarding the required IT applications
- An arrangement for the required data

Cold site

The following components are already factored in while arranging a cold site:

- The availability of space and basic infrastructure

However, for a cold site to function, it also requires the following components:

- An arrangement regarding the required IT applications
- An arrangement for the required data

Mobile site

A mobile site is a movable vehicle equipped with the necessary computer equipment. A mobile site can be moved to any warm or cold site depending upon requirements. The scale of business operations will determine the need for a mobile site.

Reciprocal agreement

In a reciprocal agreement, two organizations having similar capabilities and processing capacities agree to provide support to one another in case of an emergency. Reciprocal agreements are not regarded as very reliable. A reciprocal agreement is the least expensive as this relies solely on an arrangement between two firms.

The following table summarizes the characteristics of each alternative recovery site:

Parameters/Type of Alternate Sites	Mirrored Site	Hot Site	Warm Site	Cold Site
Space & basic infrastructure	Available	Available	Available	Available
IT Equipment for processing	Available	Available	Only few equipments available	Not Available
Database	Available	Not Available	Not Available	Not Available
Maintenance Cost	Costliest	-	-	Cheapest
Recovery Time	Fastest	-	-	Slowest

A mirrored site is the fastest mode of recovery, followed by a hot site. A cold site is the slowest mode of recovery. For a critical system, mirrored/hot sites are appropriate options, while for non-critical systems, a cold site is an appropriate option. A reciprocal agreement will have the lowest expenditure in terms of a recovery arrangement.

Self-assessment questions

1. **Which of the following is a benefit of implementing a hot site as a recovery strategy?**
    A. Low maintenance costs
    B. A site can be set up near the primary site
    C. The site can be rendered operational within a short period of time
    D. There is no system compatibility requirement

2. **Which of the following is a cost-effective solution for recovering a non-critical system?**
    A. A cold site
    B. A mirrored site
    C. A hot site
    D. A warm site

3. Which of the following is ideal for implementing a hot site as a recovery strategy?
    A. A low disaster tolerance
    B. A high RTO
    C. A high RPO
    D. A high disaster tolerance

4. Which of the following alternate sites is already provisioned with basic infrastructure, such as electric cabling, heating, ventilation and AC arrangements, and flooring, but does not have systems and other communications equipment?
    A. A cold site
    B. A warm site
    C. A hot site
    D. A mirrored site

5. A major concern associated with a warm site is:
    A. the timely availability of system hardware
    B. the timely availability of space
    C. the timely availability of electrical connections
    D. the timely arrangement of ventilation and air conditioning

6. A recovery arrangement with the lowest expenditure is:
    A. a mobile site
    B. a warm site
    C. a cold site
    D. a reciprocal agreement

7. An arrangement for just electricity and HVAC is available in:
    A. a cold site
    B. a mobile site
    C. a reciprocal agreement
    D. a warm site

8. A major concern associated with a hot site is:
    A. the timely availability of system hardware
    B. the timely availability of data
    C. the timely availability of electrical connections
    D. the timely arrangement of ventilation and air conditioning

Summary

In this chapter, we discussed various aspects of business resiliency, including the BIA, data backup, BCP and DRP plans, and testing methodologies. We also learned about various processes to evaluate the organization's ability to continue business operations.

You have now acquired the relevant knowledge and skills required should business resilience appear in the CISA exam, as well as a number of practical aspects.

In the next chapter, we will discuss various aspects of information asset security and controls.

Assessment

You can find the answers to self-assessment questions here.

Business impact analysis

1. **Answer: C. Business process owner.**
    Explanation: The most critical source is the business process owner, who possesses the most relevant information to determine system criticality. Recovery timelines can be determined on the basis of inputs from business process owners.

2. **Answer: A. To conduct a BIA.**
    Explanation: A BIA determines the impact arising from the non-availability of each system. The higher the impact, the more critical the system. A BIA is conducted on the basis of input from the business process owner. The other options will not assist directly in determining the criticality of application systems.

3. **Answer: A. To develop a business continuity strategy.**
    Explanation: Once the critical applications are identified through the BIA, the next step is to develop a strategy to recover the critical assets as soon as possible for the continuity of the business. The BCP is the next step once the strategy is developed. Testing procedures and training schedules can be designed following development of the BCP.

4. **Answer: D. A system downtime analysis.**
    Explanation: Downtime analysis, which determines the acceptable downtime, is conducted only in the BIA. The other options are determined in both the risk assessment and the BIA.

5. **Answer: B. The period of downtime.**
Explanation: Severity depends on the period of system unavailability. The higher the period of unavailability, the greater the severity of disruption. The other options do not directly impact the severity of disruption. Although a negative impact is a symptom of the incident, it is not as important as determining the severity of the disruption to service.

6. **Answer: A. A recovery strategy.**
Explanation: An appropriate recovery strategy can be designed on the basis of the BIA. The other options should be considered once the recovery strategy is in place.

7. **Answer: A. To define a recovery strategy.**
Explanation: The main objective of the BIA is to determine critical processes and define their recovery strategy. Once a recovery strategy has been identified, the other options can be considered to support the recovery strategy.

8. **Answer: B. Processes that should be recovered as a priority to ensure the organization's survival.**
Explanation: The BIA determines the most critical processes that will impact on an organization's survival. The other options are not the direct objective of the BIA.

9. **Answer: C. A BIA.**
Explanation: The BIA determines those critical assets that need to be recovered as a priority during disaster recovery of these critical assets and that are very important for the organization's survival. The other options do not prioritize the assets for recovery.

10. **Answer: B. The critical business process to prioritize recovery.**
Explanation: The identification of a critical business process is the first step to determining the priority of recovery. Once critical processes have been identified, the recovery strategy and process can be defined.

Data backup and restoration

1. **Answer: A. A full backup.**
Explanation: In a full backup, a data backup is taken every time for a full database irrespective of the previous backup. In an incremental backup, a backup is only taken of new data created since the last backup (the last backup can be either a full backup or an incremental backup). In a differential backup, a backup is only taken of data that has changed since the last full backup (the last backup should be a full backup only). The grandfather-father-son rotation is a method of media rotation and not a backup scheme.

2. **Answer: D. An incremental backup.**
   Explanation: In an incremental backup, a backup is only taken of new data created since the last backup (the last backup can be either a full backup or an incremental backup). In a differential backup, a backup is only taken of data that has changed since the last full backup (the last backup should be a full backup only).

3. **Answer: B. A differential backup.**
   Explanation: In a differential backup, a backup is only taken of data that has changed since the last full backup (the last backup should be a full backup only).

4. **Answer: A. A full backup.**
   Explanation: In a full backup, a data backup of the full database is taken every time, irrespective of the previous backup. However, a full backup scheme requires more time and media capacity for backup storage. The advantage of a full backup scheme is its ease of restoration due to its unique repository.
   Let's now understand the requirement for time and media capacity in relation to various data storage schemes:
   - Full backup: Requires more time and storage capacity compared with the other two schemes
   - Differential: Requires less time and storage capacity compared with the full backup, but more time and storage capacity compared with incremental backup
   - Incremental: Requires less time and storage capacity compared with the other two schemes

5. **Answer: A. A full backup.**
   Explanation: In a full backup, a data backup of the full database is taken every time, irrespective of the previous backup. The advantage of a full backup scheme is its ease of restoration due to its unique repository. However, a full backup scheme requires more time and media capacity for backup storage.
   Let's understand the effectiveness of the various schemes in the case of data restoration:
   - Full backup: The fastest of all three schemes
   - Differential: Slower than a full backup, but faster than an incremental backup
   - Incremental: The slowest of all three schemes

System resiliency

1. **Answer: B. Diverse routing.**
   Explanation: Diverse routing is a method of routing information through split or duplicate cables, while alternative routing is a method of routing the information through alternative cables, such as copper or fiber optic cables. Bridges and gateways are used for network extensions.

2. **Answer: B. Last-mile circuit protection.**
   Explanation: Last-mile circuit protection is used by way of redundancy for local communication, while long-haul network diversity is used by way of redundancy for long-distance communication.

3. **Answer: B. Alternative routing.**
   Explanation: Alternative routing is a method of routing the information through alternative cables, such as copper or fiber optic cables. Diverse routing is a method of routing information through split or duplicate cables. Bridges and gateways are used for network extensions.

Business continuity plan

1. **Answer: D. A preparedness test.**
   Explanation: In a preparedness test, by means of a simulated system crash, preparedness is verified in a localized environment. This is a cost-effective way to determine the adequacy of the plan. It also provides an opportunity to improve the plan in increments. It is regarded as a localized version of a full test, wherein resources are expended in the simulation of a system crash.

2. **Answer: D. Shadow file processing.**
   Explanation: In shadow file processing, exact duplicates of files are maintained, preferably at a remote site. Both the files are processed concurrently. This is used for critical data files. Shadow file processing can be implemented as a recovery mechanism for extremely time-sensitive transaction processing. Hard disk mirroring in the same server would appear to be risky if a server malfunctions. Hot and warm sites do not usually have the same real-time characteristics as a shadow file system.

3. **Answer: A. The involvement of the process owner.**
   Explanation: Process owner involvement is very important in identifying critical processes, their dependencies, and the required level of the RTO. The other options are not as important as process owner involvement.

4. **Answer: C. To integrate the BCP's assumption regarding the existence of capabilities with DRP testing.**
Explanation: It is recommended to integrate BCP and DRP testing. This comprehensive testing will provide the scope to integrate and test various assumptions pertaining to the BCP plan. For example, a BCP may assume a *work from home* scenario in the case of a disaster. However, IT may not have this kind of capability. Hence, integrated testing (BCP and DRP) will help to evaluate the correct situation.

5. **Answer: C. Test results are not documented and evaluated.**
Explanation: It is not possible to evaluate the effectiveness of the BCP if test results are not properly documented and evaluated. Ideally, the BCP should be reviewed and approved by the Board of Directors. However, the same task can be delegated to the CEO. The other options are not as important as the test results not being documented and evaluated.

6. **Answer: D. To identify the limitations of the BCP.**
Explanation: Testing the BCP will help to determine the effectiveness of the plan and to identify any gaps therein. This provides an opportunity to make improvements in the plan.

7. **Answer: C. About human safety procedures.**
Explanation: The protection of human life is a critical factor in any business continuity procedure. This takes precedence over all other elements.

8. **Answer: B. Plan test results.**
Explanation: Test results will provide reasonable assurances regarding the effectiveness of the BCP. It will provide objective evidence regarding the adequacy or otherwise of the existing BCP. The other options will not assist directly in assessing the effectiveness of the BCP.

9. **Answer: A. To determine the simplicity of the BCP.**
Explanation: Interviewing the key personnel to determine their understanding of the BCP will help the auditor to evaluate the clarity and simplicity of the BCP. Merely interviewing will not facilitate a determination of the effectiveness, adequacy, or ability of an organization.

10. **Answer: B. The impact arising from the execution of the DRPP.**
Explanation: In the absence of defined situations that can be regarded as a crisis, execution of the DRP is adversely impacted.

11. **Answer: A. To review the existing BCP for adequacy.**
Explanation: It is recommended to review the BCP for adequacy every time a risk assessment is conducted in order to ensure that the BCP is aligned with the organization's latest risk assessment.

12. **Answer: A. The level of information security requirements during a business recovery processs.**
Explanation: It is important that the BCP contains the level of information security that is required when the business recovery process is in place. The information security level may be the same, or lower, or higher, compared with what is required during normal business operations.

13. **Answer: A. An offsite facility is located at a different geographical location and is not subject to the same risks as the primary site.**
Explanation: It is important to ensure that the offsite location is not subject to the same risks as the primary site. If both the primary site and the offsite location operate from the same location, a disaster may make both of them unavailable, which could have an adverse impact on business continuity.

14. **Answer: B. To develop more comprehensive requirements.**
Explanation: If BCP requirements are integrated with the project development process, this ensures that a comprehensive set of requirements are identified and provisioned during the development stage itself.

15. **Answer: C. The use of a resilient notification system along with redundancy.**
Explanation: Redundancy is regarded as the best control for addressing the risk of the unavailability of the notification system during a disaster.

16. **Answer: A. A period of outage.**
Explanation: Activation of the BCP should be primarily based on the maximum period during which business functions can survive before the outage could threaten the attainment of business objectives. The other options are not key factors when activating the BCP.

17. **Answer: B. The results of the business continuity test.**
Explanation: The results of the business continuity test will help to evaluate the effectiveness of the BCP. The other options may not directly impact the effectiveness of the BCP.

18. **Answer: A. To perform a walkthrough of different scenarios of the plan from beginning to end.**
Explanation: A structured walkthrough helps to identify weaknesses so that gaps can be addressed accordingly. A full interruption test is the most disruptive test in terms of the impact on regular operations and business.

19. **Answer: B. A paper test.**
Explanation: A paper test is an appropriate method for testing a BCP. It is also known as a desk-based evaluation. In this type of test, key employees have a walkthrough of the BCP and identify any weaknesses in the plan, thereby providing an opportunity to improve it.

20. **Answer: B. The involvement of all user departments.**
    Explanation: The involvement of all user departments is critical for the identification and prioritization of business processes and the development of an effective continuity plan. The other options are not as important as the involvement of all user departments.

21. **Answer: D. Protect human life.**
    Explanation: The primary objective of any BCP and DRP should be to protect people. The other options are secondary aims.

22. **Answer: A. Each plan is consistent with the others**
    Explanation: It is very important that each plan has a uniform structure and language and that plans are consistent with one another. It is not feasible to have a predefined sequence because implementation depends on the nature of the disaster. All plans need not be approved by senior management. It is sufficient that a single framework is approved and that all plans should be designed as per the framework.

23. **Answer: B. A risk assessment.**
    Explanation: A risk assessment document will help in developing a BCP. It helps to understand the risks to business processes. It is recommended to review the BCP for its adequacy every time a risk assessment is conducted to ensure that the BCP is aligned with the organization's latest risk assessment.

24. **Answer: A. The responsibility for declaring a disaster is not defined.**
    Explanation: It is very important to make a key employee responsible for declaring a disaster. If a disaster is not declared by anyone, the BCP would not be invoked and thereby threaten the continuity of the business.

25. **Answer: B. Evacuation plan.**
    Explanation: The protection of human life should be the main objective of any BCP. It is important to reconcile the evacuation plan for each department's BCP to ensure that they are aligned in terms of the safety and security of staff and clients.

26. **Answer: B. Communicated to the appropriate personnel.**
    Explanation: Implementation of the BCP will only be effective if appropriate personnel are informed regarding it. The other options are not as important as communicating BCP arrangements to concerned employees.

27. **Answer: D. To manage risk while recovering from a disaster.**
    Explanation: The objective of the BCP process is to manage and mitigate the risk of disaster so that the continuity of business operations can be ensured.

28. **Answer: A. A preparedness test**
    Explanation: A preparedness test includes a phase-wise simulation of the entire environment at a very reasonable cost and helps the recovery team to understand the various challenges associated with the actual test scenario. A paper test includes a walkthrough of scenarios, but this is not as effective as a preparedness test. A full operational test is a costly and time-consuming affair and involves numerous challenges.

Disaster recovery plan

1. **Answer: B. Downtime costs increase over time.**
   Explanation: Downtime costs include a loss of sales, idle resources, salaries, and suchlike. Downtime costs increase over time. The earlier the recovery, the lower the downtime costs. Downtime costs are not related to the RPO, but recovery costs are.

2. **Answer: A. Data backup at an offsite location.**
   Explanation: Without access to backup data, it is very difficult to recover from a disaster. Data backup is a very important element of the DRP. The other factors are not as important as data backup.

3. **Answer: C. The results of the BIA are not considered in determining the DRP.**
   Explanation: The BIA determines the organization's most critical assets. If the results of the BIA are not used in designing the DRP, all the necessary critical assets may not be covered in the DRP and, as a result, the DRP may not be adequate to help an organization recover from a disaster.

4. **Answer: A. A test has not been conducted to ensure the adequacy of resources to recover from a disaster.**
   Explanation: The most critical risk is the absence of testing, which would help to identify the gaps in the DRP. Backup testing should be done as part of an overall DRP test. The other options are not as important as the lack of an overall DRP test.

5. **Answer: B. The DRP should be regularly reviewed and updated.**
   Explanation: The plan should be reviewed and updated at regular intervals to keep the same relevant and effective. Regular testing is important. However, the period of testing depends on the nature of the service and product and need not necessarily be every 6 months. The DRP should be approved by senior management, not necessarily just the CEO. The DRP need not be shared with every employee. It should be made available to all relevant employees.

6. **Answer: B. To review the SLA with the cloud service provider.**
   Explanation: It is 'essential that the service provider should have a contractual obligation (through an agreement) regarding the DRP arrangement. Without contractual obligations, it is difficult to enforce DRP requirements.

7. **Answer: B. Disk space availability at the hot site is not aligned with data utilization at the primary site.**
   Explanation: If disk space is not aligned in accordance with current requirements, this will create major issues in case of a disaster. The other options, although important, are not as critical as the alignment of disk space.

8. **Answer: A. Decrease the length of the recovery time and associated costs.**
   Explanation: One of the motives of developing the DRP is to reduce the duration of recovery and ultimately reduce the costs of recovering from a disaster. Compliance with contractual requirements is a secondary objective.

9. **Answer: C. The results of DRP tests and exercises.**
   Explanation: Tests and exercises are the most reliable evidence to determine the adequacy and effectiveness of an organization's DRP. The test results help to identify the gaps, if any, and to improve the plan by addressing those gaps. The other options are not as important as tests and exercises.

10. **Answer: D. Timely data backups and offsite storage.**
    Explanation: The availability of updated data is a key element for any DRP. All other efforts are in vain without data. The availability of a hot site will be of no use without data.

11. **Answer: The lack of process owner involvement.**
    Explanation: The DRP is based on the BIA and, without the involvement of the process owner, the BIA may not be realistic. Hence, the DRP may not be reliable if inputs from the process owner are not considered. The other options are important, but not as important as the lack of process owner involvement.

12. **Answer: B. The maximum tolerable outage.**
    Explanation: The maximum tolerable outage is the ability of an organization to tolerate a disaster. The RTO is determined on the basis of the maximum tolerable outage.

13. **Answer: A. The inability to recover from the catastrophic service disruption.**
    Explanation: If a modified DRP is not tested for its adequacy and effectiveness, a plan may not enable the organization to recover from the disaster. This is the primary risk associated with an untested plan.

14. **Answer: B. To assess whether resiliency can be established for critical information assets.**
Explanation: Resilient information assets are able to withstand the disaster and thereby prevent the problem. Preventive control is always better than corrective control. Minimizing the RTO and cost comes into play at a later stage of the disaster recovery strategy. It is not practical to remove all the threats that an organization faces.

15. **Answer: D. Reviewing the server setting configurations and comparing these with the primary site**
Explanation: The most likely reason for slower system performance seems to be poor configuration. The IS auditor should review the server configuration to determine the reason for slow performance.

16. **Answer: B. Backup systems were found to be defective during testing.**
Explanation: Defective backup systems is the critical risk. Without backup systems, the DRP may not operate in case of a real disaster. The other options are not as important as backup system failure.

17. **Answer: A. The contact details of key members of staff.**
Explanation: The most important requirement as regards the continued effectiveness of the DRP is the updated list of employees who have key responsibilities in relation to the disaster recovery procedure. The other options, although important, are not as important as an updated contact list.

18. **Answer: B. The RPO.**
Explanation: The RPO determines the maximum losses an organization can tolerate. Backup data should be taken in such a way that the latest backup supports the RPO. If the RPO is zero, then there should be real-time, online backup to ensure zero data loss.

19. **Answer: C. The maximum tolerable downtime.**
Explanation: The maximum tolerable downtime is the level of tolerance of organization when it comes to downtime. An organization cannot afford downtime beyond this period. A disaster recovery strategy is primarily influenced by the maximum tolerable downtime.

20. **Answer: A. Acceptable operational capabilities during the disaster recovery phase**
Explanation: The service delivery objective is directly related to business requirements and is the level of service to be reached during disaster recovery. It is the acceptable level of service and operational capability to be maintained from an alternate site. This is influenced by business requirements. The other options do not directly influence the service delivery objective.

21. **Answer: A. The RPO.**
    Explanation: The RPO determines the maximum losses an organization can tolerate. Backup data should be taken in such a way that the latest backup supports the RPO. If the RPO is zero, then there should be real-time, online backup to ensure zero data loss.

22. **Answer: B. A BIA.**
    Explanation: The BIA determines those critical assets and processes that need to be recovered as a priority in order for the organization to survive. Hence, disaster recovery prioritization is primarily influenced by the BIA. An RTO is part of the BIA.

23. **Answer: C. Tabletop exercises involving the procedures.**
    Explanation: A tabletop exercise involves all the key members who will go through the plan and determine whether procedures satisfy requirements. Gaps, if any, are identified and addressed to make the DRP adequate and effective as regards business requirements.

24. **Answer: B. A data restoration test.**
    Explanation: Successful data restoration is regarded as a success of disaster recovery efforts. The most reliable method would be to restore a backup to a system. Other tests will not be able to determine the success of disaster recovery efforts.

25. **Answer: D. The prioritization of processes and assets.**
    Explanation: It is very important to prioritize the functions that need to be recovered at the earliest possible juncture for the organization's survival. The DRP should cover prioritized business functions.

26. **Answer: C. A technological aspect of the BCP.**
    Explanation: The objective of the BCP is to keep business operations running, perhaps from an alternate location or by means of alternative tools and processes. The objective of the DRP is to restore normal business operations and to recover from a disaster. The BCP is the overall architecture for business continuity, whereas the DRP is regarded as a technological aspect of the BCP with more focus on IT systems and operations.

27. **Answer: B. Increase.**
    Explanation: To maintain a DRP, resources, a recovery site, testing, and other maintenance procedures will result in additional costs.

28. **Answer: B. To conduct a BIA.**
    Explanation: The first step in preparing any DRP is to conduct a BIA. A recovery strategy can be designed on the basis of the BIA. The BIA will help to determine critical business processes and systems that need to be recovered as a priority in order for the organization to survive.

DRP – test methods

1. **Answer: C. To ensure continued compatibility of the offsite facility.**
   Explanation: The main objective of testing an offsite facility is to validate the compatibility of the facility to support the organization in case of a disaster. The test results help to evaluate the adequacy and effectiveness of the offsite recovery facility.

2. **Answer: C. The recovery plan is tested regularly.**
   Explanation: Testing is the most important factor in evaluating the adequacy and effectiveness of the DRP. Also, regular testing makes the team member aware of the recovery process and helps in effective recovery during an actual disaster. Without adequate tests, other options may not be useful.

3. **Answer: B. A tabletop test**
   Explanation: A tabletop test is conducted with the aim of practicing coordination efforts and communication methodology among the relevant members of the recovery team.

4. **Answer: B. Simulation test.**
   Explanation: In the simulation type of test, a roleplay is prepared for a disaster scenario and the adequacy of the DRP is determined. It does not include activation of the recovery site.

5. **Answer: D. Structured walkthrough.**
   Explanation: A structured walkthrough includes a review of the DRP on paper. Team members review each step to evaluate the effectiveness of the DRP. Identified gaps, deficiencies, and constraints are addressed in order to improve the plan.

6. **Answer: C. Full interruption test.**
   Explanation: This type of test is the most expensive and potentially disruptive. The primary site is completely shut down and operations are conducted from the recovery site as per the DRP.

Recovery Time Objective (RTO) and Recovery Point Objective (RPO)

1. **Answer: A. The extent of acceptable system downtime.**
   Explanation: The RTO is a measure of the user's tolerance to system downtime. In other words, the RTO is the extent of acceptable system downtime. For example, an RTO of 2 hours indicates that an organization will not be overly impacted if its system is down for up to 2 hours.

2. **Answer: B. A lower RTO.**
Explanation: The RTO indicates a user's tolerance for system downtime. In the case of critical systems, an organization cannot afford to have much downtime. Hence, in the case of critical systems, generally, the RTO is zero, or near zero. A low RTO indicates that the system should be resumed at the earliest possible juncture.

3. **Answer: C. The extent of acceptable data loss.**
Explanation: The RPO is a measure of the user's tolerance to data loss. In other words, the RPO is the extent of acceptable data loss. For example, an RPO of 2 hours indicates that an organization will not be overly impacted if it loses data for up to 2 hours.

4. **Answer: B. The lower RPO.**
Explanation: The RPO indicates a user's tolerance for data loss. In the case of critical data, an organization cannot afford to endure significant data loss. Hence, in the case of critical systems, generally, the RPO is zero, or near zero. A low RPO indicates that data loss should be the minimum.

5. **Answer: B. Higher.**
Explanation: A low RPO indicates that data is critical and that it should not be lost. For example, an organization having an RPO of 0 hours needs to ensure that there should not be any data loss at all. They should invest heavily in data backup management. Hence, for a low RPO, the data maintenance costs will be higher compared with a high RPO. Thus, if the RPO is low (that is, zero or near zero), then the cost of maintaining the environment is high.

6. **Answer: C. When the RTO is lower.**
Explanation: A low RTO indicates that systems are critical and need to be resumed as soon as possible. To achieve this objective, organizations need to invest heavily in redundancy. A hot site is ideal where the RTO is lower. This will be a costly affair. On the other hand, if the RTO is high, this indicates that systems are not that critical and an organization can afford downtime to some extent. Organization need not invest in redundancy for systems with a high RTO. A cold site is ideal where the RTO is higher.

7. **Answer: C. When the RPO is lower.**
Explanation: Data mirroring is a technique where data is backed up concurrently without any time gap. A low RPO indicates that data is critical and should not be lost. For example, an organization having an RPO of 0 hours needs to ensure that there should not be any data loss at all. It should invest heavily in data backup management. Data mirroring is an ideal technique where the RPO is zero or very low.

8. **Answer: D. Implementation of a warm site that can be operational within 60 hours and where data is backed up synchronously**
   Explanation: The last two options meet the criteria of RTO and RPO. However, option D will be more cost effective compared with option C. A hot site is costlier to maintain as compared with a warm site. Options A and B do not meet the RPO of 0 hours.

9. **Answer: A. A low disaster tolerance.**
   Explanation: Disaster tolerance indicates the tolerance level of the organization to accept the non-availability of IT facilities. A hot site is recommended when disaster tolerance is low and systems should be made available as soon as possible.

Alternate recovery site

1. **Answer: C. The site can be rendered operational within a short period of time.**
   Explanation: The benefit of implementing a hot site is that it can be made operational at the earliest possible juncture. A hot site has higher maintenance costs compared to warm or cold sites. An alternate site may not be located near the primary site. Also, any kind of alternate site should have system compatibility with the primary site.

2. **Answer: A. A cold site.**
   Explanation: In a cold site arrangement, only space and basic infrastructure is required. The cost of maintaining a cold site is low compared to hot or warm sites. A cold site is the most cost-effective solution for a non-critical system. Mirrored and hot sites are appropriate for recovering critical systems as they require a greater amount of investment. A warm site is generally available at a medium cost, requires less time to become operational, and is suitable for sensitive operations.

3. **Answer: A. A low disaster tolerance**
   Explanation: Disaster tolerance indicates the ability of the organization to accept the non-availability of IT facilities. A hot site is recommended when disaster tolerance is low and systems should be made available as soon as possible.

4. **Answer: A. A cold site.**
   Explanation: In a cold site arrangement, only space and basic infrastructure is required. The cost of maintaining a cold site is low compared to hot or warm sites. A cold site is the most cost-effective solution for a non-critical system. No communication systems or computers are made available in cold sites.

5. **Answer: A. The timely availability of system hardware.**
   Space, electrical connections, and ventilation and AC arrangements have already been provisioned prior to setting up a warm site. However, it does not have all the requisite hardware devices set up in order to facilitate the resumption of services. Hence, the timely availability of hardware is a greater concern.

6. **Answer: D. A reciprocal agreement.**
   Explanation: In a reciprocal agreement, two organizations having similar capabilities and processing capacities agree to provide support to one another in case of an emergency. Reciprocal agreements are not regarded as very reliable. A reciprocal agreement is the least expensive as this relies solely on an arrangement between two firms.

7. **Answer: A. A cold site.**
   Explanation: In a cold site arrangement, only space and basic infrastructure, such as electricity and HVAC, is required. The cost of maintaining a cold site is low compared to hot or warm sites. A cold site is the most cost-effective solution for a non-critical system. No communication systems or computers are made available in cold sites.

8. **Answer: B. The timely availability of data.**
   Explanation: The following components are already factored in while arranging a hot site:
   - The availability of space and basic infrastructure
   - The availability of all business applications

   However, for a hot site to function, it requires the following additional components: An updated data backup.

5

Section 5: Protection of Information Assets

This part contains 27 percent of the CISA exam, approximately 41 questions.

This section contains the following chapters:

Information Asset Security and Control

9

Any data, system, network, and other communication structure that helps in achieving business goals and objectives is known as an information asset. Hence, securing an information asset is one of the important objectives of an organization.

The following topics will be covered in this chapter:

- Information asset security frameworks, standards, and guidelines
- Privacy principles
- Physical access and environmental controls
- Identity and access management
- Biometrics

By the end of this chapter, you will have learned that the protection of information assets involves the consideration of their **confidentiality**, **integrity**, and **availability (CIA)**.

Information asset security frameworks, standards, and guidelines

An information security framework is a set of documented policies, procedures, and processes that define how information is managed in an organization. The objective of a framework is to lower the risk and vulnerability and protect an enterprise by guarding the CIA of critical and sensitive information.

Auditing the information security management framework

An **information systems (IS)** auditor should consider the following aspects for auditing the information security management framework:

- To review the adequacy and approvals for various policies, procedures, and standards.
- To review security training and awareness programs and procedures. To determine the effectiveness of the program, it is advisable to interact with a few of the employees and evaluate their level of awareness.
- IS auditor to determine whether proper ownership has been assigned for critical processes, systems, and data. IS auditor to determine whether a data classification policy exists and evaluate its appropriateness. Also, to determine whether data custodians, such as system administration and computer operators, are responsible for storing and safeguarding the data.
- To determine whether background verification is conducted for all the new joiners and whether new users are required to sign a document abiding them with the organization's IT security policy.
- To determine whether the access rights of terminated employees are revoked immediately. Also, access rights of third-party service providers should be properly monitored and controlled.
- To determine whether an organization has an approved and documented security baseline policy and whether this security baseline is monitored for compliance.

Key aspects from the CISA exam perspective

The following table covers important aspects from the CISA exam perspective:

CISA questions	Possible answers
What is the basis for designing and developing logical access controls?	The security policy
Who is accountable for the appropriate maintenance of security controls over information assets?	Data and systems owners
What is the first step in data classification?	Establishing ownership
Who is responsible for reviewing users' access rights?	The data owner
What is the first step when reviewing an IT security baseline?	To determine the sufficiency and adequacy of the baseline

Self-assessment questions

1. **The most effective safeguard for securing software and data within an information processing facility is:**
    A. Training and awareness
    B. Logical access controls
    C. Physical controls
    D. The security committee

2. **Logical access controls are designed and developed on the basis of:**
    A. The user requirements
    B. The information system security policy
    C. Industry practices
    D. System configuration files

3. **Who among the following should be made accountable for the appropriate maintenance of security controls over information assets?**
    A. The network administrator
    B. The data and systems owners
    C. The system developer
    D. The systems operations group

4. **Which of the following is the first step in data classification?**
    A. To establish ownership
    B. To conduct critical analysis
    C. To develop an access matrix
    D. To tag classification nomenclature on assets

5. **The best method to provide access to a user is:**
    A. Authorization for access from the data owner and implementation of user authorization tables by the administrator
    B. Joint authorization by the data owner and system administrator
    C. Joint creation and update of user authorization tables by the data owner and system administrator
    D. The data owner creates and updates the user authorization tables

6. **Responsibility of granting access to data with the help of security officer resides with:**
    - A. The data owners
    - B. The system developer
    - C. The library controller
    - D. The system administrator

7. **Responsibility for reviewing users' access rights resides with:**
    - A. The data owners
    - B. The IS auditor
    - C. The library controller
    - D. The security administrator

8. **With respect to the IT security baseline, the IS auditor should first ensure:**
    - A. The documentation
    - B. Sufficiency
    - C. Audit and compliance
    - D. The process

Privacy principles

Privacy is the right of the individual to demand the utmost care of their personal information that has been shared with any organization or individual. Individuals can demand that the use of their information should be appropriate, legal, and for a specific purpose for which information is obtained.

The **Information Systems Audit and Control Association** (**ISACA**) describes several privacy principles that can be considered as a framework for privacy audits. The following are some of the privacy principles:

- Organizations should obtain appropriate consent before the transfer of personal information to another jurisdiction.
- Organizations should specify the purposes for which personal information is collected.
- Organizations are required to retain personal information only as long as necessary.
- Organizations should have appropriate security safeguards for protecting personal information.

- Organizations should have an appropriate process for reporting compliance with privacy policy, standards, and laws.
- Organizations should have an appropriate governance mechanism over the third-party service provider processing privacy data on behalf of the organization.
- Organizations should comply with applicable data protection regulations for the transfer of personal information across country borders.

Self-assessment questions

1. **An organization proposes to use its existing client database to promote its new range of products. Which of the following is an area of concern for an IS auditor?**
    A. Are there any data privacy concerns about this process?
    B. Whether the existing client database is updated
    C. Does this comply with the organization's promotional policy?
    D. Whether the client database is appropriately secured against unauthorized access

2. **Which of the following is a major concern for an offshore operation?**
    A. High cost of telecommunication setup
    B. Privacy laws preventing the cross-border flow of information
    C. Timezone differences
    D. Software development complications

3. **When transmitting PII data to a third-party service provider through the internet, an organization must ensure:**
    A. The encryption of the PII data
    B. They obtain consent from the client
    C. Privacy principles are adhered to
    D. Proper change management

4. **To determine whether an organization has complied with a privacy requirement, the IS auditor should first:**
    A. Review the IT architecture
    B. Review the standard operating procedure for IT processes
    C. Review the legal and regulatory requirements
    D. Review the risk register

Physical access and environmental controls

Physical controls aim to protect information system processing facilities through physical mediums, such as locks, fences, **closed-circuit TV (CCTV)**, and devices that are installed to physically restrict access to a facility or hardware.

Similarly, environmental controls refer to measures taken to protect systems, buildings, and related supporting infrastructure against threats associated with their physical environment. Physical and environmental safeguards are often overlooked but are very important in protecting information. Let's have a look at each of them in more detail.

Environmental controls

An IS auditor should consider the following aspect of environmental controls.

The following are four types of power failure:

- **Blackout**: Blackout indicates a complete loss of power.
- **Brownout**: Severely reduced voltage, which may place strain on electronic equipment or may even lead to permanent damage.
- **Sags, spikes, and surges**:
  - Sag is a rapid decrease in voltage level. Spikes and surges are rapid increases in voltage level. These may result in data corruption in the server or the system.
  - Sags, spikes, and surges may be prevented by using properly placed protectors.
  - Surge and spike devices help to protect against high-voltage power bursts.

  The most effective control to protect against the short-term reduction in electrical power is a power line conditioner. A power line conditioner is a device intended to improve the quality of power that is delivered to electrical equipment. It compensates for the peaks and valleys in the power supply. When the electrical supply is low, it provides its own power and maintains a constant voltage.

- **Electromagnetic interference (EMI)**: EMI is generally the result of electrical storms or noisy electrical equipment. EMI may result in system corruption or damage.

An **uninterruptible power supply** (UPS) can help to support an organization from interruptions that last from a few seconds to 30 minutes. An alternative power supply medium (such as a power generator) is most effective when there is long-term power unavailability.

The following are some of the best practices for the maintenance of an alarm control panel:

- It should be accessible to security personnel at all times.
- It should be placed in a weatherproof box.
- It should have electrical power from a dedicated and separate circuit.
- It should be placed in adherence to local regulations and requirements.

Water and Smoke Detectors

Similarly, the following are some of the best practices for the maintenance of water and smoke detectors:

- In the computer room, water detectors should be placed under raised floors and near drain holes.
- Smoke detectors should be installed above and below the ceiling tiles throughout the facilities and below the raised computer room floor.
- The location of the water and smoke detector should be highlighted for easy identification and access.
- Responsibility to be assigned to a dedicated employee for remedial action in case of an alarm. A standard operating procedure should be available.
- The location of these devices is very important and should be placed in such a way to give early warning of a fire.
- The power supply of these devices should be sufficient.
- These devices should be tested at regular intervals.

Moreover, an emergency evacuation plan should be posted throughout the facility. Electrical wiring should be placed in fire-resistant panels and conduits. This conduit should ideally lie under the fire-resistant raised computer room floor.

Fire suppression system

The following are some of the fire suppression systems.

Wet-based sprinkler (WBS)

WBS is considered more effective and reliable than dry pipes as water always remains in the system piping. However, one disadvantage is that it exposes the premises to water damage if the pipe leaks or gets damaged.

Dry pipe sprinkler

In a dry pipe sprinkler, water is not stored in the pipes. When there is a fire alarm, a pump is activated and water is sent into the system. One of the advantages of a dry sprinkler is that it does not expose the premises to water damage due to pipe leakage. It is less reliable than WBS.

Halon system

Halon gas starves the fire by removing oxygen from the air. It is not safe for humans and the environment. It is important to install an audible alarm and there should be a process to evacuate humans before the discharge of Halon gas. Popular replacements for Halon gas are FM-200 and Argonite:

- **FM-200**: FM-200 is safe for the environment as well as humans. It is the most commonly used fire suppression gas.
- **Argonite**: Argonite is a mixture of 50% Argon and 50% Nitrogen. Although it is environment-friendly and non-toxic, there have been cases where people have been suffocated by inhaling Argon.

Carbon dioxide systems

CO_2 is not safe for humans. It is mostly installed in unmanned data centers and other places where there is no presence of humans. Most countries restrict the automatic release of CO_2 gas if any human is present in the area.

Physical access control

The objective of physical access control is to restrict and control access to premises, buildings, rooms, and data centers. Examples of physical access control include door locks, security guards, access cards, and so on.

The following are a few common types of door locks.

Bolting door locks

These are traditional kinds of locks that require a metal key to open the gate. For these locks, the key should be under strict control and no one should not be allowed to duplicate the key.

Combination door locks (cipher locks)

In combination door locks, access is authorized through a numeric keypad or dial. Access numbers should be available only to authorized people. Access numbers should be changed on a frequent basis and should be mandatorily changed whenever an employee with access is transferred or terminated.

Electronic door locks

With electronic door locks, access is granted through a magnetic or embedded chip-based plastic card key. These access cards are difficult to duplicate. It is very easy to deactivate the access card in case of termination or when a card is lost. Alarms can also be configured to monitor unauthorized access However, access card issuance and management processes should be carefully controlled.

Biometric door locks

Access can be granted through any of the biometric features of the user, such as voice, retina, fingerprint, and hand geometry.

Biometric access controls are generally used for critical and sensitive facilities.

Deadman doors

Deadman doors are also known as a mantrap or airlock entrance. In these cases, two doors are used and for the second door to open, the first door must be closed and locked. Only one person is permitted in the gap between the first door and the second door.

A deadman door reduces the risk of tailgating or piggybacking wherein an unauthorized person follows an authorized person to gain unauthorized entry.

Deadman doors are also used in loading and unloading areas where outer doors open to load or unload from a truck and the inner doors cannot be opened to load or unload until the outer doors are closed and locked.

Identification badge

Employees are required to have their identification badges (photo IDs) worn and displayed when in the office. For the comfort of tracking, the badge should be of different colors for employees and visitors. Visitors are required to be escorted by a responsible staff member.

CCTV camera

Also, CCTV cameras should be placed at strategic locations. Videos and images should be retained for a sufficient period for 3 months for future requirements. For the security of a high-sensitivity workstation, the use of computer workstation locks will prevent the computer from being turned on. It is advisable not to have facilities such as computer rooms with visible or identifiable signs from the outside.

Physical security is as important as logical and should not have any scope of a loophole. It is advisable to define and document the roles and responsibilities of the personnel in charge of physical security.

Key aspects from the CISA exam perspective

The following table covers important aspects from CISA exam perspective:

CISA questions	Possible answers
What is the most effective control to protect against the long-term unavailability of electrical power?	An alternative power supply.
What is the most effective control to protect against the short-term reduction in electrical power?	A power line conditioner.

What is the most effective control to protect against a high-voltage power burst?	A surge device.
What is the risk of carbon dioxide and Halon gas?	Suffocation in a closed room (both carbon dioxide and Halon gas reduce the oxygen in the atmosphere).
What is the most effective control over visitors?	Escorting visitors.
What is the objective of having a raised floor in a computer room?	Safety of power and data cables (the floor is raised to accommodate the ventilation system, power, and data cables underneath the floor, thus protecting them from various risks and events).
What is the safest gas to be used as a fire extinguisher?	FM-200.

Self-assessment questions

1. **Which of the following is a major risk of electromagnetic emission from a computer room?**
    A. It may damage the storage device
    B. It may disrupt the processor functionality
    C. It may impact the health of employees
    D. It may be detected and displayed

2. **The most effective control to protect against short-term reduction in electrical power is:**
    A. Surge devices
    B. Spike devices
    C. A power line conditioner
    D. Alternative power supplies

3. **The most effective control to protect against the long-term unavailability of the electrical power is:**
    A. Surge devices
    B. Alternative power supplies
    C. A power line conditioner
    D. Spike devices

4. **The most effective control to protect against a high-voltage power burst is:**
    A. Surge devices
    B. Alternative power supplies
    C. A power line conditioner
    D. An uninterruptible power supply

5. **Which of the following is a major concern for the use of CO$_2$ and Halon gas as fire extinguishers?**
    A. Both of the extinguishers have a limited life span
    B. Both of the extinguishers are not suitable for computer equipment
    C. Both of the extinguishers have a risk of suffocation when used in a closed room
    D. Both of the extinguishers have a high maintenance cost

6. **What is the risk associated with the use of an access card for entering a computer room?**
    A. The risk of an unauthorized person entering behind the authorized person
    B. The risk of using duplicated access cards
    C. The risk of the absence of an audit trail
    D. The risk of delay in deactivating the access of a terminated employee

7. **The most effective control over visitor access to a data center is:**
    A. To escort the visitors
    B. To issue a visitor's badge
    C. To frisk the visitor for storage media
    D. To maintain a visitor's register

8. **Which of the following is the greatest concern for an IS auditor reviewing the fire safety arrangements of an organization?**
    A. The use of a wet pipe-based fire extinguisher in the computer room
    B. The use of a carbon dioxide-based fire extinguisher in the processing facility
    C. The use of handheld fire extinguishers in the board room
    D. Smoke detector not tested every month

9. **The prime objective of installing mantrap controlling access is to:**
    A. Prevent tailgating
    B. Prevent water leakage
    C. Control fire
    D. Prevent computer damage

10. **The objective of raising the floor in a computer room is to prevent:**
    A. Damage to the cables of computers and servers
    B. Power failure
    C. Damage from an earthquake
    D. Damage from a tsunami

11. **Which of the following is the most important concern for a badge entry access system?**
    A. Security personnel is not monitoring the badge reader for any suspected tampering
    B. Logs of access are not reviewed on a daily basis
    C. The process for promptly disabling a lost or stolen badge is not followed
    D. The backup frequency of logs is infrequent

12. **Which of the following is the most important concern for an access card entry system?**
    A. The use of a shared access card by cleaning staff
    B. The access card does not contain a label with the organization's name and address
    C. Card issuance and card reconciliation are managed by different departments
    D. Logs of access are not reviewed on a daily basis

13. **The most effective, safe, and environment-friendly fire safety arrangement in a data centre is the use of:**
    A. Halon gas
    B. Carbon dioxide
    C. Dry pipe sprinklers
    D. Wet pipe sprinklers

14. **A dry pipe fire extinguisher contains:**
    A. FM-200 gas
    B. Nitrogen
    C. Water that resides in the pipe with special water-tight sealants
    D. Water, but it enters the pipe only when a fire has been detected

15. **A wet pipe sprinkler contains**:
    A. FM-200 gas
    B. Nitrogen
    C. Water that resides in the pipe with special water-tight sealants
    D. Water, but it enters the pipe only when a fire has been detected

16. **Which of the following are the areas of most concern?**
    A. The installation of an FM-200 gas fire extinguisher in a manned data center
    B. The installation of dry pipe sprinklers in an expensive data center facility
    C. The installation of wet pipe sprinklers in an expensive data center facility
    D. The installation of a carbon dioxide gas fire extinguisher in a manned data center

17. **The safest form of a fire extinguisher that can be used in the presence of humans is:**
    A. Carbon dioxide
    B. Halon gas
    C. FM-200
    D. Argonite gas

Identity and access management

An IS auditor should review the logical access control of the organization with the prime objective of determining whether access is granted and controlled as per approved authorizations. As a CISA aspirant, you are expected to understand the concepts of identity and access management. Let's have a look at these concepts.

Logical access controls are a set of tools and protocols with the objective and purpose of the following:

- Identification
- Authentication
- Authorization
- Accountability

Access control categories

The following are the major categories of access control:

Type	Description
Mandatory access control (MAC)	Control rules are governed by an approved policy. Users or data owners cannot modify the access role.
Discretionary access control (DAC)	Control access can be activated or modified by the data owner as per their discretion.

MAC is considered more robust and stringent in terms of information security compared to DAC. To increase the effectiveness of DAC, it should be aligned in accordance with MAC.

Steps for implementing logical access

To implement logical access controls, the following chronological steps are to be followed:

1. Prepare an inventory of the IS resources
2. Classify the IS resources
3. Perform the grouping/labeling of the IS resources
4. Create an access control list

Identification of the owner of the data or application is the first step in the classification of an IS resource.

Control Effectiveness

Preventive controls are considered more effective in terms of damage control compared to detective or deterrent controls. Automated controls are considered more effective compared to manual controls. For logical access control, an automated password management tool is considered the most effective preventive control. It ensures compliance with password management policy.

As a best practice, log files should always be read-only. Edit access should not be enabled for them. The integrity of a log file is very important to treat them as an audit trail.

Default deny policy – allow all policy

Organizations can either have a default deny access control policy or an allow all access control policy. The following table shows the difference between the two:

Default Deny	Allow All
Denial of all the traffic except predefined approved traffic	Allow all the traffic except predefined restricted traffic.
Denial of all the traffic except predefined approved traffic	More prevalent where traffic is from a trusted source to access an external system such as the internet.
More prevalent where traffic is from an untrusted source to access a protected system	Also known as a discretionary access policy.

It is recommended to implement a default deny access control policy. It is more stringent and robust compared to an allow all access control policy.

Degaussing (demagnetizing)

The right kind of formatting is very critical to ensure that residual data from media cannot be recovered by an unauthorized person. To the extent possible, the media should be physically destroyed in such a way that it cannot be reused. However, it may not be economical to destroy the media, and hence for these cases, extreme care should be taken for the complete deletion of the data, and data should not be recoverable by any tool or technique.

One of these methods is to demagnetize the media record. This process involves increasing the alternating current field gradually from 0 to some maximum value and back to 0, leaving a very low residue of magnetic induction on the media. This process of demagnetization is also known as degaussing.

Naming convention

A naming convention is an agreed structure for naming assets. It helps in the effective and efficient management of access rules. Generally, assets that are critical in nature are grouped and named under sensitive categories. Rules are defined for access to sensitive categories that may be more stringent compared to other categories. This reduces the number of rules required to adequately protect resources, which in turn facilitates security administration and maintenance efforts. The owners of the data or application, with the help of the security officer, usually set up naming conventions. These conventions should promote the implementation of efficient access rules and simplify security administration.

Factor of authentication

There are three authentication factors that can be used for granting access. They are as follows:

- Something you know (for example, a password, PIN, or some other personal information)
- Something you have (for example, a token, one-time password, or smart card)
- Something you are (for example, biometric features, such as fingerprint, iris scan, or voice recognition)

Similarly, two-factor authentication means the use of two authentication methods from the preceding list. For critical systems, it is advisable to use more than one factor of authentication for granting access.

Single sign-on

Single sign-on (SSO) is a user authentication service that permits a user to use one set of login credentials (for example, a name and password) to access multiple applications. This increases the risk of a single point of failure. The impact of password compromise will be much greater since the intruder needs to know only one password to gain access to all the related applications and, therefore, causes greater concerns. It is very important to implement strong password complexity for this kind of environment.

One example of SSO is Kerberos. Kerberos is an authentication service used to validate services and users in a **distributed computing environment** (**DCE**). In the client-server environment, only users are authenticated; however, in a DCE, both users and servers authenticate themselves. At the initial logon time, the Kerberos third-party application is used to verify the identity of the client.

Advantages of SSO

The following are the advantages of SSO:

- Multiple passwords not required. This encourages users to select a strong password.
- Improves the administrator's ability to manage users' accounts.
- Reduces administrative overhead costs in resetting passwords due to a lower number of IT help desk calls about passwords.
- Reduces the time taken by users to log in to multiple applications.

Disadvantages of SSO

The following are the disadvantages of SSO:

- SSO acts as a single authentication point for multiple applications, which constitute a risk of a single point of failure.
- Support for all major operating system environments is difficult.

Key aspects from the CISA exam perspective

The following table covers important aspects from CISA exam perspective:

CISA questions	Possible answers
What is the objective of an IS auditor reviewing logical access control?	To determine whether access is granted and controlled as per the approved authorizations.
What is a major risk of shared user accounts?	Individual user accountability may not be established.
What is the first step in data classification?	Establish the data owners.
How can compliance with a password policy best be ensured?	With automated password management tools.
What is the most important consideration when reviewing system controls?	The alignment of security and performance requirements.
What is the best way to erase data?	Physical destruction. Demagnetization or degaussing in case media is to be reused.
What is the objective of using a naming convention?	The implementation of efficient access rules and to simplify security administration.
What is the first step in the implementation of logical access controls?	To prepare an inventory of IS resources.
What is the most important control for SSO?	The implementation of a strong password policy.
What is a major risk of SSO?	It acts as a single authentication point for multiple applications.
What is the most effective control against identify theft?	Two-factor authentication.

Self-assessment questions

1. **Which of the following is a prime objective for an IS auditor reviewing logical access control?**
   - A. To ensure the effectiveness of access control software
   - B. To ensure that access is granted as per an approved process

C. To ensure the protection of computer software

D. To ensure the protection of computer hardware

2. **Which of the following is a major risk of shared user accounts?**

   A. The frequent change of passwords

   B. Unauthorized access to the system

   C. The use of an easily guessable password

   D. It is difficult to establish user accountability

3. **The best method to protect sensitive data inside the server is to:**

   A. Create awareness on information security aspects

   B. Make security policies available to all the users

   C. Establish a security committee

   D. Implement logical access controls

4. **Need-to-know access control can be best ensured by:**

   A. Implementing application-level access control

   B. Encrypting databases

   C. Enabling HTTPS control

   D. Deploying network monitoring control

5. **The prime objective of data protection is to:**

   A. Comply with contractual requirements

   B. Comply with legal requirements

   C. Ensure the confidentiality and integrity of information

   D. Improve operational efficiency

6. **Which of the following is the initial step for the classification of data?**

   A. To establish data owners

   B. To conduct criticality analysis

   C. To determine an access control list

   D. To determine firewall rules

7. **Which of the following is considered a major risk in an organization's logical access control procedure?**

   A. The sharing of passwords

   B. Password files are not protected

   C. Delay in the deactivation of a resigned employee's login access

   D. Centralized issuance of logon IDs

8. **Which of the following best ensures compliance with a password policy?**
   A. A simple version of a password policy
   B. A user-friendly password policy
   C. The implementation of an automated password management tool
   D. Security awareness training for the users

9. **The availability of printing options for all users increases:**
   A. The risk of data confidentiality
   B. The risk of data integrity
   C. The risk of data availability
   D. The risk of reduced productivity

10. **Which of the following is most important when reviewing system controls?**
   A. Security and performance parameters are considered
   B. The capturing of changes in logs
   C. The availability of a change authorization process
   D. Access to system parameters is restricted

11. **Which of the following should be reviewed to determine the level of access available for different users?**
   A. System file configuration
   B. Log files
   C. Job descriptions
   D. User access review

12. **Write edit access should always be prohibited for:**
   A. Access control lists
   B. Logging criteria
   C. Log files for suspected transactions
   D. Access control analyzers

13. **Which of the following is a major aspect to be considered when reviewing telecommunication access control?**
   A. The process for capturing and monitoring logs
   B. The process for the authorization and authentication of a user
   C. The process for encrypting databases
   D. The process to control remote access

14. **Which of the following increases the effectiveness of DAC?**
    A. DAC is aligned in accordance with MAC
    B. DAC is kept independent of MAC
    C. DAC allows users to bypass MAC as per the requirements
    D. DAC is approved by the IS policy

15. **Which of the following is considered the most secure method of removing confidential data from computer storage?**
    A. Demagnetization of computer storage
    B. Formatting computer storage
    C. Deletion of data on computer storage
    D. Defragmentation of data on computer storage

16. **An IS auditor should review the router controls and settings during:**
    A. The review of physical security
    B. The review of network security
    C. The review of the backup process
    D. The review of the data center

17. **Which of the following is considered a major risk of the absence of an authorization process?**
    A. Difficult to control role-based access
    B. Multiple users can log on as a specific user
    C. User accounts can be shared
    D. Need-to-know basis access can be assured

18. **Which of the following is considered the best control for providing access rights to outsourced vendors?**
    A. To include a penalty clause in the service level agreement
    B. Temporary user accounts created for a defined role with account expiration dates
    C. Temporary user accounts created for full access for a limited period
    D. Employees of the vendors should be asked to sign a non-disclosure agreement

19. **The most important benefit of proper naming conventions for IS resources is:**
    A. It ensures that resource names are aligned as per their function
    B. It helps with defining structured access rules
    C. It helps with user management
    D. It ensures that industry standardization is maintained

20. **Which of the following is a major concern for an IS auditor reviewing a critical application?**
    A. Access is provisioned on the basis of a user role
    B. Systems are hardened
    C. Users can access and modify the database directly
    D. Multi-factor authentication for user access

21. **To implement access control, which of the following is the first step?**
    A. To categorize the IS resources
    B. To group the IS resources
    C. To implement access control rules
    D. To create an inventory of the IS resources

22. **Which of the following is a major concern for an IS auditor reviewing the general IT controls of an organization?**
    A. No restriction for connecting external laptops to the network
    B. Multi-factor authentication for user access
    C. Standalone terminals are placed at an insecure location
    D. The organization takes more than 1 month to close the audit findings

23. **Which of the following is considered the best method to prevent unauthorized access to critical databases?**
    A. Servers are placed in a restricted area
    B. Servers are placed under CCTV surveillance
    C. Online access is blocked after a specified number of unsuccessful login attempts
    D. An access card is required to access online terminals

24. **A default deny access control policy:**
    A. Allows approved traffic and rejects all other traffic
    B. Denies specific traffic and allows all other traffic
    C. Is used for allowing access from a trusted network to a protected system
    D. Allows traffic as per the discretion of the network administrator

25. **A default allow access control policy:**
    A. Allows approved traffic and rejects all other traffic
    B. Denies specific traffic and allows all other traffic
    C. Is used for allowing access from untrusted networks to external systems.
    D. Allows traffic as per the discretion of the network administrator.

26. **The most effective method to prevent unauthorized access to an unattended end user PC is:**
    A. A password-protected screensaver
    B. Automatically switching off the monitor when there is no activity
    C. CCTV surveillance
    D. To terminate a session at specified intervals.

27. **The most effective method to prevent unauthorized access to a system administration account is:**
    A. The installation of IDS
    B. To enable system lockout after three failed attempt
    C. To define password complexity rules
    D. Two-factor authentication

28. **The most important concern when conducting a post-implementation review of an organization's network is:**
    A. Mobile devices can be accessed without a password
    B. The default passwords of network devices are not changed
    C. A proxy does not exist for internal communication
    D. Email links are not encrypted

29. **The most effective method of removing data from a tape media during disposal is:**
    A. Multiple overwriting
    B. Erasing the tapes
    C. Degaussing the tapes
    D. Removing the tape header

30. **The most effective method to ensure that only authorized users can connect to the system is:**
    A. A complex password requirement
    B. SSO
    C. Two-factor authentication
    D. IP restrictions

31. **In an SSO environment, the most effective method to prevent unauthorized access is:**
    A. Log monitoring
    B. Deactivating a dormant account
    C. Implementing a strong password policy
    D. User access review

32. **Which of the following is a major risk of SSO?**
    - A. It has a single authentication point
    - B. It represents only a single point of failure
    - C. It causes administrative inconvenience
    - D. It causes user inconvenience

33. **Which of the following is the greatest risk of using SSO?**
    - A. Administrative inconvenience
    - B. Increase in administration cost
    - C. Increase in authentication time
    - D. Greater impact of password leakage

34. **The greatest advantage of the SSO process is:**
    - A. Administrative convenience for password management
    - B. Helps to avoid a single point of failure scenario
    - C. Support of all major operating system environments is easy
    - D. Helps to control network traffic

35. **The IS auditor noted a weakness through which an intruder can update the server database containing a biographic template. Auditors should recommend which of the following controls?**
    - A. Before-image/after-image logging
    - B. Reduced sign-on
    - C. Multimodal biometrics
    - D. Kerberos

36. **The most effective method to protect the organization from identity theft is:**
    - A. SSO
    - B. User-specific terminals
    - C. User access review
    - D. Two-factor authentication

37. **An organization has implemented two-factor authentication that involves a token and a PIN. Which of the following is an important rule to be included in the security policy?**
    - A. The token should not be taken out of the workplace
    - B. The token should be kept separate from the user's laptop
    - C. The PIN should be random
    - D. The PIN should not be written down anywhere

38. **Two-factor authentication is a combination of:**
    A. A smart card and PIN
    B. Fingerprint scan and iris scan
    C. PIN and password
    D. Magnetic card and badge card

39. **The greatest concern for an IS auditor reviewing a media disposal procedure is:**
    A. A disk is overwritten several times at a sector level
    B. Data is deleted and the disk is formatted
    C. A disk is destroyed by hole punching
    D. A disk is shredded in the presence of in-charge security

40. **The greatest concern for an IS auditor reviewing a user authentication procedure is:**
    A. Automatic lockout not enabled
    B. Maximum password age not defined
    C. The use of a shared account by system administrators
    D. Password history control not implemented

41. **Which of the following will not be in the scope of an IS auditor reviewing database-level access control functions?**
    A. The monitoring of the database profile creation process
    B. The process for field-level authorization
    C. The process for determining individual accountability
    D. The process for logging and monitoring database-level activities

42. **Which of the following will be in the scope of an IS auditor reviewing general operating system access control functions?**
    A. The process of logging and monitoring user activities
    B. The process of logging data communication access activities
    C. The process of authorization of a user at the field level
    D. The process of the modification of data files

Biometrics

Biometric verification is a process through which a person can be uniquely identified and authenticated by verifying one or more of their biological features. Examples of these biometric identifiers include a palm, hand geometry, fingerprints, retina and iris patterns, voice, and DNA.

Biometrics – accuracy measure

The accuracy of a biometric system determines how well a system meets the objective. Accuracy measures determine the success factor of the biometric system. In this section, we will discuss a few biometrics accuracy measures.

False acceptance rate (FAR)

This is the rate of acceptance of a false person (that is, an unauthorized person). Biometric control will not restrict the unauthorized person.

For example, if biometrics allows access to an unauthorized person, then it is referred to as false acceptance.

False rejection rate (FRR)

This is the rate of rejection of the correct person (that is, an authorized person). Biometrics will reject even an authorized person.

For example, if biometrics does not allow access to an authorized person, then it is referred to as false rejection.

Cross error rate (CER) or equal error rate (EER)

This is the rate at which the FAR and FRR are equal. A biometric system with the lowest CER or EER is the most effective system. A biometric system with the highest CER or EER is the most ineffective system.

 It must be noted that the FAR and FRR are inversely proportionate. An increase in the FAR will result in a decrease in the FRR and vice versa. Also, if the FRR increases, the FAR will decrease. The CER or EER is an adjustment point where the FAR and FRR are equal.

An IS auditor should be most concerned about the FAR as one of the critical performance indicators. The FAR has the risk of unauthorized access to the systems.

To evaluate the overall quantitative performance of a biometric system, it is important to consider the CER or EER.

The most reliable biometric identifier: Among the current biometric identifiers, a retina scan is considered the most accurate and reliable identifier with the lowest FAR. An iris scan is also considered a very reliable biometric feature.

Control over the biometric process

An IS auditor should verify that appropriate control is in place to protect the biometric information of the users. The following are some of the important aspects:

- Biometric information should be securely stored.
- Access to biometric information should only be available to authorized staff.
- The data flow between biometric devices to the server should be encrypted.
- User access should be revoked immediately on resignation or termination.

Types of biometric attacks

An IS auditor should be aware of the following attacks to exploit the weaknesses in biometric controls:

- **Replay attack**: In a replay attack, the attacker makes use of residual biometric characteristics (such as fingerprints left on a biometric device) to get unauthorized access.
- **Brute-force attack**: In a brute-force attack, the attacker sends numerous biometric samples with an objective to malfunction the biometric device.
- **Cryptographic attack**: In a cryptographic attack, an attacker attempts to obtain information by targeting algorithms or the encrypted information that transmits between biometric devices and access control systems.
- **Mimic attack**: In a mimic attack, the attacker attempts to reproduce a fake biometric feature of a genuine biometric user. For example, imitating the voice of an enrolled user.

Self-assessment questions

1. Which of the following is considered the most accurate and reliable identifier with the lowest False Acceptance Rate?
   - A. Voice wave
   - B. Face identification
   - C. Hand geometry
   - D. Retina scan

2. An IS auditor should be most concerned about which of the following biometric performance indicators?
   - A. False rejection rate
   - B. False acceptance rate
   - C. Cross error rate
   - D. Equal error rate

3. Which of the following is considered the most important overall quantitative performance indicator for a biometric system?
   - A. The percentage of employees enrolled
   - B. The false rejection rate
   - C. The false acceptance rate
   - D. The equal error rate

4. Which of the following is considered the most effective biometric system?
   - A. The highest equal error rate
   - B. The lowest equal error rate
   - C. The highest false acceptance rate
   - D. The lowest false acceptance rate

5. The accuracy of a biometric system is evaluated by:
   - A. The server utilization rate
   - B. The network connection rate
   - C. The system response rate
   - D. The false acceptance rate

6. The effectiveness of a biometric system can be best measured by evaluating:
   - A. The false acceptance rate
   - B. The cross error rate
   - C. The staff enrolled rate
   - D. The false rejection rate

7. **An IS auditor is reviewing the biometric controls for an organization's data center. The area of most concern is:**
   A. The use of a virtual private network for biometric access
   B. All restricted areas are not protected through biometric control
   C. Transit data between the biometric device and the control server is not encrypted
   D. The biometric controls were last reviewed over a year ago

8. **An IS auditor should first review which of the following biometric life cycle stages?**
   A. The termination process
   B. The enrollment stage
   C. The storage process
   D. The identification process

9. **Which of the following is considered the most effective access control mechanism?**
   A. A session-based password
   B. Iris scan
   C. Password
   D. Photo ID card

10. **Which of the following is considered the most effective access control mechanism?**
    A. A fingerprint scanner
    B. A password
    C. A cipher lock
    D. An electronic access card

11. **An attack with the unauthorized use of residual biometric information is known as:**
    A. A brute-force attack
    B. An encrypted attack
    C. A mimic attack
    D. A replay attack

12. **An attack in which the attacker attempts to reproduce the characteristics of a genuine biometric user is known as:**
    A. A mimic attack
    B. A cryptographic attack
    C. A replay attack
    D. A brute-force attack

13. **An attack in which the data transmitted between a biometric device and access control server is targeted is known as:**
    A. A mimic attack
    B. A brute-force attack
    C. A cryptographic attack
    D. A replay attack

14. **An attack in which numerous biometric samples are sent to a biometric device is known as:**
    A. A mimic attack
    B. A brute-force attack
    C. A cryptographic attack
    D. A replay attack

15. **An organization is implementing biometric control for access to its critical server. This will:**
    A. Help to completely eliminate false acceptance
    B. Require the enrollment of all the users that access a critical server
    C. Require a separate password for access to a biometric device
    D. Help to completely eliminate false rejection

Summary

In this chapter, we have discussed in detail various frameworks and standards for information assets, different access control parameters, and biometrics-related risks and controls.

We learned about relevant skills to conduct an audit in accordance with the IS audit standards and a risk-based IS audit strategy, as well as evaluating potential opportunities and threats associated with emerging technologies, regulations, and industry practices.

In the next chapter, we will discuss network-related aspects.

Assessments

You will find the answers to all self-assessment questions in this section.

Information asset security frameworks, standards, and guidelines

1. **Answer: B. Logical access controls**
   Explanation: Logical access controls are the most effective way to safeguard critical data within information processing facilities. Logical access controls are technical controls, such as authentication, encryption, firewall, IDS, and so on, which are very difficult to bypass by a layman. The security committee addresses the broader perspective of security. The other options are not as effective as logical access controls.

2. **Answer: B. The information system security policy**
   Explanation: Logical access controls are designed and developed on the basis of the approved information system security policy of the organization. The user requirements and industry practices should be considered when developing a security policy. However, the implementation of logical controls should be done in accordance with the approved security policy of the organization.

3. **Answer: The data and systems owners**
   Explanation: It is the responsibility of the appointed owner to ensure that their data and systems have appropriate security arrangements. System owners may delegate routine security responsibilities to a security administrator. However, it is the owners who remain accountable for the maintenance of appropriate security measures.

4. **Answer: A. To establish ownership**
   Explanation: Without the owner being defined, it is difficult to conduct criticality analysis or to develop an access matrix. Hence, establishing ownership is the first step in data classification.

5. **Answer: A. Authorization for access from the data owner and implementation of user authorization tables by the administrator**
   Explanation: It is the accountability and responsibility of the data owner for approving the access rights to the user. Once the user is approved, system administrators should then implement or update user authorization tables.

6. **Answer: A. The data owners**
   Explanation: It is the accountability and responsibility of the data owner for approving the access rights to the user.

7. **Answer: A. The data owners**
   Explanation: It is the accountability and responsibility of the data owner for reviewing users' access rights.

8. **Answer: B. Sufficiency**
   Explanation: An IS auditor should first ensure the adequacy and sufficiency of the baseline to address the security requirements of the organization. Other aspects, such as the documentation, process, and compliance, can be determined once sufficiency is evaluated.

Privacy principles

1. **Answer: A. Are there any data privacy concerns about this process?**
   Explanation: It is very important to ensure that the applicable data privacy laws are adhered to. For example, one of the privacy principles requires organizations to use client data only for the purpose for which it is collected. The IS should ensure that consent has been obtained from the clients for the use of their data for promotional activities.

2. **Answer: B. Privacy laws preventing the cross-border flow of information**
   Explanation: It is very important to ensure that the applicable data privacy laws are adhered to. Some privacy laws prohibit the cross-border flow of personally identifiable information. The other options are not as significant as adherence to privacy laws.

3. **Answer: C. Privacy principles are adhered to**
   Explanation: It is very important to ensure that the applicable data privacy laws are adhered to. Encryption and consent are part of the privacy requirements, but they do not address other privacy principles, such as the governance of third-party service providers, the prohibition of cross-border information, and so on. Privacy protection is necessary to ensure that the receiving party has the appropriate level of protection of personal data.

4. **Answer: C. Review the legal and regulatory requirements**
   Explanation: The first step for an IS auditor is to review the legal and regulatory requirements applicable to the organization. On the basis of that, the IS auditor can determine compliance by reviewing the processes.

Physical access and environmental controls

1. **Answer: D. It may be detected and displayed**
   Explanation: A major risk of electromagnet emission is that it may be detected and displayed by the use of sophisticated devices and thus there is the possibility of unauthorized data. Most of the electromagnetic emissions are of low frequency, so there is no impact on the health of the storage device or processor.

2. **Answer: C. A power line conditioner**
   Explanation: A power line conditioner is a device intended to improve the quality of power that is delivered to electrical equipment. It compensates for the peaks and valleys in the power supply. When an electrical supply is low, it provides its own power and maintains a constant voltage. Surge and spike devices help to protect against high-voltage power bursts. An alternative power supply medium (such as a power generator) is most effective when there is long-term power unavailability.

3. **Answer: B. Alternative power supplies**
   Explanation: An alternative power supply medium (such as a power generator) is most effective when there is long-term power unavailability. A power line conditioner is a device intended to improve the quality of power that is delivered to electrical equipment. It compensates for the peaks and valleys in the power supply. When an electrical supply is low, it provides its own power and maintains a constant voltage. Surge and spike devices help to protect against high-voltage power bursts.

4. **Answer: A. Surge devices**
   Explanation: Surge and spike devices help to protect against high-voltage power bursts. An alternative power supply medium (such as a power generator) is most effective when there is long-term power unavailability. A power line conditioner is a device intended to improve the quality of power that is delivered to electric equipment. It compensates for the peaks and valleys in the power supply. When an electrical supply is low, it provides its own power and maintains a constant voltage.

5. **Answer: C. Both of the extinguishers have a risk of suffocation when used in a closed room**
   Explanation: The protection of human life is a major element in any disaster planning. Both carbon dioxide and Halon gas reduce the oxygen in the atmosphere and thus are very dangerous for use in a closed room with employees working. In many countries, the use of Halon is prohibited.

6. **Answer: A. The risk of an unauthorized person entering behind the authorized person**

   Explanation: The risk associated with the use of an access card for entering a computer room is the risk of tailgating or piggybacking. Duplicating an access card is not an easy task. Access logs can be captured as the audit trail. Proper access control life cycle management ensures that access rights are timely terminated.

7. **Answer: A. To escort the visitors**

   Explanation: It is best practice to escort visitors all the time in the data center. This will ensure that they strictly follow the rules of the data center. The other options are good practices but not as reliable as escorting the visitors.

8. **Answer: B. The use of a carbon dioxide-based fire extinguisher in the processing facility**

   Explanation: Carbon dioxide-based extinguishers should not be used where people are present. CO_2 reduces the oxygen level from the area and hence poses a risk to humans. The other options are not as significant as the use of CO_2.

9. **Answer: A. Prevent tailgating**

   Explanation: A mantrap door is also known as a deadman door or an airlock door. It is also known as a mantrap or an airlock entrance. It uses two doors and for the second door to open, the first door must be closed and locked. Only one person is permitted in the gap between the first door and the second door. This reduces the risk of piggybacking or tailgating wherein an unauthorized person follows an authorized person through a secured entry.

10. **Answer: A. Damage to the cables of computers and servers**

    Explanation: The floor is raised to accommodate the ventilation system, power, and data cables underneath the floor. This provides the safety of the cables, which otherwise would pose a large risk if kept on an open floor. A raised floor may not directly address the other options.

11. **Answer: C. The process for promptly disabling a lost or stolen badge is not followed**

    Explanation: It is very important to immediately deactivate a badge that is lost or stolen. An unauthorized individual can enter the room using a stolen badge. The other options are not as significant as deactivating stolen or lost badges.

12. **Answer: A. The use of a shared access card by cleaning staff**

    Explanation: Accountability cannot be established in the case of the issuance of a non-personalized access card. This is the greatest concern. As good practice, access cards should not contain details of the organization to prevent unauthorized use by intruders. Segregation of duties for card issuance and reconciliation is a good practice. Logs may not be required to be reviewed on a daily basis.

13. **Answer: C. Dry pipe sprinklers**
    Explanation: Carbon dioxide and Halon are not considered safe for humans. Both dry pipe and wet pipe are effective and environmentally friendly. However, sprinklers must be dry pipes to prevent the risk of leakage in the data center.

14. **Answer: D. Water, but it enters the pipe only when a fire has been detected**
    Explanation: Dry pipe sprinklers do not have water in the pipes until an electronic fire alarm activates the water pump to send water into the system.

15. **Answer: C. Water resides in the pipe with special water-tight sealants**
    Explanation: Wet pipe systems are the most common fire sprinkler systems. A wet pipe system is one in which water is constantly maintained within the sprinkler piping.

16. **Answer: D. The installation of a carbon dioxide gas fire extinguisher in a manned data center**
    Explanation: Carbon dioxide-based extinguishers should not be used where people are present. CO_2 reduces the oxygen level in the area and hence poses a risk for humans. The other options are not as significant as the use of CO_2. FM-200 is safe to use where people are present. Both dry pipe and wet pipe sprinklers are effective and environmentally friendly. Generally, sprinklers must be dry pipes to prevent the risk of leakage in the data center. However, a major risk is the use of CO_2 where humans are present.

17. **Answer: C. FM-200**
    Explanation: FM-200 is safe to be used when people are present. FM-200 is a colorless and odorless gas. FM-200 is also environmentally friendly. It is commonly used as a gaseous fire suppression agent. Other gases are not considered safe for humans.

Identity and access management

1. **Answer: B. To ensure that access is granted as per an approved process**
   Explanation: The objective of the IS auditor reviewing logical access control is to determine whether access is granted as per an approved process. The effectiveness of access control software and the protection of computer software relates to procedures of a logical access control review, rather than objectives. The protection of computer hardware is relevant to a physical access control review.

2. **Answer: D. It is difficult to establish user accountability**
   Explanation: A major risk of shared user accounts is that user accountability cannot be determined. Logs will capture shared IDs but individual employees or people cannot be traced. The other options are not as significant as the difficulty of establishing user accountability.

3. **Answer: D. Implement logical access controls**
   Explanation: Logical access controls are the best preventive controls to ensure data integrity and confidentiality. The other options are not as effective as the implementation of logical access controls.

4. **Answer: A. Implementing application-level access control**
   Explanation: Application-level access control helps to limit access to an application as per the functionality required by users to perform their jobs. They will not be able to access any other functionality of the application. The other options will not serve this purpose.

5. **Answer: C. Ensure the confidentiality and integrity of information**
   Explanation: The main objective to protect data is to ensure that the confidentiality and integrity of the data is maintained. The other options can be considered as secondary objectives.

6. **Answer: A. To establish data owners**
   Explanation: Identification of the owner of data or an application is the first step in the classification of IS resources. The data owner is responsible for determining the criticality of the data and providing access control rules. Hence, the other options will be followed once the data owner is established.

7. **Answer: B. Password files are not protected**
   Explanations: Unprotected password files pose a major risk as unauthorized access of these files can expose the organization to major risks. Password files should always be encrypted. The other options are not as significant as the protection of password files.

8. **Answer: C. The implementation of an automated password management tool**
   Explanation: An automated password management tool will ensure that password complexity is defined as per the approved policy. It will prevent the use of passwords that are not allowed as per the policy. It will also mandate compulsory password change at a defined frequency. The other options do not directly ensure compliance with the password policy.

9. **Answer: A. The risk of data confidentiality**
   Explanation: It is difficult to control the printing of confidential documents. The availability of printing options increases the risk of confidentiality.

10. **Answer: A. Security and performance parameters are considered.**
    Explanation: The most important aspect when reviewing system controls is the consideration of the security and performance parameters. This helps to ensure that the control objectives are aligned with the business objectives. The other options are not as significant as the alignment of the security and performance parameters.

11. **Answer: A. System file configuration**
    Explanation: A review of the system configuration file will show the level of access available for different users. Both log files and user access reviews are detective in nature and may not reveal all the relevant details. Job descriptions of users will not provide details about the access level.

12. **Answer: C. Log files for suspected transactions**
    Explanation: As a best practice, log files should always be read-only. Edit access should not be enabled for them. The integrity of a log file is very important to treat log files as an audit trail. The other options may require modification and hence write access can also be provided.

13. **Answer: B. The process for the authorization and authentication of a user**
    Explanation: A major aspect is to review the process of authorization and authentication of users. This is a preventive control. Any loopholes in this process make the other controls irrelevant.

14. **Answer: A. DAC is aligned in accordance with MAC**
    Explanation: MAC rules are governed by an approved policy. Users or data owners cannot modify the access role, whereas DAC can be activated or modified by the data owner at their discretion. For DACs to be more effective, they have to be designed in accordance with MACs.

15. **Answer: A. Demagnetization of computer storage**
    Explanation: The right kind of formatting is very critical to ensure that residual data from media cannot be recovered by an unauthorized person. To the greatest extent possible, the media should be physically destroyed in such a way that it cannot be reused. However, it may not be economical to destroy the media, and hence, for these cases, extreme care should be taken for the complete eraser of the data to make sure the data cannot be recoverable by any tool or technique. One of these methods is to demagnetize the media record. This process involves increasing the alternating current field gradually from 0 to some maximum value and back to 0, leaving a very low residue of magnetic induction on the media. This process of demagnetization is also known as degaussing.

16. **Answer: B. The review of network security**
    Explanation: The router is a part of networking. Network security reviews include reviewing router access control lists, port scanning, internal and external connections to the system, and so on.

17. **Answer: A. Difficult to control role-based access**
    Explanation: In the absence of an authorization process, it will be impossible to establish and provide role-based access. The risk where many users can claim to be a specific user can be better addressed by a proper authentication process, rather than authorization. This will not directly impact the sharing of user accounts. In the absence of a proper authorization process, the principle of need-to-know cannot be established.

18. **Answer: B. Temporary user accounts created for a defined role with account expiration dates**
    Explanation: The best control would be to create user accounts temporarily only for the required roles and accounts should be disabled on a given date. The other options may not be as effective as this one.

19. **Answer: B. It helps with defining structured access rules**
    Explanation: A naming convention is an agreed structure for naming assets. It helps with the effective and efficient management of access rules. Generally, assets that are critical in nature are grouped and named under sensitive categories. Rules are defined for access to sensitive categories that may be more stringent compared to other categories. This reduces the number of rules required to adequately protect resources, which in turn facilitates security administration and maintenance efforts.

20. **Answer: C. Users can access and modify the database directly**
    Explanation: If users are allowed to modify the data directly without any authorization, it may impact the integrity of the data. Only DBA should be allowed for any backend changes to the database. The other options are not as significant as the ability of users to change the database.

21. **Answer: D. To create an inventory of the IS resources**
    Explanation: To implement logical access controls, the following chronological steps are to be followed:
    (i) Prepare an inventory of the IS resources (ii) Classify the IS resources (iii) Perform grouping/labeling of the IS resources (iv) Create an access control list.

22. **Answer: A. No restriction for connecting external laptops to the network**
    Explanation: A major concern is about unrestricted LAN connection for external laptops. Intruders can connect to the network and, using various tools and techniques, may be able to create serious damage to the IS resources. The other options are not as significant as an unrestricted LAN connection.

23. **Answer: C. Online access to be blocked after a specified number of unsuccessful login attempts**
Explanation: The most important control to prevent unauthorized access to databases is to block access after a specified number of unsuccessful login attempts. This is a preventive control. Preventive control is better than detective or deterrent controls. This will deter access through the guessing of IDs and passwords. The other options are physical controls, which may not be able to address the risk of remote attack.

24. **Answer: A. Allows approved traffic and rejects all other traffic**
Explanation: An organization can either have a default deny access control policy or an allow all access control policy. In a default deny policy, all the traffic is denied except predefined approved traffic. In an allow all policy, all traffic is allowed except predefined restricted traffic. Default deny is more prevalent where traffic is from an untrusted source to access a protected system. Allow all is more prevalent where traffic is from trusted sources to access an external system, such as the internet.

25. **Answer: B. Denies specific traffic and allows all other traffic**
Explanation: An organization can either have a default deny access control policy or an allow all access control policy. In a default deny policy, all the traffic is denied except predefined approved traffic. In an allow all policy, all traffic is allowed except predefined restricted traffic. Default deny is more prevalent where traffic is from an untrusted source to access a protected system. Allow all is more prevalent where traffic is from trusted sources to access an external system, such as the internet.

26. **Answer: A. A password-protected screensaver**
Explanation: A password-protected screensaver with a proper time interval is the best way to prevent the unauthorized access of unattended PCs. A user should lock their PC when it is not being used. Switching off the PC will not serve the same purpose as it can be switched on by anyone. CCTV cameras are a detective control and will not prevent unauthorized access. Terminating a session at a specified interval may not serve this purpose. If the screen is not locked, then anyone can access the system within a specified interval.

27. **Answer: D. Two-factor authentication**
    Explanation: Two-factor authentication means the use of two authentication methods from the following:
    i. Something you know (for example, a password, PIN, or some other personal information)
    ii. Something you have (for example, a token, OTP, or smart card)
    iii. Something you are (for example, biometric features, such as fingerprint, iris scan, or voice recognition)
    For critical systems, it is advisable to use more than one factor of authentication for granting access. IDS is a detective control and not a preventive control. The other options will not be effective if the password is compromised.

28. **Answer: B. The default passwords of network devices are not changed**
    Explanation: A major area of concern is that of the factory default password not being changed for critical network devices. Anyone can change the system configuration using a default password. The other areas are not as significant as default passwords not being changed.

29. **Answer: C. Degaussing the tapes**
    Explanation: Degaussing is the best way to erase data from a disk. The process involves increasing the alternating current field gradually from 0 to some maximum value and back to 0, leaving a very low residue of magnetic induction on the media. This is known as demagnetization or degaussing. The other options are not as secure as degaussing the tapes.

30. **Answer: C. Two-factor authentication**
    Explanation: Two-factor authentication means the use of two authentication methods from the following:
    i. Something you know (for example, a password, PIN, or some other personal information)
    ii. Something you have (for example, a token, OTP, or smart card)
    iii. Something you are (for example, biometric features, such as fingerprint, iris scan, or voice recognition)
    This provides added security and intruders need to break two levels of access. An IP address can be spoofed and cannot be considered secure. SSO increases the risk of a single point of failure.

31. **Answer: C. Implementing a strong password policy**
    Explanation: SSO is a user authentication service that permits a user to use one set of login credentials (for example, a name and password) to access multiple applications. This increases the risk of a single point of failure. It is very important to implement strong password complexity for this kind of environment. The other options are not as significant as the implementation of a strong password policy.

32. **Answer: A. It has a single authentication point**

Explanation: SSO is a user authentication service that permits a user to use one set of login credentials (for example, a name and password) to access multiple applications. This increases the risk of a single point of failure due to having only one authentication for multiple systems. However, failure can also be due to any other reason. Failure can occur at multiple points in resources, such as the data, process, or network. So, a more specific answer to this question is it has only a single authentication point.

33. **Answer: D. Greater impact of password leakage**

Explanation: SSO is a user authentication service that permits a user to use one set of login credentials (for example, a name and password) to access multiple applications. This increases the risk of a single point of failure. The impact of password compromise will be much greater since the intruder needs to know only one password to gain access to all the related applications and, therefore, cause greater problems. It is very important to implement strong password complexity for this kind of environment.

34. **Answer: A. Administrative convenience for password management**

Example: SSO makes it easy and convenient for managing passwords. However, it acts as a single point of failure and it is difficult to support all major operating system environments. SSO does not impact or control network traffic.

35. **Answer: D. Kerberos**

Explanation: Kerberos is an authentication service used to validate services and users in DCEs. In a client-server environment, only users are authenticated; however, in DCEs, both users and servers authenticate themselves. At the initial logon time, the Kerberos third-party application is used to verify the identity of the client. Multimodal biometrics are controlled against the mimicry attacks. Before-image/after-image logging is more of a detective control compared to Kerberos, which is a preventative control.

36. **Answer: D. Two-factor authentication**

Explanation: Two-factor authentication provides added security as intruders need to break two levels of access. SSO requires only one set of passwords, which increases the risk of a single point of failure. A user-specific terminal is not a practical solution when the user works from multiple devices. User access review will not help to protect from identity theft.

37. **Answer: D. The PIN should not be written down anywhere**

Explanation: A PIN is something that only the user should know. If it is written down and is compromised, the intruder can gain unauthorized access. A PIN does not necessarily need to be random. Access to a token is of no value if the PIN is kept secret.

38. **Answer: A. A smart card and PIN**
    Explanation: Two-factor authentication means the use of two authentication methods from the following:
    Something you know (for example, a password, PIN, or some other personal information)
    Something you have (for example, a token, OTP, smart card, or badge card)
    Something you are (for example, biometric features, such as fingerprint, iris scan, or voice recognition)
    Except for a smart card and PIN, all the other options are of the same authentication method.

39. **Answer: B. Data is deleted and the disk is formatted**
    Explanation: Disk formatting is not a secure way of erasing data. Data can be recovered with the use of various tools and techniques. The other options are a more secure way of data erasing and media disposal.

40. **Answer: C. The use of a shared account by system administrators**
    Explanation: The use of a shared account will not help to establish accountability for the transaction. System administrator accounts are privileged accounts and should be named and allocated to each individual. The other options are not as significant as the use of generic accounts by system administrators.

41. **Answer: C. The process for determining individual accountability**
    Explanation: Establishing individual accountability is the function of the general operating system. Creating database profiles, verifying user authorization at a field level, and logging database access activities for monitoring access violations are all database-level access control functions.

42. **Answer: A. The process of logging and monitoring user activities**
    Explanation: General operating system access control functions include logging user activities, logging events, and so on. *Choice B* is a network control feature. *Choices C* and *D* are database- and/or application-level access control functions.

Biometrics

1. **Answer: D. Retina scan**
   Explanation: Among the current biometric identifiers, a retina scan is considered the most accurate and reliable identifier with the lowest FAR.

2. **Answer: B. FAR**
   Explanation: An IS auditor should be most concerned about the FAR as one of the critical performance indicators. The FAR shows the risk of unauthorized access to systems.

3. **Answer: D. The EER**
   Explanation: To evaluate the overall quantitative performance of a biometric system, it is important to consider the CER or EER.

4. **Answer: B. The lowest EER**
   Explanation: The EER is the rate at which the FAR and FRR are equal. A biometric system with the lowest CER or EER is the most effective system. A biometric system with the highest CER or EER is the most ineffective system.

5. **Answer: D. The FAR**
   Explanation: The FAR, FRR, and CER are three main accuracy measures for a biometric control. The other options are more closely related to performance measures.

6. **Answer: A. The FAR**
   Explanations: FAR is the rate of acceptance of unauthorized persons; that is, the biometric control will allow unauthorized persons to access the system. In any given scenario, the most important performance indicator for a biometric system is the FAR. This is a fail-unsafe condition; that is, an unauthorized individual may be granted access. A low FAR is most desirable when it is used to protect highly sensitive data.

7. **Answer: C. Transit data between the biometric device and the control server is not encrypted.**
   Explanation: Data transmitted between the biometric device and the access control system should use a securely encrypted tunnel to protect the confidentiality of the biometric data. The other options are not as significant as the transmission of unencrypted data.

8. **Answer: B. The enrollment stage**
   Explanation: The process of biometric control starts with the enrollment of the users, which is followed by the storage, verification, identification, and termination processes. The users of a biometrics device must first be enrolled onto the device. This occurs through an iterative process of acquiring samples, extracting data from samples, validating the sample, and developing the final template, which is stored and subsequently used to authenticate the user.

9. **Answer: B. Iris scan**
   Explanation: Among all the controls, an iris scan can be considered as the most reliable. Fraudsters find it very difficult to bypass biometric controls. Since no two irises are alike, identification and verification can be done with confidence. The other options are not as strong as an iris scan.

10. **Answer: A. A fingerprint scanner**

    Explanation: Among all the options, the most reliable control can be considered the fingerprint scanner. The fingerprint is a biometric control that is very difficult to break. A fingerprint is hard to duplicate, easy to deactivate, and individually identifiable. Since no two fingerprints are alike (unless in very rare cases), identification and verification can be done with confidence. The other options are not as strong as a fingerprint scanner.

11. **Answer: D. A replay attack**

    Explanation: In a replay attack, the attacker makes use of residual biometric characteristics (such as fingerprints left on a biometric device) to get unauthorized access.

12. **Answer. A. A mimic attack**

    Explanation: In a mimic attack, the attacker attempts to reproduce fake biometric features of a genuine biometric user. For example, imitating the voice of an enrolled user.

13. **Answer: C. A cryptographic attack**

    Explanation: In a cryptographic attack, the attacker attempts to obtain information by targeting algorithms or the encrypted information that transmit between biometric devices and access control systems.

14. **Answer: B. A brute-force attack**

    Explanation: In a brute-force attack, an attacker sends numerous biometric samples with the objective to malfunction the biometric device.

15. **Answer: B. Require the enrollment of all the users that access a critical server**

    Explanation: For setting up a biometric control, relevant users need to enroll themselves by registration of their biometric feature. *Choice A and D* are incorrect, as the risk of false acceptance as well as the FRR cannot be eliminated completely. *Choice C* is incorrect as the biometric reader does not need to be protected in itself by a password.

10
Network Security and Control

Network security and control is an important aspect of an IS audit. In this chapter, we will discuss various components of the network, the OSI layer, and other security aspects of networking. We will also discuss and learn about the functions of each type of firewall. This chapter also deals with the **Virtual Private Network (VPN)** and **Voice over Internet Protocol (VoIP)**.

The following topics will be covered in this chapter:

- Network and endpoint devices
- Firewall types and implementation
- VPN
- VoIP
- Wireless networks
- Email security

By the end of this chapter, you will be able to understand and evaluate various risks and controls related to networking.

Network and endpoint devices

The hardening and configuration of network and endpoint devices is very important from the perspective of information security. An IS auditor should therefore be aware of the basic functioning and capability of network devices to evaluate the risk and control related to such devices. Hence, in this section, we will identify the risks associated with network security and related controls.

Open system interconnection (OSI) layers

The OSI model explains the layered steps for the network. In an OSI model, each layer is defined according to a specific function to perform. All seven layers work in a collaborative manner to transmit the data from one layer to another. The following table shows the functions of each layer:

Layer	Name	Descriptions
1st	Physical Layer	• The physical layer converts bits into voltage for transmission. • The physical layer is associated with the cables and other hardware for the physical connection of the device to the network.
2nd	Data Link Layer	• The data link layer converts the electrical voltage into a data packet and it is forwarded to the network layer. • Similarly, a data packet received from the network layer is converted into an electrical voltage and forwarded to the physical layer.
3rd	Network Layer	• The function of the network layer is to insert the IP address into the packet header and route the packet to their destination.
4th	Transport Layer	• The function of the transport layer is to provide an end-to-end data transport service and establishes a logical connection between the two devices. • The transport layer ensures the reliability of the data transfer to its destination in the proper sequence. • This layer manages traffic as per network congestion, in other words, reduces data transmission during periods of high congestion and increases transmission during periods of low congestion
5th	Session Layer	• The function of the session layer is to establish a connection between two applications, maintaining the connection and terminating the connection when required. • It is like a phone call, wherein the first connection is made and then the message is exchanged and the connection is terminated.
6th	Presentation Layer	• The function of the presentation layer is to translate the data as per the format of the application. • The presentation layer provides services such as encryption, text compression, and reformatting.
7th	Application layer	• The function of the application layer is to provide an interface and communicate directly with the end user • It includes the protocols that support the applications.

As shown in the preceding table, layers are the core of networking and they will be repeated throughout the chapter. CISA aspirants are advised to remember the sequence of each layer with the help of the following diagram:

```
┌─────────────────────────────────────────────────┐
│        Memory Technique to remember OSI Layers   │
│                                                   │
│              P D| N T | S P A                      │
│                      Or                           │
│        Please do not tell sales people anything   │
│                      Or                           │
│       Please do not teach stupid people anything  │
│                      Or                           │
│       Please do not throw sausage pizza away      │
│                      Or                           │
│    People desperately need to see Pamela Anderson │
└─────────────────────────────────────────────────┘
```

Although there will be no direct questions on the OSI layer in the CISA exam, a CISA aspirant should have a basic understanding of the OSI layer.

Networking devices

An IS auditor should have a basic understanding of the following network devices.

Repeaters

Repeaters are used to address the risk of attenuation (weakening of the signal). A repeater receives the signal from one network and it amplifies and regenerates the weak signal. Repeaters extend the signal so that a signal can cover longer distances or be received on the other side of an obstruction.

Hubs and switches

Hubs and switches are used to connect different devices for the exchange of data. A hub operates at layer 1 (physical layer), whereas a switch operates at layer 2 (data link layer) of the OSI model. A switch is regarded as a more advanced/intelligent version of the hub. A hub broadcasts the message to all connected devices, whereas a switch sends messages only to designated devices. A hub cannot store **Media Access Control (MAC)** addresses, whereas switches store MAC addresses in a lookup table.

Bridges

Bridges have the same functionality as switches. They both operate at layer 2 (data link layer) of the OSI model.

A bridge identifies the MAC address and directs the packet to its destination. It also has the ability to store the frame and can act as a storage and forward device. A bridge has only a few ports for connecting devices, whereas a switch has many ports for device connection.

Routers

A router is regarded as a more advanced/intelligent version of the switch. It operates at layer 3 (network layer) of the OSI model.

A bridge identifies the IP address and directs the packet to its destination. A router has the basic ability to monitor, control, and block network traffic. It can be regarded as a very basic level of firewall.

Routers can connect two different networks and each network remains logically separate and can function as an independent network. A router identifies the IP address, whereas a switch operates by identifying MAC addresses.

Gateway

A gateway has the capability to translate and connect different protocols and networks. It operates at layer 3 (application layer) of the OSI model. A gateway can perform much more complex tasks than connection devices such as switches and routers.

Network devices and the OSI layer

The functionality of devices depends upon the layer at which they operate. Devices operating at higher levels will be more intelligent and capable compared with devices operating at lower levels. A CISA aspirant should be aware of the layer at which various devices operate:

Device	Layer
Hub	Physical Layer (1st Layer)
Switch	Data Link Layer (2nd Layer)
Bridge	Data Link Layer (2nd Layer)
Router	Network Layer (3rd Layer)
Gateway	Application Layer (7th Layer)

A gateway operates at the seventh layer, and so is the most intelligent device, whereas hubs that operate at the first layer have limited capability.

Network physical media

Physical media refers to the physical objects that are used to transmit and store the data in a network communication. Examples of network physical media include cables, storage media, and other networking equipment.

CRM covers the following types of network physical media.

Fiber optics

Optical fiber is a thin and flexible piece of fiber made of glass or plastic. Here are their characteristics:

- It carries binary signals as flashes of light.
- Fiber optic cables are considered to be more secure than copper wire.
- Fiber optic is the preferred choice for managing long-distance networks and handling high volumes of data.
- Fiber optic is not impacted or affected by **electromagnetic interference (EMI)**.
- Fiber optic cables have very marginal transmission loss.

Twisted pair (copper circuit)

Twisted pairs are also known as copper circuits. Here are their characteristics:

- Copper wires are cheaper than fiber optics.
- There are two categories of twisted pair, that is, the **shielded twisted pair (STP)** or the unshielded twisted pair (UTP).
- STPs are less prone to EMI and cross-talks and so are more reliable than UTPs.
- A UTP is more sensitive to the effects of EMI and cross talk.
- The parallel installation of UTPs should be avoided for long distances since one cable can interfere with the signals of adjacent cables (that is what is meant by cross talk).

Infrared and radio (wireless)

Wireless communication is established through infrared or radio waves.

The following image shows various kind of networking cables:

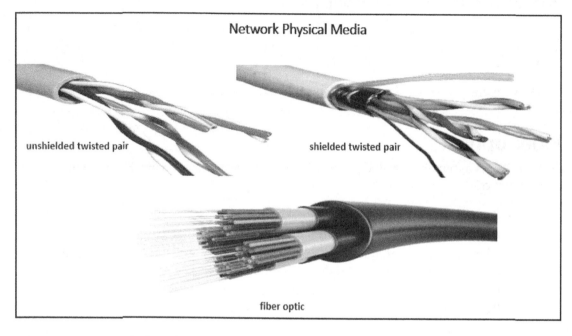

Fiber optic is regarded as the most secure cable for the purposes of data transmission.

Identifying the risks of physical network media

There are certain factors that determine the selection of particular media. IS auditors should be aware of these factors and the relevant risks that affect the performance of the media. The following are some of the major factors:

Attenuation

Attenuation is the loss or weakening of signal transmission. Attenuation can impact both wired and wireless transmissions. Distance and wire length have a direct impact on the severity of attenuation.

EMI

EMI is an interference or disturbance that impacts the quality of electrical signals. EMI is generally caused by connecting one electrical or electronic device to another, which may degrade the performance of the circuit or even stop it from functioning. With respect to network data, EMI may result in the total loss of data or an increase in the error rate. Major causes of EMI are electrical storms or noisy electrical equipment (for example, motors, fluorescent lighting, and radio transmitters).

Cross talks

Cross talk happens when the signal from one cable gets mixed up with the signal from another cable. This generally happens for UTPs of cables that run close to one another.

Network diagram

While auditing the network security aspect, an IS auditor should first review the network diagram to understand the network architecture and determine the inherent risk or a single point of failure. A network diagram is a pictorial representation of network architecture that includes computer, server, and other network devices such as cables, routers, devices, hubs, and firewalls. A network diagram includes the details of placement of each piece of network equipment and how they interact with each other.

Once the auditor is familiar with the network, it becomes easy to understand the risks and evaluate relevant controls.

Network protocols

A CISA aspirant should have a basic understanding of the following network-related protocols.

Dynamic Host Configuration Protocol

Dynamic Host Configuration Protocol (DHCP) is a protocol to manage the network configuration. A DHCP server dynamically assigns an IP address and other network configuration parameters to every device on a network so that they can communicate with other IP networks. Thus, IP address pool management is handled by the DHCP server for high-volume traffic.

One of the concerns regarding automatic IP allocation is the fact that any unauthorized individual can connect to the corporate network. Hence, physical network ports should not be kept open and strong restrictions should be in place to access the network port.

Transport Layer Security and Secure Socket Layer

Transport Layer Security (TLS) and **Secure Socket Layer** (SSL) are the protocols operating at the transport layer. They are used for privacy and data security while communicating over the network. Both protocols make use of cryptographic functions to protect the confidentiality, reliability, and integrity of private documents traveling through the internet. SSL is now deprecated as the same is vulnerable to attack.

Transmission Control Protocol and User Data Protocol

Transmission Control Protocol (TCP) and **User Data Protocol** (UDP) are the protocols operating at the transport layer. TCP is considered a reliable and connection-oriented protocol. TCP ensures that data packets are delivered to the destination. TCP provides for enhanced error checking and correction. If a data packet is corrupted or lost during transmission, TCP resends the packet. It delivers the packet in a sequence.

UDP is considered a connectionless protocol. UDP has unreliable service and data packets may arrive out of order, be corrupted, or may get dropped, and the destination does not acknowledge every packet it receives. One advantage of UDP is that it allows for reduced latency as it does not perform error checking.

Secure Shell and Telnet

Secure Shell (SSH) and Telnet are remote terminal control protocols. Through these protocols, a user can connect to the terminal from a remote location. For instance, Mr. A of the USA can access the computer of Mr. B of India through these protocols.

SSH provides authentication and secure transmission for remote connection. However, it must be noted that Telnet traffic is not encrypted by default. It is advisable to use SSH in place of Telnet. If Telnet is used, it is advisable to use a dedicated leased line to reduce the security risk.

Key aspects from CISA exam perspective

The following table covers the key aspects from the perspective of the CISA exam:

CISA questions	Possible answers
What is the most secured and reliable transmission media	Fiber Optic
What is the best security for telecommunication network	Dedicated lease lines
While auditing the network security aspect, what an IS auditor should first review?	Network diagram
Name a connectionless and unreliable protocol.	UDP
Which OSI layer route packets between the nodes?	Network layer
Which OSI layer is primarily concerned with the reliability of data transfer between the systems?	Transport layer

Self-assessment questions

1. **Which of the following is regarded as the most secure transmission medium?**
   - A. Fiber optic wires
   - B. A UTP
   - C. A twisted-pair wire
   - D. A copper wire

2. **A device that is primarily installed as a security measure to prevent unauthorized traffic among the different segments of the network is:**
   - A. a switch
   - B. a hub
   - C. a firewall
   - D. a router

3. **An enterprise has installed a wireless local area network connection port in its conference room for internet access. Which of the following is the best control to protect the production server from unauthorized access?**
   - A. Enable encryption for network traffic
   - B. Separate the VLANs for the conference and production environments
   - C. Enable a logon procedure to connect with the network
   - D. Only a laptop with an updated antivirus should be allowed to connect to the network

4. **Which of the following is a major concern regarding the use of the DHCP?**
   A. Use of the application layer firewall
   B. Access to the network port is not restricted
   C. Antivirus software is updated every month
   D. Two-factor authentication is implemented

5. **The most effective medium for providing security for a telecommunication network is:**
   A. broadband
   B. dedicated leased lines
   C. a dial-up connection
   D. a public network

6. **An organization allows visitors to access its wireless internet by means of a generic user ID and password. Which of the following is the best control to address the risk?**
   A. Physical separation of the visitor's network and the company network
   B. The installation of a firewall between the visitor's network and the company network
   C. A password change every day
   D. The installation of IDS to protect the company network

7. **Which of the following is looked at first by an IS auditor when reviewing the security of the local area network?**
   A. The authentication factor
   B. The penetration testing report
   C. A user access review
   D. A diagram of the network

8. **The most effective method for restricting an unauthorized internet site is:**
   A. the installation of an IDS
   B. the use of a content filtering proxy server for outbound traffic
   C. the use of a content filtering proxy server for inbound traffic
   D. the installation of client software on each PC computer to restrict web content

9. **A defense-in-depth arrangement can be illustrated by:**
    A. the use of two centralized firewalls to monitor traffic
    B. the use of a centralized firewall as well as a host-level firewall on each computer
    C. the use of a centralized firewall as well as logical access control on each computer
    D. the use of security guards for perimeter security

10. **The best control for an internet-based business that is seeking confidentiality, reliability, and integrity of the data is:**
    A. a router
    B. an **intrusion detection system (IDS)**
    C. a secure socket layer
    D. an intrusion protection system

11. **Which of the following documents is accorded the highest priority for review by the IS auditor while reviewing network security?**
    A. The user access review
    B. The configuration, wiring, and schematic diagram
    C. The list of servers
    D. The redundancy procedure

12. **Which should be determined first by an IS auditor while reviewing network security?**
    A. The factor of authentication
    B. The firewall configuration
    C. An evaluation of the vulnerability assessment report
    D. The network entry points

13. **Which of the following is a feature of the UDP?**
    A. UDP is a connection-oriented protocol
    B. UDP provides enhanced latency
    C. UDP provides unreliable service and packets may arrive out of order
    D. UDP provides for enhanced error checking and correction

14. **Disabling the dynamic host configuration protocol:**
    A. is not suitable for high-volume traffic
    B. will automatically allot IP addresses to any device on the network
    C. reduces the risk of unauthorized access to networks
    D. is not suitable for wireless networks

15. An organization has one wired as well as one wireless local area network (WLAN). A wired network is used to store and transmit sensitive data, and a wireless network is used for other general purposes. A few employees with wireless access are required to access customer information. Which of the following is the best way to separate both the networks?

   A. Separate both networks physically

   B. Implement a firewall between both networks

   C. Implement an IDS between both networks

   D. Implement a VLAN between both networks

16. Which of the following is an IS auditor's first step in reviewing access control for client server environments?

   A. Determining the network access point

   B. Determining placement of the firewall

   C. Determining the authentication system

   D. Determining logical access control

17. Which of the following will help to protect a network from acting as a zombie in a denial-of-service attack?

   A. Deny all incoming traffic with the source address of the critical host

   B. Deny all incoming traffic with the spoofed source IP

   C. Deny all incoming and outgoing traffic for the critical host

   D. Deny all outgoing traffic with the external source address

18. Which of the following is regarded as a major concern in a firewall configuration?

   A. A default configuration setting has not been changed

   B. Denying all traffic expect approved traffic

   C. Allowing all traffic except restricted traffic

   D. The setting of a firewall for the VPN endpoint

19. Which of the following is regarded as a major concern for an organization when allowing visitors to use its network?

   A. The guest network is not separated from the production network

   B. Only single-factor authentication is implemented

   C. An IDS is not installed

   D. A firewall allows all traffic except restricted traffic

20. **Which of the following devices will help to best restrict the accessing of forbidden websites on a user's PC?**
    A. A router
    B. A stateful inspection
    C. An IDS
    D. A web content filter

21. **Which of the following is the most appropriate security control for implementing a wireless local area network (WLAN)?**
    A. Enable an SSID for the network
    B. Enable a DHCP
    C. Physical security of wireless access points
    D. Enable an SNMP to monitor the network

22. **Which should be identified first by an IS auditor while reviewing network security?**
    A. Determine the importance of network devices in topology
    B. Determine the lack of network devices
    C. Determine the placement of network devices
    D. Determine the integration of network devices

23. **Which of the following is the most appropriate action by network administrators in addressing user feedback regarding slow networks?**
    A. Segment the network to improve the speed
    B. Change the internet service provider
    C. Use a protocol analyzer to analyze the performance of the network and related devices
    D. Increase the bandwidth of the internet connection

24. **Which of the following is the best control for remote sites connected to the headquarters of the organization over the internet via Telnet?**
    A. Implement two-factor authentication
    B. A dedicated leased line for remote connection
    C. A firewall configuration to allow only a remote IP
    D. Appropriate network administrator training

25. **A disturbance that can impact both wired and wireless communication is:**
    A. surges
    B. cross talk
    C. attenuation
    D. multipath interference

26. **A disturbance that can be caused by the length of cable is:**
    A. surges
    B. cross talk
    C. attenuation
    D. EMI

Firewall types and implementation

A firewall is a network security system designed to prevent unauthorized access to networks. It monitors and controls incoming and outgoing network traffic as per defined rules. A firewall can be implemented either in software or hardware form.

The prime objective of a firewall is to allow only authorized uses of the system and network and thereby restrict unauthorized access.

CRM covers the following types and implementations of firewall:

Types of Firewall	Types Firewall Implementation
• Packet Filtering Router • Statefull Inspection • Circuit-Level • Application-Level	• Dual Homed Firewall • Screened Host Firewall • Screened Subnet Firewall (DMZ)

CISA aspirants need to understand the basics of each of the preceding types and firewall implementation methods.

Types of firewall

The following are the basic characteristics of the different types of firewall.

Packet filtering router

A packet filtering router is the simplest and earliest version of the firewall.

It tracks the IP address and port number of both the destination and source and takes action (either to allow or deny the connection) as per defined rules.

A packet filtering router operates at the network layer of the OSI framework.

Stateful inspection

A stateful inspection firewall monitors and tracks the destination of each packet that is being sent from the internal network. It ensures that the incoming message is in response to the request that went out of the organization. A stateful inspection firewall operates at the network layer of the OSI framework.

Circuit-level

A circuit-level firewall works on the concept of a bastion host and proxy server:

- It provides the same proxy for all services.
- It operates a session layer of the OSI.

Application-level

An application-level firewall provides a separate proxy for each application. Here are a few of its characteristics:

- It operates at the application layer of the OSI.
- It controls the application such as FTP and http.
- An application-level firewall is regarded as the most secure type of firewall.

What is a bastion host?

The objective of a bastion host is to protect the network of the organization from outside exposure. Only bastion hosts are made available on the internet and it is the only system that can be addressed directly from the public network. Bastion hosts are heavily forfeited against attack.

Both application- and circuit-level firewalls work on the concept of bastion hosting.

The following are some of the common characteristics of a bastion host:

- The operating system of a bastion host is hardened and only essential services are activated for the bastion host. Vulnerabilities are removed as far as possible.
- Generally, an additional level of authentication is required before a user is allowed to access proxy services.
- Bastion hosts are configured in such a way that access is allowed only for specific hosts.

What is a proxy?

Let's understand the concept of a proxy from the following diagram:

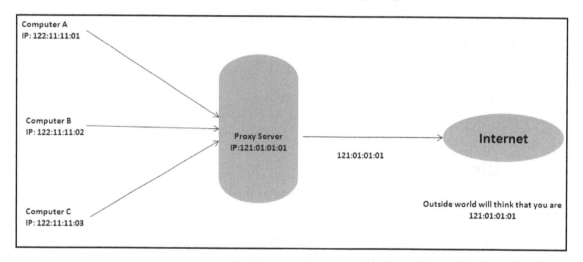

A proxy can be regarded as a middleman. A proxy stands in between the internal and external networks.

No direct communication will be allowed between the internal and external networks. All communication will pass through the proxy server.

The outside world will not have the addresses of the internal networks. It can recognize only proxy servers.

Proxy technology operating at the session layer is referred to as circuit-level proxy, while proxy technology operating at the application layer is referred to as an application-level proxy.

Types of firewall implementation

The following three types of firewall implementation are relevant to the CISA exam.

Dual-homed firewall

The following are the characteristics of a dual-homed firewall:

- A dual-homed firewall consists of one packet filtering router.
- It also has one bastion host with two **Network Interface Cards** (**NICs**).
- The following diagram illustrates the concept of a dual-homed firewall:

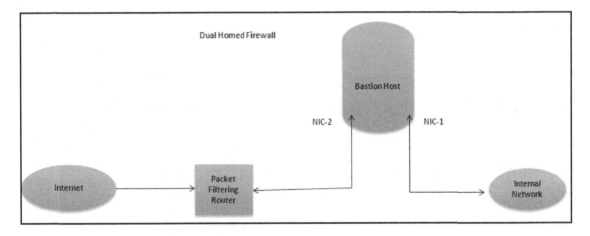

As can be seen in the preceding diagram, a dual-homed firewall consists of one packet filtering router and one bastion host with two network interface cards.

Screened host firewall

The following are the characteristics of a screened host firewall:

- A screened host firewall consists of one packet filtering router.
- It also has one bastion host.
- The following diagram illustrates the concept of a screened host firewall:

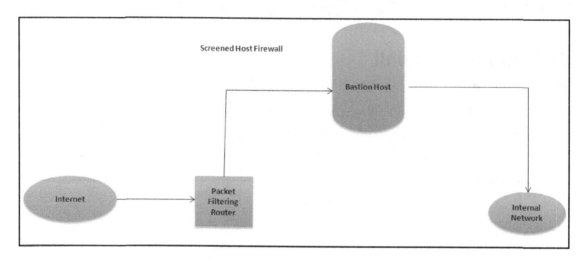

As can be seen in the preceding diagram, the screened host firewall consists of one packet filtering router and one bastion host.

Screened subnet firewall (demilitarized zone)

The following are the characteristics of a screened subnet firewall:

- A screened subnet firewall consists of two packet filtering routers.
- It also has one bastion host.
- Of the preceding firewall implementations, a screened subnet firewall (demilitarized zone) is regarded as the most secure type of firewall implementation.

The following diagram illustrates the concept of a screened subnet firewall:

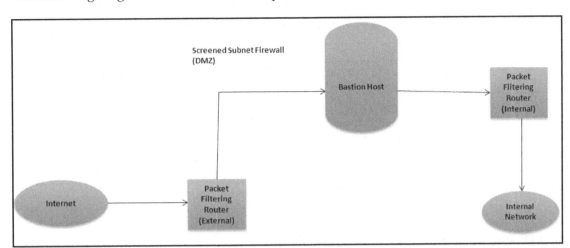

As can be seen in the preceding diagram, the screened subnet firewall consists of two packet filtering routers and one bastion host. A screened subnet firewall is regarded as one of the most robust firewall arrangements.

Firewall and the corresponding OSI layer

An IS auditor should have a basic understanding of the OSI layer for each type of firewall. The following table illustrates the type of firewall and their corresponding OSI layer:

Firewall	OSI Layer
Packet Filtering Firewall	Network Layer (3rd Layer)
Statefull Inspection Firewall	Network Layer (3rd Layer)
Circuit-Level Firewall	Session Layer (5th Layer)
Application-Level Firewall	Application Layer (7th Layer)

CISA aspirants should be aware of the OSI layer for each firewall type. The functionality of the firewall improves with the increase in layers. An application-level firewall that operates at the seventh layer is regarded as the most robust firewall.

Key aspects from the CISA exam perspective

The following table covers the key aspects from the perspective of the CISA exam:

CISA question	Possible answer
What is the objective of firewall?	To connect only authorized users to trusted networks (thereby restricting unauthorized access)
The most secured type of firewall is:	Application-level (as it works on the application layer of the OSI model)
The most secured implementation technique is:	Screened subnet firewall (DMZ)
The most stringent and robust configuration setting in the firewall is:	Deny all traffic and allow specific traffic
The firewall that permits traffic from external source only if it is in response to traffic from internal hosts is:	Stateful inspection

Self-assessment questions

1. **Which of the following firewall settings is regarded as the most robust?**
    A. To allow all traffic and reject specific traffic
    B. To deny all traffic and allow specific traffic
    C. To decide dynamically based on network availability
    D. To control traffic at the discretion of the network engineer

2. **A packet filtering firewall works at:**
    A. the network layer of the OSI
    B. the data layer of the OSI
    C. the application layer of the OSI
    D. the session layer of the OSI

3. **The most robust and stringent firewall system implementation is:**
    A. a screened host firewall
    B. a dual-homed firewall
    C. a screened subnet firewall
    D. a stateful inspection firewall

4. **A firewall system with an enhanced degree of control is:**
   A. a stateful gateway
   B. a packet gateway
   C. an application gateway
   D. a circuit gateway

5. **Which of the following firewall structures will provide the best protection to a network from an internet attack?**
   A. A packet filtering router
   B. A circuit-level gateway
   C. A screened subnet firewall
   D. A screened host firewall

6. **Which of the following firewalls permits traffic from external sources only if it is in response to traffic from internal hosts?**
   A. An application-level gateway firewall
   B. A stateful inspection firewall
   C. A packet filtering router
   D. A circuit-level gateway

7. **Which of the following firewalls will help in restricting the downloading of files through File Transfer Protocol?**
   A. A router
   B. A packet filter
   C. An application gateway
   D. A stateful inspection

8. **Which of the following firewalls provides the best protection to internet-based critical servers against hacking?**
   A. A circuit gateway
   B. A packet filter
   C. An application gateway
   D. A stateful inspection

9. **Which of the following is the most important consideration while reviewing the implementation of a firewall?**
   A. A documented information security policy
   B. A vendor supporting firewall implementation
   C. The effectiveness of the firewall in enforcing security policy
   D. Firewall algorithms

10. **Which of the following is the most common error while implementing a firewall?**
    A. Users are not trained in the rules of firewalls
    B. Improper due diligence for vendor selection
    C. Incorrect configuration of access lists
    D. Antivirus software is not updated on a frequent basis

11. **Which of the following is regarded as the first step in installing a firewall in a large organization?**
    A. To develop a security policy
    B. To develop an access control list
    C. To analyze firewall functionality
    D. To configure the firewall settings

12. **A firewall is primarily installed with the objective of:**
    A. connecting different networks
    B. preventing authorized users from accessing the LAN
    C. connecting authorized users to trusted network resources
    D. acting as a proxy server for improving the speed of access to authorized users

13. **Which of the following is regarded as a major concern when installing a firewall in a large organization?**
    A. The adoption of an SSL
    B. The frequent updating of firewall rules on the basis of changing requirements
    C. Firewall monitoring is outsourced to a third-party service provider
    D. A firewall is placed on top of the commercial operating system with all installation options

14. **The best auditing procedure for ascertaining correct firewall configuration is:**
    A. to review logs of failed attempts
    B. to review the approved access control list
    C. to review firewall change management policy
    D. to review parameter settings

15. **A firewall is primarily installed to prevent:**
    A. unauthorized traffic from an external network
    B. unauthorized traffic from the internal network
    C. delays in internet connectivity
    D. delays in system processing

16. **The most effective method for maintaining the integrity of a firewall log is:**
    A. to provide access only to network administrators
    B. to capture logs in two separate media
    C. to make a network administrator responsible for backing up log records
    D. to capture logs at a dedicated third-party log server

VPN

A VPN is used to extend a private network through use of the internet in a secure manner. It provides a platform for remote users to get connected to the organization's private network.

The prime objective of VPN technology is to enable remote users and branch offices to access applications and resources available in private networks of organizations. A VPN is created by establishing a virtual point-to-point connection through the use of dedicated circuits or with tunneling protocols.

VPN technology, if properly configured, will reduce the risk associated with sensitive data traveling in an open public network.

Types of VPN

The following are some of the VPN connection types:

Type	Description
A remote access VPN	• Through a remote VPN, authorized users can connect to the corporate network from anywhere. • A VPN ensures that information is secured on the open internet
An intranet VPN	• An intranet VPN is used to connect branch offices within an enterprise WAN.
An extranet VPN	• An extranet VPN is used to connect business partners and provide limited access to each other's corporate networks.

The following are some of the advantages of a VPN:

- A VPN helps organizations to expand their corporate network in a cost-efficient way.
- A VPN provides a platform to authorized remote users in terms of a secure and effective way of connecting to corporate networks.

- A VPN provides a platform for secure communication with business partners.
- A VPN provides a platform for efficient and effective supply chain management.

VPNs – security risks

The following are some of the risks associated with the use of a VPN:

- The risk of malware entering the network through remote access.
- One of the overriding risks of a VPN is that firewalls cannot adequately examine the encrypted VPN traffic.
- If a remote computer is compromised, an intruder may send malicious code through a VPN to enter inside the organization's private network.
- The risk of poor configuration management.

VPNs – technical aspects

A VPN provides a platform to hide the information from the sniffer on the internet. Instead of using expensive dedicated leased lines, a VPN relies on public IP infrastructure, which is cost efficient. To protect the data, a VPN encrypts the packets with **IP Security Standards (IP Sec)**.

A VPN uses IPSec tunnel mode or IPSec transport mode. IPSec tunnel mode is used to encrypt the entire packet, including the header. The IPSec transport mode is used to encrypt only the data portion of the packet. A VPN uses the data encapsulation or tunneling method to encrypt the traffic payload for secure transmission of the data.

Key aspects from the perspective of the CISA exam

The following table covers the key aspects from the perspective of the CISA exam:

CISA questions	Possible answer
What is the most prevalent risk of virtual private network?	The entry of malicious code into the network
Which is the most secured and cost-effective method for remote access?	A VPN

Self-assessment questions

1. **In a VPN, which of the following is the area of most concern?**
    - A. Computers connected to the network that are located within the enterprise's perimeter
    - B. Computers connected to the network that are located at remote offices
    - C. Computers connected to the network that are located at an employee's home
    - D. Computers connected to the network that are located at an enterprise's backup site

2. **Which of the following ensures security in a VPN?**
    - A. Data diddling
    - B. Data encapsulation
    - C. Data hashing
    - D. Data compression

3. **The function of a VPN is to:**
    - A. implement security policies
    - B. compress data traveling in the network
    - C. hide data traveling in the network
    - D. verify the content of the data packet

4. **Which of the following is the most prevalent risk of using a VPN for remote login?**
    - A. The entry of malicious code in the network
    - B. The unauthorized access of data while in the network
    - C. Logon spoofing
    - D. The adverse impact on network availability

5. **For a small organization, the most economical and secure method for connecting a private network over the internet is:**
    - A. a dedicated leased line
    - B. a VPN
    - C. a broadband connection
    - D. VoIP

6. **The most comprehensive method for protecting a remote access network with multiple and diversified systems is:**
   A. a firewall
   B. a VPN
   C. an IDS
   D. a demilitarized zone

Voice over Internet Protocol (VoIP)

VoIP is the transmission of voice and other content over IP networks. It is also known as IP telephony or internet telephony. It is made possible by digitalizing the sounds into IP packets and transmitting them through a network layer, where it is again decoded to sound. VoIP is a cost-effective solution for long-distance costs. VoIP can be operated from IP infrastructure and very little additional telephony infrastructure is required.

A CISA aspirant is required to understand the following aspects of VoIP:

- It is very important to consider a backup arrangement for a VoIP system as data traffic normally has less reliability. A backup arrangement is required to ensure that communication is not interrupted in the case of an undesirable event impacting the network service.
- Bandwidth capacity should be determined for voice traffic to ensure quality of the service.
- VoIP infrastructure should be designed in consideration of laws and regulations, as certain countries have banned the use of VoIP. The risk of transmitting sensitive PII data through VoIP should also be considered. SMS messages may be in breach of certain regulations, such as HIPAA or PCI requirements.
- Traditional telephone lines are considered more secure than internet-based VoIP. IP packets may not be as secure as physical wire security of traditional phone lines.

In the absence of effective security controls, a VoIP environment is subject to the following:

- The theft of data
- The loss of productivity due to the unavailability of the infrastructure
- Fines and penalties as a result of using corporate VoIP for unlawful activity
- Security breaches

VoIP infrastructure should have the following level of control:

- Firewall arrangements for network traffic
- Data encryption
- Updated patches and antivirus for VoIP infrastructure
- Need-to-know access
- The use of VLAN to segregate VoIP from telephone systems and the implementation of firewalls between these two types of infrastructure
- The use of **session border controllers** (**SBCs**) to provide security to VoIP traffic, monitor DoS attacks, and to provide network address and protocol translation features

A distributed **denial-of-service** (**DDoS**) attack aims at bringing down the VoIP infrastructure of the organization. In case the organization does not have a backup arrangement, this can have a severe impact. DDoS can disrupt the organization's ability to communicate internally as well as externally.

A session border controller is deployed to protect VoIP networks. The aims of session border controllers are to:

- protect the session from malicious attacks, such as a **denial-of-service** attack (**DoS**) or DDoS
- prevent toll fraud or premium rate fraud
- encrypt signals
- provide quality of service

VoIP toll fraud, or premium rate fraud, refers to a situation where an intruder hacks the VoIP system and takes over part of a VoIP phone network to use it for their own calls.

Key aspects from the CISA exam perspective

The following table covers the key aspects from the CISA exam perspective:

CISA questions	Possible answers
Which is the best method to ensure the security and reliability of Voice over Internet Protocol (VoIP) and data traffic?	Segregation of VoIP infrastructure using VLAN
How can data traffic over VoIP be eavesdropped?	Address Resolution Protocol is corrupted
What is the primary requirement while considering a VoIP service?	Reliability and quality of VoIP service

Which is the most appropriate access control for the VoIP system?	Role-based access control
What is the objective of the session border controller?	The objective of the session border controller is to: • Protect the session from malicious attacks such as a denial-of-service attack (DoS) or distributed DoS. • Preventing Toll fraud or premium fraud • Encryption of signals • Provide the quality of service
What is the Toll fraud?	VoIP toll fraud or premium rate fraud refers to a situation where intruder hacks the VoIP system and take over part of a VoIP phone

Self-assessment questions

1. **Which of the following is the best method to ensure the security and reliability of VoIP and data traffic?**
   A. Segregation of VoIP infrastructure using the VLAN
   B. The use of two-factor authentication
   C. Traffic encryption
   D. The availability of backup power

2. **Which of the following poses a major risk when using the VoIP system as a sole means of voice communication?**
   A. Failure of the hardware device
   B. Premium rate fraud
   C. A DDoS attack
   D. Toll fraud

3. **Which of the following is a major concern as regards the cabling arrangements for a VoIP system?**
   A. The same cable type is used for LAN as well as telephone
   B. Networking wires are not arranged and labeled
   C. VoIP infrastructure is not connected to an uninterrupted power supply
   D. Power and telephone equipment are separated

4. **VoIP system traffic can be eavesdropped if:**
   A. only single-factor authentication is implemented
   B. VLAN is used for data transmission
   C. default passwords are used for the analog phone
   D. the address resolution protocol is corrupted

5. **Which of the following should be primarily considered for use in a VoIP system?**
   - A. A cryptographic function used for the VoIP service
   - B. The availability of the VoIP service
   - C. The reliability and quality of the VoIP service
   - D. The privacy of the VoIP service

6. **Which of the following access control methods is most appropriate for a VoIP** system?
   - A. Department-based access control
   - B. Hierarchy-based access control
   - C. Role-based access control
   - D. Privilege access control

7. **The most important control in addressing the DoS attack on a VoIP system is:**
   - A. a router
   - B. an IDS
   - C. an access control server
   - D. session border controllers

8. **Which of the following is a major concern as regards the VoIP system?**
   - A. The same cable type is used for LAN as well as telephone
   - B. There is a common administrator for both telephone and network
   - C. A LAN switch is not connected to a UPS
   - D. Only single-factor authentication is required to access the VoIP

Wireless networks

A network connection not involving the use of a cable or wire is known as a wireless network. A wireless network is a computer network that uses wireless data connections between communication endpoints (nodes). Cell phone networks and wireless local area networks are examples of wireless networks.

CISA aspirants should be aware of the following controls regarding the protection of wireless (Wi-Fi) security:

- To enable MAC filtering
- To enable encryption

- To disable SSID
- To disable DHCP

Let's discuss each of these in detail:

Enabling MAC filtering

Each system/PC/laptop/mobile has a unique identification number, which is known as the MAC address. This control will help us to allow access to only selected and authorized devices. Hence, the router will restrict other unauthorized devices in terms of accessing the network. Blacklist features can be used to specifically reject some MAC addresses.

A router has the option to enable MAC filtering, as indicated in the following screenshot:

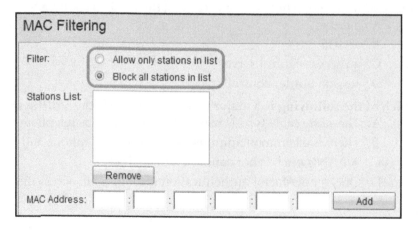

An organization can either allow only specific devices to be connected and block all other devices, or it can block specific devices and allow all other devices.

Enabling encryption

Encryption is the process of converting data into an unreadable form. The process of encryption helps to scramble the data we send through the wireless network into a code. Encryption is an effective way of restricting intruders when it comes to accessing the wireless network. **Wi-Fi Protected Access (WPA)** and **Wired Equivalent Privacy (WEP)** are the two main types of encryption. WPA 2 is the strongest encryption standard for wireless connection. These encryption methods only protect data in transit and not data on the device.

Disabling a service set identifier (SSID)

An SSID is the name of a wireless network broadcast by a router. When a wireless device searches the area for wireless networks, it will detect and display a list of all available SSIDs:

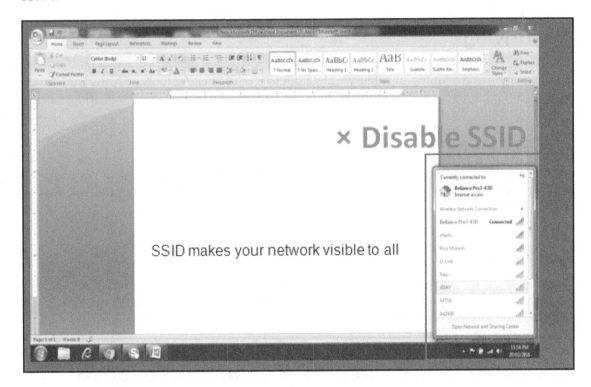

Such open broadcasting is not required or necessary unless it is purposefully done to promote Wi-Fi, as in case of a hotel/restaurant/lounge/mall and so on.

Disabling DHCP

DHCP is a network management tool. It automatically assigns an IP address to each device connected to the network, which will help said devices to communicate with other IP networks. If DHCP is disabled, then the IP address can be configured manually, that is, the static IP, and this helps to reduce the risk of unauthorized access.

Common attack methods and techniques for a wireless network

The following are some common attack methods for wireless networks.

War driving

War driving is a technique used by a hacker to search wireless networks from a moving car or vehicle by using a laptop or other wireless devices with hacking tools or software. The same technique is used by IS auditors to test the wireless security of an organization.

War walking

War walking is a similar process to war driving, where hackers search wireless networks by walking with their devices instead of driving. This is commonly practiced in public areas, such as malls, hotels, and city streets.

War chalking

War chalking is a technique of drawing a mark or symbol in a public area indicating the existence of an open wireless network. These symbols are subsequently used by others to exploit weak wireless networks.

Key aspects from the CISA exam perspective

The following table covers the key aspects from the CISA exam perspective:

CISA questions	Possible answers
What are the best practices for wireless security?	• To enable MAC filtering • To enable encryption • To disable SSID • To disable DHCP
Which encryption key provides the best security for data transmitted through the wireless network? (Dynamic or static key)	Dynamic (a dynamic key is changed frequently and hence considered more secure than a static key)
Which technique is used by a hacker to search wireless networks from a moving car or vehicle by using hacking tools and software? (The same technique is used by an IS auditor to test the wireless security.)	War driving

Which is the strongest encryption standard for the wireless connection?	WPA - 2 (Wi-Fi Protected Access)
Which protocol automatically assigns an IP address to each device connected to the network?	Dynamic Host Control Protocol
Why should DHCP be disabled?	DHCP automatically assigns an IP to each device. If the DHCP is disabled, then the IP address needs to be configured manually, in other words, a static IP, and this helps to reduce the risk of unauthorized access.
Which encryption key is considered as the most secure? (MAC-based Pre-shared key or a randomly generated PSK)	A randomly generated PSK is stronger than a MAC-based PSK (MAC address of a computer is fixed and often accessible)

Self-assessment questions

1. **The security of wireless networks against unauthorized access can be improved by disabling:**
    A. MAC address filtering
    B. Encryption
    C. WPA-2 (Wi-Fi Protected Access Protocol)
    D. SSID broadcasting

2. **Which of the following techniques is more relevant for testing the wireless (Wi-Fi) security of an organization?**
    A. WPA-2
    B. War dialing
    C. War driving
    D. Social engineering

3. **In reviewing a wireless network, what should an IS auditor be more concerned with?**
    A. System hardening of all wireless clients
    B. SSID broadcasting has been enabled
    C. WPA-2 (Wi-Fi Protected Access Protocol) encryption is enabled
    D. DHCP is disabled at all wireless access points

4. **Which of the following statements is true when DHCP is disabled for wireless networks?**

    A. It increases the risk of unauthorized access to the network

    B. It decreases the risk of unauthorized access to the network

    C. It automatically provides an IP address to anyone

    D. It disables an SSID

5. **The best method for ensuring the confidentiality of the data transmitted in a wireless LAN is to:**

    A. restrict access to predefined MAC addresses

    B. protect the session by means of encryption with static keys

    C. protect the session by encrypting it with dynamic keys

    D. initiate the session by means of an encrypted device

6. **The risk of which of the following attacks increases while using wireless infrastructure to use mobile devices within the organization?**

    A. Port scanning

    B. Social engineering

    C. Piggybacking

    D. War driving

7. **Which of the following encryption methods will BEST protect a wireless network in the case of a man-in-the-middle attack?**

    A. A WEP

    B. A MAC-based **pre-shared key (PSK)**

    C. A randomly generated PSK

    D. An SSID

Email security

In this digital world, email is a widely used mode of official communication for both internal and external communication. A lot of critical and sensitive information is shared through email. It is very important to secure email communication.

The following are some email-related risks and controls:

- Relying only on SMTP is not relatively secure as email security requires an end-to-end method, such as the use of digital signatures or the use of integrity checks at the transport level.

- Social engineering attacks such as phishing and spear phishing can be addressed through security awareness training of employees.
- Email attachments should be scanned by anti-malware software.
- Users should be trained on the security aspect of using email.
- Mail servers should be properly hardened and configured as per the organization's security policy and guidelines.
- The implementation of encryption technologies to protect user authentication and mail data should be considered.
- The use of digital signatures to authenticate users in an untrusted network environment. Digital signatures are a good method for securing email transmissions because they cannot be forged on account of being encrypted.
- The installation of firewalls, routers, and IDSes to protect the mail server.

Key aspects from the CISA exam perspective

The following table covers the key aspects from the CISA exam perspective:

CISA questions	Possible answers
What is the objective of web and email filtering tools?	To prevent viruses and spam
What is the best method for ensuring email authenticity?	A digital signature

Self-assessment questions

1. **The use of digital signatures in an email application will:**
    A. assist in the detection of spam messages
    B. provide assurances regarding content confidentiality
    C. improve network speed
    D. reduce the bandwidth capability

2. **The organization can guarantee authenticity of the email to the recipient by:**
    A. the use of two-factor authentication
    B. encrypting all email communication
    C. installing an email antivirus scanner
    D. digitally signing all email communication

3. **The objective of a web and email filtering tool is:**
   A. to restrict viruses and spam
   B. to improve employee productivity
   C. to ensure data confidentiality
   D. to ensure data integrity

Summary

In this chapter, we learned about the identification of network-related risks and pertinent controls. We discussed different components of the network, including repeaters, hubs, switches, routers, and firewalls. We also learned about the basic structure of OSI layers and network physical media.

In the next chapter, we will discuss cryptography and other emerging technologies, such as cloud computing, mobile computing, virtualization, and the Internet of Things. In cryptography, we will discuss the elements of public key infrastructure and the functions of symmetric as well as asymmetric keys.

Assessments

You will find the answers to the questions in this section.

Network and endpoint devices

1. **Answer A: Fiber optic wires**
   Explanation: Optical fiber is a thin and flexible piece of fiber made of glass or plastic. Fiber optic cables are considered to be more secure than copper wire. Fiber optic is the preferred choice for managing long-distance networks and handling high volumes of data. Fiber optics are not impacted or affected by EMI. Fiber optic cables have very marginal transmission loss.

2. **Answer C: A firewall.**
   Explanation: A firewall is primarily installed as a security measure to prevent unauthorized traffic among the different segments of the network. Hubs, routers, and switches do have a limited capability to block traffic, but they are not primarily installed as a security measure.

3. **Answer B: Separate the VLANs for the conference and production environments.**

   Explanation: An open connection point in the conference room is a risk as it can be accessed by anyone in the conference room and an intruder can attempt to access the production server through it. The best method of preventing this is to have a separate network for conferences that allows users to access the internet without any risk of unauthorized access to production servers.

4. **Answer B: Access to a network port is not restricted.**

   Explanation: A DHCP server dynamically assigns an IP address and other network configuration parameters to every device on a network in order that they can communicate with other IP networks.

   One of the concerns of automatic IP allocation is that any unauthorized individual can connect to the corporate network. Hence, physical network ports should not be kept open and strong restrictions should be in place to access the network port.

5. **Answer B: Dedicated leased lines.**

   Explanation: A dedicated leased line is regarded as the most effective medium as there is no sharing of lines or intermediary entry points. The risk of interception is very low in dedicated lines as compared with other media.

6. **Answer A: Physical separation of the visitor's network and the company network.**

   Explanation: The best way to secure the company network from intrusion is to keep the visitor' network physically separate. Other options may not be as secure as the separation of the network. Firewall and IDSes have to be properly configured and are subject to multiple risks.

7. **Answer D: A diagram of the network.**

   Explanation: The first arrangement that should be reviewed by the IS auditor is a network diagram. A network diagram is a pictorial representation of the network architecture that includes computer, server, and other network devices, such as cables, routers, devices, hubs, and firewalls. A network diagram includes the details of placement of each network equipment and how they interact with each other. While auditing the network security aspect, the IS auditor should first review the network diagram to understand the network architecture and determine inherent risks or a single point of failure.

8. **Answer B: The use of a content filtering proxy server for outbound traffic.**
   Explanation: A content filtering proxy server will be the best way to filter the unauthorized internet site. Proxy servers that monitor outbound traffic can block the restricted internet sites. Use of a content filtering proxy server for inbound traffic is used to monitor and control access to corporate sites. The installation of client software on each PC computer to restrict web content is less effective compared with centralized proxy servers. The purpose of an IDS is to detect the intrusion.

9. **Answer C: The use of a centralized firewall as well as logical access control on each computer.**
   Explanation: A defense-in-depth security arrangement includes the use of multiple security mechanisms that support and complement each other. The failure of one device can be compensated by the security features of another. By using two different products – the firewall and logical access control, the probability of failure is reduced and the defensive structure becomes deeper. This is like two lines of defense. The other options involve only one kind of product.

10. **Answer C: A secure socket layer.**
    Explanation: A secure socket layer uses a cryptographic function to protect the confidentiality, reliability, and integrity of private documents traveling through the internet. The function of IDS and IPS is for intrusion detection and prevention, while the function of the router is to route internet traffic.

11. **Answer B: The configuration, wiring, and schematic diagram.**
    Explanation: It is important to have an understanding of network configuration, network cabling, and the use of other network devices for a review of network security. The other options are not as important as a review of the configuration, wiring, and schematic diagram.

12. **Answer D: The network entry points.**
    Explanation: The first arrangement that should be reviewed by the IS auditor is a network diagram. A network diagram will help the auditor to determine network entry points, the placement of various network devices, and how they interact with each other. This will help the auditor to determine the level of inherent risk and plan their audit accordingly.

13. **Answer C: UDP provides an unreliable service and packets may arrive out of order.**
    Explanation: The UDP is regarded as a connectionless protocol. The UDP has an unreliable service and data packets may arrive out of order, be corrupted, or may get dropped, and the destination does not acknowledge every packet it receives. One advantage of the UDP is that as it does not perform error checking, it allows for reduced latency.

14. **Answer C: Reduces the risk of unauthorized network access.**
    Explanation: DHCP is a protocol to manage the network configuration. A DHCP server dynamically assigns an IP address and other network configuration parameters to every device on a network so that they can communicate with other IP networks. Hence, IP address pool management is effected by the DHCP server for high-volume traffic. It is suitable for both wired and wireless networks. One of the concerns of automatic IP allocation is that any unauthorized individual can connect to the corporate network. Hence, disabling the DHCP protocol reduces the risk of unauthorized network access.

15. **Answer B: Implement a firewall between both networks.**
    Explanation: The best way to separate both networks is to implement a firewall between the networks. A firewall will allow only authorized users on the wireless network to access the wired network. A VLAN would be less secure than a firewall. The function of an IDS is to detect an intrusion. If both networks are physically separated, then it would not be possible for authorized wireless users to access the data.

16. **Answer A: Determine the network access point.**
    Explanation: A client server environment may have multiple access points and it is important to first determine all the network access points in order to evaluate the risk of unauthorized access. Once the IS auditor is aware of all the access points, we can evaluate other options.

17. **Answer D: Deny all outgoing traffic with external source address.**
    Explanation: In a zombie attack, compromised computers will send huge amounts of traffic to outside networks. But in this case, the source address will be other than the internal IP range. Denying the traffic of the source address external to the network will afford protection from a DoS attack.

18. **Answer A: A default configuration setting has not been changed.**
    Explanation: The default configuration not being changed poses a major risk. Default configurations are published openly and intruders can use the same for access purposes. The other options are not as important compared with the default configuration not being changed.

19. **Answer A: The guest network is not separated from the production network.**
    Explanation: The best way to secure the company network from intrusion is to keep the visitor network physically separate. Other options may not be as secure as separation of the network. Firewalls and IDSes have to be properly configured and are subject to multiple risks. Single-factor authentication is subject to the risk of passwords being compromised.

20. **Answer D: A web content filter.**
Explanation: A web content filter allows or rejects web traffic on the basis of rules. It is the most effective way to restrict access to forbidden websites and the user's stateful inspection will not be helpful as it does not look into site classification or website content. The function of the IDS is to detect the network intrusion. Routers do have a basic ability to filter, but web content filters are more effective than routers.

21. **Answer C: Physical security of wireless access points.**
Explanation: It is important to have restricted access to wireless devices such as routers in order to protect the same from misconfiguration or theft. If access points are not physically protected, intruders can change the configuration and gain access to the network. An SSID, DHCP, and SNMP should be disabled for the protection of wireless security.

22. **Answer A: Determine the importance of network devices in topology.**
Explanation: The first procedure is to determine the use and importance of network devices in the topology. Once the auditor becomes familiar with the topology, he may evaluate appropriate placement, integration, and the lack of network devices.

23. **Answer C: Use a protocol analyzer to analyze the performance of network and related devices.**
Explanation: In this scenario, the first step should be to identify the root cause of the problem. The use of a protocol analyzer will help to determine the exact nature of the issue, which can be either a configuration issue or a device malfunction. Subsequent action can be taken once the problem is known.

24. **Answer B: A dedicated leased line for remote connection.**
Explanation: It must be noted that Telnet traffic is not encrypted by default. It is advisable to use SSH in place of Telnet. If Telnet is used, it is advisable to use a dedicated leased line to reduce the security risk. Two-factor authentication, as well as firewall and network administrator training, will not address the security risk of transmission channels.

25. **Answer C: Attenuation.**
Explanation: Attenuation is the loss or weakening of signal transmission. Attenuation can impact both wired and wireless transmissions. Distance and wire length have a direct impact on the severity of attenuation. The other factors generally impact wired transmission only.

26. **Answer C: Attenuation.**
Explanation: Explanation: Attenuation is the loss or weakening of signal transmission. Attenuation can impact both wired and wireless transmissions. Distance and wire length have a direct impact on the severity of attenuation. The other factors generally do not have any correlation with the length of the wire.

Firewall types and implementation

1. **Answer B: To deny all traffic and allow specific traffic.**
   Explanation: The most stringent and robust configuration setting in firewall rules is 'deny all traffic and allow specific traffic' (as against 'allow all traffic and deny specific traffic'). This will restrict unknown traffic as regards entering critical systems and networks.

2. **Answer A: The network layer of the OSI.**
   Explanation: The diagram shown in the chapter illustrates the type of firewall and their corresponding OSI layer.

3. **Answer C: A screened host firewall.**
   Explanation: Of the preceding firewall implementations, a screened subnet firewall (demilitarized zone) is regarded as the most secure type of firewall implementation. A screened subnet firewall consists of two packet filtering routers. It also has one bastion host. It provides the greatest security environment. A screened subnet firewall is also used as a **demilitarized zone (DMZ)**.

4. **Answer C: An application gateway.**
   Explanation: An application-level firewall works on the concept of a bastion host and proxy server. It operates at the application layer of the OSI. An application-level firewall is regarded as the most secure type of firewall. Therefore, an application gateway works in a more detailed (granular) way than the others.

5. **Answer C: A screened subnet firewall.**
   Explanation: A screened subnet firewall is regarded as the most robust structure that provides a stringent security environment. A screened subnet firewall consists of two packet filtering routers. It also has one bastion host. It acts as a proxy and a direct connection between the internal and external networks is not allowed. A screened subnet firewall is also used as a demilitarized zone (DMZ).

6. **Answer B: A stateful inspection firewall.**
   Explanation: A stateful inspection firewall monitors and tracks the destination of each packet that is being sent from the internal network. It ensures that the incoming message is in response to the request that went out of the organization. A stateful inspection operates at the network layer of the OSI.

7. **Answer C: An application gateway.**
   Explanation: An application-level firewall works on the concept of a bastion host and proxy server. It operates at the application layer of the OSI. It controls the application such as FTP and HTTP. An application-level firewall is regarded as the most secure type of firewall.

8. **Answer C: An application gateway.**
   Explanation: An application-level firewall works on the concept of a bastion host and proxy server. It operates at the application layer of the OSI. An application-level firewall is regarded as the most secure type of firewall. It permits or denies network traffic by analyzing each packet in detail at the application level of the OSI.

9. **Answer: The effectiveness of the firewall in enforcing security policy.**
   Explanation: The effectiveness of firewalls in supporting information security policy is the most important factor. If the firewall is not aligned in line with IS policy, the other factors will not have an impact. Documented IS policy is important, but if the firewall does not support its enforcement, then the policy is of little value.

10. **Answer C: Incorrect configuration of access lists.**
    Explanation: It is very important to update the current access list. This aspect is generally neglected and therefore has the greatest scope for errors at the time of initial installation. Other options do not directly impact firewall implementation.

11. **Answer A: To develop a security policy.**
    Explanation: The first step in installing a firewall is to design and develop an information security policy. On the basis of approved information security policy, other options can be considered.

12. **Answer C: Connecting authorized users to trusted network resources.**
    Explanation: The primary objective of a firewall is to allow only authorized uses of the system and network and thereby restrict unauthorized access.

13. **Answer D: A firewall is placed on top of the commercial operating system with all installation options.**
    Explanation: Keeping all installations open for a firewall is a major risk for the organization. Fire security can be compromised in such a situation. The adoption of SSL is a good practice. Firewall rules should be changed as per business requirements. The monitoring of firewalls by an outsourced firm is not a major concern if appropriate controls are in place.

14. **Answer D: To review parameter settings.**
    Explanation: The best audit procedure for ascertaining correct firewall configuration is to review parameter settings. This will help to determine whether approved configurations as per security policy have actually been implemented. The other options do not provide strong auditing evidence as compared with a review of parameter settings.

15. **Answer A: Unauthorized traffic from an external networks.**
    Explanation: A firewall is a network security system designed to prevent unauthorized access to networks. It monitors and controls incoming and outgoing network traffic as per defined rules. Primarily, firewalls are meant to prevent unauthorized external traffic from gaining access to an organization's network.

16. **Answer D: To capture logs at a dedicated third-party log server.**
    Explanation: The most effective method for maintaining the integrity of a firewall log is to capture logs at a dedicated third-party log server. Network administrators will not have access to third-party servers, and so independence can be ensured. As a best practice, network administrators should not have access to logs. Capturing logs in two different media, in itself, does not ensure the integrity of logs.

Virtual Private Network (VPN)

1. **Answer C: A computer connected to the network that is located at the employee's home.**
   Explanation: Home computers are generally not hardened from a security perspective. Also, they are not subject to enterprise security policy. Once a computer is hacked, an intruder may penetrate the enterprise's network. Enterprises have sufficient control on computers within their perimeter, remote offices, and back up sites.

2. **Answer B: Data encapsulation.**
   Explanation: A VPN uses data encapsulation or the tunneling method to encrypt the traffic payload for secure transmission of the data. A VPN uses the IPSec tunnel mode or IPSec transport mode. The IPSec tunnel mode is used to encrypt the entire packet, including the header. The IPSec transport mode is used to encrypt only the data portion of the packet. Mere data hashing and compression will not ensure data confidentiality. Data diddling is an attack method.

3. **Answer C: To hide data traveling in the network.**
   Explanation: The objective of a VPN is to hide data from the sniffer. A VPN uses data encapsulation or the tunneling method to encrypt the traffic payload for secure transmission of the data.

4. **Answer A: The entry of malicious code in the network**.
   Explanation: One of the prevalent risks of a VPN is that firewalls cannot adequately examine the encrypted VPN traffic. If a remote computer is compromised, an intruder may send malicious code through a VPN to enter inside the organization's private network. Unauthorized access can be controlled through encryption. Logon spoofing can be addressed by means of two-factor authentication. A VPN does not directly impact the availability of the network.

5. **Answer B: A VPN.**
   Explanation: A VPN is the most effective and secure way of connecting a private network over the internet. The primary objective of VPN technology is to enable remote users and branch offices to access applications and resources available in an organization's private network. A VPN is created by establishing a virtual point-to-point connection through the use of dedicated circuits or with tunneling protocols. VPN technology, if properly configured, will reduce the risk associated with sensitive data traveling in an open public network. Dedicated leased lines are quite expensive to maintain. The other options are not sufficiently secure compared with a VPN.

6. **Answer B: A VPN.**
   Explanation: A VPN is used to extend a private network through the use of the internet in a secure manner. It provides a platform for remote users to get connected to the organization's private network. The primary objective of VPN technology is to enable remote users and branch offices to access applications and resources available in an organization's private network. A VPN is created by establishing a virtual point-to-point connection through the use of dedicated circuits or with tunneling protocols. Firewall, IDS, and DMZ are used to filter and control traffic between internal and external networks.

Voice over Internet Protocol (VoIP)

1. **Answer A: The segregation of VoIP infrastructure using a VLAN.**
   Explanation: The best way to protect the VoIP and data traffic is to segregate the VoIP using a VLAN. This will help to protect against network-based attacks and other issues. The other options are not as effective as segregating the VoIP infrastructure.

2. **Answer C: A DDoS attack.**
   Explanation: A DDoS attack aims at bringing down the VoIP infrastructure of the organization. In case an organization does not have a backup arrangement, this will have an adverse impact on the continuity of voice communication. The risk of hardware failure can also apply to telephony lines and is not a unique risk to VoIP infrastructure. Premium rate and toll fraud involve unauthorized long-distance calls and may have some financial impact, but not as severe as a DDoS attack.

3. **Answer C: The VoIP infrastructure is not connected to an uninterrupted power supply.**
   Explanation: VoIP uses standard network cabling for voice communication. If network switches do not get power, a telephone will not get power either, and so it is very important to have an arrangement for an uninterrupted power supply. Use of the same type of cable for both LAN and telephone does not possess any risk. In fact, this is regarded as an advantage for VoIP infrastructure. Separate power and telephone equipment is a good practice. Improper networking wires entail some risk, but the major concern will be the unavailability of UPS.

4. **Answer D: The address resolution protocol is corrupted.**
   Explanation: The address resolution protocol is a communication protocol used to map IP and MAC addresses. It sends traffic to a designated port. Attackers may corrupt the ARP by a technique known as ARP poisoning. A corrupted ARP then sends the traffic to all the ports (instead of only designated ports) and the attacker can eavesdrop on traffic. The other options may not directly enable the attacker to eavesdrop on the traffic.

5. **Answer C: The reliability and quality of the VoIP service.**
   Explanation: The primary consideration when using a VoIP system is to have a reliable and quality VoIP service. VoIP (voice over IP) is the transmission of voice and other content over IP networks. VoIP is a cost-effective solution for long-distance costs. However, it should provide a reliable and quality service. The others are important aspects to be considered, but the main requirements will be the reliability and quality of the VoIP service.

6. **Answer C: Role-based access control.**
   Explanation: Like any other critical applications, a VoIP system can be best protected by using role-based access control (RBAC). RBAC can be provisioned as per the role or function of the employees and only need-to-know access should be made available. The other options are not as effective as role-based access control.

7. **Answer D: Session border controllers.**
   Explanation: A session border controller is deployed to protect the VoIP networks. The objective of a session border controller is to:
   - Protect the session from malicious attacks, such as DoS or DDoS attacks.
   - Prevent toll fraud or premium rate fraud
   - Protect the IP packets against malfunctioning
   - Encrypt signals

8. **Answer C: The LAN switch is not connected to a UPS.**
   Explanation: A VoIP uses standard network cabling for voice communication. If network switches do not get power, a telephone will not get power either, and so it is very important to have an arrangement for an uninterrupted power supply. Use of the same type of cable for both LAN and telephone does not possess any risk. In fact, this is regarded as an advantage for VoIP infrastructure. The other options possess some risk, but the major concern will be the unavailability of a UPS.

Wireless networks

1. **Answer D: SSID broadcasting.**
   Explanation: An SSID is the name of a wireless network broadcast by a router. When a wireless device searches the area for wireless networks, it will detect and display a list of all available SSIDs. Disabling SSID broadcasting enhances security by making it more difficult for unauthorized users to find the network. MAC filtering and WPA-2 should be enabled (and not disabled) for better security control.

2. **Answer C: War driving.**
   Explanation: War driving is a technique used by a hacker to search wireless networks from a moving car or vehicle by using a laptop or other wireless devices with hacking tools or software. The same technique is used by IS auditors to test the wireless security of an organization. WPA-2 is an encryption standard and not a technique for testing security.

3. **Answer B: SSID broadcasting has been enabled.**
   Explanation: Disabling SSID broadcasting enhances security by making it more difficult for unauthorized users to find the network. In any given scenario, the following are the best practices for wireless (Wi-Fi) security:
   1. Enabling MAC address filtering.
   2. Enabling encryption to protect data in transit.
   3. Disabling SSID broadcasting.
   4. Disabling DHCP.

4. **Answer B: It decreases the risk of unauthorized access to the network.**
   Explanation: DHCP is a network management tool. It automatically assigns an IP address to each device connected to the network, which will help them to communicate with other IP networks. If DHCP is disabled, then the IP address can be configured manually, that is, a static IP, and this helps to reduce the risk of unauthorized access.

5. **Answer C: Protect the session by encrypting it with dynamic keys.**
   Explanation: In any given scenario, using dynamic keys for the session encryption protects the confidentiality of the data transmitted in a wireless LAN. Dynamic keys reduce the risk of the key being compromised and the message being decrypted as the encryption key is changed frequently. Options A and D will not ensure data confidentiality while in transit. Encryption of the data on the connected device addresses the confidentiality of the data on the device, not the wireless session.

6. **Answer D: War driving.**
   Explanation: War driving is a technique used by a hacker to search wireless networks from a moving car or vehicle by using a laptop or other wireless devices with hacking tools or software. The same is done by driving or walking in and around buildings, with a wireless Ethernet card set in promiscuous mode, and a powerful antenna to penetrate wireless systems from outside.

7. **Answer: A randomly generated PSK.**
   Explanation: An SSID is not an encryption technique. The MAC address of a computer is fixed and often accessible. A randomly generated PSK is stronger than a MAC-based PSK. WEP has been shown to be a very weak encryption technique and can be cracked within minutes. The SSID is broadcast on the wireless network in plain text.

Email security

1. **Answer A: Help in detecting spam messages.**
   Explanation: A digital signature helps to authenticate users in an untrusted network environment. Digital signatures are a good method of securing email transmissions because they cannot be forged as they are encrypted. A digital signature is used to track the sender. It helps to detect spam messages. A digital signature does not provide confidentiality. It does not impact the network speed and bandwidth capability.

2. **Answer D: Digitally signing all email communication.**
   Explanation: A digital signature helps to authenticate users in an untrusted network environment. Digital signatures are a good method of securing email transmissions because they cannot be forged as they are encrypted. A digital signature is used to track the sender. Through digital signatures, an organization can provide assurances regarding the authenticity of the email.

3. **Answer A: To restrict viruses and spam.**
   Explanation: Web and email filtering tools help to prevent viruses and spam. It cannot ensure data confidentiality or data integrity.

11
Public Key Cryptography and Other Emerging Technologies

In this chapter, we will concentrate on public key cryptography, and other important aspects of information asset security and control. An IS auditor is required to have a thorough understanding of elements of public key infrastructure. They should also have the ability to evaluate the functioning of public key cryptography and other technologies.

The following topics will be covered in the chapter:

- Public key cryptography
- Elements of public key infrastructure
- Cloud computing
- Virtualization
- Mobile computing
- **Internet of Things (IoT)**

At the end of the chapter, CISA aspirants will be able to understand and evaluate various aspects of public key infrastructure and other technology.

Public key cryptography

Encryption is the process of converting data into an unreadable code so it cannot be accessed or read by any unauthorized person. This unreadable data can again be converted into readable form by a process of decryption. Different types of algorithms are available for encryption and decryption. In this section, we will look at various aspects of public key cryptography.

Let's understand the concepts of symmetric and asymmetric encryption and the difference between the two.

Symmetric encryption versus asymmetric encryption

Encryption can be of two types, that is, symmetric encryption or asymmetric encryption. The following table will help us to understand the difference between the two terms:

Symmetric Encryption	Asymmetric Encryption
A single key is used to encrypt and decrypt the messages	Two keys are used: one for encryption and another for decryption.
The Key is said to be symmetric because the encryption key is the same as the decryption key.	Messages encrypted by a private key can be decrypted only by the corresponding public key. Similarly, messages encrypted by the public key can be decrypted only by the corresponding private key.
Comparatively faster computation and processing.	Comparatively slower computation and processing.
Comparatively symmetric encryption process is cheaper.	Comparatively symmetric encryption process is costlier.
A major disadvantage of the symmetric encryption process is sharing of the key with other parties.	No such challenge is faced in asymmetric encryption as two separate keys are used.

The major challenge in symmetric encryption is the exchange of keys as both the sender and receiver use the same key.

Encryption keys

In an asymmetric environment, a total of four keys are available with different functions.

The following table indicates who possesses the different keys:

Type of Key	Availability
Sender's private key	The Key is available only with the sender.
Sender's public key	The key is available in the public domain. The public key can be accessed by anyone.
Receiver's private key	The key is available only with the receiver.
Receiver's public key	The key is available in public domain Public key can be accessed by anyone.

The keys discussed here are used to achieve the following objectives:

- Confidentiality
- Authentication and non-repudiation
- Integrity

Confidentiality

In asymmetric encryption, two keys are used – one for encryption and the other for decryption. Messages encrypted by one key can be decrypted by the other key. These two keys are known as private keys and public keys. The private key is available only to the owner of the key and the public key is available in the public domain.

Messages can be encrypted by the following means:

- **Receiver's public key**: If a message is encrypted by using the public key of the receiver, then only the receiver can decrypt it as they are the only one with access to their private key. This will ensure message confidentiality as only the owner of the private key can read the message.
- **Receiver's private key**: The sender will not be in possession of the receiver's private key and hence this option is not feasible.
- **Sender's public key**: If a message is encrypted using the public key of the sender, then it can be decrypted only by using the private key of the sender. The receiver will not be in possession of the sender's private key and hence this option is not feasible.
- **Sender's private key**: If a message is encrypted by using the private key of the sender, then anyone with a public key can decrypt it. The public key is available in the public domain and hence anyone can decrypt the message. This will not ensure the confidentiality of the message.

Hence, for message confidentiality, the receiver's public key is used to encrypt the message and the receiver's private key is used to decrypt the message.

Authentication

Authentication is ensured by verifying and validating some unique features of the sender. In the normal course of things, we validate a document by verifying the signature of the sender. This signature is unique for everyone. Similarly, for digital transactions, the private key is unique for each owner. Only the owner is in possession of their unique private key and no one else.

Each private key has a corresponding public key. A third person can authenticate the identity of the owner with the use of a public key. When the objective is to authenticate the sender of the message, the sender's private key is used to encrypt the hash of the message. The receiver will try to decrypt it with the use of the sender's public key, and if it is successfully decrypted, it indicates that the message is genuine, and the sender is authenticated.

Hence for the authentication of the message, the sender's private key is used to encrypt the message and the sender's public key is used to decrypt the message.

Non- Repudiation

Similarly, non-repudiation refers to a situation wherein the sender cannot take back their responsibility for the digital message or transaction. Non-repudiation is established once the sender is authenticated. Hence, for non-repudiation, the same concept of authentication will apply.

This means that for the non-repudiation of the message, the sender's private key is used to encrypt the message and the sender's public key is used to decrypt the message.

Integrity

Integrity refers to correctness, completeness and accuracy of the data. Same concept of authentication and non-repudiation will apply to integrity. This means to ensure the integrity of the message, the sender's private key is used to encrypt the message and the sender's public key is used to decrypt the message.

The following figure will help us to understand the use of different keys to achieve each of the preceding objectives:

Objective	Use of Keys	What to encrypt
Confidentiality	Receiver's public key	Full message
Authentication/Non-repudiation	Sender's private key	Hash of the message
Integrity	Sender's private key	Hash of the message
Confidentiality & authentication/non-repudiation	• For confidentiality: use of the receiver's public key to encrypt the full message • For authentication (non-repudiation): use of sender's private key to encrypt the hash of the message	
Confidentiality, Integrity & Authentication/non-repudiation	• For confidentiality - use of receiver's public key to encrypt full message • For integrity, authentication (non-repudiation): use of sender's private key to encrypt the hash of the message	

Let's learn about the hash of the message.

The hash of the message

A hash value is a digital code of the message content. Some important features and functionality of the hash value are as follows:

- It is arrived at by using a different algorithm.
- A hash value is also known as a message digest.
- The hash value is unique for each message.
- A slight change in message/content will produce a different hash value.
- A hash value is used to ensure the integrity of the message/content.

A hash value is used for the creation of a digital signature. A hash value, when encrypted with the sender's private key, becomes a digital signature. A digital signature is used to determine the integrity of a message and the authentication of the sender (that is, non-repudiation).

Combining symmetric and asymmetric methods

The most efficient use of **Public Key Infrastructure (PKI)** is to combine the best features of asymmetric and symmetric methods. The challenge of asymmetric encryption is that it is an expensive and time-consuming process. Though symmetric encryption is comparatively much faster, it possesses the challenge of sharing the symmetric key with other parties. To combine the benefits of both and address their challenges, the following process is recommended:

1. For faster and inexpensive computation, encrypt the entire message with the help of a symmetric key.
2. Encrypt the symmetric key with the public key of the receiver.
3. Send the encrypted message (step 1) and the encrypted symmetric key (step 2) to the receiver.
4. The receiver will decrypt the symmetric key using their private key.
5. The receiver will use a symmetric key to decrypt the full message.

Thus, when a combined method is used, the symmetric key encrypts the full message and the receiver's public key encrypts the symmetric key.

Key aspects from the CISA exam perspective

The following table covers important aspects from CISA exam perspective:

CISA questions	Possible answers
How can message confidentiality be ensured in asymmetric encryption?	Use of the receiver's public key for encryption and use of the receiver's private key for decryption
How can message authentication be ensure in asymmetric encryption?	Use of the sender's private key to encrypt the message/hash and use of the sender's public key to decrypt the message/hash
How can message non-repudiation be ensured in asymmetric encryption?	Use of the sender's private key to encrypt the message/hash and use of the sender's public key to decrypt the message/hash
How can message integrity be ensured in asymmetric encryption?	Use of the sender's private key to encrypt the hash and use of the sender's public key to decrypt the hash
What increases the cost of cryptography?	Long asymmetric keys
How can symmetric and asymmetric methods be combined for strong encryption at the optimum cost?	• Use of symmetric key to encrypt full message • Use of receiver's public key to encrypt the symmetric key

Self-assessment questions

1. **For asymmetric encryption, message confidentiality can be ensured by:**
    A. Using a private key for encryption and using a public key for decryption
    B. Using a public key for encryption and using a private key for decryption
    C. Using a public key for encryption as well as decryption
    D. Using a private key for encryption as well as decryption

2. **In public key encryption, the sender of the message is authenticated by:**
    A. Using the receiver's private key to encrypt the hash of the message and using the receiver's public key to decrypt it
    B. Using the sender's public key to encrypt the hash of the message and using the sender's private key to decrypt it
    C. Using the sender's private key to encrypt the hash of the message and using the sender's public key to decrypt it
    D. Using the receiver's public key to encrypt the hash of the message and using the receiver's private key to decrypt it

3. **In public key encryption, content integrity is ensured by:**
   A. Using the sender's private key to encrypt the hash of the message and using the sender's public key to decrypt it
   B. Using the sender's public key to encrypt the hash of the message and using the sender's private key to decrypt it
   C. Using the receiver's private key to encrypt the hash of the message and using the receiver's public key to decrypt it
   D. Using the receiver's public key to encrypt the hash of the message and using the receiver's public key to decrypt it

4. **In public key encryption, how can you ensure the confidentiality of a message and also, at the same time, authenticate the sender of the message?**
   A. By using the receiver's public key to encrypt the hash of the message and thereafter using the sender's public key to encrypt the message
   B. By using the sender's private key to encrypt the hash of the message and thereafter using the receiver's private key to encrypt the message
   C. By using the receiver's public key to encrypt the hash of the message and thereafter using the sender's private key to encrypt the message
   D. By using the sender's private key to encrypt the hash of the message and thereafter using the receiver's public key to encrypt the message

5. **In public key encryption, message authenticity and confidentiality are best achieved by encrypting the message by using:**
   A. The receiver's public key and using the sender's private key to encrypt the hash of the message
   B. The receiver's private key and using the sender's public key to encrypt the hash of the message
   C. The sender's public key and using the receiver's private key to encrypt the hash of the message
   D. The sender's private key and using the receiver's public key to encrypt the hash of the message

6. **Which of the following provides assurance about email authenticity?**
   A. Using the sender's public key to encrypt the prehash code
   B. Using the sender's private key to encrypt the prehash code
   C. Using the receiver's public key to encrypt the prehash code
   D. Using the receiver's private key to encrypt the prehash code

7. **Using the sender's private key to encrypt the message as well as the message hash will ensure:**
   A. Authenticity and privacy
   B. Confidentiality and integrity
   C. Authenticity and integrity
   D. Confidentiality and privacy

8. **An organization sending invoices to clients via email wants to ensure the emails are not modified in transit. With which of the following will the organization achieve this objective?**
   A. By using the firm's private key to encrypt the hash of the invoice.
   B. By using the firm's public key to encrypt the hash of the invoice
   C. By using the client's private key to encrypt the hash of the invoice
   D. By using the client's private key to encrypt the invoice

9. **An organization uses public key infrastructure for its communication server where there is one private key for the server and an associated public key is made available to the customer. This ensures:**
   A. A customer's authenticity
   B. The website's authenticity
   C. Non-repudiation from customer
   D. The certification of the authority's authenticity

10. **Cryptographic cost increases with:**
    A. The application of a long asymmetric key
    B. The application of symmetric encryption instead of asymmetric encryption
    C. The encryption of a hash as compared to the encryption of a full message
    D. The application of a short asymmetric key

11. **The efficient use of PKI is ensured by encrypting:**
    A. The receiver's private key
    B. The sender's private key
    C. The complete message
    D. The symmetric session key

12. **Which of the following is the most effective process to ensure message integrity, confidentiality, and non-repudiation?**

    A. Using the sender's private key to encrypt the message digest, using a symmetric key to encrypt the message and using the receiver's public key to encrypt the symmetric key

    B. Using the sender's private key to encrypt the message digest, using a symmetric key to encrypt the message, and using the receiver's private key to encrypt the symmetric key

    C. Using the sender's private key to encrypt the message digest, using a symmetric key to encrypt the message, and using the sender's private key to encrypt the symmetric key

    D. Using the sender's private key to encrypt the message digest, using the symmetric key to encrypt the message, and using the sender's public key to encrypt the symmetric key

Elements of PKI

Public key infrastructure is a set of rules and procedures for the creation, management, distribution, storage, and use of digital certificates and public key encryption.

PKI terminology

Before moving on to discuss the elements of PKI, you should have a basic understanding of the following terms with respect to public key infrastructure. Here are some terminologies to get yourself acquainted with:

- **Digital Certificate**: A digital certificate is an electronic document used to prove the ownership of a public key. A digital certificate includes information about the key, the owner of the key, and the digital signature of the issuer of the digital certificate. It is also known as a public key certificate.
- **Certifying Authority (CA)**: A Certifying Authority is an entity that issues digital certificates.
- **Registration Authority (RA)**: A Registration Authority is an entity that verifies user requests for digital signatures and recommends the certifying authority to issue it.

- **Certificate Revocation List (CRL)**: A CRL is a list of digital certificates that have been revoked and terminated by the certifying authority before their expiry date and these certificates should no longer be trusted.
- **Certification Practice Statement (CPS)**: A CPS is a document that prescribes practices and processes for the issuing and management of digital certificates by the certifying authority. It includes details such as the controls that should be in place, the method for validating applicants, and the usage of certificates.
- **Public Key Infrastructure**: Public key infrastructure is a set of roles, policies, and procedures for the issuance, maintenance, and revocation of public key certificates.

Processes involved in PKI

The issuance of a public key takes place with the following different steps:

1. The applicant applies for a digital certificate to be issued by the CA.
2. The Certifying Authority delegates the verification process to the RA.
3. The Registration Authority verifies the correctness of the information provided by the applicant.
4. If the information is correct, the Registration Authority recommends that the Certifying Authority issues the certificate.

The Certifying Authority issues the certificate and manages it through its life cycle. The Certifying Authority also maintains the details of certificates that have been terminated or revoked before their expiry date. This list is known as the Certificate Revocation List (CRL). The Certifying Authority also maintains a document called a **Certification Practice Statement (CPS)** containing the Standard Operating Procedure (SOP) for the issuance and management of a certificate.

Certifying Authority versus Registration Authority

You can differentiate between the Certifying Authority and Registration Authority with the help of the following figure:

Certifying Authority	Registration Authority
The Certifying Authority is responsible for the issuance and management of digital certificates.	Registration Authority is delegated with the function of verifying the correctness of information provided by applicants.

The Certifying Authority delegates some of the administrative functions such as verification of information provided by applicants.	After authentication of information, Registration Authority recommends Certifying Authority for issuance of the certificate.
The Certifying Authority authenticates and validates the holder of the certificate after issuance of the certificate.	Registration Authority authenticates information of the applicant before issuance of the certificate.

An Registration Authority has the following functions:

- To verify and validate the information provided by the applicant.
- To verify that the applicant is in possession of a private key and that it matches the public key requested for a certificate. This is known as **proof of possession (POP)**.
- To distribute physical tokens containing private keys.
- To generate shared secret keys during the initialization and certificate pickup phase of registration.

Key aspects from the CISA exam perspective

The following table covers important aspects from CISA exam perspective:

CISA questions	Possible answers
Which authority manages the life cycle of digital certificates?	Certifying Authority
What are the functions of an Registration Authority?	• To verify and validate the information provided by the applicant. • To verify that applicant is the possession of the private key and that matches the public key requested for a certificate. This known as **proof of possession (POP)**. • To distribute physical tokens containing private keys • To generate shared secret keys during initialization and certificate pick up phase of registration
What is the name of the procedural document that details how to deal with compromised private keys?	Certification Practice Statement

Self-assessment questions

1. **Which of the following manages the life cycle of a digital certificate?**
   A. Registration Authority
   B. Certifying Authority
   C. Public key authority
   D. Private key authority

2. **Which of the following is a function of the Registration Authority?**
   A. To issue the digital certificate
   B. To manage the certificate throughout its life cycle
   C. To document and maintain certificate practice statements
   D. To validate the information of the certificate applicant

3. **Which of the following authorities manages the life cycle of a digital certificate to ensure the existence of security in a digital signature?**
   A. Certifying Authority
   B. Registration Authority
   C. Certification practice statement
   D. Public key authority

4. **A Certifying Authority can delegate the process of:**
   A. Certificate issuance
   B. Certificate life cycle management
   C. Establishing a link between the applicant and the public key
   D. The maintenance of the certificate revocation list

5. **Which of the following is considered a weakness in a public key infrastructure process:**
   A. The centralized location of the Certifying Authority
   B. A transaction can be executed from any device
   C. The user's organization is also the owner of the Certifying Authority
   D. The availability of multiple data centers to manage the certificate

6. **Which of the following is a function of the Registration Authority?**
   A. The issuance of the certificate
   B. The validation of information provided by the applicant
   C. Signing the certificate to achieve authentication and non-repudiation
   D. Maintaining the certificate revocation list

7. **The procedural aspect of dealing with a compromised private key is prescribed in:**
    A. The certificate practice statement
    B. The certificate revocation list
    C. The certificate disclosure statement
    D. The applicant disclosure form

8. **Which of the following is a function of a Certifying Authority?**
    A. Ensuring the availability of a secured communication network based on certificates
    B. Validating the identity and authenticity of the certificate owner
    C. Ensuring that both communicating parties are digitally certified
    D. Hosting the private keys of subscribers in the public domain

Cloud computing

Cloud computing is the practice of using remote servers hosted on the internet to store, manage, and process data, rather than a local server or a personal computer. Cloud computing simply means the use of computing resources as a service through networks, typically the internet.

With cloud computing, users can access computing resources via the internet from anywhere, for as long as they need, without worrying about the maintenance or the management of actual resources.

The following are some of the characteristics of cloud computing:

- It provides the capability for organizations to access the data or application from anywhere, anytime, and from almost any device.
- It provides the capability for the organization to scale the IT resources as per the business requirements at the optimum cost.
- It provides the capability to monitor, control, and report the usage of the resources.

Resources such as storage, processing power, memory, network bandwidth, and virtual machines can be used through cloud computing.

Cloud computing – deployment models

The following are important details of deployment models of cloud computing.

The private cloud

A private cloud is used for the exclusive benefit of the organization. A private cloud is considered the most secure type of deployment as it can be controlled and centralized by the organization. A cloud server is either deployed on-premises or off-premises.

The public cloud

The public cloud is open to all on the basis of pay per use. The public cloud is considered highly scalable as services can be reduced or increased as per the requirements of the organization.

It is very important to consider the following requirements for the use of the public cloud:

- Legal and regulatory compliance (such as data localization)
- Backup
- Right to audit
- Security requirements

The community cloud

Cloud services are used by specific communities of consumers who have shared concerns. They can be managed by the organization or a third party. Data may be stored with the data of a competitor.

The hybrid cloud

The community cloud is a combination of the private and the public cloud. An organization initially uses the private cloud and then, for additional requirements, the public cloud is used.

It makes cloud storage complex as more than one model is used.

Cloud computing – the IS auditor's role

An IS auditor should consider the following risks and security control for a cloud arrangement:

- Ensure compliance with relevant laws, regulations, and standards.
- Ensure compliance with privacy laws that restrict the movement of personal data to an offshore location.
- To ensure the availability of information systems and data on a continuous basis. To evaluate the business continuity and disaster recovery plan of the cloud service provider.
- To ensure the integrity and confidentiality of information and sensitive data while stored and in transit.
- To ensure that the SLA includes clauses with respect to data ownership, data custody, and security administration related to cloud deployment models.
- To ensure the inclusion of the right to audit clause in the SLA.

Self-assessment questions

1. **Which of the following is the best way to verify a cloud service provider's physical security arrangements?**
    - A. Verify the **Content Security Policy's (CSP)** physical security policy and ensure that it is aligned with the enterprise's security policy
    - B. Verify a copy of independent security reviews or audit reports of the CSP
    - C. Bind the CSP through a contract to align with the enterprise's security policy and to implement necessary controls to ensure it is complied with
    - D. Verify the CSP's disaster recovery plans and ensure that they contain the necessary arrangements to protect assets

2. **Which of the following is the most important clause in a contract with a cloud service provider?**
    A. The contract should specify that, upon contract expiration, a mandatory data wipe will be carried out in the presence of a representative of the enterprise
    B. The contract should also include non-compete clauses
    C. The contract should include a "right to audit" clause
    D. The contract should restrict the movement of data within permitted territories, as per relevant laws and regulations

3. **The IS auditor reviews the terms of the contract with the Cloud Service Provider. Which of the following is the most important consideration?**
    A. Clarity with respect to data ownership, data custody, and IPR-related requirements
    B. Clarity with respect to non-disclosure requirements
    C. Clarity with respect to data backup requirements
    D. Clarity with respect to data access requirements

4. **Which of the following would be of most concern to the IS auditor with respect to the storage of personal customer information in cloud environments?**
    A. An inadequate disaster recovery procedure
    B. The data in the multi-tenancy environment being accessed by competitors
    C. An inadequate incident management procedure
    D. Inadequate business continuity arrangements

5. **The IS auditor is reviewing the terms of the contract with the cloud service provider. Which of the following is the most important consideration?**
    A. Physical security
    B. Compliance with legal requirements
    C. The data disposal policy
    D. The application disposal policy

6. **Which cloud deployment method is considered the most secure and has very few chances of data leakage?**
    A. Public cloud
    B. Private cloud
    C. Community cloud
    D. Hybrid cloud

Virtualization

Virtualization makes it possible to run multiple operating systems simultaneously on a single computer. It refers to the act of creating a virtual (rather than an actual) version of system-related hardware. With the use of virtualization, organizations can increase the efficiency and reduce the cost of IT operations. Virtual resources such as the server, desktop, Operating System, storage, and networks can be created with the help of virtualization tools.

The most important element of virtualization is the hypervisor, which aids in the creation of virtual resources.

Some important terms for virtualization are as follows:

- Hypervisor: Software or hardware used to create virtual resources
- Host: The original computer
- Guest: Virtual resources created by a hypervisor

The following are some of the risks of virtualization:

- The improper configuration of hypervisors may allow unauthorized access to guests.
- Attackers may be able to gain unauthorized access with the help of mechanisms called guest tools.
- Poor control of access to hypervisors.
- An attack on the host may impact all the guests as well.
- Performance issues with the host may impact all the guests as well.
- The risk of data leakage between guests if there is poor control for memory release and allocation.

The following are important control requirements for a virtualized environment:

- Strong access control for the hypervisor dashboard and services
- The proper hardening of hypervisors and the guest OS by disabling unused features and ports
- Encrypted hypervisor management communications
- Regular patch updates for the hypervisor
- The synchronization of the host as well as the guest to a trusted time server
- The disabling of hypervisor services such as file sharing between the host and the guest (if not used)

- The capturing of logs and proper monitoring of security events for hosts as well as guests
- File integrity monitoring of the hypervisor to monitor for signs of compromise

Mobile computing

Mobile computing is the use of devices that do not require a physical connection to process, transfer, or store data.

Examples of mobile devices include smartphones, laptops, USB storage devices, digital cameras, and other similar technologies.

The following are some of the controls to reduce the risks related to mobile computing:

- Use **mobile device management (MDM)** solutions.
- Store only data and applications on the device that are absolutely necessary for processing.
- Data stored on mobile devices should be backed up regularly to the organization's server.
- All mobile computing devices should be registered for tracking and monitoring control.
- Mobile devices that are stationed at a location should be physically locked.
- All mobile devices should be installed with anti-malware software.
- Use strong encryption mechanisms for data stored on mobile devices.
- Enable access control for mobile devices. Two-factor authentication can be used to further enhance security.
- Organizations should have documented policies that restrict the usage of devices to official and approved purposes only.
- Any loss or theft of a mobile device must be treated as a security breach and reported immediately in accordance with security management policies and procedures.
- Mobile devices should be allowed to connect to the organization's network through some secure channel, such as a VPN.

- Some MDM solutions provide remote wipe and lock features in case a mobile device is lost or stolen. These features help to protect confidential data on lost mobile devices.
- MDM should include the tracking of a wide variety of devices and should capture all access and activity logs.

Internet of Things (IoT)

IoT is a concept wherein devices have the ability to communicate and transfer data with each other without any human interference. IoT is an emerging concept and is being gradually adopted by organizations.

Although a specific risk of IoT depends on how it is used, an IS auditor should consider the following risks with respect to IoT:

- The impact of IoT on the health and safety of human life
- Regulatory compliance with respect to the use of IoT
- The impact of IoT on user privacy
- The impact of IoT on device vulnerabilities

Summary

In this chapter, we learned about relevant skills to conduct audits in accordance with IS audit standards and a risk-based IS audit strategy and to evaluate potential opportunities and threats associated with emerging technologies, regulations, and industry practices.

In the next chapter, we will discuss various security testing and monitoring tools and techniques. We will also learn about different kinds of attacks and how to prevent them.

Assessments

The answers to the questions are given here.

Public key cryptography

1. **Answer: B. Using the public key for encryption and using the private key for decryption**

   Explanation: In asymmetric encryption, two keys are used – one for encryption and the other for decryption. Messages encrypted by one key can be decrypted by another key. These two keys are known as private keys and public keys. A private key is available only to the owner of the key and a public key is available in the public domain. Let's evaluate each option:

   - A. Using the private key for encryption and using the public key for decryption – if a message is encrypted by the private key of the owner, anyone can decrypt it using the public key (as the public key is easily available), hence, the confidentiality of the message cannot be ensured.
   - B. Using the public key for encryption and using the private key for decryption – if a message is encrypted by using the public key, then only the person with the private key can decrypt it. This will ensure message confidentiality as only the owner of the private key can read the message.
   - Options C and D are not valid as, in asymmetric encryption, two keys are required for encryption and decryption.

2. **Answer: C. Using the sender's private key to encrypt the hash of the message and using the sender's public key to decrypt it**

   Explanation: Authentication is ensured by verifying and validating some unique features of the sender. In the normal course of things, we validate a document by verifying the signature of the sender. This signature is unique for everyone. Similarly, for digital transactions, a private key is unique for each owner. Only the owner is in possession of his unique private key and no one else. Each private key has a corresponding public key. A third person can authenticate the identity of the owner with the use of a public key. When the objective is to authenticate the sender of the message, the sender's private key is used to encrypt the hash of the message. The receiver will try to decrypt it with the use of the sender's public key and, if successfully decrypted, it indicates that the message is genuine and the sender is authenticated.

3. **Answer: A. Using the sender's private key to encrypt the hash of the message and using the sender's public key to decrypt it**
   Explanation: A hash value is a unique code for a given message. The hash value is unique for each message. A slight change in message/content will produce a different hash value. The hash value is used to ensure the integrity of a message with details as follows:
   - The hash value is encrypted using the sender's private key. The sender will send (i) messages and (ii) the encrypted hash to the receiver.
   - On receiving the message, the receiver will (i) decrypt the received hash by using the public key of the sender and (ii) re-compute the hash of the message, and if the two hashes are equal, then it proves that the message's integrity has not been tampered with.

4. **Answer: D. Using the sender's private key to encrypt the hash of the message and thereafter using the receiver's public key to encrypt the message**
   Explanation: For authentication, encrypt the hash of the message with the sender's private key. For confidentiality, encrypt the message with the receiver's public key.

5. **Answer: A. Using the receiver's public key and using the sender's private key to encrypt the hash of the message**
   Explanation: For confidentiality, encrypt the message with the receiver's public key. For authentication, encrypt the hash of the message with the sender's private key.

6. **Answer: B. Using the sender's private key to encrypt the prehash code**
   Explanation: To provide assurance about email authenticity, the hash of the message should be encrypted with the sender's private key.

7. **Answer: C. Authenticity and integrity**
   Explanation: Using the sender's private key to encrypt the message as well as the message hash will ensure authenticity and integrity. It will not ensure confidentiality or privacy as anyone having a public key can decrypt the message.

8. **Answer: A. Using the firm's private key to encrypt the hash of the invoice**
   Explanation: A hash value is a unique code for a given message. The hash value is unique for each message. A slight change in message/content will produce a different hash value. A firm can ensure the integrity of an invoice by implementing the following process:
   - The hash value of the invoice is to be encrypted using the sender's private key. The firm will send (i) the invoice and (ii) the encrypted hash of the invoice to the client.
   - On receiving the message, the client will (i) decrypt the received hash by using the public key of the sender and (ii) re-computing the hash of the invoice and if the two hashes are equal, then it proves that the message's integrity has not been tampered with.

9. **Answer: B. The website's authenticity**
   Explanation: When a link is established between an organization's website and the customer's computer, the customer's computer validates the private key of the website with the use of the associated public key. This helps to determine the authenticity of the website.

10. **Answer: A. Applying a long asymmetric key**
    Explanation: The cost of a symmetric key (only one key is used) is lower compared to an asymmetric key (two keys are used). For the encryption and decryption of long asymmetric keys, more processing time and costs are involved compared to short asymmetric keys. A hash is shorter than the original message, hence the cost of encrypting only the hash is lower.

11. **Answer: D. A symmetric session key**
    Explanation: The most efficient use of PKI is to combine the best features of asymmetric as well as symmetric methods. The Challenge of asymmetric encryption is that it is an expensive and time-consuming process. Though symmetric encryption is comparatively much faster, it has the challenge of sharing the symmetric key with other parties. To combine the benefits of both and address their challenges, the following process is recommended:
    1. Step 1: For faster and inexpensive computation, encrypt the entire message with the help of a symmetric key.
    2. Step 2: Encrypt the above symmetric key with the public key of the receiver.
    3. Step 3: Send the encrypted message (step 1) and encrypted symmetric key (step 2) to the receiver.
    4. Step 4: The receiver will decrypt the symmetric key using its private key.
    5. Step 5: The receiver will use a symmetric key to decrypt the full message.

12. **Answer: A. Using the sender's private key to encrypt the message digest, using the symmetric key to encrypt the message, and using the receiver's public key to encrypt the symmetric key**
    Explanation:
    1. Integrity and non-repudiation: the sender's private key is used to encrypt the hash/message digest.
    2. Confidentiality: The most efficient use of PKI is to combine the best features of asymmetric as well as symmetric methods. The challenge of asymmetric encryption is that it is an expensive and time-consuming process. Though symmetric encryption is comparatively much faster, it possesses the challenge of sharing the symmetric key with other parties. To combine the benefit of both and address their challenges, the following process is recommended:
        1. Step 1: For faster and inexpensive computation, encrypt the entire message with the help of a symmetric key.
        2. Step 2: Encrypt the symmetric key with the public key of the receiver.
        3. Step 3: Send the encrypted message (step 1) and the encrypted symmetric key (step 2) to the receiver.
        4. Step 4: The receiver will decrypt the symmetric key using his private key.
        5. Step 5: The receiver will use a symmetric key to decrypt the full message.

    Thus, for confidentiality, use a symmetric key to encrypt a message, and use the receiver's public key to encrypt the symmetric key.

Elements of public key infrastructure

1. **Answer: B. Certifying Authority**
   Explanation: A Certifying Authority is an entity that issues digital certificates. The Certifying Authority is responsible for the issuance and management of digital certificates.

2. **Answer: D. To validate the information of the applicants for a certificate**
   Explanation: Registration Authority has the following functions:
   - To verify and validate the information provided by the applicant.
   - To verify that the applicant is in possession of a private key and that it matches the public key requested for a certificate. This is known as proof of possession (POP).
   - To distribute physical tokens containing private keys.
   - To generate shared secret keys during the initialization and certificate pickup phase of registration.

3. **Answer: A. Certifying Authority**
   Explanation: A certifying authority is an entity that issues digital certificates. The Certifying Authority is responsible for the issuance and management of digital certificates.

4. **Answer: C. Establishing a link between the applicant and their public key**
   Explanation: The Certifying Authority delegates some of the administrative functions, such as the verification of the information provided by applicants. The Registration Authority is delegated with the function of verifying the correctness of information provided by applicants. The Registration Authority verifies that the applicant is in possession of a private key and that it matches the public key requested for the certificate. This is known as proof of possession (POP).

5. **Answer: C. The user organization is also the owner of the Certifying Authority**
   Explanation: This indicates that there is a conflict of interest as the user and owner of the certificate are the same. The independence of the Certifying Authority will be impaired in this scenario and this is considered a major weakness.

6. **Answer: B. The validation of the information provided by the applicant**
   Explanation: A Registration Authority has the following functions:
   - To verify and validate the information provided by the applicant.
   - To verify that the applicant is in possession of a private key and that it matches the public key requested for a certificate. This is known as **proof of possession (POP)**.
   - To distribute physical tokens containing private keys.
   - To generate shared secret keys during the initialization and certificate pickup phase of registration.

7. **Answer: A. The certificate practice statement**
   Explanation: A certification practice statement is a document that prescribes the practices and processes of issuing and managing digital certificates by the Certifying Authority. It includes details such as the controls in place, the method for validating applicants, and the usage of certificates.

8. **Answer: B. Validating the identity and authenticity of the certificate owner**
   Explanation: A Registration Authority has the following functions:
   - To verify and validate the information provided by the applicant.
   - To verify that the applicant is in possession of a private key and that it matches the public key requested for a certificate. This is known as **proof of possession (POP)**.
   - To distribute physical tokens containing private keys.
   - To generate shared secret keys during the initialization and certificate pickup phase of registration.

Cloud computing

1. **Answer: B. Verify a copy of independent security reviews or audit reports of the CSP**
   Explanation: The best way to ensure is to obtain and verify an independent security review or audit report of the CSP. Other options are not sufficient in themselves to verify physical security arrangements.

2. **Answer: D. The contract should restrict the movement of data to within permitted territories as per relevant laws and regulations**
   Explanation: It is very important to validate and verify whether the regulations of the locations (where infrastructure is located) are aligned with the enterprise's requirements. The contract should include terms to restrict the movement of assets to within approved locations. Other options are also important but option (D) should be considered as the most important clause in a contract with a cloud service provider.

3. **Answer: A. Clarity with respect to data ownership, data custody, and IPR-related requirements**
   Explanation: It is very important that contracts should have proper clarification with respect to data ownership, data custody, and other IPR-related requirements.

4. **Answer: B. The data in the multi-tenancy environment being accessed by competitors**
   Explanation: Considering various laws and regulations that require the privacy/confidentiality of customer information, unauthorized access to information and data leakage are the major concerns.

5. **Answer: B. Compliance with legal requirements**

    Explanation: The most important considerations are legal requirements, laws, and regulations. Other options are also important but option (B) should be considered as the most important clause in a contract with a cloud service provider.

6. **Answer: B. Private cloud**

    Explanation: The private cloud is considered the most secure deployment method.

12
Security Event Management

Security assessment is the process of identifying, implementing, and managing various security tools and techniques. This chapter will help us to evaluate the organization's information security policies and practices and determine risks associated with the information system by understanding different attack methods and techniques.

The following topics will be covered in this chapter:

- Security awareness training and programs
- Information system attack methods and techniques
- Security testing tools and techniques
- Security monitoring tools and techniques
- Incident response management
- Evidence collection and forensics

Security awareness training and programs

Automated controls alone cannot prevent or detect security incidents. Knowledge, experience, and awareness on the part of employees play a key role in mitigating information security risk. Security awareness programs are a very important element in IT risk management.

Employees should be educated on various aspects of security events to minimize the impact. Security awareness programs should include do's and don'ts regarding password frameworks, email usage, internet usage, social engineering, and other relevant factors.

Participants

Security awareness training should be provided to all employees irrespective of their job functions or designations and authority. All employees within the organization should be aware of security requirements.

For those job functions where critical data is processed or critical assets handled, enhanced levels of training should be provided. Functions such as OS configuration, programmers, network engineers, job schedulers, and other critical functions should be provided with information security training at regular intervals.

Security awareness methods

Security awareness can be imparted to employees and third-party contractors in the following ways:

- Workshop and training programs
- Security tips via email
- Documented security policies and procedures
- NDAs with employees and third-party vendors
- Awareness through newsletters, posters, screensavers, and suchlike
- Documented security roles and responsibilities
- Simulated drills and security scenarios

Social engineering attacks

In a social engineering attack, an intruder attempts to obtain sensitive information from users by means of their social and psychological skills. They attempt to manipulate individuals into divulging confidential information such as passwords. This kind of attack can best be restricted and addressed by educating users through frequent security awareness training.

Evaluating the effectiveness of security programs

It is important for an IS auditor to evaluate the effectiveness of various security programs. Interaction and interviews with employees will help an IS auditor to evaluate the state of awareness of information security requirements. Overall security depends on the knowledge of those employees who are in the field. Also, an increase in valid incident reporting indicates that employees are aware of the importance of security and are proactively following the incident reporting procedure.

Key aspects from the CISA exam perspective

The following table covers important aspects from CISA exam perspective:

CISA questions	Possible answers
Which technique is used to obtain the passwords without technical tools or programs?	Social engineering
What is the most effective way to minimize the impact of social engineering attacks?	Security awareness training
Risk of a phishing attack can be best addressed by:	User education

Self-assessment questions

1. **Which of the following techniques is used to obtain passwords without technical tools or programs?**
    A. A backdoor attempt
    B. A social engineering attempt
    C. A man-in-the-middle attempt
    D. Password sniffing

2. **The most effective way to minimize the impact of social engineering attacks is by means of:**
    A. the installation of a firewall
    B. stringent physical security
    C. security awareness training
    D. penetration testing

3. **The most effective way to evaluate the effectiveness of security awareness training is:**
   - A. to review the security training calendar
   - B. to review the job description
   - C. to ask the security team
   - D. to interact with a number of employees

4. **Which of the following is the most important aspect of a security awareness program?**
   - A. to organize training at frequent interval
   - B. to provide training related to password complexity
   - C. to organize training on employee's on-boarding
   - D. to provide security policy to all the employees

5. **The effectiveness of a security awareness program is best indicated by:**
   - A. users having signed and acknowledged the acceptable usage policy
   - B. the number of users attending the awareness program
   - C. the inclusion of security responsibility in job descriptions
   - D. an improvement in incident reporting

6. **The most important criterion in determining the adequacy of an organization's security awareness program is:**
   - A. the fact that the security policy is available to all employees
   - B. an appropriate level of funding of security initiatives
   - C. awareness among senior management regarding the protection of critical information assets
   - D. the availability of job descriptions relating to information security accountability

7. **The risk of phishing attacks can best be addressed by:**
   - A. educating users
   - B. two-factor authentication
   - C. penetration testing
   - D. IDS

8. **One factor resulting in the success of social engineering is:**
   A. system error
   B. confidentiality
   C. technical expertise
   D. judgement error

Information system attack methods and techniques

An IS auditor should be aware of the following methods and techniques in relation to information system attacks:

Alteration attack: In this type of attack, the data or code is altered or modified code without authorization. Cryptographic code is used to prevent alteration attacks.

Botnets: Botnets are compromised computers, also known as zombie computers. They are primarily used to run malicious software for DDoS attacks, adware, or spam.

Buffer overflow: A buffer overflow, or buffer overrun, is a common software coding mistake that an attacker could exploit in order to gain access to the system. This error occurs when there is more data in a buffer than it can handle, causing the data to overflow into adjacent storage. Due to this, an attacker gets an opportunity to manipulate the coding errors for malicious actions. A major cause of buffer overflow is poor programming and coding practices.

Denial-of-Service attack (DoS): A DoS attack intends to shut down a network or machine by flooding the same with traffic. In a DoS attack, a single computer is used to flood a server with TCP and UDP packets. In a **Distributed Denial-of-Service (DDoS)** attack, multiple systems are used to flood the target system. The targeted network is bombarded with packets from multiple locations.

Data diddling: Data diddling is a type of attack in which data is altered as it enters a computer system. This is done mostly by a data entry clerk or a computer virus. Data is altered before computer security is able to protect the data. Dada diddling requires very little technical knowledge. Apparently, there are no preventive controls for data diddling and so the organization needs to rely on compensatory controls.

Dumpster diving: Dumpster diving is a technique for retrieving sensitive information from the trash or a garbage bin. To address the risk of dumpster diving, employees should be made aware of this kind of risk by way of frequent security awareness training. A document discarding policy should be in place that should define appropriate methods for discarding various pieces of information. One example is the use of a shredder to discard documents. The following diagram indicates how dumpster diving is performed:

In a dumpster diving attack, the intruder looks for critical information in a garbage bin

Organizations should take the utmost care and avoid disposing of sensitive documents and other information in the garbage.

War dialing: War dialing is a technique in which tools are used to automatically scan a list of telephone numbers to determine the details of a computer, modems, and other machines.

War driving: War driving is a technique for locating and getting access to wireless networks with the aid of specialized tools. An intruder drives or walks around the building while equipped with specialized tools to identify unsecured networks. The same technique is used by IS auditors to identify unsecured networks and thereby test the wireless security of an organization.

Eavesdropping: Eavesdropping is a process in which an intruder gathers the information flowing through the network via unauthorized methods. Using a variety of tools and techniques, sensitive information, including email addresses, passwords, and even keystrokes can be captured by intruders.

Email attacks and techniques: Here are a few types of email attacks and techniques:

- **Email bombing**: In this technique, abusers repeatedly send an identical email to a particular address.
- **Email spamming**: In this attack, unsolicited emails are sent to thousands of users.
- **Email spoofing**: In this attack, the email appears to originate from some other source and not the actual source. This is often an attempt to trick the user into disclosing sensitive information.

Juice jacking: In this type of attack, data is copied from a device attached to a charging port (mostly available at public places). Here, charging points also act as data connections. This type of attack is also used to insert malware in the attached devices:

Juice jacking – High risk at public charging points

Interrupt attack: In this type of attack, the operating system is invoked to execute a particular task, thereby interrupting ongoing tasks.

Flooding: This is a type of DoS attack that brings a network down by flooding it with huge amounts of traffic. The host's memory buffer cannot handle this huge volume of traffic.

Malicious codes

Trojan horse: In this attack, malicious software is disguised as legitimate software. Once installed in the system, it starts taking control of the user's system.

Logic bomb: A program is executed when a certain event happens. For example, a logic bomb can be set to delete files or databases at a future date.

Trapdoor: This is also known as backdoor attack. In this method, malware is placed inside the application. This malware is used to bypass normal security measures and gain unauthorized access to applications.

Man-in-the-middle attack: In this attack, the attacker interferes while two devices are establishing a connection. Alternatively, the attacker actively establishes a connection between two devices and pretends to be each of them to be the other device. In case any device asks for authentication, it sends a request to the other device and the response is then sent to the first device. Once a connection is established, the attacker can communicate and obtain information as desired.

Masquerading: In this type of attack, an intruder hides their original identity, acting as someone else. This is done in order to access systems or data that are restricted. Impersonation can be implemented by both people and machines.

IP spoofing: In IP spoofing, a forged IP address is used to break a firewall. IP spoofing can be regarded as the masquerading of a machine.

Message modification: In this type of attack, a message is captured and altered and deleted without authorization. These attacks can have a serious impact; for example, a message is sent to a bank to make a payment.

Network analysis: In this type of attack, an intruder creates a repository of information pertaining to a particular organization's internal network, such as internal addresses, gateways, and firewalls. Intruders then determine what service and operating system are running on the targeted system and how it can be exploited.

Packet replay: In this type of attack, an intruder captures the data packet as data moves along the vulnerable network.

Pharming: In this type of attack, website traffic is redirected to a bogus website. This is done by exploiting vulnerabilities in DNS servers. Pharming is a major concern for e-commerce websites and online banking websites.

Piggybacking: In this type of attack, an intruder follows an authorized person through a secure door and so is able to enter a restricted area without authentication. Piggybacking is regarded as a physical security vulnerability:

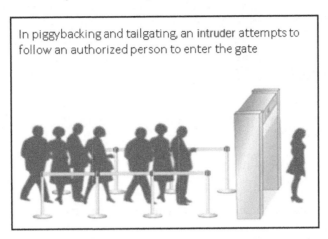

In piggybacking and tailgating, an intruder attempts to follow an authorized person to enter the gate

Piggybacking is also known as tailgating.

Password sniffing: The password sniffer is a small program that listens to all traffic in the attached network(s), builds data streams out of TCP/IP packets, and extracts usernames and passwords. These passwords are then used to gain unauthorized access to the system.

Parameter tampering: The unauthorized modification of web application parameters with a malicious intent is known as parameter tampering. As the hidden files in the web page are not visible, developers may feel safe to pass the data without proper validation. This creates a risk as an intruder may intercept the hidden data and may modify the parameter for malicious purposes.

Privilege escalation: In a privilege escalation attack, high-level system authority is obtained by employees through some unauthorized methods by exploiting security flaws.

Race condition: This is also known as **time-of-check** to **time-of-use** (TOC/TOU) attack. In this attack, intruders exploit a small window between the time when services are used and the time when security controls are applied. The greater the time gap between the time of use and the time of service, the greater the chances of race condition attacks.

Salami: In this technique, a small amount of money is sliced from a computerized transaction and transferred to unauthorized accounts.

Social engineering: In a social engineering attack, an attempt is made to obtain sensitive information from users by tricking and manipulating people. In a social engineering attack, the attacker does not require any technical tools and techniques to obtain information. Social engineering is generally conducted through dialogue, interviews, inquiries, and other social methods of interaction. The objective of social engineering is to exploit human nature and weakness in order to obtain critical and sensitive information. As a result of adequate and effective security awareness training, the consequences of social engineering attacks can be minimized.

Shoulder surfing: In a shoulder surfing attack, an intruder or a camera captures the sensitive information by looking over the shoulder of the user entering the details on the computer screen.

Passwords entered in the computer screen should be masked to prevent shoulder surfing attacks.

Traffic analysis: In traffic analysis, communication patterns between entities are studied and information is deduced.

Virus: A virus is a type of malicious code that can self-replicate and spread from one computer to another. A virus can take control of a user's computer and can delete or alter sensitive files. It can also disrupt system functioning.

Worms: Worms are destructive programs that can destroy sensitive data. However, worms do not replicate like viruses.

Biometric attacks

The following are some of the attacks for targeting biometric devices and systems:

- **Replay attack**: In a replay attack, an attacker makes use of residual biometric characteristics (such as fingerprints left on a biometric device) to obtain unauthorized access.
- **Brute-force attack**: In a brute-force attack, an attacker sends numerous biometric samples with the aim of causing the biometric device to malfunction.
- **Cryptographic attack**: In a cryptographic attack, an attacker attempts to obtain information by targeting algorithms or the encrypted information that is transmitted between biometric devices and access control systems.
- **Mimic attack**: In a mimic attack, an attacker attempts to reproduce a fake biometric feature of a genuine biometric user.

CISA aspirants should also understand the difference between active and passive attacks. Passive attacks are types of attacks in which only information is captured but does not modify, insert, or delete the traffic. Examples of passive attacks include traffic analysis, network analysis, and eavesdropping. Active attacks attempt to alter system resources or affect their operations. Active attacks involve some modification of the data stream or the creation of false statements.

Key aspects from the CISA exam perspective

The following table covers important aspects from CISA exam perspective:

CISA questions	Possible answers
In which type of attack, internet traffic appears to originate from the internal IP of the organization?	IP spoofing
Which type of risk is exposed due to a hidden fie on webpage?	Parameter tampering
In which kind of attack, no technical tools and techniques are required to extract information?	Social Engineering
What is the best way to reduce the risk of shoulder surfing?	Password screen should be masked
Inherent risk for date entry process for which there are no preventive control	Data diddling
What are the example of passive attacks?	Traffic analysis/network analysis/eavesdropping
Which technique is used to test the wireless security?	War driving
In which type of attack, computers are used as zombie to perform DDOS, spam or other kind of attacks?	Botnet
Which attack has the capability to circumvent two-factor authentication?	Man in the middle
What is the primary risk due to poor programming and coding practices?	Buffer overflow
URL shortening services increase the risk of which attack?	Phishing

Assessment

1. **The use of hidden files on web pages to save certain information of client sessions can expose the risk of:**
   A. race conditions
   B. parameter tampering
   C. flooding
   D. juice jacking

2. **An attack in which internet traffic appears to originate from the internal IP of the organization is known as:**
    A. a DDoS attack
    B. parameter tampering
    C. spoofing
    D. port scanning

3. **Which of the following can be regarded as a significant risk for VoIP infrastructure?**
    A. A DDoS attack
    B. Social engineering
    C. Juice jacking
    D. Premium rate fraud

4. **In which of the following types of attacks does an employee run a task scheduler without authorization to access restricted applications?**
    A. Privilege escalation
    B. Race condition
    C. Social engineering
    D. Buffer overflow

5. **Which of the following techniques does not require any tools or techniques to obtain critical information?**
    A. Privilege escalation
    B. Race condition
    C. Social engineering
    D. Buffer overflow

6. **The most effective way to reduce the consequences of a social engineering attack is:**
    A. to implement robust physical security
    B. to implement robust logical security
    C. to provide security awareness training
    D. to prepare information security policy

7. **Passwords entered in the computer screen should be masked to prevent:**
    A. juice jacking
    B. tailgating
    C. shoulder surfing
    D. impersonation

8. **A mandatory process of reading an employee's ID badge at the entrance door is designed to prevent:**
    A. shoulder surfing
    B. piggybacking
    C. race condition
    D. dumpster diving

9. **Which of the following techniques is regarded as an inherent risk in the data entry process for which apparently there is no preventive control?**
    A. Shoulder surfing
    B. Data diddling
    C. Race condition
    D. Dumpster diving

10. **Which of the following is regarded as a passive cybersecurity attack?**
    A. Traffic analysis
    B. Juice jacking
    C. Denial of service
    D. IP spoofing

11. **A password sniffing attack can:**
    A. help an intruder act as another party
    B. help an intruder bypass physical security
    C. help an intruder gain unauthorized access to a system
    D. help an intruder perform impersonation

12. **Which technique is used to test the wireless security of an organization?**
    A. War driving
    B. Juice jacking
    C. War dialing
    D. Social engineering

13. **Which of the following is used for distributed denial-of-service?**
    A. Phishing techniques
    B. Logic bombs
    C. Botnets
    D. Social engineering

14. **Wireless infrastructure increases which of the following risks?**
    A. Port scanning
    B. War driving
    C. War dialing
    D. Backdoor

15. **In which of the following attacks is residual biometric information used to gain unauthorized access?**
    A. A brute-force attack
    B. An encrypted attack
    C. A mimic attack
    D. A replay attack

16. **Which of the following methods has the ability to circumvent two-factor authentication?**
    A. DDoS
    B. Man in the middle
    C. Juice jacking
    D. Brute force

17. **The risk of which of the following increases due to poor programming and coding practices?**
    A. Juice jacking
    B. Social engineering
    C. Buffer overflow
    D. Brute force

18. **Which of the following risks increases due to URL shortening services?**
    A. Social engineering
    B. Phishing
    C. Vishing
    D. DDOS

19. **Social engineering can succeed on account of:**
    A. a technical error
    B. an error in judgement
    C. a highly qualified intruder
    D. a computer error

20. **Which of the following techniques is used to gather information about encrypted data being transmitted over the network?**
    A. DDOS
    B. IP spoofing
    C. Traffic analysis
    D. Masquerading

21. **Which of the following is the most effective approach in addressing the risk of dumpster diving?**
    A. Security awareness training
    B. A documented discarding policy
    C. Placing CCTV above bins
    D. Purchasing high-speed shredders

Security testing tools and techniques

An auditor should be aware of various security testing tools and techniques to determine the security environment of the organization. To evaluate the security risks and controls, an auditor should be well versed in auditing techniques.

General security controls

An IS auditor can adopt the following testing techniques for security controls:

Terminal controls

The following are some of the important aspects with respect to terminal controls:

- An auditor should obtain access cards and keys and attempt to enter the restricted area. This will ensure that access controls are effective and operational.
- An auditor should determine and verify whether the terminal list has been updated and reconciled with addresses and locations. The IS auditor should select a few terminals and try to locate them in the network diagram.
- An auditor should verify whether any unsuccessful attempts to access the terminals are monitored at regular intervals and whether appropriate action is taken against the violation of access rules.

Logon IDs and passwords

The following are some of the important aspects with respect to logon IDs and passwords:

- Auditors should ensure compliance with a clear desk and clear screen policy. Login IDs and passwords should not be openly available or written on the desk.
- Auditors should use social engineering techniques to determine user awareness regarding password confidentiality.
- Auditors should also determine password complexity and password rules configured in the system and these should be reconciled with the approved password policy of the organization. Auditors should ensure that the vendor-provided default password is changed immediately.
- Passwords should be changed immediately when first logging on. Also, a procedure for the mandatory password change at frequent intervals should be enforced for all users. Auditors should verify password policy to determine the password change procedures.
- Auditors should determine whether the password table is in an encrypted form. To test this, the auditor should work with the system administrator and attempt to view the internal password table.
- Application logs should be verified to ensure that logon IDs and passwords are not captured in a readable form.
- As an auditor, you should verify whether a given password is masked on the screen. It should not be visible.

Authorization process

To review the authorization process, an access list should be obtained. Then, sample forms should be verified to ensure approval by the appropriate authority. Authorization should be provided on a need-to-know basis. Auditors should match the current roles of the employees vis-à-vis access granted for a few samples.

Automatic logoff

Auditors should verify whether an automatic logoff procedure is enabled for unattended terminals. Auditors should wait for the terminal to disconnect following the established period of inactivity.

Account lockout

Auditors should verify whether an account lockout facility is being enabled for unsuccessful access attempts. Auditors should purposefully enter the wrong password a number of times. Accounts should be locked after a predefined number of unsuccessful attempts. Also, the auditor should verify the process of activating the account.

Controls on bypassing software and utilities

Auditors should verify the fact that system utility programs that have the capability to bypass normal logon procedures are restricted and available only on a need-to-know basis.

Auditors should determine control over the following programs that can bypass normal logon procedures:

- **Bypass label processing (BLP)**: BLP bypasses the reading of file labels by computer. This may impact access control as most of the access rules are based on file labels.
- System exits: These programs are used for maintenance of the application. They generally exist outside of the computer security system and, thus, are not restricted or reported in their use.
- Privileged logon IDs: These are generally administration IDs with unlimited access.

Log capturing and monitoring

To test the effectiveness of the log capturing and monitoring process, the IS auditor should select a sample of security reports and look for evidence of follow-up and investigation of access violations. It is important that logs should not be allowed to be edited, modified, or deleted in order to preserve their integrity.

Time synchronization

It is important that all devices should have a common time. The objective of all computer clocks being synchronized to a common time network is to support incident investigation processes. If the timestamp is not the same on all devices, this will impact the process of investigating an incident. The audit trail may not be effective and reliable.

Network penetration tests

In penetration testing, the IS auditor uses the same techniques as used by hackers to gain access to critical systems/data. This helps the auditor to determine the security environment of the organization. Penetration testing helps to identify the risk relevant to the confidentiality, integrity, and availability of information systems. The objective of penetration testing is to verify the control environment of the organization and to take corrective action in case a deficiency is noted. Penetration testing should only be performed by experienced and qualified professionals.

Aspects to be covered within the scope of the audit

From an audit risk perspective, the following aspects need to be covered within the scope of auditing penetration testing:

- Precise details of IP addresses need to be included in the scope of the audit.
- Details of the testing technique (SQL injection/DoS/DDoS/social engineering, and so on) should be provided.
- The day and time of the attack (that is, either during office hours or after office hours) should be included.
- It is the responsibility of the penetration tester/auditor to provide appropriate warning prior to the simulation so as to avoid false alarms being raised with law enforcement bodies.

Types of penetration tests

The following are some of the penetration tests that can be used to evaluate the security environment of an organization:

External testing

In external testing, an attack is conducted on the target's network perimeter from outside the target's system (that is usually the internet).

Internal testing

In internal testing, an attack is conducted on the target from within the perimeter. This is done to determine the security risk if an actual intruder happens to be within the organization.

Blind testing

In a blind testing type of attack scenario, the tester is provided with limited or no knowledge of the target's information systems. Here, the tester is regarded as blind as they do not have any knowledge of the target environment. Such a test is expensive because detailed analysis, study, and research is required for an attack.

Double blind testing

Double blind testing is the extension of blind testing, wherein the administrator and security staff at the target organization are also unaware of the test. Both the tester and security team are blind as no one is aware of the test details. It simulates a real kind of attack. This helps to evaluate the incident handling and response capability of the target organization.

Targeted testing

In targeted testing, both the target's IT team and penetration testers are aware of the testing scenarios. A penetration tester is aware of the target details and network structure.

Risks associated with penetration testing

The following are some of the risks associated with penetration testing

- A pentest attempt by an unqualified auditor may have an adverse impact on the target's system.
- Sensitive information relating to the target environment gathered during penetration testing can be misused by the tester.
- Inappropriate planning and timing of the attack may cause the system to fail.
- This is a simulation of a real attack and may be restricted by law or regulations. Such attacks without appropriate approvals may have an adverse impact.

Threat intelligence

Threat intelligence is intelligent information about likely attacks on the basis of an analysis of current trends. This information is organized and provided by the service providers and **Computer Emergency Response Teams (CERTs)**. Threat intelligence is designed to help an organization understand common and severe external threats, such as zero-day threats, **advanced persistent threats (APTs)**, and other security exploits. Threat intelligence provides in-depth information about **indicators of compromise (IOC)** and thus helps the organization to protect itself from attacks.

Key aspects from the CISA exam perspective

The following table covers important aspects from CISA exam perspective:

CISA questions	Possible answers
What is the best way to protect an unattended PC?	Password-protected screen saver
What kind of penetration testing indicates a real kind of attack and to determine the incident response capability of the target?	Double blind testing
What is the most important control to preserve the integrity of logs?	Read-only access (edit and delete access should be disabled)
What is the first step once the password is compromised?	Change of password

Self-assessment questions

1. **The most effective method for preventing unauthorized access to an unattended computer is:**
    - A. to mandate two-factor authentication
    - B. to mandate termination of the user session following a predefined interval
    - C. to switch off the monitor automatically
    - D. to mandate a password-protected screensaver

2. **What course of action should an IT auditor take having observed that password complexity rules are as stringent for business as compared to system developers?**
    - A. To report this as an audit observation
    - B. To determine whether this complies with policy
    - C. To recommend that password rules should be equal
    - D. To recommend the implementation of a password management tool

3. The penetration testing type that indicates a real kind of attack and determines the incident response capability of the target is:
   A. double blind testing
   B. internal testing
   C. external testing
   D. blind testing

4. The greatest concern for an IS auditor conducting a post-implementation review is:
   A. Mobile devices are not password protected
   B. Internal communication is not encrypted
   C. Vendor-provided default passwords are not changed
   D. A proxy server is not used for outbound traffic

5. Which of the following is the most important control for preserving the integrity of transaction logs?
   A. A transaction log should be set up as 'write once' and 'read many' drives
   B. Take a backup of the log on a daily basis
   C. Review the log on a daily basis
   D. Document change management policy for transaction logs

6. Which of the following is the greatest concern in terms of logical access security of a remote session?
   A. Shared logon IDs are used
   B. Support for remote login is provided by a third party
   C. A user access review is not conducted on an annual basis
   D. Authentication passwords are not encrypted

7. Which of the following should have only read access?
   A. A log capturing policy
   B. Log monitoring rules
   C. Access control rules
   D. Security log files

8. What should be the first step undertaken by an organization when it realizes that a password for one of its critical systems has been compromised?
   A. Immediate change of the password
   B. Intimation of the incident management team
   C. Immediate change of the login name
   D. Immediate deletion of the account

9. **The greatest concern while reviewing logical access control for an application is:**
    A. Developers have access to the production database
    B. Password complexity is not defined
    C. The use of shared accounts by the administration team
    D. A file containing a list of user IDs and associated passwords exists in plain text

10. **To determine the preparedness of an organization in terms of incident handling and its response capability, a penetration test is conducted as:**
    A. internal testing
    B. blind testing
    C. double blind testing
    D. walkthrough testing

11. **Which of the following is the area of greatest concern for a physical security arrangement?**
    A. An emergency exit route is blocked
    B. A fire drill report is not reviewed
    C. The UPS is not tested
    D. The data center does not have CCTV monitoring

Security monitoring tools and techniques

Monitoring security events is a very important aspect of information security. Two important monitoring tools are **Intrusion Detection Systems (IDS)** and **Intrusion Prevention Systems (IPS)**. IDS only monitor, record, and provide alarms about intrusion activity, whereas IPS also prevent intrusion activities.

Let's study each of them in detail.

Intrusion detection system

An IDS helps to monitor a network (network-based IDS) or a single system (host-based IDS) with the aim of recognizing and detecting an intrusion activity.

Network-based and host-based IDS

The following table differentiates between network-based and host-based IDS:

Network-based IDS	Host-based IDS
It monitors activities across the network	It monitors the activities of a single system or host.
Comparatively, network-based IDS have high false positives (in other words, a high rate of false alarms)	Host-based IDS have low false positives (in other words, a low rate of false alarms)
Network-based IDS are better at detecting attacks from outside.	Host-based IDS are better at detecting attacks from inside.
Network-based IDS inspect the content and header information of all packets moving across the network and identify irregular behavior.	Host-based IDS detect activities on a hast computer, such as the deletion of files and the modification of programs

Components of the IDS

The following table shows the various components of the IDS:

Components	Description
Sensors	The function of the sensors is to collect the data. Data can be in the form of network packets, log files and so on.
Analyzers	The function of the analyzers is to analyze the data and determine the intrusion activity.
Administration console	An administration console helps the administrator to control and monitor IDS rules and functions.
User interface	A user interface supports the user in viewing the results and carrying out the necessary tasks.

Limitations of the IDS

The following are some of the limitations of the IDS:

- IDS operate on the basis of policy definition. Weaknesses in policy definitions weaken the function of the IDS.
- IDS cannot control application-level vulnerabilities.
- IDS cannot control the backdoor into an application.
- IDS cannot analyze the data that is tunneled into an encrypted connection.

Types of IDS

The following are the types of IDS:

Signature-based

In signature-based IDS, the IDS looks for specific predefined patterns to detect intrusion. Patterns are stored as signatures and they are updated at frequent intervals. They are also known as rule-based IDS.

Statistical-based

Statistical-based IDS attempt to identify abnormal behavior by analyzing the statistical algorithm. Any abnormal activity is flagged as an intrusion. For example, if normal logon hours are between 7 a.m. and 5 p.m. and if logon is performed at 11 p.m., it will raise this as an intrusion. Statistical IDS generate the most false positives compared with other types of IDS.

Neural network

Neural networks work on the same principle as statistical-based IDS. However, they possess the advanced functionality of self-learning. Neural networks keep updating the database by monitoring the general pattern of activities. Neural networks are most effective in addressing problems that require consideration of a large number of input variables.

Placement of IDS

Network-based IDS can be placed either between a firewall and an external network (that is, the internet) or between a firewall and the internal network. This can be seen in the following diagram:

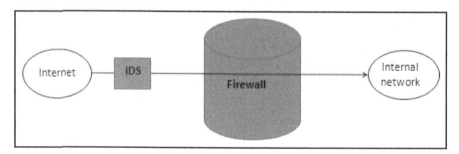

If an IDS is installed between a firewall and external network, it will be able to identify all the intrusion attempts irrespective of whether intrusion packets bypassed the firewall:

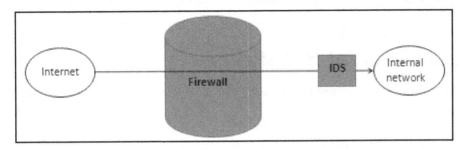

If an IDS is installed between a firewall and an internal network, it will be able to detect only those attempts that bypassed the firewall rules.

Intrusion prevention system

IPS have the ability to not only detect the intrusion attempts, but also to prevent the impact of the intrusion attack.

Honey pots and honey nets

A honey pot is a decoy system set up to attract the hacker and intruders. The purpose of setting a honey pot is to capture the details of intruders in order to proactively strengthen the security controls. High-interaction honeypots provide a real environment to attack, whereas a low-interaction honeypot provides limited information.

A honey net is a combination of linked honey pots. A honey net is used for large network setups.

Key aspects from the CISA exam perspective

The following table covers important aspects from CISA exam perspective:

CISA questions	Possible answers
Which IDS has the capacity to update its database and self-learn?	Neural network-based IDS
Component of IDS that collects the data	Sensor
Which IDS has the highest number of false alarms?	Statistical based IDS

A setup to capture information pertaining to the intruder in order to proactively strengthen security controls is known as:	Honey pot
What is the first action performed by an intruder/attacker in preparation for a system attack?	To gather information

Self-assessment questions

1. **An IDS that observes the general pattern of activities and updates its database is a:**
   - A. neural network-based IDS
   - B. statistical-based IDS
   - C. signature-based IDS
   - D. role-based IDS

2. **Which of the following parts of an IDS collects the data?**
   - A. Console
   - B. Sensor
   - C. Analyzer
   - D. Interface

3. **The IDS with the highest number of false alarms is:**
   - A. the neural network-based IDS
   - B. the statistical-based IDS
   - C. the signature-based IDS
   - D. the host-based IDS

4. **A major concern for an auditor verifying an IDS is:**
   - A. the number of false alarms
   - B. not being able to identify the intrusion activity
   - C. the use of automated tools for log capturing and monitoring
   - D. the fact that an IDS is placed between an internal network and a firewall

5. **The best place to incorporate an intrusion detection system to detect an intrusion that bypasses the firewall is:**
   - A. between a firewall and an external network
   - B. between a firewall and an internal network
   - C. between an external network and an internal network
   - D. alongside a firewall

6. **A characteristic of an IDS is:**
    A. to collect evidence relating to intrusion activity
    B. to route traffic as per defined rules
    C. to block restricted websites
    D. to act as access control software

7. **The most frequently encountered problem with respect to an IDS is:**
    A. a false rejection rate
    B. a false acceptance rate
    C. false positives
    D. DDoS attacks

8. **The risk of intrusion attacks and network penetration can be detected on the basis of unusual system behavior by:**
    A. a hub
    B. packet filters
    C. a switch
    D. an IDS

9. **Which of the following is the most important control in terms of detecting the intrusion?**
    A. access control procedures
    B. automatic logoff of inactive computers
    C. the monitoring of unsuccessful login attempts
    D. account lockout following a specified number of unsuccessful login attempts

10. **Which of the following is the most important concern with respect to IDS?**
    A. Many false alarms generated by statistical-based IDS
    B. A firewall is installed between the IDS and the external network
    C. The IDS is used to detect encrypted traffic
    D. Zero-day threats are not identified by signature-based IDS

11. **The most important factor impacting the effectiveness of the neural network is:**
    A. A neural network detects all known types of intrusion
    B. A neural network flags all activities that are not normal
    C. A neural network monitors the general pattern of activities and creates a database and attacks problems that require consideration of a large number of input variables

    D. A neural network solves the problem where a large database is not required

12. **An organization whose aim is to protect the public-facing website on its server should install the network IDS:**
    A. in a demilitarized zone
    B. on the same web server where the website is hosted
    C. between a firewall and an external network
    D. in the organization's internal network

13. **To prevent the installation of a rootkit on a web server hosting an application, which of the following should be installed?**
    A. packet filtering
    B. a network-based IDS
    C. the latest operating system patch
    D. a host-based IPS

14. **Which of the following helps to capture information for proactively strengthening security controls?**
    A. A honeypot
    B. A proxy server
    C. An IDS
    D. An IPS

15. **Which of the following systems can block a hacking attempt?**
    A. An IPS
    B. A router
    C. A switch
    D. An IDS

16. **Which of the following is the first action to be performed when preparing a system attack?**
    A. Capture information
    B. Erase evidence
    C. Initiate access
    D. Launch a DoS attack

17. **After a firewall, which of the following is regarded as the next line of defense for network security?**
    A. Anti-malware software
    B. A router
    C. A switch
    D. An IDS

18. **A major concern for a poorly configured IPS is the fact that:**
    A. an administrator has to verify high instances of alarms
    B. critical services or systems are blocked due to false alarms
    C. the network slows down
    D. the IPS is expensive

Incident response management

Incident response management policy is very important in minimizing the damage from an incident and in recovering the operations at the earliest possible juncture.

Roles and responsibilities for incident management should be clearly defined. The following are some of the important functions relating to incident management:

- A coordinator to liaison with process owners
- An executive officer to oversee the incident response capability
- Security experts to investigate the incident
- A public relations team to manage the reputation for both internal and external stakeholders

The incident reporting procedure should be clearly defined, documented, and made available to all employees and relevant stakeholders.

Teams of experts should be available to investigate the incident to arrive at the root cause for preventive action. To address incidents properly, it is necessary to collect evidence as soon as possible after the occurrence. Legal advice may be needed in the process of evidence collection and protection.

Computer Security Incident Response Team

A **Computer Security Incident Response Team (CSIRT)** or **CERT** should be established within the organization with clear roles and responsibilities. They should act as a centralized authority to evaluate and monitor all the incidents and issues related to information security. Learning from incidents should be documented for preventive as well as corrective actions.

Further, tools and techniques should be in place to identify and detect the incidents in real-time that could be acted on immediately to prevent further damage.

Key aspects from the CISA exam perspective

The following table covers important aspects from CISA exam perspective:

CISA questions	Possible answers
The primary objective of an incident response plan is:	To minimize the duration and impact of system outages and security incidents
The most important factor in improving the incident response process is:	Simulated testing of incident response plan at regular interval
A plan to detect and recover from an attack is known as:	Incident response plan
The best indicator to determine the effectiveness of the incident response team is:	Financial impact per security incident
A uniform time across all devices helps in the investigation of an incident	Support incident investigation

Self-assessment questions

1. **An auditor's first step when suspecting the occurrence of an incident should be:**
    - A. to switch off the system
    - B. to do nothing and verify the effectiveness of the incident response team
    - C. to conduct a detailed investigation of the incident
    - D. to report the incident to management immediately

2. **The primary objective of an incident response plan is:**
    A. to ensure appropriate communication to management
    B. to reduce the impact of system outages and incidents on business
    C. to facilitate better public relations management
    D. to reduce the cost of incident handling

3. **The most important aspect while recovering from an attack is:**
    A. to activate a business continuity plan
    B. to activate an incident response plan
    C. to activate an alternate site
    D. to hire expert investigators

4. **The most important factor in improving the incident response process is:**
    A. a walkthrough of the incident response plan at regular intervals
    B. to train team members at regular intervals
    C. to document all incidents
    D. to simulate the testing of the incident response plan at regular intervals

5. **A document that contains a plan to detect and recover from an attack is:**
    A. a business continuity plan
    B. a disaster recovery plan
    C. an incident response plan
    D. an IT operating process

6. **Which of the following is a major concern in terms of disseminating a detailed description of incident threats to users?**
    A. Information can be used to launch an attack
    B. The loss of reputation
    C. High instances of security alerts
    D. Threats can be ignored

7. **The effectiveness of the incident response process can be determined by:**
    A. the business and financial impact of each security incident
    B. the number of new patch installations
    C. team size
    D. the number of assets included in a penetration test

4. The **objective of synchronizing all computer clocks to a common time network is:**

        A. to remove duplicate transactions

        B. to comply with audit requirements

        C. to support the incident investigation process

        D. to have accurate timestamps on email messages

Evidence collection and forensics

Digital evidence can be used in legal proceedings provided it has been preserved in its original state. Evidence loses its integrity if the chain of custody is not maintained. The chain of custody refers to the process of identifying, preserving, analyzing, and presenting evidence in such a manner that it demonstrates the reliability and integrity of the evidence.

Chain of custody

The following are some of the major considerations when demonstrating the chain of custody:

Identify

This refers to the practice of the identification of evidence. This process should not impact the evidence's integrity. Evidence should not be altered or modified in any way.

Preserve

This refers to the process of preserving the evidence, such as the imaging of original media. This process should be followed in the presence of an independent third party. The process of preserving evidence should be documented for further reference.

Analyze

This refers to the process of interpreting and analyzing the evidence. This process should be performed on an image copy and not on the original evidence.

Present

This refers to the process of presenting the evidence to various authorities. This process should not impact the integrity of the evidence. Evidence should not be altered or modified in any way.

Key elements of computer forensics

The following key elements of computer forensics should be considered by an IS auditor during audit planning:

Data protection

An incident response procedure and plan should be in place to ensure that the required information is not deleted or altered.

Data acquisition

All required information should be transferred in a controlled environment. Write blocker devices should be used to ensure that electronic media is write-protected. Volatile data such as open ports, open files, user logons, and other data helps to determine the status of the system. This information is lost when the computer is shut down.

Imaging

Imaging is a process of copying data bit for bit so as to avoid inflicting damage on the original data. It is used to obtain residual data such as deleted files and other information. Imaging is helpful when multiple analyses are performed. Imaging copies the disk surface sector by sector.

Extraction

The extraction process involves the identification and selection of data from imaged data.

Interrogation

Interrogation is the process of obtaining relevant data, such as IP addresses, telephone numbers, and other details from extracted data.

Ingestion/normalization

Using the normalization process, information is converted to a format that can be understood by an investigator. Binary or hexadecimal data is converted into readable characters or in other formats suitable for data analysis tools.

Reporting

Reporting involves the presentation of findings in a structured way. It includes details such as the objective and purpose of the review, the review process to be followed, and conclusions arising from the review. Reporting should not be ambiguous and open to misinterpretation and be able to be utilized in legal proceedings.

Protection of evidence

An IS auditor should consider the following safeguards in order to protect evidence:

- Affected systems should not be rebooted. Rebooting the system could result in the loss or corruption of evidence.
- It is recommended to copy one or more images of the affected system.
- As far as is possible, analysis should be performed on an image of the evidence and not on the original evidence.
- Preservation of the chain of custody to ensure integrity of the evidence.

Self-assessment questions

1. **The primary consideration of an IS auditor when evaluating a fraudulent transaction is:**
   A. to remain unbiased while evaluating the evidence
   B. the independence of the IS auditor
   C. to determine the source of the evidence
   D. to ensure that the integrity of the evidence is maintained

2. **An IS auditor is reviewing the incident management process of an organization. Which of the following is the primary concern?**
   A. End users are not trained in incident reporting processes
   B. The chain of custody is not followed for evidence integrity
   C. The incident management process is not reviewed every year
   D. A post-incident review is not conducted for each incident

3. **Which of the following is the most important factor for an IS auditor investigating an incident?**
   A. The incident reporting procedure
   B. The data recovery procedure
   C. The chain of custody for evidence
   D. Reporting to external agencies

4. **Which of the following will have the greatest impact on the collection and preservation of forensic evidence for an incident?**
   A. Isolating the system from the network
   B. Rebooting the system
   C. Taking images from the original image
   D. Copying memory content

5. **The most important criterion is ensuring that evidence is admissible in court is that:**
   A. the data is timestamped from a reliable source
   B. the data is logged automatically
   C. the data is encrypted
   D. the data is verified for integrity

Summary

In this chapter, we discussed various aspects of security awareness training and programs, security testing, and monitoring tools and techniques. We also learned to evaluate incident management policies and practices.

We also discussed how to evaluate evidence collection and the forensics process. Digital evidence can be used in legal proceedings provided it has been preserved in its original state. Evidence loses its integrity if the chain of custody is not maintained. The chain of custody refers to the process of identifying, preserving, analyzing, and presenting evidence in such a manner that it demonstrates the reliability and integrity of the evidence.

With this chapter, you have acquired the relevant skills and knowledge required to pass the CISA exam as well as perform IS audits. It is strongly recommended to refer the key aspects mentioned at the end of each topic and practice self-assessment questions in order to excel in the CISA exam.

Assessments

You can find the answers to the self assessment questions in this section.

Security awareness training and programs

1. **Answer: B. Social engineering attempt**
   Explanation: In a social engineering attack, an intruder attempts to obtain sensitive information from users through their social and psychological skills. They attempt to manipulate people to divulge confidential information such as passwords. The other options require some kinds of tools and software to capture the passwords.

2. **Answer: C. Security awareness training**
   Explanation: In a social engineering attack, an intruder attempts to obtain sensitive information from users through their social and psychological skills. They attempt to manipulate people to divulge confidential information such as passwords. This kind of attack can best be restricted and addressed by educating users through frequent security awareness training.

3. **Answer: D. To interact with a number of employees**
   Explanation: Interaction and interviews with employees will help an IS auditor to evaluate the state of awareness of information security requirements. Overall security depends on the knowledge of those employees who are in the field. The other options may not be directly helpful in evaluating the effectiveness of security awareness training.

4. **Answer: A. Organize training at frequent intervals**

   Explanation: The most important aspect of a security awareness program is to organize the awareness program at regular intervals. One-time training programs may not be effective. Security requirements should be reiterated at regular intervals. Just providing a security policy to all employees will not serve the purpose. Password complexity should be inbuilt into the system and it should be enforced automatically.

5. **Answer: D. Incident reporting has been improved**

   Explanation: The reporting of incidents indicates that employees are aware of the importance of security and proactively report incidents. Other options are not as effective as evaluating the incident reporting process.

6. **Answer: D. The availability of job descriptions containing the accountability of information security**

   Explanation: The inclusion of information security roles and responsibilities is very important in demonstrating the maturity of a security program. It ensures that staff are well aware of their accountability vis-à-vis information security. The other options are important aspects as regards the success of a security program, but they are not as important as job descriptions that require all the staff to be responsible for information security.

7. **Answer: A. Educating users**

   Explanation: Security awareness is the best method to address the risk of phishing. Educating users will help to address the risk of visiting the untrusted website or email links. Users should be trained at frequent intervals to be aware of suspicious web pages and links. Phishing is a kind of social engineering attack that cannot be directly controlled by other options.

8. **Answer: D. An error of judgement**

   Explanation: In a social engineering attack, an intruder attempts to obtain sensitive information from users through their social and psychological skills. They attempt to manipulate people to divulge confidential information such as passwords. Due to an error of judgement, the user provides critical information to the intruder. This kind of attack can best be restricted and addressed by educating users through frequent security awareness training.

Information system attack methods and techniques

1. **Answer: B. Parameter tampering**
   Explanation: The unauthorized modification of web application parameters with a malicious intent is known as parameter tampering. As the hidden files in the web page are not visible, developers may feel safe to pass the data without proper validation. This creates a risk as the intruder may intercept the hidden data and may modify the parameter for malicious purposes.

2. **Answer: C. Spoofing**
   Explanation: In IP spoofing, a forged IP address is used to break a firewall. In this type of attack, an intruder hides their original identity and acts as someone else. Intruders generally make use of spoofed internal IPs to get access to systems or data that are restricted for outside IPs. IP spoofing can be regarded as the masquerading of a machine.

3. **Answer: A. A DDoS attack**
   Explanation: Distributed denial-of-service attacks intend to shut down a network or machine by flooding the same with traffic. A DDoS attack is regarded as a significant risk for VoIP infrastructure. Premium rate fraud occurs when the phone system is compromised and used for making long-distance calls. However, a more significant risk is a DDoS attack. Juice jacking and social engineering do not directly have any impact on VoIP infrastructure.

4. **Answer: A. Privilege escalation**
   Explanation: In a privilege escalation attack, high-level system authority is obtained by a number of unauthorized methods by exploiting security flaws. In this example, a security flaw in the task scheduler is exploited by employees to gain unauthorized access to restricted applications.

5. **Answer: C. Social engineering**
   Explanation: In a social engineering attack, an attempt is made to obtain sensitive information from users by tricking and manipulating people. In a social engineering attack, the attacker does not require any technical tools and techniques to obtain information. Social engineering is generally conducted through dialogue, interviews, inquiries, and other social methods of interaction.

6. **Answer: C. The provision of security awareness training**
   Explanation: The objective of social engineering is to exploit human nature and weakness to obtain critical and sensitive information. By means of adequate and effective security awareness training, the consequences of a social engineering attack can be minimized. Other options will not help to directly address the impact of social engineering attacks.

7. **Answer: C. Shoulder surfing**
   Explanation: In a shoulder surfing attack, an intruder or camera captures the sensitive information by looking over the shoulder of the user entering the details on the computer screen. Passwords entered on the computer screen should be masked to prevent shoulder surfing attacks.

8. **Answer: B. Piggybacking**
   Explanation: In this type of attack, an intruder follows an authorized person through a secure door and so is able to enter a restricted area without authentication. Piggybacking is regarded as a physical security vulnerability.

9. **Answer: B. Data diddling**
   Explanation: Data diddling is a type of attack in which data is altered as it enters a computer system. This is done mostly by a data entry clerk or a computer virus. Data is altered before computer security is able to protect the data. Data diddling requires very little technical knowledge. There are no preventive controls for data diddling and so the organization needs to rely on compensatory controls.

10. **Answer: A. Traffic analysis**
    Explanation: Passive attacks are types of attacks in which only information is captured but does not modify, insert, or delete the traffic in an active way. Examples of passive attacks include traffic analysis, network analysis, and eavesdropping. The other options are examples of active attacks.

11. **Answer: C. To help an intruder gain unauthorized access to a system**
    Explanation: The password sniffer is a small program that listens to all traffic in the attached network(s), builds data streams out of TCP/IP packets, and extracts usernames and passwords. This password is then used to gain unauthorized access to the system.

12. **Answer: A. War driving**
    Explanation: War driving is a technique for locating and getting access to wireless networks with the aid of specialized tools. An intruder drives or walks around the building while equipped with specialized tools to identify unsecured networks. The same technique is used by IS auditors to identify unsecured networks and thereby test the wireless security of an organization.

13. **Answer: C. Botnets**
    Explanation: A botnet is a network of zombie computers controlled by intruders. Botnets can be used to perform DDoS, spam, and other types of attack.

14. **Answer: B. War driving**

    Explanation: War driving is a technique that is designed to exploit the weakness of a wireless infrastructure. It is a technique for locating and getting access to wireless networks with the use of specialized tools such as wireless Ethernet cards. An intruder drives or walks around the building to identify unsecured networks.

15. **Answer: D. A replay attack**

    Explanation: In a replay attack, an attacker makes use of residual biometric characteristics (such as fingerprints left on a biometric device) to obtain unauthorized access.

16. **Answer: B. Man in the middle**

    Explanation: In this attack, the attacker interferes while two devices are establishing a connection. In case any device asks for authentication, it sends a request to another device and then a response is sent to the first device. Once a connection is established, the attacker can communicate and obtain information as required, thereby circumventing the two-factor authentication.

17. **Answer: C. Buffer overflow**

    Explanation: A buffer overflow, or buffer overrun, is a common software coding mistake that an attacker could exploit to gain access to the system. This error occurs when there is more data in a buffer than it can handle, causing the data to overflow into adjacent storage. Due to this, an attacker gets an opportunity to manipulate the coding errors for malicious actions. A major cause of buffer overflow is poor programming and coding practices.

18. **Answer: B. Phishing**

    Explanation: A URL shortening service converts long URLs (web addresses) into short versions. Hackers attempt to fool users by using URL shortening services to create URLs resembling genuine websites. This is done to spread malicious software or collect sensitive data by way of phishing.

19. **Answer: B. An error of judgement**

    Explanation: Social engineering succeeds due to errors in judgement on the part of an employee who provides sensitive information to intruders. Intruders establish a level of trust with the user/employer and take advantage.

20. **Answer: C. Traffic analysis**

    Explanation: In traffic analysis, an intruder attempts to capture and analyze the nature of the traffic flow between hosts, the frequency of messages, their length, the length of the session, and other relevant information. Through all of this information, an intruder attempts to understand and guess the type of communication. This is typically done when messages are encrypted.

21. **Answer: A. Security awareness training**
Explanation: Dumpster diving is a technique in which an intruder attempts to gather sensitive information from bins and other areas where documents are not properly discarded. Users should be appropriately trained on discarding sensitive information. In the absence of security awareness training, other options may not be effective in preventing the risk of dumpster diving.

Security testing tools and techniques

1. **Answer: D. To mandate a password-protected screensaver**
Explanation: Password-protected screensavers will help to log off the computer following a predefined period of inactivity. This is the most effective method to protect an unattended computer. Other options will not prevent access to unattended computers if the unattended computer is not locked. Computers that are switched off can easily be switched on and if the screen is not password protected, unauthorized access cannot be prevented.

2. **Answer: B. To determine whether this complies with policy**
Explanation: An IS auditor's first step is to determine compliance with policy. Considering the compensatory control, policy may allow for different password rules. Auditors should take further action after considering the adequacy and effectiveness of policy.

3. **Answer: A. Double blind testing**
Explanation: Double blind testing is the extension of blind testing, wherein the administrator and security staff at the target organization are also unaware of the test. It stimulates a real kind of attack. This helps to evaluate the incident handling and response capability of the target organization. In double blind testing, both the tester and security team are blind as no one is aware of the test details.

4. **Answer: C. Vendor-provided default passwords are not changed**
Explanation: Of greatest concern is the use of vendor-provided default passwords. These can be easily exploited by an intruder. The other options are not as important as default passwords not being changed.

5. **Answer: A. A transaction log should be set up as 'write once' and 'read many drives'**
Explanation: It is important that logs should not be allowed to be edited, modified, or deleted in order to preserve their integrity. A backup and review of logs does not, by itself, ensure the integrity of transaction logs.

6. **Answer: D. Authentication passwords are not encrypted**
   Explanation: The transmission of passwords to an authentication server in a clear form increases the risk of compromise involving the password. Hackers can capture the password with the aid of specialized tools and techniques and the password can be misused. The other options are not as important as unencrypted passwords.

7. **Answer: D. Security log files**
   Explanation: It is important that logs should not be allowed to be edited, modified, or deleted in order to preserve their integrity. Log policy, rules, and access control rules may need to be changed in keeping with changes in business processes.

8. **Answer: A. The immediate changing of the password**
   Explanation: The organization should change the compromised password immediately. Changing a login name or deleting an account should be considered after studying the impact of the same on business processes. Intimation to the incident management team is an important step. However, passwords should be changed immediately to prevent any damage.

9. **Answer: D. A file containing a list of user IDs and associated passwords exists in plain text**
   Explanation: The greatest concern will relate to unencrypted password files. This makes all passwords visible in clear text, and the disclosure of this file can expose organizations to significant damage. The other options are not as important as unencrypted password files.

10. **Answer: C. Double blind testing**
    Explanation: Double blind testing is the extension of blind testing, wherein the administrator and security staff at the target organization are also unaware of the test. It stimulates a real kind of attack. This helps to evaluate the incident handling and response capability of the target organization. In double blind testing, both the tester and security team are blind as no one is aware of the test details.

11. **Answer: A. An emergency exit route is blocked**
    Explanation: The blockage of an emergency exit is a major risk for safeguarding human life. In the event of any accidents, if emergency exits are not available, then human lives are at stake. The other options are not as important as the blockage of emergency exits.

Security monitoring tools and techniques

1. **Answer: A. A neural network-based IDS**
   Explanation: Neural networks work on the same principle as statistical-based IDS. However, they possess the advanced functionality of self-learning. Neural networks keep updating the database by monitoring the general pattern of activities.

2. **Answer: B. Sensor**
   Explanation: The function of sensors is to collect data. Data can be in the form of network packets, log files, and suchlike. The function of an analyzer is to analyze the data and determine the intrusion activity. An administration console helps the administrator to control and monitor IDS rules and functions. A user interface supports the user to view the results and carry out the requisite tasks.

3. **Answer: B. A statistical-based IDS**
   Explanation: A statistical-based IDS attempts to identify abnormal behavior by analyzing the statistical algorithm. Any abnormal activity is flagged as an intrusion. For example, if normal logon hours are between 7 a.m. and 5 p.m. and if logon is performed at 11 p.m., it will raise this as an intrusion. Statistical IDS generate the most false positives compared with other types of IDS.

4. **Answer B. Not able to identify the intrusion activity**
   Explanation: If an IDS is not able to identify and detect the intrusion activity, this will be an area of most concern. It defeats the core purpose of installing the IDS. Attacks will remain unnoticed if not identified by the IDS and so no corrective and preventive action can be taken in relation to such attacks. The number of false alarms is not as significant as the IDS not being able to detect the intrusion attack. Options C and D are not areas of concern.

5. **Answer: B. Between a firewall and an internal network**
   Explanation: If an IDS is installed between a firewall and an internal network, it will be able to detect only those attempts that bypassed the firewall rules. If an IDS is installed between a firewall and an external network, it will be able to identify all the intrusion attempts irrespective of whether intrusion packets bypassed the firewall.

6. **Answer: A. To collect evidence relating to intrusion activity**
   Explanation: An IDS helps to monitor a network (network-based IDS) or a single system (host-based IDS) with the aim of recognizing and detecting an intrusion activity. The function of an IDS is to analyze the data and determine the intrusion activity. An IDS does not provide features in the same way as the other options.

7. **Answer: C. False positives**

   Explanation: The identification of false positives is one of the routine and frequent issues in the implementation of an IDS. An IDS operates on the basis of policy definition. Weakness of policy definitions weakens the function of an IDS. False acceptance and rejection rates are associated with biometric implementation. DDoS is a type of attack and is not an issue in the operation of an IDS.

8. **Answer: D. An IDS**

   Explanation: An IDS attempts to identify abnormal behavior by analyzing the statistical algorithm. Any abnormal activity is flagged as an intrusion. Hubs and switches are the networking devices for routing. A packet filter is a type of firewall to restrict blocked traffic.

9. **Answer: C. The monitoring of unsuccessful login attempts**

   Explanation: The most important control in identifying and detecting the intrusion is to actively monitor the unsuccessful login attempts. The other options will not directly assist in detecting the intrusion.

10. **Answer: A. Many false alarms generated by statistical-based IDS**

    Explanation: High instances of false alarms indicate that the IDS configuration needs to be further tuned. The major impacts of poorly configured IDS would be on business processes or systems that need to be closed due to false alarms. This could have an adverse impact on business profitability. An IDS cannot read the encrypted traffic. However, it can be compensated by the next-generation firewall. The other options are not as important as the blocking of critical services and systems.

11. **Answer: C. A neural network monitors the general pattern of activities and creates a database and attacks problems that require consideration of a large number of input variables**

    Explanation: Neural networks work on the same principle as statistical-based IDS. However, they possess the advanced functionality of self-learning. Neural networks keep updating the database by monitoring the general pattern of activities. Neural networks are most effective in addressing problems that require consideration of a large number of input variables.

12. **Answer: A. In a demilitarized zone**
    Explanation: Public-facing websites are placed in a demilitarized zone to safeguard the internal network from external attacks. IDS should be placed in the same demilitarized zone. An IDS monitors the network traffic to detect any intrusion. Network-based intrusion would not be installed in a web server just like a host-based IDS. Placing the IDS outside the firewall would not be helpful in protecting the website specifically.
    Placing an IDS in an internal network is a good way of ensuring that the website is not prone to internal attacks. However, an IDS would normally be placed in a demilitarized zone.

13. **Answer: D. A host-based IPS**
    Explanation: The most effective method is to install a host-based IPS. A host-based IPS will prevent activities on the host computer or server, such as the deletion of files and the modification of programs. A network-based IDS will be able to detect irregular traffic, but if signatures are not updated or traffic is encrypted, it may bypass the IDS. Regular operating system patch updates will address the vulnerabilities. However, host IPS are more effective at preventing unauthorized installation, and are unable to prevent rootkit installation. Packet-filtering firewalls will not be able to restrict the rootkit if the incoming IP is correct.

14. **Answer: A. A honeypot**
    Explanation: A honey pot is a decoy system set up to attract the hacker and intruders. The purpose of setting a honey pot is to capture the details of intruders in order to proactively strengthen the security controls.

15. **Answer: A. An IPS**
    Explanation: IPS have the ability to not only detect intrusion attempts, but also to prevent the impact of intrusion attacks. IDS only monitor, record, and provide alarms relating to intrusion activity, whereas IPS also prevent intrusion activities. Routers and switches are devices used for network routing.

16. **Answer: A. To capture information**
    Explanation: The first step that an intruder takes is to capture and gather relevant information about the target environment. On the basis of this information, they attempt various techniques to gain access and once the objective is accomplished, they try to evade the evidence.

17. **Answer: D. An IDS**
    Explanation: A network-based IDS is regarded as the next line of defense after a firewall. IDS monitor, record, and provide alarms relating to intrusion activity that bypasses the firewall. IDS have a greater capability to identify abnormal traffic as compared with anti-malware software. Routers and switches are devices used for network routing.

18. **Answer: B. Critical services or systems are blocked due to false alarms**
Explanation: A major impact of poorly configured firewalls would be on business processes or systems that need to be closed due to false alarms. This could have an adverse impact on business profitability. The other options are not as important as the blocking of critical services and systems.

Incident response management

1. **Answer: D. To report the incident to management immediately**
Explanation: It is most important that the auditor should report the details of the incident to management immediately. Auditors should not switch off the system directly as this may impact the evidence. Let the IT expert work on the solution.

2. **Answer: B. To reduce the impact of system outages and incidents on business**
Explanation: The main objective of the incident response plan is to reduce the impact of system outages on the business process. Through a well-defined incident management process, an organization can recover from the incident at the earliest possible juncture with a minimum business impact.

3. **Answer: B. Activating the incident response plan**
Explanation: The first step is to activate the incident response plan. The main objective of the incident response plan is to reduce the impact of system outages on the business process. Through a well-defined incident management process, an organization can recover from the incident at the earliest possible juncture with a minimum business impact. The services of experts are obtained once the incident has been identified. Considering the nature of the incident, the next step may be to activate business continuity plans and alternate sites.

4. **Answer: D. The simulated testing of the incident response plan at regular intervals**
Explanation: Simulation-based testing helps to understand the challenges of incident response plans in real-life scenarios. It helps to determine the weak areas and provides scope for improvement. The other options are not as important as simulated testing.

5. **Answer: C. An incident response plan**
   Explanation: An incident response plan includes a process for identifying, managing, and recovering from an incident. Through a well-defined incident management process, an organization can recover from the incident at the earliest possible juncture with a minimum business impact. A business continuity plan includes a process for ensuring the continuity of critical business services. A disaster recovery policy and an IT operating process do not include a plan to detect and recover from an attack.

6. **Answer: A. Information can be used to launch the attack**
   Explanation: As a practice, the CSIRT disseminates the roles and responsibilities of users to address the threats. However, detailed information pertaining to the threat may be used to launch the attack. Only the minimum amount of information required should be released. The other options are not as important as the use of information to launch the attack.

7. **Answer: A. The business and financial impact of each security incident**
   Explanation: The best way to determine the effectiveness of the performance of an incident response procedure is to evaluate the business and financial impact of each security incident. The number of patches and assets covered under penetration is not the responsibility of the incident response team. Instead, it is the responsibility of the security team.

8. **Answer: C. To support the incident investigation process**
   Explanation: If the timestamp is not the same on all devices, this will impact the process of investigating an incident. The audit trail may not be effective and reliable. The other options are not the objective of synchronized timings.

Evidence collection and forensics

1. **Answer: D. To ensure that the integrity of the evidence is maintained**
   Explanation: Digital evidence can be used in legal proceedings provided it has been preserved in its original state. Evidence loses its integrity if the chain of custody is not maintained. A major obligation on the part of the auditor is to ensure that the integrity of the evidence is maintained. The other options, although important, are not as important as the aspect of maintaining the integrity of the evidence.

2. **Answer: B. The chain of custody is not followed for evidence integrity**
Explanation: Digital evidence can be used in legal proceedings provided it has been preserved in its original state. Evidence loses its integrity if the chain of custody is not maintained. The chain of custody refers to the process of identifying, preserving, analyzing, and presenting evidence in such a manner that it demonstrates the reliability and integrity of the evidence.

3. **Answer: C. The chain of custody for evidence**
Explanation: Digital evidence can be used in legal proceedings provided it has been preserved in its original state. Evidence loses its integrity if the chain of custody is not maintained. The chain of custody refers to the process of identifying, preserving, analyzing, and presenting evidence in such a manner that it demonstrates the reliability and integrity of the evidence. The other options are important, but not as important as the chain of custody.

4. **Answer: B. Rebooting the system**
Explanation: Rebooting the system could result in the loss or corruption of the evidence. The other options, if performed with due care, may not have a direct impact on evidence integrity.

5. **Answer: D. Data is verified for integrity**
Explanation: It must be ensured that data is in its original form and has not been tampered with. Integrity of the data is the most important criterion in ensuring that evidence is admissible in the court of law. The other options are important, but not as important as data integrity.

Other Books You May Enjoy

If you enjoyed this book, you may be interested in these other books by Packt:

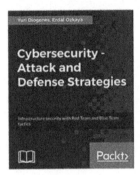

Cybersecurity – Attack and Defense Strategies - Second Edition

Yuri Diogenes, Erdal Ozkaya

ISBN: 9781838827793

- The importance of having a solid foundation for your security posture
- Use cyber security kill chain to understand the attack strategy
- Boost your organization's cyber resilience by improving your security policies, hardening your network, implementing active sensors, and leveraging threat intelligence
- Utilize the latest defense tools, including Azure Sentinel and Zero Trust Network strategy
- Identify different types of cyberattacks, such as SQL injection, malware and social engineering threats such as phishing emails
- Perform an incident investigation using Azure Security Center and Azure Sentinel
- Get an in-depth understanding of the disaster recovery process
- Understand how to consistently monitor security and implement a vulnerability management strategy for on-premises and hybrid cloud
- Learn how to perform log analysis using the cloud to identify suspicious activities, including logs from Amazon Web Services and Azure

Microsoft Exam MD-100 Windows 10 Certification Guide
Jeroen Burgerhout

ISBN: 9781838822187

- Deploy Windows 10 in a variety of ways
- Manage local users, groups, and devices
- Configure networking and remote connectivity
- Gain insights into Windows 10 maintenance
- Customize different Windows 10 features
- Become an expert at troubleshooting and recovery
- Get to grips with managing log files
- Monitor and manage Windows security

Leave a review - let other readers know what you think

Please share your thoughts on this book with others by leaving a review on the site that you bought it from. If you purchased the book from Amazon, please leave us an honest review on this book's Amazon page. This is vital so that other potential readers can see and use your unbiased opinion to make purchasing decisions, we can understand what our customers think about our products, and our authors can see your feedback on the title that they have worked with Packt to create. It will only take a few minutes of your time, but is valuable to other potential customers, our authors, and Packt. Thank you!

Index

Made in the USA
Coppell, TX
16 June 2023

18170350R00326